W9-ACS-844

THE SIXTIES PAPERS

Documents of a Rebellious Decade

udith Clavir Albert

Stewart Edward Albert

The Sixties Papers

Documents of a Rebellious Decade

The Sixties Papers

Documents of a Rebellious Decade

Judith Clavir Albert

and

Stewart Edward Albert

WITHDRAWN

PRAEGER SPECIAL STUDIES • PRAEGER SCIENTIFIC

New York • Philadelphia • Eastbourne, UK
Toronto • Hong Kong • Tokyo • Sydney

Library of Congress Cataloging in Publication Data
Main entry under title:

The sixties papers.

1. United States—Social conditions—1960–1970—
Addresses, essays, lectures. 2. Social movements—
United States—Addresses, essays, lectures. 3. Radical-
ism—United States—Addresses, essays, lectures.
I. Albert, Judith Clavir, 1943–   II. Albert, Stew-
art Edward, 1939–
HN65.S563   1984   306′.0973   84–15105
ISBN 0-03-063616-7
ISBN 0-03-063617-5 (pbk.)

Published in 1984 by Praeger Publishers
CBS Educational and Professional Publishing
A Division of CBS, Inc.
521 Fifth Avenue, New York, New York 10175 U.S.A.

© 1984 by Praeger Publishers

456789   145   987654321

Printed in the United States of America

Contents

SECTION 5 — THE COUNTERCULTURE   401

SECTION 6 — THE WOMEN'S REBELLION   459

List of Photographs
and Their Captions

For Jessica Pearl Clavir Albert

Preface

The need for this anthology became apparent when one of us discovered, in the process of assigning readings for a social movements course that, with the exception of some women's liberation documents, most of the important and original sixties writings were out of print. We also discovered that current sympathetic scholarship, tends to be specialized, and that conservatives who interpret the 1960s focus overwhelmingly on drugs, riot, and streetfighting and diminish the role of ideas.

The 1960s were much more than an emotional outburst. So many documents were authored, articles were written, and positions were debated. The 1960s was a time when truly new ideas were articulated, and everything in our country was up for debate—from foreign policy to sex. Nothing except the need for change was taken for granted. It was a period of utopian visions and practical reforms, of hope and paranoia, of pacifism and violence, of democratic ideals and police state repression. In this anthology we try to present a cross section of the thinking, values, attitudes, and passions that strongly influenced a generation.

We treat the various social movements as an integrated phenomenon. It is impossible to understand the peace movement without considering the formative influence of the civil rights movement. The revolutionary outlook of many SDS members is difficult to interpret unless seen in the context of black insurrections, black power, and the Black Panther Party. The egalitarianism of the women's liberation movement has strong roots in the participatory democracy of the early new left. The social movements of the 1960s all tended to create each other. In each section we tried to reflect this dynamic interaction.

We based our choice of selections on four criteria: the degree of an article's influence or representative character; if the piece was still available elsewhere; the cost demanded by publishers for reprinting; and our belief that the reading offered something relevant for the 1980s. While we could not reprint all documents in their entirety for reasons of space and cost, we did try to single out the central statement of each author. Although many of the documents are excerpted, we have, of course, left their linguistic style and phrasing intact. We had special access to West Coast underground newspapers, but most of the articles selected were widely reprinted in many other radical publications. The great majority of documents presented here were originally produced between the late 1950s and 1971. We also included a few later pieces that offer insightful reflections by activists about their role in the decade's protest.

Like many of the sixties generation, we, the authors of this book, participated in and were affected by all the social movements treated in the volume. In the early 1960s we marched for civil rights and listened to speeches by Fannie Lou Hamer and Martin Luther King. We attended forums where Malcolm X spoke about black nationalism and revolution. In the mid-1960s we were speaking, demonstrating, and writing in favor of free speech and against U.S. military involvement in Vietnam. By the end of the decade we were supporting black power and the Black Panther Party and helping to found the Yippies and the women's liberation movement. We started an underground newspaper, organized conferences, ran for public office, were teargassed in Chicago in the summer of 1968, were jailed on numerous occasions, traveled to North Vietnam and Cuba, and dissolved and later reestablished our personal relationship. We met militants from SDS, the Young Lords, Rising Up Angry, Redstockings, La Huelga, the Young Patriots, the White Panther Party, and the many different peace activists who worked in the national antiwar movement, as well a radicals from other countries—France, Germany, Iran, Palestine, Israel, Denmark, Japan, and Vietnam. Beginning in 1960 and continuing for the next 16 years, our FBI files show we were the subjects of an increasingly thorough government investigation and surveillance. We, like many of our compatriots, were at the center of a political, social, and cultural movement that changed both American society and our own lives in enduring ways.

Our experiences in the 1960s and the recollections and views of over 100 veteran activists with whom we consulted while preparing this volume determined our choice of selections and encouraged an ecumenical emphasis. Of course, everyone who was involved has their *own* sixties, and the choice of selections is our sole responsibility.

We wish to thank the following people for giving us access to their personal libraries: Al Haber, Mike Smith, Art Goldberg, Joe Blum, and Michael Rossman. For their ideas and encouragement, we also want to thank: Barbara Haber, David Harris, Steve Hamilton, Janet Kranzberg, Martin Kenner, Camilla Smith, Marty Schiffenbauer, Merry Kassoy, Marilyn Milligan, Leslie Bacon, Annie Popkin, Jeanne Friedman, Jane Brunner, Wendell Brunner, Jack Kurzweil, Michael Ochs, Jay Levin, Jonah Raskin, George Fischer, Roz Baxandall, Beverley Axelrod, Pat Richardz, Charles R. Garry, Abe Peck, Arthur Naiman, Noreen Banks, Carole Cullen, Michael Oliver, K.W., Jean Raisler, Al Copeland, Paul Krassner, Daphne Muse, Phil Hutchings, Nancy Barrett, Peter Clapp, Jeff Jones, Eleanor Stein, Ellen Ray, Bill Schapp, Margie Ratner, Bill Kunstler, Michael Ratner, Harriet and Leo Clavir, and our editor, Lynda Sharp. We also wish to thank the kind and helpful women at the Berkeley Public Library.

* * *

President Ronald Reagan built his political career in California and nationally by attacking sixties radicalism and its effects. Much of his presidency can be seen as an attempt to undo the social reforms and attitudinal changes that emerged from that decade. Opposition to Reagan—from the gender gap of women's dissatisfaction to Reverend Jesse Jackson's push for civil rights and black power in the 1980s, from the nonviolent disruptions of the antinuclear movement to the militancy of those who oppose U.S. intervention in Central America—has its inspirational origins in sixties protest. This book is about the 1960s, but the concepts and ideas presented herein also shed a clarifying light on our present lives.

Judy Clavir Albert, a.k.a. Gumbo

Stew Albert

May 1984

About the Editors

Judy Clavir Albert has taught sociology and Women's Studies at the University of Oregon and at Mills College in Oakland, California. She holds a Ph.D. from the University of Toronto, Canada. Stew Albert has worked as a private investigator and journalist. He has a Bachelor's degree from Pace University.

In the late 1960s Judy was a founder of the Berkeley women's movement. Adopting the name "Gumbo," she became an organizer for the 1968 Chicago antiwar demonstrations, visited Hanoi with a women's peace delegation, and traveled around the country agitating against the war and for the liberation of women.

Stew Albert was an original Yippie, an unindicted co-conspirator in the Chicago Conspiracy Trial of 1969, and an early supporter of the Black Panther Party. In 1970 he ran for sheriff of Alameda County and received 70,000 votes.

In 1975 Judy discovered a homing device on her car. The Alberts, who had been labeled in government documents as "recidivist new leftists," sued the Federal Bureau of Investigation and won an out-of-court settlement.

The editors are married and have a daughter, Jessica Pearl.

About the Contributors

Ti-Grace Atkinson is preparing her dissertation in philosophy for Columbia University on the subject of women and oppression.

F.J. Bardacke lives in a small town in central California and is involved in efforts to democratize the Teamsters Union.

Frances M. Beale lives in Berkeley, California, recently worked for a civil rights organization for the disabled, and currently covers black news for the Marxist-Leninist newspaper *Frontline*.

Julian Beck and Judith Malina continue to travel the world with the Living Theatre.

Konstantin Berlandt is a prominent leader of the gay liberation movement in San Francisco.

H. Rap Brown lives in Atlanta, Georgia, is a practicing Muslim, and manages a health food store.

Stokely Carmichael lived in Africa for a number of years. He frequently visits the United States and remains active in the black movement.

Dave Dellinger lives in Vermont and continues to write and speak out against American militarism and war.

Diane DiPrima's most recent work of poetry is *Loba*, published by Wingbow Press in 1978.

Bernardine Dohrn recently passed the New York State Bar examination and continues to be politically active.

Don Duncan's current whereabouts are unknown.

Karen Durbin is a senior editor at the *Village Voice.*

Lee Felsenstein, formerly of Osborne Computers, developed the concept of using television screens as monitors for personal computers.

W.H. Ferry, one of the authors of *The Triple Revolution,* resides in Scarsdale, New York.

Shulamith Firestone is rumored to be living in New York City.

The Fort Hood Three served time in jail. One is currently a construction worker living in the Bronx, another writes for a Communist Party newspaper, and the third is a farmer.

Allen Ginsberg is the director of the Poetics department at the Naropa Institute in Boulder, Colorado.

Al Haber, one of the original authors of the Port Huron Statement, lives in Berkeley, California.

Casey Hayden lives in Atlanta, Georgia and is active in civil rights issues.

Tom Hayden is currently state assemblyman from Santa Monica, California, a leader of the Campaign for Economic Democracy, and is married to movie star Jane Fonda.

Ho Chi Minh died on September 3, 1969. The city of Saigon in Vietnam was named after him.

Abbie Hoffman lives in upstate New York and New York City, organizing in defense of clean rivers and against American foreign policy.

Erika Huggins lives in Oakland, California and works for an advocacy organization trying to create more effective laws against rape and sexual abuse.

Naomi Jaffe's current whereabouts are unknown.

Martin Luther King, Jr. was assassinated in Memphis, Tennessee on April 4, 1968.

Mary King lives in Washington, D.C. and continues to organize.

Anne Koedt is a feminist artist living and working in New York City.

Paul Krassner pursues his career as a stand-up comic in Los Angeles and San Francisco.

Keith Lampe, a.k.a. Ponderosa Pine, has his roots in Bolinas, California.

Norman Mailer's most recent best selling novel is *Ancient Evenings,* published by Warner in 1984.

Joy Marcus is director of the Center to Prevent Nuclear Annihilation in Half Moon Bay, California.

Herbert Marcuse died on July 29, 1979.

Kate Millett is a New York City artist who continues to agitate for feminist causes.

C.W. Mills, author of many books, including *The Power Elite,* died on March 20, 1962. His last public act was to oppose America's involvement in the Bay of Pigs invasion.

Robin Morgan lives in New York City. Her most recent book is *The Anatomy of Freedom,* published by Doubleday in 1984.

Linda Morse, the Conspiracy Trial witness, became a physician and lives in San Francisco.

Huey P. Newton lives in Oakland, California and works in Hollywood.

Phil Ochs committed suicide on April 9, 1976. He was recently the subject of a film documentary, *Chords of Fame.*

Carl Oglesby lives in Boston, Massachusetts. He was a founder of the Assassination Information Bureau.

Shin'ya Ono, whose current whereabouts are unknown, is Yoko Ono's cousin.

Genie Plamondon was last seen running for public office in Ann Arbor, Michigan.

Paul Potter died of cancer in July 1984. He had recently worked on Kathy Boudin's defense committee.

Patricia Robinson is a clinical social worker in private practice working in upstate New York in the same communities that inspired the documents reprinted here.

Jerry Rubin worked for a stockbroker, organized social gatherings for business people, and is now interested in health foods and life extension.

Ed Sanders, author of *The Family* (published by Dutton in 1971), a widely read study of Charles Manson, lives in Woodstock, New York and writes poetry.

Robert Scheer is a journalist with the *Los Angeles Times* and author of the best-selling book *With Enough Shovels*, published by Random House in 1982.

Bobby Seale lives in Philadelphia, is enrolled in a graduate program at Temple University, and is the author of a forthcoming cookbook, *Barbecuing With Bobby*. He continues to speak out on political issues.

Gary Snyder continues to write poetry and work in the ecology movement.

Valerie Solanis's current whereabouts are unknown.

The Wall Street Journal no longer publishes editorials criticizing U.S. imperialism.

Malcolm X was assassinated on February 21, 1965 in New York City.

CONSIDERING THE 1960s

Finding the 1960s in the 1950s

The beginnings of 1960s protest can be found in a few dissenting voices from the 1950s. Despite current highly sentimental remembrances of that decade, America in the 1950s was a nation dominated by personal conformity, political paranoia and a cold war. Government leaders and newspaper editorialists encouraged Americans to believe that Russia was preparing for a nuclear conquest of the United States. The Soviets, it was said, were being abetted by domestic spies and communist sympathizers. While American soldiers were confronting the "red menace" on Korean battlefields, many on the home front believed that subversives were infiltrating into the mainstream of national life.[1] In 1951 a federal judge sentenced two alleged Communists, Julius and Ethel Rosenberg, to death for conspiracy to spy against the United States. He blamed the couple for causing the Korean War "with casualties of 50,000," declaring "who knows that millions more innocent people may pay the price of your treason."[2] In this highly charged climate, practically any eccentricity in lifestyle or fundamental criticism of the United States was considered suspect and unpatriotic.

Throughout the 1950s powerful public and private groups waged campaigns of censorship against political and sexual nonconformists, purging present and former Communist party members, freethinkers, and homosexuals from institutions of government, education, and culture. Hollywood films that portrayed sexual activity were edited under pressure from censors or subjected to national boycotts. Perhaps American prudishness was most pointedly expressed at the end of the decade when Lucille Ball, playing a married woman on television, became pregnant. Her scriptwriters used her condition as part of the show's plot, but network executives would not permit the word "pregnant" to be spoken on the air.

America's great fear began to subside when the Korean War ended in 1953. The Soviet Union's long-time ruler, Joseph Stalin, had died a few months earlier, and his successors appeared more flexible in foreign policy matters. In 1952 General Dwight D. Eisenhower had been elected president, and by the middle of the decade, Ike, as he was affectionately known, was having a soothing effect on America. The demogoguery and national insecurity of the early 1950s began to give way to a mood of self-satisfied boastfulness while the prevailing economic boom prompted an ongoing celebration of "our way of life."

Leading American sociologists of the 1950s, most importantly Talcott Parsons, glorified the stability, adaptability, and social equilibrium they saw as inherent in the American social system. Another sociologist, Daniel Bell, coined the phrase "the end of ideology" to describe a dynamic, open, and pragmatic America that, he claimed, was solving its social problems by means of tremendous technological development and moderate social reforms. By the middle of the 1950s most Americans, from respected intellectuals to gossip columnists in tabloids, seemed to agree that the United States was *the greatest country on earth.*

NEW REBELS

Despite the celebration, large numbers of Americans were leading impoverished and angry lives. Little had changed to improve the political and social position of black people since the abolition of slavery. Although the Supreme Court had ruled in favor of the National Association for the Advancement of Colored People (NAACP), declaring in May 1954 that legal segregation in public education was unconstitutional, the majority of black children were poor, still went to segregated schools, and received inferior education. Black life in the South was restricted by an all-encompassing, legally sanctioned system of racial separation.

In December 1955 a black woman, Rosa Parks, refused to relinquish her seat to a white passenger on an Alabama bus and was jailed for this act of defiance.[3] Her protest sparked a successful black boycott of the city's bus system. The demonstrations soon were led by a young minister named Martin Luther King, Jr., who advocated a philosophy of nonviolent resistance to unjust authority. Dr. King's oppositional and spiritual outlook was influenced by the autobiographical perspectives of Mohandas Gandhi and the transcendentalist writings of Henry David Thoreau.

King believed that black people and their white supporters would have to find a way both to break the laws of segregation and return love for racist hatred. The black protest movement, which would reach massive proportions in the 1960s, found a powerful inspiration in the leadership of Martin Luther King.

In addition to the concerns of black people, the typical American was forced to take note of increasing discontent among the nation's youth. The causes and potential cures of "juvenile delinquency" were a much discussed subject in the press and academia. Hollywood was criticized for producing films that seemed to make folk heroes of youthful offenders. Popular movies such as *The Wild One* with Marlon Brando and *Rebel Without a Cause* starring James Dean, Natalie Wood and Sal Mineo portrayed attractive young people in trouble with the law. When the real-life Dean was killed in an automobile accident, he became an overnight cult figure among teenage girls and boys. Many feared that juvenile delinquency was being encouraged by the jarring rhythms of rock and roll. It was particularly galling to many white Americans that their children so enthusiastically embraced a type of music created primarily by black artists. When Elvis Presley began to sing exactly in the style of black performers, he became an instant sensation. The early Presley combined his surly and hostile lyrics with wild pelvic gyrations, conveying an overwhelming impression of aggressive male sexuality that appealed to many young people and horrified their parents.[4] The growing gap between young and middle-aged Americans in the 1950s foreshadowed what was to be a worldwide youth revolution in the 1960s.

In the mid-1950s, some American intellectuals and artists were involved in their own form of personal and literary rebellion. In the fall of 1955 Allen Ginsberg, a young poet, gave the first public reading of his epic work *HOWL*. The poem evoked images of a brutal, avaricious, warlike, and dangerously repressed America. Despite its biting tone, *HOWL* held out the hope of redemption through compassion, faith in the holiness of all, humor, and orgasmic sexuality. Ginsberg and his literary and personal associates, including Peter Orlovsky, Jack Kerouac, Diane Di Prima, William Burroughs, and Neal and Carolyn Cassady, became publicly identified as "the beat generation." Some members of this group faced legal difficulties because the sexually explicit content of their work challenged 1950s censorship laws. The beat lifestyle, chronicled by Kerouac in his best-selling novel *On the Road*, was one of frequent sexual encounters, endless traveling, marijuana smoking, mystical reveries and revelations, cool jazz, and joyous homecomings.[5] The beats' message of freedom and independence was infectious for many educated young Americans. Some, who sought to be "with it," adopted sloppy forms of dress, rough language, and severe makeup and were popularly derided as "beatniks."[6] The beat beneration would continue to have influence in the 1960s when a new movement of rebels combined the bohemianism of the 1950s with radical politics, psychedelic drugs, and a love of rock and roll.

By the late 1950s a small number of radical scholars were putting forward a systematic critique of American society. Sociologist C. Wright Mills analyzed and condemned a national power elite consisting of interpenetrating military, industrial, and corporate hierarchical structures. He passionately rejected the commonly held view that political power was dispersed democratically throughout the American polity. Economists Paul Sweezy, Leo Huberman, and Paul Baran, writing for *Monthly Review*, a magazine with extremely small circulation, challenged the widely held belief that the foreign policy of the United States was based on benevolence and that America was seeking to protect the world from communist aggression. In contrast, these independent Marxists argued that the American capitalist system was breeding imperialism, war, poverty, exploitation, and social decay. Historian William Appleman Williams described American diplomacy as a "tragedy" because of the nation's longstanding tendency to solve its social problems through military and economic conquest. Psychologist Eric Fromm asserted that life in America was becoming a "joyless quest for joy." These scholars and several others, including Paul Goodman, David Reissman, Michael Harrington, and journalist I.F. Stone, castigated American society in strong and convincing terms. For the most part, however, the radical critics shared with mainstream proponents of the status quo a belief in the long-term stability of the American system.

One significant dissenter was the author Norman Mailer. In his essay "The White Negro," Mailer foresaw the imminence of black and youth rebellion, male/female war, and a pervasive tendency for white middle class intellectuals to adopt the hip style of the black lumpenproletariat. He predicted that out of the pain and psychic brutality of American life would come a generation of violent, angry, and potentially political rebels. In the 1950s Mailer was almost alone in seeing that America was on the brink of a fierce social upheaval.

Sit-Ins, SNCC, and the Emergence of Political Rebellion

On February 1, 1960 four black college students sat down at a lunch counter in Greensboro, North Carolina. Because they had located themselves in the "whites-only" section, the young people were refused service. The store manager declared that he would not accommodate "colored" since doing so would violate Woolworth's policy of adhering to local segregationist custom. The four remained seated until the store's closing. Growing numbers of students, mostly blacks and a few whites, joined in the nonviolent protest. By the end of the week, in an atmosphere of rising community hostility and racist violence by the Ku Klux Klan, the Woolworth's store was temporarily shut down.

The improvisational sit-in movement spread rapidly and began to threaten the imperturbability of Eisenhower's America. By April 1960 an estimated 50,000 people had participated in sit-ins or support demonstrations at lunch counters in 100 southern cities and at least 3,600 demonstrators had been arrested.[7] Commentators had to recall union-led factory sit-ins of the 1930s to find any precedent for such discordant and combative behavior. With the end of the 1950s, a decade dominated by fear, repression, cultural superficiality, and individual acts of nonconformity, a new style of political rebellion was beginning to take hold and, by its presence, suggested that the coming period might be very different from the quiescence of the previous period.

THE STUDENT NON-VIOLENT CO-ORDINATING COMMITTEE

The Student Non-Violent Co-Ordinating Committee (SNCC)[8] was founded at a conference held in Raleigh, North Carolina in April,

6

1960. Attending the gathering were sit-in activists who wished to develop a black-led association that espoused nonviolence and would link southern civil rights groups into a network of communication and support. These young militants also wanted to protect their organization from domination by the older, patriarchal, church-based civil rights groups led by the prestigious Dr. Martin Luther King. Ella Baker, a close associate of Reverend King's, played a major role in calling the SNCC conference, but she actively supported the young people in their efforts not to be controlled or manipulated. The Student Non-Violent Co-Ordinating Committee was inaugurated in an atmosphere of generational revolt.

Within a year, fewer sit-ins were taking place and SNCC activists determined that a new tactical approach was needed. They decided to stimulate the black civil rights movement by deliberately provoking confrontations with segregationists, local police, the southern power structure, and eventually with the federal government. In the rural South of the early 1960s almost all black people were denied the right to vote by means of costly poll taxes and rigged literacy and intelligence tests mandated by state laws.[9] Racist domination was imposed by systematic terror carried out by the Ku Klux Klan and the White Citizens Councils. Lynching was still practiced in Mississippi. By organizing integration and voter registration drives in rural Georgia, Alabama, and Mississippi, SNCC brought its campaign for racial equality into the heartland of bedrock white supremacy. SNCC activists knew they were risking their lives by moving into the deep South. This kind of commitment was referred to as "putting your body on the line."

In the summer of 1961 interracial groups called "Freedom Riders," organized by SNCC and the Congress of Racial Equality (CORE), took buses into Alabama and Georgia. When the travelers stopped at bus terminals, they were assaulted by mobs, and some were arrested as they tried to integrate lunch counters, public bathrooms, separate drinking fountains, and waiting rooms. Another part of SNCC's political strategy was to encourage and aid disenfranchised blacks by establishing Freedom Schools to help adults pass literacy tests. Black children who attended these schools were taught to read and write, and they learned Freedom songs and black history. By the summer of 1964 hundreds of young white students had come to Mississippi and joined with SNCC as part of the Mississippi Summer Project. Together with many volunteers from black colleges, they assisted with the voting rights campaign and taught in the Freedom Schools.

Some leading SNCC activists had been strongly influenced by the French existentialist philosopher Albert Camus, who argued that the means through which social change is accomplished must be harmonious with the desired ends.[10] SNCC members aimed for this moral consistency by trying to live each day in an egalitarian manner. Even though many of them came from prosperous middle-class families or had been educated at leading black universities, SNCC organizers learned to speak and dress like the poorest sharecroppers and to defer to them in important matters of policy. SNCC's passion for social and political equality was expressed in its slogan: "Let the people decide."

Despite SNCC's commitment to the moral imperative of day-to-day democracy, women in the organization were treated in a politically and personally inconsistent manner. They shared fully in the risks and dangers but were denied equal access to the decision-making process and were regularly given menial and secretarial tasks.[11] Two female activists resisted being put in a secondary status and, in an unsigned memo circulated at a SNCC retreat in 1964, equated white supremacy with male domination and compared their disadvantaged position to that of black people in American society.

Both male and female SNCC workers lived under constant threat of violence. By the end of the summer of 1964 over 1,000 protesters had been arrested and 37 black churches had been bombed or otherwise damaged. Fifteen people were murdered and four were wounded.[12] During July the killings of civil rights workers Michael Schwerner, Andrew Goodman, and James Chaney (two whites and a black) occupied newspaper headlines. The American people looked on while the FBI and federal marshalls dredged the Mississippi swamps looking for corpses. But massive national publicity did not stop the killing. Nine months after the triple murder, following a SNCC-initiated series of demonstrations in Alabama, a white civil rights worker, Viola Liuzzo, was shot to death by the Ku Klux Klan.

As a result of moral and political pressure brought on the government by the highly publicized beatings and deaths of civil rights workers and by numerous protests, including a demonstration by 500,000 people in Washington D.C., the White House and Congress could no longer evade their constitutional responsibilities.[13] On August 6, 1965 the Voting Rights Act was signed into law, and the following year a comprehensive civil rights act was passed. This legislation committed the federal government to abolish legal segregation and supervise voter registration in the South. SNCC's policy of tactical confrontation had proved to be politically effective.

SNCC's style of organizing, its democratic values, and its identification with poor people of color had a lasting effect on 1960s radicalism and served as a model of political rebellion throughout the decade. Many activists admired the organization's bravery and equalitarian ethics, and they sought to reenact that courage in their own lives, by accepting jail, beatings, tear gas, shootings, and occasionally death in the service of their ideals. SNCC would prove a powerful exemplar for what would come to be called the new left.

The Rise of a New Left

STUDENTS FOR A DEMOCRATIC SOCIETY
AND PARTICIPATORY DEMOCRACY

In June 1962 Students for a Democratic Society (SDS), an organization of radical college students, collectively wrote and published the *Port Huron Statement*, a document that offered the vision and philosophic rationale for a new left.[14] The statement portrayed American society as undemocratic and militaristic. It declared that the rise of bureaucracy, mechanization, and the worship of material objects created an American way of life that was lonely, estranged, and isolated. Elaborating on a theory propounded by the critical sociologist C. Wright Mills that the personal life of individuals and the social life of nations are interdependent, SDS called for a society based on love and community in which all members would be equally involved in formulating the political decisions that shape their private lives. This egalitarian image of community, which SDS shared with SNCC, was termed "participatory democracy." The idea would become a linchpin for new left thought and protest activity.

The term "new left" was loosely used to distinguish its advocates from the traditional or "old" left, which was composed of the Communist party, Socialist party, Social Democrats and various Trotskyist groups. Both old and new left had in common a declared passion for social justice, but new leftists believed they were more concerned than the old radicals with arriving at political decisions by democratic means and not manipulating those whom they were trying to organize. The traditional left looked to industrial workers as the primary agents of social change, while new leftists, at one time or another, thought of everyone except industrial workers and the power elites as potential rebels. The old left was ideologically influenced primarily by Karl Marx, Friedrich Engels, and V.I. Lenin; alternatively, the new radicals discov-

10

ered wisdom in a highly eclectic assortment of personalities, including Albert Camus, Gandhi, Fidel Castro, Bob Dylan, Mao Tse Tung, Che Guevara, Emma Goldman, and the Beatles.

Members of SDS were optimistic about the potential political power of young people. The 1960 census showed that 15 per cent of the American people were between the ages of 14 to 24, and the percentage of college students was the highest in history.[15] SDS members predicted that many of these youths would be angered and rebellious over their complete political unimportance within American society. In addition, the new leftists shared SNCC's philosophic view that poor people could be effectively encouraged to organize themselves. A widely read pamphlet entitled *The Triple Revolution* convinced SDS members that the number of poor people would dramatically increase in the coming decade because of massive unemployment created by the new technology of automation and computers.

By the summer of 1964, with the goal of creating an "interracial movement of the poor," SDS activists launched the Economic Research Action Projects (ERAP) in the impoverished black, white, and racially mixed neighborhoods of ten cities across America.[16] Emulating SNCC's Mississippi approach, they tried to establish community-controlled grass-roots organizations that would encourage poor residents to confront local power structures. ERAP members attempted to solidify their community ties by calling meetings, offering the poor needed information, as well as by fundraising, working with unemployed people and welfare mothers, and providing childcare or lawyers.

Like SNCC, SDS's internal democracy was not complete. Women and men shared equally in political accomplishments, but men dominated the meetings and, while women made up at least one-third of the organization's membership, there was only one woman on the ERAP executive committee.[17] Nonetheless, many SDS women acquired a commitment to participatory democracy that would continue to inspire them when they became activists in a later women's liberation movement.

Despite the dedication of its young participants, only a small number of poor people joined in ERAP activities. Contrary to the predictions made by the authors of *The Triple Revolution*, American unemployment declined in the latter half of the decade due to a war-induced prosperity. It was American military intervention in Vietnam, not economic collapse, that would come to govern the direction of protest in the 1960s.

While some SDS members, including Tom Hayden, were living with poor black people in Newark, and some, like Rennie Davis, were making common cause with white Appalachians in Chicago, still others devoted themselves to organizing demonstrations against the war in Vietnam. On April 17, 1965 national news commentators were stunned when 25,000 people, most of whom were young, heeded the call of SDS and poured into Washington D.C. to oppose American intervention in Asia. Never before had so many Americans protested their country's participation in an ongoing foreign war.

SDS quickly became a highly publicized object of both emulation and scorn. The organization's antimilitarist analysis of American foreign policy, formerly available only in mimeographed pamphlets, suddenly began appearing in the daily press. SDS grew rapidly, and by December 1966 could boast 265 chapters.[18] It would become the largest and most broadly based membership organization of radical protest in the 1960s.

SIT-INS COME NORTH: THE FREE SPEECH MOVEMENT

In the fall of 1964 a confrontation erupted between the administrators of the University of California at Berkeley and the student body. The conflict began when veterans of the Freedom Rides together with students who had been influenced by SNCC's moral style and new left ideas publicly raised money for the civil rights movement on the University of California campus.[19] The protesters also recruited students to sit-in at local businesses and demand that more blacks be hired. University officials responded to outside pressures by banning all political activity not directly concerned with campus affairs. As students started speaking out against this political repression, they found themselves questioning the impersonal and bureaucratic character of academic life. The students satirized their condition by carrying signs proclaiming "Do Not Fold, Spindle, Staple, or Mutilate." The alienation that many experienced while attending what the university's president had termed a "knowledge factory" became a highly emotional source of protest. Free Speech Movement leader Mario Savio articulated the sentiments of many by declaring that "There's a time when the operation of the machine becomes so odious, makes you so sick at heart, that you can't take part. And you've got to put your bodies upon the gears and upon the wheels, upon the levers, upon all the apparatus, and you've got to make it stop."[20]

The Free Speech Movement (FSM) ended with a massive sit-in and the arrest of 801 persons. Because of widespread support enjoyed by the movement among students, many faculty members, and liberal members of the Berkeley community, the young new leftists emerged from the sit-in with more political rights than they orginally sought. Forms of protest that had developed in the southern freedom struggle were now effectively transplanted into an entirely different region and social milieu. The FSM served as a model of campus protest until the more violent disruptions of the late 1960s.

JFK AND THE SANCTIONING OF PROTEST

By 1965 America was a changed country. Commitment, idealism, and dissent had come to replace the patriotic apathy of the 1950s. This new condition had been created by the activities of the civil rights movement, the new left, and through the tentative support given to protest by a new American president.

The presidency of John Fitzgerald Kennedy was a time of rising expectations. In his 1960 inauguration speech Kennedy declared that the "torch" was passing to a new generation. The president was in his

early forties, as were many of his closest advisors, and possessed a glamorous, exuberant spirit that the press likened to King Arthur's Court and dubbed "Camelot." Kennedy called on Americans to "ask not what your country can do for you, ask what you can do for your country" and offered service in the newly established Peace Corps as an opportunity for altruistic expression. He condemned the existence of widespread poverty in America and initiated the first food stamp program. Kennedy publicly supported the civil rights movement and, while urging tactical moderation. maintained a personal dialogue with Martin Luther King.[21]

In contrast to his experimental domestic reforms, JFK pursued a traditional cold war foreign policy of active confrontation with the Soviet Union. Kennedy sharply escalated the production of nuclear missiles and began sending U.S. troops into Vietnam to oppose a developing communist insurgency.[22] By the fall of 1962 President Kennedy and Soviet Premier Nikita S. Khrushchev were involved in a political and military confrontation, known as the Cuban missile crisis—an event that many believed brought the world to the brink of nuclear war.[23]

The Kennedy years were a time of innovation in popular culture, especially music. An increasingly vapid rock and roll was being replaced on the hit charts by "folk rock" and protest songs. Drawing on the radical folk tradition of the Weavers and Woody Guthrie, groups like Peter, Paul, and Mary and the Kingston Trio began singing "songs of social significance." The young poet and musician Bob Dylan gained overnight fame with his timely and bitter ballads excoriating warmakers and racists. His prophetic "The Times They Are a Changin'" would become akin to a national anthem for sixties protesters. Dylan was part of a talented new movement of young artists including Joan Baez and Phil Ochs who combined lively performance with new left political commitment.

On November 22, 1963 JFK was assassinated. His successor, Lyndon Baines Johnson, tried to maintain the Kennedy mix of domestic liberalism and cold war combativeness. Johnson was initially successful, and, when he ran for president in 1964 against a conservative, Barry Goldwater, he received the qualified endorsement of Students for a Democratic Society.[24] But LBJ's programs, policies, and eventually his entire presidency would be destroyed on the battlefields of Vietnam.

The Mass Culture of Rebellion

THE ANTIWAR MOVEMENT

In the second half of the 1960s America was engulfed both by a war and an antiwar movement. Military intervention in the small Asian country of Vietnam was officially defended as being in the vital interests of the United States. According to President Johnson, the presence of American combat troops in South Vietnam would stop the spread of "godless communism," defend democracy, and preserve international security. But many Americans disagreed, and President Johnson and his successor Richard Nixon faced an unparalleled movement of organized opposition to their wartime policies.

The antiwar movement was extraordinary for its size, duration, and capacity to disrupt and divide American society. During the latter part of the 1960s, massive antiwar demonstrations, some with as many as 500,000 participants, were taking place in Washington and New York.[25] Supportive protests by up to 25,000 people were held simultaneously in smaller cities across the country. Many of these events were organized by the National Mobilization Against the War—a coalition of radical pacifists, SDS members, independent new leftists, countercultural revolutionaries, women's peace movement activists, trade unionists, and representatives of old left communist organizations. Marchers chanted, sang peace songs, and carried placards that bore such slogans as "Peace Now," "Bring the Boys Home," "Give Peace a Chance," and "War is Not Healthy For Children and Other Living Things." University campuses became major centers of antiwar protest and the site of teach-ins, marches, sit-ins, moratoriums, occupations of official buildings, and by 1968, extremely violent confrontations with police and bombings of ROTC buildings. In scenes reminiscent of the early civil rights conflicts, police used teargas, clubbed, and by the end of the decade, shot and killed antiwar demonstrators. Americans in the tens of

15

thousands avoided the draft by fleeing to Canada and Sweden. As the war in Indochina escalated, young people joined in a movement to resist the draft. Heavyweight boxing champion Cassius Clay changed his name to Muhammad Ali and refused induction, saying "No Viet Cong ever called me nigger." The Resistance, an antidraft organization, counselled and supported those who chose jail, exile, or fugitive status rather than military service. Some young men assumed aliases, and a few became full-time activists in the antiwar movement. Leaders of the anti-draft resistance, including David Harris, Stanford student body president, received stiff prison sentences for refusing to be inducted.[26] Opposition to the war spread into the United States Army. The military forces experienced low morale; soldiers were smoking marijuana, frequenting movement-sponsored coffee houses, and refusing to fight. Some appeared to be in a state of near mutiny. By the decade's conclusion rumors of *fragging*, which refers to the act of killing a superior officer using a fragmentation grenade, were being brought home by returning GIs. Former soldiers and some still in the armed forces established a group called Vietnam Veterans Against the War (VVAW) and, in an act of collective protest, threw their combat medals over a Capitol Building fence.[27]

Not since the Civil War had American society been so divided. From the perspective of the antiwar movement, the United States government and armed forces seemed like some cruel Goliath trying, in General Curtis LeMay's unfortunate phrase, to "bomb Vietnam back into the Stone Age."[28] Night after night millions watched the carnage of war on television and saw images of burning villages, children with face and limbs disfigured, communist prisoners of war being tortured and killed, and unidentified bodies floating down the Mekong River. Television news began giving extensive coverage to antiwar demonstrations in America and Saigon, to Buddhist nuns and monks immolating themselves in protest, and to the nightly "body count" of dead and wounded.[29] Since Congress had never officially declared war against the communist-led Democratic Republic of Vietnam, journalists were able to report on the conflict in a relatively uncensored manner. Many Americans saw on their television screens a version of war quite different from that glorified in the lofty phrases of official propaganda.

President Johnson fueled the antiwar movement by the poor quality of his leadership, which some compared to that of a "riverboat gambler."[30] He appeared insincere and was unable to rally the country with a sense of moral purpose. It was in reaction to Johnson's presidency that the term "credibility gap" was originally coined, to make a distinction between what government officials were claiming and what was actually happening. As LBJ raised the number of American troops in Vietnam from 20,000 to 250,000, he came to be hated by the antiwar movement. In turn, he denounced peace activists, calling them "nervous nellies."[31] Demonstrators responded in kind by chanting "Hey, Hey, LBJ, How many kids did you kill today?"

By the late 1960s many new leftists were experiencing a depth of alienation from American society that could be measured by their willingness to identify with the person and cause of the country's officially defined enemy—North Vietnam's President Ho Chi Minh. Ho gained many Western supporters by quoting from the American Declaration of Independence to justify Vietnam's revolution. Disappointed in their own country, many new left militants began to shift their emotional allegiance to the communist side. During marches many would defiantly chant, "Ho Ho Ho Chi Minh, the NLF is gonna win!"[32]

ORGANIZING TEACH-INS

During 1965, young people who were angered at the widening Asian conflict began forming grass-roots antiwar organizing committees in many college towns. On hundreds of campuses, these groups sponsored teach-ins—events that were an important force in galvanizing antiwar sentiment around the country.[33]

The first all-night teach-in was presented by students, faculty and SDS activists at the University of Michigan in March 1965, shortly after a major escalation in the bombing of North Vietnam. Two months later, the Vietnam Day Committee (VDC) of Berkeley, California held a 36-hour marathon event. The declared purpose of the teach-in was to present both sides of the Vietnam issue, and some prowar academics and representatives of the State Department appeared to offer their opinions. But it was the antiwar speakers, such as pediatrician Benjamin Spock, satirist Paul Krassner, and author Norman Mailer, among others, who won over most of the 12,000 people in the audience. Bolstered by their successful event, the VDC organizers continued to promote rallies against the war, as well as marches of tens of thousands of people and nonviolent blockades of troop trains. Ronald Reagan, who was at that time running for governor of California, angrily summed up the VDC's influence on campus life as being one of "sex, drugs and treason."[34] On the night of April 8, 1966 the VDC office was bombed and completely destroyed by persons unknown.[35] The organization never recovered. By this time, the civil rights tactics of nonviolent confrontation did not seem to be having any real effect in preventing the continued expansion of the Vietnam War, and some grass-roots activists began doubting whether their commitment to peaceful marches and teach-ins could ever change the policy of the seemingly implacable Johnson administration.

THE PSYCHEDELIC COUNTERCULTURE

By 1966 a psychedelic youth culture was beginning to attract attention. It fascinated many new leftists and offered them a stylistic identity distinctly different from that of any previous generation of radicals. The surprising birthplace of this countercultural lifestyle was Harvard University in the early 1960s. Professors Timothy Leary and Richard Alpert were experimenting on themselves and their students by taking a hallucinogenic drug called lysergic acid diethylamide, soon to become known as LSD or "acid." Those who ingested the substance would subject themselves to unusual states of consciousness, more closely resembling the varieties of religious experience than the ordinary condition of being "high," "stoned," or drunk. After Harvard fired Leary and Alpert for unprofessional conduct in 1963, Leary moved to a mansion in Millbrook, New York, provided for him by a rich scion of the Mellon family and founded a religion, the League for Spiritual Discovery, which used LSD as its sacrament. The former professor became an overnight sensation and "guru," influencing thousands to take LSD and admonishing his followers to "tune-in, turn-on and drop out."

Most of the young people who found Leary's dictum persuasive came not to his mansion but to the city of San Francisco. The Bay area, which had played host in the 1950s to the beat generation, often cast a tolerant eye on the bohemian eccentricities of artists, writers, and poets. In the easygoing San Francisco environment, the appearance of drugged, long haired, "hippies" and "flower children" was not a cause of immediate concern.[36]

Hippies dubbed their LSD experiments "tripping" because the many hours of hallucinations could feel like a momentous journey. The acid user might see dreamlike visions—each containing its own mood or message. He or she might feel alternatively holy, magical, silly, paranoid, hilarious, or like a genius with cosmic insight. For a few, using LSD was a terrifying and dangerous practice, and, in rare instances, individuals suffered psychotic episodes; some committed suicide.

Many LSD users, however, experienced such an exciting sense of inner freedom that they chose not to return to their routine existence. In 1965 thousands of young people began moving to the low-rent Haight-Ashbury section of San Francisco and living "communally" in the neighborhood's large Victorian houses. Citizens of the Haight earned their rent, food, drug, and entertainment money by panhandling, selling psychedelic and "underground" newspapers, holding odd jobs, "dealing" drugs, making candles, sandals, jewelry, and clothing to sell on street-corners, and by getting on the welfare rolls. Some of the more successful counterculturalists opened small businesses, including psychedelic "head shops," record stores, and bookshops. New and inventive forms of dress became the norm. The hippies wore bells and spangles, long hair, feathers, beads, earrings and buttons, paisley skirts, shirts, blouses, ties and pants—an eclectic free form of imaginative fashion. These lively styles spread into new left circles; multicolored clothing and long hair quickly replaced the SNCC "uniform" of denim jeans and workshirts as popular rebel attire.

Counterculturalists also developed a unique set of sexual mores and gender role expectations. While those women who performed traditional tasks were idealized as "earth mothers," others could practice a new sexual freedom.[37] Because LSD tended to break down inhibitions and stimulate erotic urges, flower children easily found partners for numerous and multiple sexual encounters. Janis Joplin, a local Haight-Ashbury blues singer, urged her listeners to "get it while you can." For women, the ability to seek out and aggressively pursue sexual relationships was an especially drastic departure from customary values; many felt free to enjoy the physical aspects of sex without being encumbered by romantic requirements. Flower children celebrated the values of physical pleasure, affection, sharing, noncompetitiveness, and the absolute personal freedom to experiment with their life. Many believed that a chemically synthesized drug was fostering a utopian community, dedicated to spiritual possibility, body pleasure, human solidarity, and peace.

The Haight-Ashbury influence spread rapidly to nearby radical Berkeley, to cities all across the United States and Canada, and into Europe and Japan. "Acid-rock" groups signed contracts with major record companies and soon the western world became aware of such Haight-Ashbury favorites as the Jefferson Airplane, Big Brother and the Holding Company with Janis Joplin, and the Grateful Dead. The Beatles, who had earlier become famous with a straightforward rock and roll sound, now switched to psychedelic rhythms and in their 1966 album *Revolver* urged their fans to "turn off your mind, relax and float downstream."[38]

Within a year, however, life in the Haight became difficult. The California legislature had declared LSD illegal, and San Francisco's tolerance was wearing thin. Prompted by law enforcement officials, businessmen, and distressed parents, the police began "hassling" and arresting hippies. Making things worse was the presence of organized criminal syndicates, intent on capturing the drug trade. They began threatening and killing the independent dealers and selling an expensive LSD, adulterated with amphetamines and poisonous contaminants. Many acid users were hospitalized because of "bum trips," "freakouts," and physical injuries. In this fearful and unhospitable environment, reports of rape, suicide, and theft were common. The social fabric of the psychedelic community was tearing apart.

Thousands of flower children moved to rural areas seeking a more peaceful setting for their lifestyle. While some returned to their hometowns hoping to "turn on" old friends, others would involve themselves in political activity, linking up with those new leftists who had taken LSD and shared similar experiences. But by 1967 young radicals were not only being influenced by the hippie message of "love and good vibes," but they were hearing an angrier voice that was coming from many of their former allies in SNCC and the civil rights movement.

BLACK POWER

America was undergoing an economic boom in the mid-1960s. Yet despite prosperity and the passage of civil rights legislation, most black people in northern ghettoes still lived in poverty, hopelessness, and a de facto segregation as complete as the more overt segregation found in the South. During the summer of 1964, Harlem, the symbolic capital of black America, had exploded in rioting. This unexpected urban uprising was quelled with extreme police violence. The black novelist James Baldwin received tremendous media attention when he predicted more and bloodier rebellions declaring that the Harlem riots were just the beginning of America's "long, hot summer."

This confrontational mood was articulated most eloquently by Malcolm X. An ex-convict and former minister in the Nation of Islam, or Black Muslims, Malcolm X was a persuasive speaker who mixed typically tough New York City street corner oratory with poetic wit. His speeches drew large, enthusiastic crowds. In Malcolm X's view, black people needed to take political, cultural, and military control over their communities. The militant leader advocated self-defense and the establishment in America of a separate black nation that would develop close ties with Africa. He believed that white America had, because of its racist history, brought the Harlem riots and the assassination of President John F. Kennedy on itself.[39] Malcolm X was himself assassinated in New York City on February 21, 1965, but his perspective would continue to have a heuristic influence on black and white radicals for the remainder of the decade.

Between 1964 and 1967, 101 major riots and scores of minor disruptions took place in cities across the country. Police made 28,932 arrests.[40] On April 4, 1968, Martin Luther King was murdered by a white racist in Memphis, Tennessee. Black rage at his death spurred simultaneous nationwide rioting. By the end of 1968, the decade's racial upheavals had led to a total of 208 deaths and $792.8 million worth of property destruction.[41] The amount of damage and extent of popular participation led many observbers to describe the disturbances as a black insurrection.

During the period of riots and rising black anger, SNCC fired its white staff workers and emerged as a national voice for black radicalism.[42] SNCC chairperson, Stokely Carmichael, popularized the slogan "Black Power." The phrase struck a responsive chord among black people and quickly became both a political demand and a rallying cry. In 1967 H. Rap Brown, who had succeeded Carmichael as the organization's chairperson, expressed SNCC's frustration with nonviolence and gradualism and declared that black people should form paramilitary groups to fight in support of rioters.[43]

"Black power" also came to have a distinct cultural expression. Many black people began wearing their hair in a full, natural style called an afro and began dressing in multicolored dashikis. They took up the study of Swahili, the most widely spoken language in Africa. Some abandoned Christianity as a "slave religion" and embraced forms of Islam. This upsurge of black pride and cultural nationalism was expressed succinctly by the slogan "Black is beautiful."

PANTHER POWER

The Black Panther Party (BPP) became, for a few years, the leading voice of black militancy in America. By 1970 the party, based in Oakland, California, claimed a widely circulated weekly newspaper, children's schools, free breakfast and health care programs, 30 chapters, and 10 community centers across the country.[44] The BPP borrowed its name and symbol from a SNCC-sponsored group in Lowndes County, Alabama and proposed a ten-point economic and political program for black liberation. Party co-founder Huey P. Newton sought to give a pragmatic significance to the black power slogan. According to the Panther leader, black power should mean more than a change in pride, consciousness, and culture. Power required the revolutionary will to alter forcefully the circumstances of black life; it was "the ability to define phenomena and make them act in a desired manner."

The Panthers urged black people not to engage in rioting. Spontaneous uprisings, they believed, were hurting the black community more than damaging the "white power structure." The disorders had been successfully contained within ghettoes; many more blacks than whites had been killed; and much property owned by blacks was being destroyed. Rather than riots, the Panthers called for armed self-defense and a strategy of urban guerrilla warfare. Insurrectionary struggle would be directed against the police, whom the Panthers denounced as an "occupying army in the black community."

Police were ridiculed by Panthers and labeled "pigs." The Panther newspaper regularly contained cartoons in which police, landlords, and other "enemies of the people" were portrayed as greedy, fly-infested creatures. The "pigs" were always contrasted unfavorably with "the people," who were portrayed as noble, brave, self-sacrificing, and no longer willing to suffer racism.[45] The phrase "pig" became a popular black militant and new left term; it was used extensively as a symbolic description of the entire American social system.

In 1967, Huey Newton was arrested and charged with murdering a policeman.[46] The Black Panther Party, under the direction of Eldridge Cleaver (author of the best-seller *Soul on Ice*) and Party co-founder Bobby G. Seale, organized a campaign to free the jailed leader. Nationwide rallies drew large, multiracial audiences, and the presence of Marlon Brando and other celebrities ensured thorough media coverage. At these well-attended gatherings, Panther cadre marched in formation, wearing berets and black leather jackets and chanting in unison, "Free Huey or the sky's the limit!"

The Party broadened its efforts to win white support. The chance to work with black militants was a boon to those new leftists who had been feeling politically adrift since their expulsion from SNCC. White radicals were attracted by the Panthers' popularity in black communities and the organization's military charisma.[47] Many new leftists adopted a generally uncritical attitude toward the Black Panther Party. Some followed the Panthers' suggestion and purchased weapons; a few relinquished previous commitments to pacifism. They also ignored the early Party's complete male domination.[48]

The Black Panther Party was a hierarchical organization governed by a central committee composed almost exclusively of men. The official title of the only woman member, Kathleen Cleaver, was communications secretary. Nonetheless Panther women in the rank and file spent considerable time together under what became increasingly difficult circumstances, and, as a result, they formed close bonds, special loyalties to one another, and a reliable network of friendship and support. By the late 1960s, after a spate of jailings and killings of male leaders, several Panther women, including singer Elaine Brown and young poet Erika Huggins, became major leaders in the organization.

At the end of the decade, FBI Director J. Edgar Hoover announced that the Black Panther Party had replaced the Communist party as the greatest threat to national security. He launched a full-scale counter-intelligence program (COINTELPRO) aimed at "disrupting and neu-tralizing" the group.[49] FBI special agents sought to divide the Panther organization by spreading false rumors and misinformation. They com-posed letters to Party members implicating Panther leaders in stealing from the Party treasury, taking money from the police, maintaining secret Swiss bank accounts, and having sexual liaisons with white women. Local police forces were encouraged to launch raids against Panther headquarters. On December 4, 1969 the Chicago police shot to death two Panther leaders, Fred Hampton and Mark Clark, in an armed assault on their apartment.

The Panthers began falling prey to a siege mentality. The Party was wracked by harmful purges, distrust, and political splits.[50] By 1972, the Black Panther Party had ceased functioning as a national organization. It remained active in its home base of Oakland, California, running candidates for public office, continuing to publish its newspaper, and administering a variety of schools and service programs.

1968: The Movement

In 1968 increasingly large numbers of young people became engaged in political protest and were attracted to a countercultural lifestyle.[51] In campus towns and large cities across the country, a dissident community emerged; it was called by many names but most frequently was referred to as "The Movement." This phenomenon was rooted in many sources, including SNCC's early idea of community, new left participatory democracy, Black Panther anger, and the Haight-Ashbury's experimental attitude toward drugs, sexual freedom, and exotic fashions of dress.

The Movement was ecumenical in its social composition; it consisted of individuals who were usually separated from each other by class, age, racial and cultural differences. Although students continued to predominate, the Movement came to include GIs, older radicals, gay rights activists, disabled people, high school students, women's liberation militants, youth culture dropouts, senior citizens, and alienated children of the very rich and of the working class. Movement ranks included college professors, ministers, Native American medicine people, old time labor organizers, Mexican-American farm workers, show business personalities, Puerto Rican nationalists, nuns, priests, members of the lumpenproletariat, and children of generals, of CIA officials, and of the Mafia. All these people were joined together in a highly charged atmosphere of personal change and political confrontation.

Movement activists started to publish hundreds of cooperatively run newspapers that were independent, community based, politically rebellious, pro-psychedelic, and sexually explicit. These journals collectively named themselves the "underground press," and, at their peak, enjoyed an estimated 2 million readers.[52] The alternative press supplemented its coverage by subscribing to the Liberation News Service, which provided a packet of articles, cartoons, and photographs. To expand radical media further, new left cinematographers formed Newsreel, and began producing and distributing radical film documentaries. The major media became fascinated by the new and colorful Movement lifestyle and began giving it considerable coverage.[53] This extensive publicity brought many new recruits but also served to stir up greater hostility among the majority of Americans who were still opposed to protest.

Amidst increasing opposition to his war policies, Lyndon Johnson announced in the spring of 1968 that he would not run for a second term as president, in order to facilitate peace negotiations in Vietnam. Leaders of the antiwar movement viewed the president's decision as a partial victory that created for them a tactical dilemma. They had planned to demonstrate at the upcoming Democratic convention in Chicago, but since the nomination would possibly go to Senator Robert Kennedy, a peace candidate, many antiwar activists were no longer sure that their protest would serve a useful purpose. When Robert Kennedy was gunned down after winning the California primary, the political situation changed dramatically. Now there was little likelihood that the Democratic party would give its presidential nomination to an advocate of peace. Many activists became convinced that demonstrations at the Democratic convention were imperative. For them, it was "On to Chicago!"

COLUMBIA UNIVERSITY

In the months preceding the Democratic convention, the confrontational spirit of 1968 took hold at Columbia University in New York City. The prestigious Ivy League institution was engulfed by protest, and all official educational and extracurricular activities were brought to a halt. The hostilities commenced when Columbia's trustees decided to construct a campus gymnasium on university-owned land in neighboring Harlem's Morningside Park. Black students and their community supporters denounced this plan as an imperious intrusion that would result in the removal of already scarce community recreational facilities. The local SDS chapter, led by Mark Rudd, joined the protest and added demands that the university democratize its academic procedures and sever its official ties to the Department of Defense. As negotiations were proceeding, black and white students barricaded themselves into separate campus buildings. The radicals ate, slept, made love, held meetings, and practiced participatory democracy inside the occupied buildings. The walls of these "communes" were decorated with posters of Stokely Carmichael, Malcolm X, Ho Chi Minh, and Che Guevara.

After eight days of disruption, university administrators requested that the New York City police clear the five occupied buildings. The police proceeded to club, kick, and punch the occupiers, injuring 100 students and faculty members, and arresting nearly 700.[54] Horrified at

the brutality and what they considered Columbia University's betrayal of its proclaimed civility in favor of "police barbarism," the university community went on strike, and classes could not be resumed that semester. The Columbia strike was a dramatic signal that some members of America's young intellectual elite were renouncing the privileges of their status and rebelling against racism, the Vietnam War, and other perceived injustices of American life.

CHICAGO: THE WHOLE WORLD WAS WATCHING

In the last week of August 1968, while millions watched on television, a ferocious battle between police and antiwar demonstrators unfolded in the streets of Chicago during the Democratic National Convention. The Democrats picked Chicago for their convention site because the city appeared to be effectively protected from what seemed to them a wild, uncontrollable, violent, nihilistic, and irresponsible protest movement. Memories of a massive antiwar sit-in on the steps of the Pentagon in October 1967 and recent images of the crisis at Columbia and, in May, of a nationwide student and worker uprising in France were cause for alarm. Chicago was tightly ruled by one of the last old-time political bosses, Mayor Richard J. Daley. The power of his Democratic machine and police force was virtually unchallengeable, and the mayor had recently declared that rioters and looters would be shot on sight.

Mayor Daley refused to grant permits for some of the planned protests. Soon, frightening rumors spread through the peace movement: Chicago's sewers were being prepared for use as jails, and dogs were being trained to attack demonstrators. A public debate broke out in antiwar ranks. A heterogeneous collection of individuals and groups, including some SDS chapters, various pacifists and liberals, the *Rolling Stone* magazine's editorial writers, and an assortment of rock personalities argued against going to Chicago. Influenced by the Kennedy and King assassinations, they fearfully predicted that many protesters would be shot and killed during the Democratic convention. The demonstration's proponents, including National Mobilization leaders Dave Dellinger, Tom Hayden, and Rennie Davis, answered the criticism by affirming their nonviolent intentions. The greater the numbers of people who came to Chicago, they argued, the less chance there would be of police assault. It was likely that Richard Daley would grant permits at the last minute in any case, since officials typically acted in a deliberately evasive manner when negotiating with protest leaders.

Mayor Daley remained adamant in his refusal to grant permits. His unyielding position may perhaps be explained by what appears to have been an FBI-directed counterintelligence disinformation project.[55] FBI agents informed the mayor and his representatives of bizarre conspiracies in which Democratic candidates would be assassinated by leftists and the city's water supply poisoned with hallucinogenic drugs. Mayor Daley's office never granted requests for permits to march or sleep in a city park. The outcome of his decision would be chaos in the streets.

THE YIPPIES

Among the groups involved in confrontations during the Democratic convention was the Youth International Party, better known as the Yippies. A loosely knit association with no formal structure, the Yippies consciously blended new left and libertarian ideas with hippie lifestyle and a talent for media manipulation. They sought to turn comedy, play, theatrics, and acid-rock music into new forms of political protest. This innovative mix would attract many young people who had already experienced the surrealistic excitement of hallucinogenic drugs.

Yippie tacticians Jerry Rubin, Abbie Hoffman, and satirist Paul Krassner believed that television was potentially the most effective agent of social change because of its global influence on human consciousness. Persuaded by Marshall McLuhan's views on the determining importance of electronic communications, they maintained that the media could be seduced into providing even greater coverage of radical events if those activities were made entertaining.[56]

The Youth International Party came to be publicly identified with its charismatic male personalities. Those few Yippie women who became known in the media did so at least in part because they were girlfriends or wives of men. Despite this masculine ascendancy, many freewheeling women who rejected traditional conformist values could find in Yippie philosophy a compelling appeal for personal freedom.

The unpredictable Yippies had previously brought the New York Stock Exchange to a halt by tossing money at stockbrokers. In another act of "guerrilla theatre," they had thrown soot in the faces of public utility executives. Now the Yippies declared they would defy Mayor Daley's threats and hold a Festival of Life in Chicago, at which time a live, four-legged pig would be nominated for president of the United States.

LINCOLN PARK

Only a small number of protesters came to Chicago during convention week. It was estimated that 5,000 people arrived from out of town, and another 5,000 were local residents. Peace activists and Yippies were joined by SDS members, whose leaders had a last minute change of heart and encouraged members to participate. Additionally, followers of antiwar candidate Eugene McCarthy defiantly united with the demonstrators when the senator's presidential hopes were crushed on the convention floor.[57] The protesters' ranks were further enlarged by black residents of Chicago who supported a Poor People's March organized by comedian Dick Gregory. Unexpectedly, the Blackstone Rangers, a well-known Chicago youth gang, involved themselves in numerous rallies, marches, and protest activities.[58]

Chicago's Lincoln Park was a gathering place for demonstrators. Young protesters spent their days painting antiwar placards, practicing Japanese "snake dancing" and karate, smoking marijuana, forming "affinity groups," debating tactics, and listening to orators and rock music. The militants were determined to ignore the mayor's denial of permits and remain in the park. Their right to sleep under the stars had become a symbolic confrontational issue.

A POLICE RIOT

Mayor Richard Daley was equally determined. Every night throughout convention week he ordered his police to clear the park. An unusual armored vehicle, protected with its own barbed wire shield and guided by rotating searchlights, led the way for advancing lines of masked helmeted police who lobbed rounds of tear gas at those who fled. The poet Allen Ginsberg was gassed as he and a group of disciples sat on the grass and attempted to subdue the violence by chanting "OMMMMM." A group of ministers carrying large crosses tried to calm the police but were ignored. Everyone ran to escape the gas and avoid arrest. Some radicals reacted by fanning out into the surrounding streets, fighting with police in hand-to-hand combat, lighting fires in trash cans, throwing rocks, and smashing windows.

As the week progressed, the police became increasingly violent, often indiscriminantly assaulting news reporters, television camerapeople, bystanders, and even convention delegates. When the street fighting escalated, Lyndon Johnson called out the National Guard, which proceeded to roll tanks through the riotous city. Troops with fixed bayonets took positions outside the Hilton Hotel, which housed many delegates. In that same week, the Soviet Union invaded Czechoslovakia. Images of Russian tanks and U.S. Army bayonets appeared side by side on front pages of the daily press. Some Chicago demonstrators responded by spraypainting "Czechago" on walls and tanks, while others, like folk singer Phil Ochs, urged the troops to throw down their weapons.[59]

Although some Chicago police maintained a professional decorum and attempted to restrain their fellow officers, others engaged in uncontrolled brutality. A report for the National Commission on the Causes and Prevention of Violence concluded that a "police riot" had taken place in Chicago between August 21-28, 1968.[60] Since members of the press had been battered along with protesters, the national television networks had made the unprecedented decision to provide live, unedited coverage of these bloody scenes. With cameras pointing at them, the harassed demonstrators chanted, "The whole world is watching."

THE NIXON ADMINISTRATION
AND POLITICAL REPRESSION

In November 1968 Richard M. Nixon was elected president of the United States. Nixon had, in the early 1950s, advanced his political career by investigating what he called "communist infiltration" of the United States government; now he played to voters' fears of disruptive radical activity by asserting that "bums" and anarchists were bent on destroying American society.

Immediately after his election, Nixon and John Mitchell, the attorney general, directed federal prosecutors to seek grand jury indictments against key organizers of the convention demonstrations. FBI Director J. Edgar Hoover publicly acknowledged the activities of 2,000 special agents, located on college campuses and in communities nationwide, whose job it was to question participants in the Chicago violence. Hoover informed his operatives that their investigative work might culminate in a political "show trial" and give the government a desirable opportunity to "neutralize and hamper" the new left.[61] FBI agents began expanding the bureau's clandestine counterintelligence program against the Movement by spreading rumors and falsehoods concerning radicals to parents, lovers, friends, neighbors, political associates, employers, landlords, and the media.[62] Attorney General Mitchell authorized wiretaps and break-ins into the offices and homes of radicals, their friends, and families. In this increasingly repressive atmosphere, federal and state grand juries began to subpoena Movement activists and imprison those who would not answer questions.[63] House and Senate committees added to the government's campaign of harassment by demanding that Movement organizers testify at their highly publicized hearings.[64] Local police intelligence bureaus, known as "red squads," began to receive increased federal funding that enabled them to coordinate programs to repress the new left with other national law enforcement agencies.[65] Both President Nixon and Vice-President Spiro T. Agnew sought, through belligerent public references, to arouse popular anger against protesters. This agitation by the country's two highest elected officials once inspired New York construction workers to beat up antiwar marchers. Finally, with Richard Nixon's direct encouragement, college presidents began to suspend and expel students who were found to be in violation of campus rules because of their involvement in demonstrations.[66] Men who suffered this academic punishment lost their student deferments and became eligible for the draft.

Richard Nixon's program of political repression was qualitatively different from anything American protest movements had recently experienced. The assaults were concerted, coordinated, well financed, and thorough. By 1969, the American government, under the urging of its president, was in an all out war against dissent.

1969: "The Revolution"

Despite the repressive policies of the Nixon administration, the radical protest movement seemed to prosper for approximately three years after the Chicago violence. The underground press had increased from only five weekly newspapers in 1967 to 150 community-based papers by 1969.[67] A national radical press, including magazines such as *Ramparts* and *Leviathan* and newspapers such as *The Movement* or *The National Guardian*, sometimes scooped established publications on their coverage of the Vietnam War and other issues. The year 1969 began with a series of student strikes and campus building seizures led by black undergraduates who demanded that university officials hire more black faculty and initiate black studies programs. Disturbances occurred at San Francisco State, the University of Wisconsin in Madison, Harvard, and many other schools. Black students publicly brought guns onto the Cornell campus to dramatize their cause. The number of local SDS chapters had grown to 304 by 1969, even though its national organization was on the brink of political disintegration.[68] In June of 1969 thousands of gays rioted, threw bricks, and set fire to police cars in New York city, to protest police harassment of homosexuals.[69] This rebellion became a national symbol of new gay pride and resistance. The antiwar movement held its largest demonstration of the decade, a peace march of 500,000 people, in Washington, D.C. during November 1969.

In that year, partially as a result of police brutality in Chicago, many Movement activists ceased referring to themselves as "new leftists." Their earlier commitment to participatory democracy lessened and was superceded by "the revolution" as a preeminent value. Some advocated variations of classical Marxist-Leninist proletarian revolution, with an emphasis on Chinese-style Maoism, and took jobs in factories to engage in union organizing. But for most activists, the revolution was something vague. The phrase could mean joining a rural commune or driving trucks for an urban food cooperative. Using the word as a self-description might signify that a young rebel was in absolute opposition to all governmental policies, or it might mean just growing long hair and eating health foods. For some, revolution meant becoming a pacifist and rejecting all forms of violence; for others, who believed in the inevitability of "armed struggle," it demanded taking target practice. Many, acting in the name of revolution, broke up their marriages and monogamous sexual relationships. For women, not wearing a bra or not shaving their legs was part of the revolution. Attending free universities and liberation schools or sending children to alternative daycare centers was, for some, revolutionary. Rock music that produced anger and euphoria in its listeners was hailed as revolutionary.[70] Public nudity and the use of hallucinogenic drugs were boasted of as revolutionary acts. Rebellion against one's parents and rejection of their values and lifestyle was often seen as a sine qua non of revolutionary faith. Supporting Third World guerrillas was a revolutionary obligation. And finally, for some, having a good time in "uptight" American society was, in itself, the revolution.

Movement participants shared an emboldening sense of having broken with the dominant institutions of American society. These new revolutionaries replaced loyalty to the American government with a highly emotional commitment to social change. They regarded Vietnamese guerillas as heroes. Posters of Indochinese women carrying guns were widely circulated, and, at antiwar demonstrations, thousands of protesters displayed the red, yellow, and blue flag of the National Liberation Front of South Vietnam. The wartime heroism of Asian fighters in their David and Goliath confrontation with the technological superiority of a powerful country inspired in many Movement activists a romantic view of revolution. Rejecting the possibility of gradual and peaceful reform in America, the new militants proudly proclaimed that they would make a "revolution in our lifetime."[71]

PEOPLE'S PARK

The largest community-based uprising of 1969 began in April, when a group of young radicals started to fashion a park on property belonging to the University of California at Berkeley. Thousands of students and other local residents joined in its construction by laying sod, planting flowers, landscaping, building benches and swings, cooking, playing music, and just "hanging out" in what would come to be called People's Park. Campus officials declared that this unauthorized use of university land would not be tolerated. With the active support of Governor Ronald Reagan, they directed police to build a barbed wire fence around the park. For a week, thousands battled with local police, Alameda County sheriffs, and eventually with the National Guard. The People's Park supporters were beaten, fired upon with deadly force, or arrested en masse. Police helicopters dropped tear gas on the entire city of Berkeley. For the first time in the sixties, police received official sanction to use guns against white demonstrators. An estimated 100 protesters were wounded by shotgun blasts and one youth, James Rector, was killed.

In its brief existence, People's Park was for many a perfect representation of the Movement's utopian impulse. Moderate and conservative fraternity and sorority members who worked in the park because they believed it was a constructive community achievement were shocked to discover that the University would resort to such brutal methods. Radicals of all ages were attracted to People's Park and to the mixture of voluntary hard work, creative planning, individual initiative, collective decision making, and play that it provided. Community anger at the park's destruction sparked a peaceful protest march of 25,000, but university officials adamantly refused to remove their fence.[72]

WOODSTOCK

The most well-attended countercultural event of 1969 was the Woodstock Music Festival, which took place on a farm in the Catskill Mountains of New York State in mid-August 1969. Woodstock became the Festival of Life that the Yippies had not been permitted to hold in Chicago; it exemplified the peaceful aspirations of an entire generation of young Americans. For three days and nights, 500,000 people lived together in cow pastures, listening and dancing to an array of the popular rock artists of the 1960s. Although the festival promoters had intended to charge admission, it was the gate crashers who prevailed. In accord with the Movement's anticommercial values, the decade's most significant rock concert was free.

"Woodstock" would enter the American language as a countercultural synonym for community. The festival's celebrants dined on food cooked in collective kitchens and treated their "bad LSD trips" in cooperatively run medical tents. There were no reported incidents of violence. So communal was the quality of work and play that it prompted

Yippie Abbie Hoffman to write a book, *Woodstock Nation*, in which he celebrated the spirit of Woodstock as the quintessence of his decade's cultural rebellion.[73]

PUTTING A DECADE ON TRIAL

It was not the harmony of Woodstock but the continuing violence and repression in Chicago that had the greatest impact on the Movement in 1969. Early in that year a federal grand jury had indicted seven organizers of the Chicago demonstrations and the chairman of the Black Panther Party for conspiracy to incite a riot during the Democratic National Convention. Both the federal prosecutors and the defendants used the long trial for political ends. If the government's intent was to intimidate and weaken the Movement, as FBI Director J. Edgar Hoover had stated, then Yippie defendant Jerry Rubin saw the Conspiracy Trial as an opportunity to increase the scope of radical activity. He accepted his indictment gladly, declaring it to be "the Academy Award of protest."[74]

WEATHERMAN: DAYS OF RAGE

The Chicago Conspiracy Trial opened in the last week of September 1969 amidst politically motivated streetfighting. These riots, proclaimed the "Days of Rage," were planned and led by a revolutionary group called Weatherman who took their name from a Bob Dylan refrain that proclaimed, "You don't need a weatherman to know which way the wind blows."[75] Weatherman was directed by former SDS leaders who now believed that large demonstrations, electoral political activity, and other forms of peaceful protest could not end the war or bring about any significant social change. Weather leaders Bernardine Dohrn and Jeff Jones argued that young people should stop marching and instead remake themselves into urban guerrillas, who would fight in solidarity with black and Third World revolutionaries against the American government and its "racist empire." To further their military strategy, several hundred members of Weatherman rampaged in Chicago's streets for several days. In one "action," a helmeted band of Weatherwomen assaulted the police.[76] These were the first known instances of sixties protest in which large numbers of demonstrators carried out a planned attack on police.

By the fall of 1969 Weatherman was emerging as the most famous surviving offshoot of Students for a Democratic Society. SDS had recently succumbed to internal divisions and, as the organization split into warring factions, any sense of common purpose had broken down.[77] Inflammatory rhetoric, verbal abuse, and even physical violence replaced SDS's former practice of consensus, lengthy discussion, and participatory democracy. Weatherman emerged from this political strife with a clandestine organization termed the Weather Underground, and, for the next few years, provoked much controversy, debate, and grudging admiration in Movement circles by carrying out highly publicized bombings of government buildings in a determined campaign to "bring the war home."

THE TRIAL

As the Conspiracy Trial proceeded, a modern morality play unfolded inside the Chicago courtroom. It pitted the defendants and their attorneys, who represented the political and cultural rebellion of a decade, against prosecutors and a judge, who embodied the conservative beliefs that had dominated the 1950s. This clash of values and personalities caused all involved parties to set aside judicial logic and procedure. As the trial progressed, the courtroom was periodically enmeshed in an alternately cruel and comic pandemonium.

The Chicago 8, as they were called in the press, personified a cross section of 1960s protest. Dave Dellinger, a lifelong pacifist and founder of the national anti-Vietnam War movement, was, in his fifties, the oldest of those indicted. Tom Hayden and Rennie Davis had been influential SDS leaders and participants in the ERAP projects. John Froines and Lee Weiner were involved in local organizing activities. Abbie Hoffman had been a SNCC worker and one of the Youth International Party's originators. Jerry Rubin was a former member of the Vietnam Day Committee in Berkeley and a Yippie. Bobby Seale, a co-founder of the Black Panther Party, was the party's chief public spokesperson.

The elderly Judge Hoffman consistently ridiculed and ruled against these defendants.[78] He would routinely upbraid chief defense counsel

William M. Kunstler for leaning against a lectern while addressing the court. The judge always misspoke the name of defense co-counsel Leonard Weinglass. Julius Hoffman's autocratic manner and open bias served as an ongoing provocation to the eight radical defendants and their attorneys.

The Chicago 8 decided to present a defense that would offer evidence of improper police and government conduct and put on display radical political ideas and the countercultural lifestyle. "The Conspiracy" called to the stand such well-known figures as civil rights leader Jesse Jackson; poet Allen Ginsberg; singers Judy Collins, Phil Ochs, Arlo Guthrie, and Country Joe McDonald; women's peace movement activist Cora Weiss; LSD guru Timothy Leary; and writer Norman Mailer. A former pacifist who had observed police brutality in Chicago, testified that she could no longer believe in the possibility of nonviolent social change. News reporters, photographers, and even a member of the British Parliament gave articulate descriptions of how they had been abused by the Chicago police.[79]

Government prosecutor Thomas Foran responded to the defendants' strategy by denouncing their lawyers as "mouthpieces" and calling the defendants "evil men." Foran was not judicially admonished for making these prejudicial statements in the jury's presence. Nor was Judge Hoffman any more sympathetic when the defense called former Attorney General Ramsey Clark to the stand. Clark had opposed the conspiracy indictment because he believed the Chicago riots were, in the main, caused by police overreaction. Judge Hoffman refused to let Clark appear before the jury and derided his testimony as "irrelevant." Despite this hostile courtroom atmosphere, seven of the eight defendants managed to present most of their legal arguments. But the fortunes of the eighth, Black Panther leader Bobby Seale, were different.

Friction between the judge and the Panther leader had been brewing from the trial's inception. Bobby Seale requested that proceedings be delayed because his attorney, Charles R. Garry, was ill. Seale also requested that he be allowed to act as his own lawyer. Both requests were denied. Seale persisted in trying to defend himself, to cross-examine witnesses, and to raise procedural objections. Judge Hoffman repeatedly directed the Panther to remain silent, but Seale, who maintained that he was exercising his constitutional rights, refused. Finally the judge decreed that Bobby Seale be bound to his chair and gagged.

For many courtroom observers, the chaining of Black Panther Bobby Seale recalled images of nineteenth century slavery. Several altercations between federal marshals and the other defendants erupted in the courtroom. Spectators were ejected for verbal outbursts. After three embarrassing days for the United States legal system, Judge Hoffman declared a mistrial in the case of Bobby Seale and sentenced him to an unprecedented four and one-half years in prison for contempt of court. The Chicago 8 became the Chicago 7.

The Conspiracy Trial did not restrain the radical movement. In fact, the trial offered the defendants an opportunity for communicating revolutionary ideas to considerable numbers of people. This turn of events occurred at a time when the protest movement had been weakened by the demise of SDS. But as the defendants traveled across America, speaking on numerous campuses, they attracted large, enthusiastic audiences. Those same people who had been unsuccessful in bringing great numbers of demonstrators to Chicago during convention week were now mobbed at rallies and pursued for autographs. Movie stars like Dustin Hoffman and John Voight sought them out. Nicholas Ray, the legendary director of James Dean's film *Rebel Without a Cause*, appeared with his camera in Chicago, looking for a new rebel to lionize.

At the end of the five-month trial, and even before the jury rendered its verdict, Judge Hoffman sentenced all the defendants and their lawyers to jail for contempt of court. The Chicago 7 had prepared for the expected conviction by mobilizing their supporters for "The Day After" or TDA demonstrations. When five of the seven defendants were found guilty, youth riots took place in numerous cities, with protesters marching in the streets, chanting "You can jail the revolutionaries, but you can't jail the revolution."

With the exception of Bobby Seale, who was awaiting trial on a different charge, the conspiracy defendants were soon released on bail.[80] The convictions were eventually reversed by a higher court on the grounds of Judge Hoffman's numerous procedural errors and open hostility to the defendants. The Chicago Conspiracy Trial was, because of its symbolism and publicity, the most important of a number of such political trials that occurred with increasing frequency by the end of the 1960s.[81]

For the next few years, most of the Chicago 7 remained highly visible celebrities. Their influential role soon came to be resented by many activists, especially women, who rebuked the seven for being a media-created, white male elite who did not make themselves accountable to any Movement constituency. The expressions "heavy" and "revolutionary superstar" were frequently used to describe the seven. Given traditional new left egalitarian values, these phrases connoted a perception that the Conspiracy defendants had been elevated to positions of leadership without Movement participation or approval. Eventually the term "heavy" came to be incorporated into radical nomenclature and was frequently applied to anyone in Movement circles who achieved some degree of influence and power.

1970: The Women's Rebellion

By 1970 the movement for gender democracy had taken strong hold within the ranks of radical protest. During the early 1960s, women had occasionally tried to lessen their inequality within new left organizations; but these advocates of sexual egalitarianism were for the most part isolated from each other and ignored by the majority of male and female activists.[82] Up until the middle of the decade, women had filled a minority of important positions inside radical organizations, and a few, like the Free Speech Movement's Bettina Aptheker, were prominent leaders. By the late 1960s women were observing that their influence and status within radical protest groups were rapidly declining, and that the Movement was becoming almost completely male dominated. By January 1967, only 18 out of 99 SDS national committee delegates were women.[83] The large antidraft movement was, by its nature, male centered and had taken as one of its slogans "Girls say yes to boys who say no." The influential Black Panther Party was directed by an all-male leadership. Finally, by 1970, the Chicago Conspiracy Trial had produced a closed circle of white male radical celebrities.

WOMEN'S LIBERATION

In 1968 a small number of women began agitating for equality both within the protest movement and in the whole of American society. Borrowing from the revolutionary rhetoric of the time, the militant women named their new movement "women's liberation." On September 7, 1968 one of the first women's liberation demonstrations took place at the Miss America Pageant in Atlantic City, New Jersey.

47

Some participants chose this activity as a symbolic alternative to involvement in the demonstrations that had occured a week earlier at the Democratic National Convention in Chicago. Two hundred women marched outside the convention hall and threw bras, high-heeled shoes, and other "instruments of torture" into a "freedom trash can." Inside the hall, demonstrators brought the pageant to a momentary halt by hanging a women's liberation banner from the balcony. And, in the style of those counterculturalists who had, a week previously, nominated a pig for president, the pageant protesters crowned a live sheep Miss America.[84]

Women activists began meeting in small groups to decide on the new movement's goals, tactics, and theoretical analysis. Topics of discussion included consciousness raising, the abolition of beauty standards, birth control and abortion, complaints about boyfriends and husbands, experiences of rape and sexual harassment, female sexuality and lesbianism, the monotony of secretaial tasks, appropriate responses to being called a "chick" or an "old lady," and the joys of repairing one's own Volkswagen. These gatherings, from which men were excluded, were held in an extremely egalitarian manner, recalling the participatory democracy practiced in early SNCC and SDS meetings. Many female militants had been civil rights and student activists and brought to women's politics a longstanding new left commitment to equality. Only now the principle would be applied to gender.

Women's liberationists were coming to the conclusion that their experience of sixties protest had been marred by a painful situation in which the language of liberation was spoken on behalf of everyone who was oppressed—but not for women. They felt that women were not receiving sufficient credit for their contributions to building the Movement and were now being denied access to its policy-making processes. In Movement organizations, women were being treated as secretaries, supporters, sex objects, and, occasionally, targets of misogynistic verbal abuse, but not as complete human beings and equal partners. Movement men, it was asserted, were replicating the hierarchical relationships of American society rather than living the alternative. Similar experiences, new friendships, and an emerging communality of viewpoint linked the militants together in an exhilarating bond of "sisterhood."

Liberation theorists believed that all personal problems had a political cause. Any woman's difficulties were seen as endemic to the secondary position of all. If individual women fought for more personal

power, their struggle could lead to a democratic restructuring of American society. The new militants argued that without women reinterpreting their sense of self they could not effectively participate in a movement for radical political transformation and, conversely, that without the occurrence of major social change it would be impossible for women to truly experience a liberated consciousness. The interrelatedness of personal problems and social change, which had been discussed in the earlier sociological writings of C. Wright Mills, was now used to interpret women's oppression. In 1969, women activists began insisting that "the personal is political."[85]

NEW LEFTISTS AND SEPARATISTS

As the message of women's liberation began spreading outside Movement environs, an angry disagreement emerged. Some women believed that activists should continue to champion women's issues within existing movements for social change. Others, now describing themselves as "radical feminists," formed a separatist movement.[86] These radicals claimed that sixties protest was "hopelessly sexist," dismissed antiwar causes as "male-defined," and labeled women who continued to devote themselves to such activities as "male-identified." Many feminists used the anticolonialist ideas of black nationalism to justify their complete break with men. Just as black militants, in order to control their own organization, forced all white people out of SNCC, so, the female separatists argued, women ought to establish a similar independence by purging men from their lives. Some advocated lesbianism as the politically preferred form of female sexual activity. In an influential 1970 manifesto, former Yippie Robin Morgan called on Movement women to abandon boyfriends and husbands and to "free our sisters, free ourselves."[87]

Those critics who experienced women's involvement in sixties protest as entirely oppressive tended to deny the liberatory effects of activism. The Movement's culture and politics offered women an opportunity to act in a variety of nontraditional roles and to acquire an assortment of skills, ranging from media broadcasting to martial arts. In the milieu of protest, women lived free from the pressures of having to marry and bear children or take up stereotypical careers. They were motivated to question all traditional institutions of American society: the family, schools, motherhood, as well as the government. As a result of sixties activism, many Movement women developed greater self-reliance, charisma, self-confidence, networks of friendship, and social mobility. Participation in protest inspired many to believe that their actions and ideas would contribute to "changing the world."

PROTESTING

From 1968 to 1971 women organized large demonstrations calling for legalized, "free abortion on demand," and an end to job discrimination, pornography, and violence against women. Women organized sit-ins at Playboy owner Hugh Hefner's clubs and private mansion. Some occupied the offices of daily newspapers to protest sexist and degrading advertising and editorial policies. In 1970 liberationists took managerial control of The Rat, a New York City underground newspaper, and fired all male staff. Other underground newspapers began to show a much greater concern with women's issues and sharply reduced their revenues by dropping all pornographic advertising. A variety of women's newspapers with such titles as It Ain't Me Babe, Up From Under, off our backs, and No More Fun and Games commenced publication. Such influential books as Shulamith Firestone's *Dialectic of Sex*, Kate Miller's *Sexual Politics*, Toni Cade's *The Black Woman*, and Marge Piercy's *Dance the Eagle to Sleep* all appeared in 1970.[88] In 1971 5,000 women descended on the Pentagon in an antiwar demonstration, many carrying placards bearing the portrait of Vietnamese communist diplomat Madame Binh. Women's liberation organizations, such as Boston's Bread and Roses, took over campus buildings and temporarily converted them into women's centers. University authorities were compelled to permit the establishment of accredited Women's Studies programs. The FBI, which had initially been uninterested in women's liberation, now took investigative note of this new movement and, by 1971, considered it threatening enough to justify collecting files on women's political activities and infiltrating agents and informers into the movement's ranks.

THE WOMEN'S MOVEMENT

By 1972 images of "liberated" women were appearing in mass advertising, and Ms. magazine, with its commercial format, was building a large circulation. Women smokers were told by Virginia Slims, "You've come a long way, baby," and the cigarette company was sponsoring a women's golf tournament. The traditional stereotype of female passivity was being partially replaced in popular culture by a more independent image.

The women's liberation movement was in a state of decline by 1973, replaced by a more moderate and ecumenical movement. It was led by feminists who had dropped the radical label "liberation" and worked within the mainstream of American political life. This new movement concentrated its efforts on successfully legalizing abortion, trying to win support for the Equal Rights Amendment, and creating a feminist scholarship. Many early women's liberation activists joined this cause. Others ceased political activity to pursue private goals. A few continued to agitate for lesbian separatism, and some remained active in leftist politics, although in an increasingly isolated movement.

The Decade Ends

The 1960s concluded with a rapid series of violent acts. In November 1969 U.S. Army Lieutenant William Calley was officially accused of covering up a massacre in which unarmed residents of a Vietnamese village were killed by American soldiers and their bodies thrown into a ditch. A few days before Calley was charged, 5,000 antiwar demonstrators besieged the U.S. Justice Department in a scene that Attorney General John Mitchell described as looking "like the Russian revolution."[89] In the early morning hours of December 4, 1969, Chicago police raided the apartment of a sleeping Black Panther leader, Fred Hampton, killing him and an associate, wounding two women Panthers, and riddling the apartment with bullets.[90] In that same month the peaceful image of Woodstock was challenged at the Rolling Stones concert in Altamont, California, when Hells Angels motorcycle gang members battered spectators and stabbed a black man to death. It was also in December 1969 that the world discovered Charles Manson and his commune associates, who were indicted in California for brutally murdering movie star Sharon Tate and several of her houseguests without apparent purpose. Manson, who had once lived in the Haight-Ashbury, espoused countercultural values to defend his savage lifestyle.

The constant barrage of brutality was well publicized by the media and seemed to substantiate SNCC leader H. Rap Brown's statement that "violence is as American as cherry pie."[91] Many radicals came to believe that American society could only be changed by "revolutionary violence," a term they would apply to politically motivated bombings, "trashing," streetfighting, and the burning of a bank in Santa Barbara, California.[92] It was conservatively estimated that at least 174 bombings took place on campuses between the fall of 1969 and the spring of 1970.[93] Between 1969 and 1972, the Weather Underground took credit for over 14 bombings, including assaults on the Pentagon, the Capitol Building, and the National Guard headquarters in Washington D.C.; they also took credit for helping Timothy Leary escape from a California prison.[94] While only an extremely small number of people actually participated in these acts, a mystique of weaponry started developing within the Movement, and, by the early 1970s, there arose a mythic glorification of the American outlaw. Bob Dylan had previously given moral sanction to outlaw life by proclaiming that "to live outside the law you must be honest" and the Jefferson Airplane released a song that declared "We are all outlaws in the eyes of Amerika."[95] The underground and radical press frequently displayed pictures of such notorious figures as Billy the Kid, John Dillinger, Belle Star, and Pretty Boy Floyd. Hollywood promoted the trend by producing such popular films as *Bonnie and Clyde, Butch Cassidy and the Sundance Kid, the Wild Bunch,* and *Ned Kelly* (which starred Mick Jagger). These productions showed the bandit protagonists as benevolent figures and celebrated the romance of outlaw violence.[96] In 1970 a Yippie and self-proclaimed outlaw ran for sheriff in Alameda County, California, using a shotgun and a hashish pipe for his representative symbols and received close to 70,000 votes.

Radical pacifists responded to the cycle of government repression and Movement militarism by reasserting their commitment to nonviolent civil disobedience. These pacifists, including Conspiracy Trial defendant Dave Dellinger, insisted that the protest movement could win much wider support and gain greater political power if it refused to "play the government's game" and did not respond in kind to violent assault. These views found widespread support among peace activists, especially the many who had discontinued political activity because of their concern with both government and radical violence. In May 1970 pacifists and their allies organized an antiwar demonstration attended by 120,000 people, 413 of whom were arrested for committing acts of nonviolent civil disobedience in the streets of Washington, D.C.[97]

Peaceful sentiment also found popular cultural expression. An album of music from the Woodstock festival and a film of that event were internationally acclaimed, and many people still found inspiration in the dream of a Woodstock nation. Many individuals attempted to affirm a new commitment to nature by moving to the country. Earth Day was celebrated in April 1970, and some antiwar activists found ecology to be their ultimate and best cause.

THE MOVEMENT FADES

In the early 1970s, the protest movement entered into a sharp decline. FBI agents sought to take advantage of this condition by creating division and fomenting paranoia within Movement ranks.[98] Additionally, a series of politically motivated killings carried out by police and the National Guard in 1969 and the early 1970s sapped morale and spread fear among many radicals. The violent deaths of Panther leaders, of prison author George Jackson in San Quentin, of 32 rebellious prisoners in Attica, New York, and especially the shooting of four white students at Kent State University on May 4, 1970, followed ten days later by the killings of two black students in Jackson, Mississippi, served chilling notice on activists that the politics of confrontation had become a life-threatening activity.

Although there had been a successful 1971 Mayday peace protest in Washington, D.C. and large nationwide demonstrations following the massive bombing of Cambodia in 1972, the number and size of such occurrences was noticeably decreasing. By the early 1970s many of

the most important organizations of the 1960s, including SNCC, SDS, and the Black Panther Party, had dissolved or existed in a smaller, less militant form. The underground press began losing readers, and by 1975 the majority of alternative newspapers had ceased publication. The once-cohesive Movement community was rapidly becoming fragmented and atomized. A variety of bitter ideological divisions and internecine conflicts emerged between women and men, gays and straights, blacks and whites, rank and file and leaders, pacifists and terrorists, communists and participatory democrats. The sense of trust, which had previously characterized the radical community's social relations, was replaced by paranoia and a narrow political sectarianism.[99] Nixon's intransigence and a seemingly unstoppable war produced a sense of futility in many activists. The president's ordering of high tonnage bombing raids in Indochina obscured from notice the important beginning of American troop withdrawal. Some believed the Movement had failed in its purpose. Many individuals became self-doubting, suspicious of the motives of friends, lovers, and comrades, and fearful of real or imagined police agents. In this increasingly hostile and divided environment, activists experienced an anomic breakdown of Movement norms, solidarity, and community.

By 1973, with over 58,000 American soldiers dead, President Nixon concluded the full withdrawal of U.S. troops. Two years later, Vietnamese communist troops captured Saigon and declared its name to be Ho Chi Minh City. The revolutionary forces had achieved complete political and military victory.

The two major issues that had gripped people's imagination and passions for a decade had been successfully resolved. Legal segregation had been abolished, and the war in Vietnam was over. Yet many radicals took little pleasure in these victories and were unable, at that moment, to appreciate their own political accomplishments. By the early 1970s they had developed such an unrealistic expectation of imminent "total revolution" that nothing short of the overthrow or abolition of the American government would offer satisfaction.

In contrast to this millenarian approach, many other veterans of the 1960s began adopting a gradualist view. More moderate and traditional forms of dissent gained acceptance, as former protesters and counterculturalists went back to school, took up careers, obtained full-time jobs, and began to "work within the system." Some SNCC workers and new leftists allied themselves with Senator George

McGovern, who in 1972 won the Democratic party's presidential nomination as a peace and civil rights candidate.

When looking over the 1960s we can see that, while liberal presidents Kennedy and Johnson occupied the White House, the national political consensus affirmed idealism and social and economic reform. In this permissive milieu, a mass culture of rebellion took hold. Protesters, whose defiant philosophy was rooted in the prophetic visions and critical ideals of a few wayward poets, preachers, and radical intellectuals, started gaining adherents and power. They espoused citizens' participation in political decision-making, intellectual and emotional openness, pluralism, cultural experimentation, and a democracy of daily life. Out of this dissident community grew a massive social phenomenon of opposition to the war and support for civil rights, which by 1968 was called the Movement. When, during the Nixon administration, American opinion turned approvingly toward conservatism and political repression, the Movement, as if in imitation of the national mood, and in a dramatic shift away from its original ideals, became intolerant and rigid. Within three years after Nixon's election, the Movement was weakened and eventually destroyed, not only becaue of government assult, but because many of its militants had begun to embrace a variety of sectarian ideologies and had become isolated from their base of support among students and young people. The Movement no longer seemed to represent a moral and democratic alternative to the dominant society, but rather it increasingly took on, within its own ranks, an authoritarianism not so different from that which it was trying to oppose. Yet many individual activists retained their commitment to the Movement's original democratic and rebellious values and continued to involve themselves in grass-roots community scenarios for social change.

NOTES

1. This frame of mind came to be termed "McCarthyism" after Joseph McCarthy, a junior senator from Wisconsin, who was notorious for his Senate Committee's investigations of radicals and his demagogic claims about communist infiltration of the government.

2. For opposing views on the Rosenberg case, see Walter and Miriam Schnier, *Invitation to an Inquest* (New York: Pantheon, 1983); and Ronald Radosh and Joyce Milton, *The Rosenberg File: A Search For The Truth* (New York: Holt, Rinehart and Winston, 1983).

3. See Cynthia Brown's interview with Rosa Parks in *Southern Exposure*, "Stayed on Freedom," Spring 1981, pp. 16–17.

4. For 1960s commentaries on Presley's role, see especially Eldridge Cleaver, *Soul on Ice* (New York: McGraw Hill, 1968), pp. 194–95; and Jerry Rubin, *Do It!* (New York: Simon and Schuster, 1970), pp. 17–20.

5. For a woman's personal recollections of Kerouac and the beats see Joyce Johnson, *Minor Characters* (New York: Houghton Mifflin, 1983).

6. The term "beat" was never precisely defined. It could refer to the beat of jazz, to beatific consciousness, to losing, or whatever meaning its users chose to give it.

7. See Clayborne Carson, *In Struggle: SNCC and the Black Awakening of the 1960s* (Cambridge, Mass.; Harvard University Press, 1981), p. 11; Howard Zinn, *SNCC, The New Abolitionists* (New York: Alfred Knopf, 1965), pp. 16–17.

8. Pronounced Snick.

9. There were instances when blacks with Ph.D.'s were denied the vote because of their "illiteracy."

10. See especially Albert Camus's essay "Neither Victims Nor Executioners," *Liberation*, March 1960.

11. For an in-depth perspective on gender and politics in SNCC and Students for a Democratic Society (SDS) see Sara Evans, *Personal Politics: The Roots of Women's Liberation in the Civil Rights Movement and the New Left* (New York: Alfred A. Knopf, 1979).

12. Ibid., p. 73.

13. At the massive August 1963 march on Washington, Martin Luther King, who gave the keynote address, articulated vision of multiracial unity in his "I Have a Dream" speech.

14. The document was initially drafted by SDS leaders Al Haber and Tom Hayden.

15. Kirkpatrick Sale, *SDS* (New York: Vintage Books, 1974), p. 20.

16. Ibid., p. 114. For an in-depth analysis of the ERAP Projects see Wini Breines, *The Great Refusal: Community and Organization in the New Left: 1962–68* (New York: Praeger, 1982), chapter 7.

17. Evans, *Personal Politics*, p. 151.

18. Sale, *SDS*, p. 307.

19. The Free Speech Movement was held together by an 86-member executive committee composed of a highly diverse grouping of political organizations and individuals. Approximately one-third of the committee members were women.

20. Speech by Mario Savio to 6,000 people at Sproul Hall, University of California, noon, December 2, 1964. From Hal Draper, *Berkeley: The New Student Revolt* (New York: Grove Press, 1965), p. 98.

21. The Kennedy administration's friendship with King was not totally pure. Attorney General Robert F. Kennedy gave the FBI permission to wiretap King's telephone. See David J. Garrow, *The FBI and Martin Luther King Jr: From Solo to Memphis* (New York: W.W. Norton and Company, 1981), p. 73.

22. The original American forces in Vietnam were described as "advisors."

23. For a CIA insider's view of these events, see Victor Marchetti, "The Missile Crisis at the CIA," in Lynda Rosen Obst, *The Sixties* (New York: Random House/Rolling Stone, 1977), pp. 76–78.

24. SDS changed Johnson's official campaign slogan. In the new left organization's public statement, "All the Way with LBJ" became "Half the Way with LBJ."

25. When, in a telephone interview on May 4, 1983, we asked FBI Special Agent Manuel Marquez, Jr. to estimate the number of antiwar demonstrations that had taken place between 1964–70, he replied, "Information as to the number of antiwar demonstrations is not retrievable. We kept no running tally, and local police departments did not keep a running total."

26. For his portrait of the antiwar and antidraft movements see David Harris, *Dreams Die Hard* (New York: St Martin's Press, 1982).

27. VVAW was founded in the spring of 1968, and the demonstration, known as Dewey Canyon 2, took place between April 17–22, 1970.

28. Curtis LeMay with MacKinley Kantor, *Mission With LeMay* (Garden city, N.Y.: Doubleday, 1965), p. 565.

29. Saigon was then the capital city of the Republic of South Vietnam.

30. Milton Viorst, *Fire in the Streets: America in the 1960s* (New York: Simon and Schuster, 1979), p. 384.

31. Ibid., p. 385.

32. The NLF stands for National Liberation Front of South Vietnam. It was considered the political arm of the communist guerrillas and was commonly known as the Vietcong.

33. For an account of the teach-in movement, see Ron Radosh and Louise Menashe, *Teach-ins USA* (New York: Praeger, 1967).

34. Joseph Lyford, *The Berkeley Archipelago* (Chicago: Regnery Gateway, 1982), p. 27. This book offers an explicitly hostile account of Berkeley radicalism in the 1960s and 1970s.

35. See Seth Rosenfeld, "Of Spies and Radicals: The FBI In Berkeley," *The Daily Cal's Weekly Magazine*, June 4, 1982.

36. As in the case of the term "beatnik," the words "hippie" and "flower children" were coined and popularized by local San Francisco newspaper columnists.

37. Gene Anthony, commenting recently on a young hippie woman's role, states, "Phyllis Wilner's destiny was to serve." In Gene Anthony, *The*

Summer of Love: Haight-Ashbury at Its Highest (Millbrae, Calif.: Celestial Arts, 1980), p. 34. At that time, birth control devices were readily available.

38. For an interpretation of the relationship between 1960s protest activity and the music and literature of the period, see Morris Dickstein, *Gates of Eden: American Culture in the Sixties* (New York: Basic Books, 1977).

39. Malcolm X described the Kennedy assassination as "chickens coming home to roost."

40. *U.S. News and World Report*, November 13, 1967, p. 53.

41. *Ibid.*, October 7, 1968, pp. 29–30.

42. For an analytical history of black power and black radicalism, see Robert L. Allen, *Black Awakening in Capitalist America* (Garden City, N.Y.: Doubleday, 1969).

43. H. Rap Brown was subsequently indicted on a variety of federal and state charges, but he chose not to appear for trial and became a federal fugitive. Other SNCC workers adopted a more moderate political approach and took employment in the Johnson administration's poverty programs.

44. *The Black Panther* 4, no. 3 (June 29, 1970): 22.

45. Popular Panther slogans emphasizing this point were "The spirit of the people is greater than the man's technology" and "The pigs of the power structure are oinking at the people."

46. After three trials, charges against Newton were dropped.

47. The Panthers' popularity among black Americans can be measured by a survey that showed 30.6 per cent of black enlisted men planned to "join a militant black group like the Panthers" when they returned home. First reported by Wallace Terry II in the *New York Times* and reprinted in *The Black Panther*, July 4, 1970, p. 18.

48. Panther supporters also ignored Eldridge Cleaver's qualified rationale for rape and other violent acts against women, which was evidenced in his book *Soul on Ice*, pp. 13–15.

49. The FBI director's fear of all black militants, including Martin Luther King and Malcolm X, led him to warn against the "rise" of a black nationalist "messiah" who might lead a violent revolution that could result in the destruction of American society. See *Counterintelligence Program Against Huey P. Newton* and *Counterintelligence Programs Internationally* made available by the law offices of Garry, Dreyfus, and McTernan in San Francisco. See also: the COINTELPRO files available from the Grand Jury Project in New York City; and Garrow, *The FBI and Martin Luther King*.

50. An especially destructive and violent example was the falling out between New York City Panthers and the West Coast leadership.

51. A Yankelovitch poll showed that 27 percent of their "forerunner" college students identified with the left, and 21 percent of the "forerunner" group expressed sympathy for the Vietcong. See *Fortune*, January 1969, p. 71.

52. Personal conversation with Abe Peck of the School of Journalism, Northwestern University on November 5, 1983. Peck is the author of a forthcoming book on the underground press to be published by Pantheon.

53. For a positive and contemporaneous view of this media interest, see Rubin, Do It!; and Abbie Hoffman, Revolution for the Hell of It (New York: The Dial Press, 1968). For a recent critical analysis of media influence, see Todd Gitlin, The Whole World is Watching (Berkeley: the University of California Press, 1980).

54. Columbia Daily Spectator, April 30, 1968.

55. FBI memoranda that provide evidence for this view were located by researchers of Jerry Rubin's main FBI file obtained under the Freedom of Information Act. See especially the FBI "White Paper," which evaluates the Bureau's performance during the Chicago convention. These files are in the possession of the Center for Constitutional Rights in New York City. National COINTELPRO operations against the new left were authorized by President Johnson in the spring of 1968.

56. See Marshall McLuhan, Understanding Media (New York: McGraw Hill, 1964).

57. Many college students had rallied to Senator McCarthy's cause; some had cut their hair in order to campaign in middle-class neighborhoods. This was referred to as going "Clean for Gene."

58. For an eyewitness account of the convention week disturbances, see Norman Mailer, Miami and the Siege of Chicago (New York: New American Library, 1968).

59. None took his suggestion. The performer had sung his "I Ain't Marching Anymore" to the guards.

60. See Daniel Walker and the National Commission on the Causes and Prevention of Violence, Rights in Conflict: The Violent Confrontation of Demonstrators and Police in the Parks and Streets in Chicago During the Democratic National Convention (New York: Bantam, 1968). This document is commonly referred to as the "Walker Report."

61. William M. Kunstler with Stewart E. Albert, "The Great Conspiracy Trial of '69," The Nation, September 29, 1979, pp. 257, 273–76.

62. U.S., Congress, Senate, Select Committee to Study Government Operations With Respect to Intelligence Activities, Hearings, vol. 6, 94th Cong., 1st sess., 1975. This group is usually described as the "Church Committee."

63. Among those subpoenaed were Tom Hayden, Jerry Rubin, and Abbie Hoffman.

64. See David Weiss, The American Police State (New York: Random House, 1976), pp. 382–83.

65.   For a discussion of the federalization and militarization of local police forces during this period, see *The Iron Fist and the Velvet Glove* (Berkeley: Center for Research on Criminal Justice, 1975).

66.   Sale, *SDS*, p. 642.

67.   From a personal conversation with Abe Peck, November 5, 1983.

68.   Sale, *SDS*, p. 529.

69.   For a history of the gay movement and its relationship to the women's movement and the new left, see John D'Emilio, *Sexual Politics, Sexual Communities: The Making of a Homosexual Minority in the United States, 1940–1970* (Chicago: University of Chicago Press, 1983).

70.   See especially John Sinclair, *Guitar Army* (New York: Douglas Book Corporation, 1972).

71.   Philosophic support was provided to these militants in the writings of Herbert Marcuse, "Repressive Tolerance," in Robert P. Wolff, Barrington Moore, and Herbert Marcuse, eds., *A Critique of Pure Tolerance* (Boston: Beacon Press, 1966), pp. 81–123.

72.   Several years later the fence was torn down by demonstrators. The fence was never rebuilt, but a course in the study of People's Park is currently offered for credit at the University of California at Berkeley.
University of California at Berkeley.

73.   See Abbie Hoffman, *Woodstock Nation* (New York: Random House, 1969).

74.   Rubin, *Do It!*, p. 196.

75.   Bob Dylan, "Subterranean Homesick Blues," on his album *Bringing It All Back Home*, 1965.

76.   See Susan Stern, *With the Weathermen: The Personal Journal of a Revolutionary Woman* (Garden City, N.Y.: Doubleday, 1975), pp. 127–146.

77.   For an in-depth discussion of the disintegration of SDS and the origins of Weatherman, see Sale, *SDS*, pp. 511–650. See also Harold Jacobs, *Weatherman* (Ramparts Press, 1970); and Jonah Raskin, *The Weather Eye* (New York: Union Square Press, 1974).

78.   Judge Hoffman's hostility to the defendants predated the trial. Some of the reasons for this may have been due to FBI briefings. See Kunstler and Albert, "Great Conspiracy Trial," pp. 257, 273–76.

79.   For complete trial testimony, see Judy Clavir and John Spitzer, *The Conspiracy Trial* (Indianapolis/New York: Bobbs-Merrill, 1970).

80.   Seale was transferred to Connecticut, where, along with Erika Huggins, he stood trial for murder. After a hung jury, the charges were dismissed. The case provoked numerous demonstrations on the Panthers' behalf.

81.   Such conspiracy trials included, among others: the January 1968 indictment and subsequent trial of Dr. Benjamin Spock, Reverend William Sloan Coffin and three others in Boston, Massachusetts; the Oakland Seven

trial in California, January 1969; the trial of the Panther 21 in New York City in April 1969; the Seattle Conspiracy Trial in Washington, April 1970; the Harrisburg, Pennsylvania trial of Reverends Phillip and Daniel Berrigan, and Sister Elizabeth McAllister in May 1971; and the trial of eight members of the Vietnam Veterans Against the War in Gainesville, Florida in January 1973.

82. For a discussion of this condition in SDS and SNCC, see Evans, *Personal Politics*, pp. 24–59.

83. *New Left Notes*, January 13, 1967, p. 5.

84. Some of the demonstrators later questioned the propriety of not being sensitive to the feelings of the beauty contestants. See Carol Hanish, "A Critique of the Miss America Protest," in Shulamith Firestone and Anne Koedt, eds., *Notes from the Second Year* (New York: Firestone and Koedt, 1970) pp. 86–88. See also Redstockings, *Feminist Revolution* (New York: Random House, 1978).

85. See Leslie Cagan's personal account of her political biography "Something New Emerges" and Ann Popkin's essay, "The Personal Is Political," both in Dick Cluster, ed., *They Should Have Served That Cup of Coffee: 7 Radicals Remember the 60s* (Boston: South End Press, 1979), pp. 181–258.

86. For a discussion of these events, see Jo Freeman, *The Politics of Women's Liberation* (New York: David McKay, 1975), pp. 134–42.

87. Robin Morgan, "Goodbye to All That," *The Rat*, February 9–23, 1970, pp. 6–7. For the author's later view, see Robin Morgan, *Going Too Far* (New York: Random House, 1977), pp. 115–22.

88. Marge Piercy continued to offer a fictional rendering of women in the Movement. See her novels, *Small Changes* (Greenwich, Conn.: Fawcett, 1976); and *Vida* (New York: Summit Books, 1979).

89. Sale, *SDS*, p. 633. See also Dave Dellinger, *More Power Than We Know* (New York: Anchor, 1965). The protesters had broken away from a large, peaceful antiwar rally.

90. This assault was carried out with no apparent fear of extensive and embarrassing publicity. There were many prominent journalists in Chicago who were covering the Conspiracy Trial at the time of the Hampton and Clark killings.

91. H. Rap Brown, *Die Nigger Die!* (New York: The Dial Press, 1969), p. 144.

92. An analytic justification for political violence was provided in the revolutionary writings of Algerian psychoanalyst Frantz Fanon. See especially his book, *The Wretched of the Earth* (New York: Grove Press, 1963). The radical slang term "trashing" was used to describe the deliberate destruction of property by demonstrators. It was a form of political vandalism.

93. Sale, *SDS*, p. 632.

94. Weather Underground, *Prarie Fire: The Politics of Revolutionary Anti-Imperialism*, 1974, pp. 4–5.

95.   From "Absolutely Sweet Marie" on Dylan's 1966 album *Blonde on Blonde*. Dylan's 1967 musical tribute to the desperado John Wesley Harding, on an album of the same name, was now being listened to by male and female radicals for political inspiration.

96.   For an influential study of *social banditry*, explaining the historic popularity of outlaws, see E.J. Hobsbawm, *Primitive Rebels* (New York: W.W. Norton and Son, 1959).

97.   Dellinger, *More Power Than We Know*, p. 149.

98.   See Garry, Dreyfus, and McTernan, Counterintelligence Program; and Nelson Blackstock, *COINTELPRO: The FBI's War on Political Freedom* (New York: Random House, 1975).

99.   For an exhaustive critique of sectarian and rigid approaches to ideology, see Stanley Aronowitz, *The Crisis in Historical Materialism* (New York: Praeger, 1981). See also his article, "Remaking the American Left," *Socialist Review* January–February 1983 and May–June 1983.

THE PAPERS

1   PROPHETIC VISIONS: FORMATIVE IDEAS

We begin this anthology with a segment of the poem HOWL by Allen Ginsberg. First published in 1956, HOWL's stirring evocation of individual freedom and cultural transcendence inspired members of the beat generation to experiment with their lives. The poem continued to be lionized by the cultural and political rebels of the 1960s. For many of its readers, HOWL provided the first inkling that an alternate lifestyle existed outside the limits of middle-class values.

The Causes of World War III, written by C. Wright Mills in 1958, analyzed the sociological basis of a drift toward war between the United States and the Soviet Union. His imaginative portrayal of the American "power elite" and his call for a "new" left offered young radicals of the late 1950s a body of thought profoundly critical of American society yet independent of traditional Marxist categories. His Letter to the New Left, written in 1960, gave an intellectual rationale and a sense of personal legitimacy to those students whose nonconforming ideas had previously been ridiculed as immature and uninformed by their professorial elders. Mills's prescient views of the dangers of global war seem especially relevant now.

Norman Mailer's "The White Negro" appeared in Dissent magazine in the summer of 1957. The piece links together divergent forms of cultural and political alienation and prophesies a coming social apocalypse. Mailer's ideas, especially his championing individual acts of violence, were alternatively defended and attacked throughout the decade by radical and feminist writers. In the 1960s Mailer became a widely read literary advocate for the new left.

HOWL

Allen Ginsberg

for Carl Solomon

I

I saw the best minds of my generation destroyed by madness, starving
   hysterical naked,
dragging themselves through the negro streets at dawn looking for an
   angry fix,
angelheaded hipsters burning for the ancient heavenly connection to
   the starry dynamo in the machinery of night,
who poverty and tatters and hollow-eyed and high sat up smoking in
   the supernatural darkness of cold-water flats floating across the
   tops of cities contemplating jazz,
who bared their brains to Heaven under the El and saw Mohammedan
   angels staggering on tenement roofs illuminated,
who passed through universities with radiant cool eyes hallucinating
   Arkansas and Blake-light tragedy among the scholars of war,
who were expelled from the academies for crazy & publishing obscene
   odes on the windows of the skull,
who cowered in unshaven rooms in underwear, burning their money in
   wastebaskets and listening to the Terror through the wall,
who got busted in their pubic beards returning through Laredo with a
   belt of marijuana for New York,
who ate fire in paint hotels or drank turpentine in Paradise Alley, death,
   or purgatoried their torsos night after night

with dreams, with drugs, with waking nightmares, alcohol and cock and endless balls....

* * *

II

What sphinx of cement and aluminum bashed open their skulls and ate up their brains and imagination?

Moloch! Solitude! Filth! Ugliness! Ashcans and unobtainable dollars! Children screaming under the stairways! Boys sobbing in armies! Old men weeping in the parks!

Moloch! Moloch! Nightmare of Moloch! Moloch the loveless! Mental Moloch! Moloch the heavy judger of men!

Moloch the incomprehensible prison! Moloch the crossbone soulless jailhouse and Congress of sorrows! Moloch whose buildings are judgement! Moloch the vast stone of war! Moloch the stunned governments!

Moloch whose mind is pure machinery! Moloch whose blood is running money! Moloch whose fingers are ten armies! Moloch whose breast is a cannibal dynamo! Moloch whose ear is a smoking tomb!

Moloch whose eyes are a thousand blind windows! Moloch whose skyscrapers stand in the long streets like endless Jehovahs! Moloch whose factories dream and croak in the fog! Moloch whose smokestacks and antennae crown the cities!

Moloch whose love is endless oil and stone! Moloch whose soul is electricity and banks! Moloch whose poverty is the specter of genius! Moloch whose fate is a cloud of sexless hydrogen! Moloch whose name is the mind!

Moloch in whom I sit lonely! Moloch in whom I dream Angels! Crazy in Moloch! Cocksucker in Moloch! Lacklove and manless in Moloch!

Moloch who entered my soul early! Moloch in whom I am a consciousness without a body! Moloch who frightened me out of my natural ecstasy! Moloch whom I abandon! Wake up in Moloch! Light streaming out of the sky!

Moloch! Moloch! Robot apartments! invisible suburbs! skeleton treasuries! blind capitals! demonic industries! spectral nations! invincible madhouses! granite cocks! monstrous bombs!

They broke their backs lifting Moloch to Heaven! Pavements, trees, radios, tons! lifting the city to Heaven which exists and is everywhere about us!

Visions! omens! hallucinations! miracles! ectasies! gone down the American river!

Dreams! adorations! illuminations! religions! the whole boatload of sensitive bullshit!

Breakthroughs! over the river! flips and crucifixions! gone down the flood! Highs! Epiphanies! Despairs! Ten years' animal screams and suicides! Minds! New loves! Mad generation! down on the rocks of Time!

Real holy laughter in the river! They saw it all! the wild eyes! the holy yells! They bade farewell! They jumped off the roof! to solitude! waving! carrying flowers! Down to the river! into the street!

* * *

FOOTNOTE TO HOWL

Holy! Holy! Holy! Holy! Holy! Holy! Holy! Holy! Holy! Holy! Holy! Holy! Holy! Holy! Holy!

The world is holy! The soul is holy! The skin is holy! The nose is holy! The tongue and cock and hand and asshole holy!

Everything is holy! everybody's holy! everywhere is holy! everyday is in eternity! Everyman's an angel!

The bum's as holy as the seraphim! the madman is holy as you my soul are holy!

The typewriter is holy the poem is holy the voice is holy the hearers are holy the ecstasy is holy!

Holy Peter holy Allen holy Solomon holy Lucien holy Kerouac holy Huncke holy Burroughs holy Cassady holy the unknown buggered and suffering beggars holy the hideous human angels!

Holy my mother in the insane asylum! Holy the cocks of the grandfathers of Kansas!

Holy the groaning saxophone! Holy the bop apocalypse! Holy the jazzbands marijuana hipsters peace & junk & drums!

Holy the solitudes of skyscrapers and pavements! Holy the cafeterias filled with the millions! Holy the mysterious rivers of tears under the streets!

Holy the lone juggernaut! Holy the vast lamb of the middle-class! Holy the crazy shepherds of rebellion! Who digs Los Angeles IS Los Angeles!

Holy New York Holy San Francisco Holy Peoria & Seattle Holy Paris Holy Tangiers Holy Moscow Holy Istanbul!

Holy time in eternity holy eternity in time holy the clocks in space holy the fourth dimension holy the fifth International holy the Angel in Moloch!

Holy the sea holy the desert holy the railroad holy the locomotive holy the visions holy the hallucinations holy the miracles holy the eyeball holy the abyss!

Holy forgiveness! mercy! charity! faith! Holy! Ours! bodies! suffering! magnanimity!

Holy the supernatural extra brilliant intelligent kindness of the soul!

The Causes of World War III

C. Wright Mills

WAR BECOMES TOTAL—AND ABSURD

To reflect upon war is to reflect upon the human condition, for that condition is now most clearly revealed by the way in which World War III is coming about. The preparations for this war are now pivotal features of the leading societies of the world. The expectation of it follows from the official definitions of world reality. In accordance with these definitions power elites decide and fail to decide; publics and masses fatalistically accept; intellectuals elaborate and justify. The drift and the thrust toward World War III is now part of the contemporary sensibility—and a defining characteristic of our epoch.

Most of the causes of World War III are accepted as "necessity"; to expect its coming is considered "realism." Politicians and journalists, intellectuals and generals, businessmen and preachers now fight this war—and busily create the historical situation in which it is viewed as inevitable. For them "necessity" and "realism" have become ways to hide their own lack of moral and political imagination. Among the led and among the leaders moral insensibility to violence is as evident as is the readiness to practice violence. The ethos of war is now pervasive. All social and personal life is being organized in its terms. It dominates

Excerpts from *The Causes of World War III*. Copyright © 1958 by C. Wright Mills. Reprinted by permission of Simon & Schuster, a division of Gulf & Western Corporation.

the curious spiritual life of the peoples of Christendom. It shapes their scientific endeavor, limits their intellectual effort, increases their national budgets, and has replaced what was once called diplomacy. The drive toward war is massive, subtle, official, and self-directed. War is no longer an interruption of peace; in fact, peace itself has become an uneasy interlude between wars; peace has become a perilous balance of mutual terror and mutual fright.

* * *

Many scholars say—and many more feel—that only a fool would now publicly discuss the causes of war and the roads to peace. They believe that the human mind cannot grapple successfully with the total and ultimate issues involved, that any inquiry not more "specialized" is bound to be inadequate. Yet many, perhaps in fear of being thought Unpatriotic, become nationalist propagandists; others, perhaps in fear of being thought Unscientific, become nationalist technicians. Neither type seems able to transcend the official terms in which the world encounter is now defined. As propagandists, they are no more enlightening than any other propagandists, as technicians, they are committed in advance to some one or another narrow range of policy which they would elaborate and justify. As a result, such knowledge and skills as many students of man and society have are largely wasted so far as the human problems of war and peace are concerned.

Yet all significant problems of contemporary man and society bear upon the issues of war and the politics of peace; and the solution to any significant problem in some part rests upon their outcome. I do not believe that these issues are now as dreadfully complicated as everyone so readily tends to assume. But regardless of that, is it not precisely the task of the intellectual, the scholar, the student, to confront complications? To sort out insistent issues in such a way as to open them up for the work of reason—and so for action at strategic points of intervention? Is it not our task continually to make the new beginning?

The epoch in which we live is pivotal; the tradition of classic social analysis is clear. We must respond to events; we must define orienting policies. Should we fail to do so we stand in default of our intellectual and of our public duties; we abdicate such role as reason may have in human affairs. And this we should be unwilling to do.

* * *

ON FATE AND DECISION

In what sense may it be said that men make history, and in what sense, if in any, are historical events, such as war inevitable? Some believe that events are overwhelming; that men are trapped by circumstances, even if circumstances are in some collective way made by men. But others stress the causal role of explicit decisions in the making of history. For them, events are not overwhelming; events are themselves shapable—and often shaped—by the deliberate decisions of identifiable circles of men.

To the question of fate and decision, I think we cannot give one answer that holds for all of human history. To argue about history-making in general is to throw away our chance to understand the history-making of any given epoch. It is less useful, for example, to argue about the causes of war in general or the causes of any previous war than about what is now causing World War III. For to know the causes of the First or of the Second World War is not necessarily to know much about those of the Third. The guide rule for adequate social analysis, especially today, is that we cannot merely assume that there are Forces independent of the structure of a given epoch that are acting upon History or that if there were we could grasp them. Neither can we assume that "War" is a unitary phenomenon, always caused by uniform forces and decisions. We can best understand the causes of World War III not by studying history as the recorded past but by examining, in Paul Sweezy's phrase, "the present as history." Every epoch has its own kinds of history-making—and its own forms of war and peace, and of the conditions that lie between the two. The causes of war and the conditions of peace must be considered as historically specific to a given epoch.

So we must rephrase our question: Is war, today, a matter of blind drift, of overwhelming events, of historical destiny? Or is it a matter of men making decisions, and if so, which men?

* * *

Power has to do with whatever decisions men make about the arrangements under which they live and about the events which make up the history of their times. Events that are beyond human decisions do happen; social arrangements do change without benefit of explicit decision. But in so far as such decisions are made—and in so far as they could be but are not made—the problem of who is involved in making them—or in not making them—is the basic problem or power. It is also the problem of history-making, and so of the causes of war.

The relevant means of power now include the facilities of industrial production and of military violence, of political administration and of the manipulation of opinion. According to the reach, the centralization, and the availability of such means of power, we must determine the roles of explicit decision and the mechanics of fate in the making of history.

In those societies in which the means of power are rudimentary and decentralized, history *is* fate. The innumerable actions of innumerable men modify their local milieus, and thus gradually modify the structure of society as a whole. These modifications—the course of history—go on behind men's backs. History is drift, although in total "men make it."

But in those societies in which the means of power are enormous in scope and centralized in form a few men may be so placed within the historical structure that by their decisions about the use of these means they modify the structural conditions under which most men live. Nowadays such elites of power make history—"under circumstances not chosen altogether by themselves," yet compared with other men, and with other periods of human history, these circumstances do indeed seem less overwhelming.

I am contending that "men are free to make history" and that some men are now much freer than others to do so, for such freedom requires access to the means of decision and of power by which history can now be made. To assume that men are equally free to make history is to assume that they are equal in power. But power is a hierarchy; the shape of that hierarchy is itself subject to historical change, and at any given moment of history it opens to different men different opportunities to exercise their wills in the making of history. What to powerless men is an overwhelming event to men of power is a decision to be made or an abdication to commit. It is a challenge, an obstacle, an opportunity, a struggle, a fear, a hope. In our time if men do not make history, they tend increasingly to become the utensils of history-makers and the mere objects of history-making. But those who do have access to the new means of power, and yet define their situation as one of fate—do they not stand now in objective default?

* * *

THE PERMANENT WAR ECONOMY

Since the end of World War II many in elite circles have felt that economic prosperity in the U.S. is immediately under-pinned by the war economy and that desperate economic—and so political—problems might well arise should there be disarmament and genuine peace. Conciliatory gestures by the Russians are followed by stockmarket selling. When there is fear that negotiations may occur, let alone that a treaty structure for the world be arranged, stocks, by their jitters, reflect what is called a "peace scare." When unemployment increases and there is demand that something be done, government spokesmen regularly justify themselves by referring first of all to increases in the money spent and to be spent for war preparations. Thus with unemployment at 4.5 million in January 1958, the President proclaimed that war-contract awards will rise from $35.6* billion of 1957 to the $47.2 billion of 1958.

These connections between economic conditions and war preparations are not obscure and hidden; they are publicly and regularly reported. And they are definitely among the causes for elite acceptance of the military metaphysic and hence among the causes of World War III.

Behind these well-reported facts are the structural connections between the privately incorporated economy and the military ascendancy. Leading corporations now profit from the preparation of war. In so far as the corporate elite are aware of their profit interests—and that is their reponsible business—they press for a continuation of their sources of profit, which often means a continuation of the preparation for war. As political advisers and as centers of power, higher business and higher military circles share an interest in the felt need for armament and for its continual and wasteful development. We cannot assay with accuracy the casual weight of this personnel and their interests, but the combination of a seemingly "permanent war economy" and a "privately incorporated economy" cannot reasonably be supposed to be an unambiguous condition for the making of peace.

I am *not* suggesting that military power is now only, or even mainly, an instrument of economic policy. To a considerable extent, militarism has become an end in itself and economic policy a means of it. Moreover,

---

*"Billion" is used in the American sense, i.e. 1,000 million.

whatever the case in previous periods of capitalism, in our immediate times war in each country is being prepared in order to prevent another country from becoming militarily stronger. "There is much justification," E.H. Carr has noted, "for the epigram that 'the principal cause of war is war itself.'" Perhaps at no previous period has this been so much the case as now, for the means of a war, and war as a means, have never before been so absolute as to make war so economically irrational.

But we must remember that true capitalist brinkmanship consists of the continual preparation for war, just short of it; and that such brinkmanship does have economic functions of important capitalist consequence. Moreover, it is by no means clear that the American elite realize the economic irrationality of war itself. In the meantime, an expensive arms race, under cover of the military metaphysic and in a paranoid atmosphere of fright, is an economically attractive business. To many utopian capitalists, it has become The Business Way of American Life.

* * *

The economic boom of World War II—and only that—pulled the U.S.A. out of the slump of the thirties. After that war a flood of pentup demand was let loose. To this was added the production of war materials of conventional and unconventional sort. The result, as everyone knows, was the great American prosperity of the last decade.

In the winter of 1957–8 another recession began in the United States. By late March, some six million were unemployed. The mechanics of this recession were generally familiar. There was an "overextension" of capitalist investment in the early fifties, perhaps due to favorable tax amortization; then the rate of capital formation dropped. There was an increase in the installment debt—a mortgaging of future income— especially during 1955. At the same time there has been an arrogant rigidity of prices set by corporate administrators. In fact some prices (for example, steel) were administered up rather than down—even in the face of declining demand—and production was cut.

To this old capitalist folly, Dr. John Blair has recently revealed, there has now been added a rather direct link between "the mode of compensation" for corporation executives and the rigidity or even the

*See "Report of the Subcommittee on Antitrust and Monopoly," S. Res. 1957, 85th Congress, First Session (U.S. Government Printing Office, 1958).

increase of the prices they administer. The stock options given these executives connect their income and wealth to dividends or to the market value of common stock, thus avoiding taxes payable on salaries. Price increases, it is well known, tend to raise stock prices. The long-term compensation of the business elite is thus tied to rising prices and to rising stock values, rather than to lower costs and lower prices.*

The recession could of course be fought by vigorous price reductions, even imposed by government price controls; by a cut in taxes to increase purchasing power, and by a very large public-works program, perhaps for school facilities. Such means, which are theoretically at the disposal of the capitalist slump-fighter, are now generally accepted by liberal and by conservative economists. Perhaps such means would be economically adequate. They do not, however, seem to be politically acceptable to everyone involved in the decisions; they do not seem to be altogether acceptable to the capitalists of the Eisenhower Administration.

There is always another way open to them: expenditures for war as a capitalist subsidy and as a countervailing force to capitalist slump. Such expenditures have been most efficiently wasteful, and they often seem to be politically unarguable.

It is not relevant to my argument that any particular recession either deepen or be overcome. My point is that slump—for so long as it is felt as a threat—will further harden the militarist posture of the U.S. elite, and that this elite has attempted and will attempt to overcome it by still larger military expenditure. It is of course not that simple, but neither is it so complex as to be incomprehensible. International tensions, incidents, crises do not just happen. The definitions of world reality held by both sides of the encounter, as well as continual default, enter into such international affairs. Slump in America will stiffen these war-making definitions and will serve as additonal excuse for the continued lack of decision; it will increase the tension; it will make more likely and more frightening the incidents; it will sharpen the perilous crisis. The fear of slump in America cannot reasonably be considered a context that will increase the American elite's contribution to the making of peace. In their interplay with Soviet decision-makers it is more likely to increase their contribution to the thrust and the drift toward World War III.

Yet it is a hard fact for capitalism that the new weaponry, the new kinds of war preparations, do not seem to be as economically relevant to subsidizing the defaults and irrationalities of the capilatist economy as the old armament and preparations. The amount of money spent is large enough, but it tends to go to a smaller proportion of employees, to the technician rather than to the semi-skilled. The people who make missiles and bombs will probably not put into comsumption as high a ratio of their incomes as would the more numerous makers of tanks and aircraft. Accordingly, the new type of military pump-priming will not prime as much; it will not carry as great a "multiplier effect"; it will not stimulate consumption or subsidize capitalism as well as the older type. It is a real capitalist difficulty, and the military expenditures may indeed have to be great to overcome it.

* * *

Imperialism has generally meant the politican and, if need be, the military protection of businessmen and their interests in foreign areas. The political protection need not include the conquest of colonies; the military protection need not involve the establishment of bases and garrisons. But regardless of the manner of the protection extended, imperialism by definition involves the interplay of economic, political, and military institutions and men. No event of significance can be understood without understanding how these interests come to points of clash or of coincidence. "The international system" of the world today cannot be understood without understanding the changing forms of their interplay.

In thinking about "imperialism" we must be prepared to develop different theories for different kinds of political economies. The pre-1914 situation, for example, was quite different from the post-1945 scene, in which two superstates of quite distinctive structure confront each other around the world, and in which specific ruling coalitions of economic, political, and military agents are quite unique.

Both Russia and America have been "imperialistic" in the service of their ideas and in their fears about military and political security. It is in the economic element that they differ.

The economic aim of Soviet imperialism after the second World War was simply booty. Such imperialism consists of the political control of an area with the aim of (1) accumulating valuable capital goods or (2) extracting agricultural and other "surpluses"—as in the Stalinist exploitation of Eastern Europe. Such efforts, as in capitalist imperialism, result in keeping the "colonial" country from industrialization, in keeping it a producer of raw materials. The economic nature of Soviet imperialism does not arise from any "contradiction" in the Soviet economy; economically, it is simply brutal conquest. But as the Soviet economy is further industrialized, this kind of imperialist temptation and drive loses its strength. The reverse is the case with capitalist imperialism.

The aim of capitalist imperialism is, at first, to open up markets for the export of "surplus" consumer goods, and to use the colonial country as a producer of raw materials which the industrial nation needs in its manufacturing. Manufactured goods, in turn, are sold to the backward country. In due course, however, the backward region becomes a sphere for the investment of capital accumulated by the advanced nation. Such export of capital requires, in the capitalist view, that the risk be limited by political guarantees. Only when the state will assure the capitalist that it will support and protect him can such risky investments be undertaken on any scale. After the investment is made there is naturally an expectation or a demand that it be backed up politically. Only a highly organized capitalist group can expect to exert such influence within and upon the state....

* * *

ON PSYCHOLOGICAL CAUSES

The strategic causes of World War III, I have been arguing, are direct and immediate. Only if we assume a direct and immediate democracy of power can we assume that "the people" have an immediate and active part in such history-making decisions as are involved in this *thrust*. Neither for the Soviet Union nor for the United States can we make such an assumption; the part of people in general in the *thrust* is at most permissive or hampering. In the U.S.A., in fact, publics are becoming politically indifferent, they are being rapidly transformed into masses; and these masses are becoming morally as well as politically insensible.

Yet many commentators hold the view that the opinions of innumerable people, or even generic "human nature," are among the causes of war. More recently, psychologists and anthropologists have ascribed war to "misunderstandings" between "peoples" or, more sophisticatedly, to "the tensions arising from differences in national character." This is a very old view, although it now masquerades in the garb of social science.

Rousseau and Kant argued that since wars were waged by princes in their own interests and not in that of their peoples, there would be no wars under a republican form of government, More recently, many men of goodwill have publicized the view that war is due to a "failure of understanding," that peace is a matter of rationally convincing enough of the public that war is absurd.

To hold such a view, I believe, requires us to assume that people in general are directly responsible for history-making, and so for war-making; it is to assume that a direct and total democracy of power prevails, rather than a condition in which history-making power is decisively centralized. Such notions, once they are fully elaborated, turn out, I believe, to be variations of the idea of fate which I have already explained in a sociological way. Often enough, too, those who hold such views come to talk of tragic guilt, usually that of "other people," rather than of political responsibility. Such programs for peace often come down, contradictorily, to educational programs—usually directed toward the people of nations whose elites have behaved badly and stupidly.

The vague notion that war is due to tense differences of "national character," along with the assumption that power rests with the people, seems to me more than mistaken and less than useful. It is part of the nationalist trap. Increased "understanding" may just as well lead to more intelligent hatred as to greater love. To have understood better the Nazi character and outlook would not necessarily have led to avoidance of war with Nazis.

* * *

The issues of war and peace cannot be reduced to a naive psychology of "peace through better understanding among peoples." It is not the aggression of people in general but their mass indifference that is the point of their true political and psychological relevance to the thrust toward war. It is neither the "psychology of peoples" nor raw "human nature" that is relevant; it is the moral insensibility of people who are selected, molded, and honored in the mass society.

In this new society there has come about a situation in which many who have lost faith in prevailing loyalties have not acquired new ones, and so they pay no attention to politics of any kind. they are not radical, not liberal, not conservative, not reactionary. They are inactionary. They are out of it. If we accept the Greek definition of the idiot as an altogether private man, then we must conclude that many American and many Soviet citizens are now idiots. This spiritual condition—and I choose the phrase with care—is the key to many contemporary problems as well as to much political bewilderment. Intellectual "conviction" and moral "belief" are not necessary, in either the ruled or the rulers, for a ruling power to persist and even to flourish. The prevalence of mass indifference is surely one of the major political facts about the Western societies today.

As it concerns the thrust toward war this indifference is best seen as moral insensibility: the mute acceptance—or even unawareness—of moral atrocity; the lack of indignation when confronted with moral horror; the turning of this atrocity and this horror into morally approved conventions of feeling. By moral insensibility, in short, I mean the incapacity for *moral* reaction to event and to character, to high decision and to the drift of human circumstance.

* * *

This insensibility was made dramatic by the Nazis; but the same lack of human morality prevailed among fighter pilots in Korea, with their petroleum-jelly broiling of children and women and men. And is not this lack raised to a higher and technically more adequate level among the brisk generals and gentle scientists who are now planning the weapons and the strategy of World War III?

* * *

ON FATE AND THE RADICAL WILL

What I have been trying to say to intellectuals, preachers, scientists—as well as more generally to publics—can be put into one sentence: Drop the liberal rhetoric and the conservative default; they are now parts of one and the same official line; transcend that line.

There is still a good deal of talk, so fashionable several years ago, about the collapse of "right" and "left"; about "conservative" and "radical" being no longer viable as intellectual and political orientations. Much of this talk, I believe, is part of the default of intellectual workmen, a revelation of their lack of imagination. As a political type, the conservative, in common with the indifferent, is generally content "to be like other men and to take things as they are," for he believes that the status quo has been built slowly and that as such it is as beneficent an arrangement as can fairly be expected. In brief, and in the consistent extreme, the conservative is a man who abdicates the willful making of history.

The radical (and even the liberal) is a man who does not abdicate.

He agrees that many human events, important events at that, may indeed be the results of so many little acts that they are indeed part of fate. But he also sees that more and more events in our epoch are not matters of fate; that they are the results of decisions made and not made by identifiable men who command the new means of decision and of power.

Given these means of administration, production, violence, it seems clear that more and more events are due less to any uncontrollable fate than to the decisions, the defaults, the ignorance—as the case may be—of the higher circles of the superstates. To reflect upon the present as history is to understand that history may now be made by default. Understanding that, we no longer need accept historical fate, for fate is a feature of specific kinds of social structure, of irresponsible systems of power.

These systems can be changed. Fate can be transcended. We must come to understand that while the domain of fate is diminishing and in fact becoming organized as irresponsibility. We must hold men of power variously responsible for pivotal events, we must unmask their pretensions—and often their own mistaken convictions—that they are not responsible.

Our politics, in short, must be the politics of responsibility. Our basic charge against the systems of both the U.S.A. and the U.S.S.R. must be that in differing ways they both live by the politics of irresponsibility.

In East and in West, nowadays, the idea of responsibility is in a sad condition. It is either washed away in Liberal rhetoric, or it becomes a trumped-up bloody purge. But we must hold to it; we must be serious about it; we must understand that to use it requires knowledge and inquiry, continual reflection and imagination.

Those who decide should be held responsible to those men and women everywhere who are in any grievous way affected by decisions and defaults. But by whom should they be held responsible? That is the immediate problem of political power. In both East and West today, the immediate answer is: By the intellectual community. Who else but intellectuals are capable of discerning the role in history of explicit history-making decisions? Who else is in a position to understand that now fate itself must be made a political issue?

No longer can fate be used either as excuse or as hope; neither our hopes nor our fears are part of anything inevitable: we are on our own. Would it not be elementary honesty for the intellectual to realize this new and radical fact of human history and so at least consider the decisions that he is in fact making, rather than to deny by his work that any responsible decisions are open to him?

Democracy requires that those who bear the consequences of decisions have enough knowledge to hold decision-makers accountable. If men hope that contemporary America is to be a democratic society, they must look to the intellectual community for knowledge about those decisions that are now shaping human destiny. Men must depend upon knowledge provided by this community, for by their own private experience they can know only a small portion of the social world, only a few of the decisions that now affect them.

Yet leading intellectual circles in America as elswhere have not provided true images of the elite as men in irresponsible command of unprecedented means of power. Instead, they have invented images of a scatter of reasonable men, overwhelmed by events and doing their best in a difficult situation. By its softening of the political will, the conservative mood of the intellectuals, out of which these images have arisen, enables men to accept public depravity without any private sense of outrage and to give up the central goal of Western humanism, so strongly felt in nineteenth-century American experience: the audacious control by reason of man's fate.

Letter to the New Left

C. Wright Mills

We have frequently been told by an assorted variety of dead-end people that the meanings of left and of right are now liquidated, by history and by reason. I think we should answer them in some such way as this:

The *Right*, among other things, means what you are doing: celebrating society as it is, a going concern. *Left* means, or ought to mean, just the opposite. It means structural criticism and reportage and theories of society, which at some point or another are focussed politically as demands and programs. These criticisms, demands, theories, programs are guided morally by the humanist and secular ideals of Western civilization—above all, the ideals of reason, freedom and justice. To be "left" means to connect up cultural with political criticism, and both with demands and programs. And it means all this inside *every* country of the world.

Only one more point of definition: absence of public issues there may well be, but this is not due to any absence of problems or of contradictions, antagonistic and otherwise. Impersonal and structural changes have not eliminated problems or issues. Their absence from many discussions is an ideological condition, regulated in the first place by whether or not intellectuals detect and state problems as potential *issues* for probable publics, and as *troubles* for a variety of individuals. One indispensible means of such work on these central tasks is what can only be described as ideological analysis. To be actively left, among other things, is to carry on just such analysis.

Excerpts from C. Wright Mills, "Letter to the New Left," *The New Left Review*, September/October 1960. Reprinted with permission.

To take seriously the problem of the need for a political orientation is not, of course, to seek for A Fanatical and Apocalyptic Vision, for An Infallible and Monolithic Lever of Change, for Dogmatic Ideology, for A Startling New Rhetoric, for Treacherous Abstractions, and all the other bogeymen of the dead-enders. These are, of course, "the extremes," the straw men, the red herrings used by our political enemies to characterize the polar opposite of where they think they stand.

They tell us, for example, that ordinary men cannot always be political "heroes." Who said they could? But keep looking around you; and why not search out the conditions of such heroism as men do and might display? They tell us that we are too "impatient," that our "pretentious" theories are not well enough grounded. That is true, but neither are our theories trivial. Why don't they get to work to refute or ground them? They tell us we "do not really understand" Russia and China today. That is true; we don't; neither do they. We at least are studying the question. They tell us we are "ominous" in our formulations. That is true: we do have enough imagination to be frightened, and we don't have to hide it. We are not afraid we'll panic. They tell us we are "grinding axes." Of course we are: we do have, among other points of view, morally grounded ones, and we are aware of them. They tell us, in their wisdom, that we do not understand that The Struggle is Without End. True: we want to change its form, its focus, its object.

We are frequently accused of being "utopian" in our criticisms and in our proposals and, along with this, of basing our hopes for a new left *politics* "merely on reason," or more concretely, upon the intelligentsia in its broadest sense.

There is truth in these charges. But must we not ask: What now is really meant by *utopian?* And is not our utopianism a major source of our strength? *Utopian* nowadays, I think, refers to any criticism or proposal that transcends the up-close milieux of a scatter of individuals, the milieux which men and women can understand directly and which they can reasonably hope directly to change. In this exact sense, our theoretical work is indeed utopian—in my own case, at least, deliberately so. What needs to be understood, and what needs to be changed, is not merely first this and then that detail of some institution or policy. If there is to be a politics of a new left, what needs to be analyzed is the *structure* of institutions, the *foundation* of policies. In this sense, both in its criticisms and in its proposals, our work is necessarily structural, and so—*for us,* just now—utopian.

This brings us face to face with the most important issue of political reflection and of political action in our time: the problem of the historical agency of change, of the social and institutional means of structural change. There are several points about this problem I would like to put to you.

* * *

V

First, the historic agencies of change for liberals of the capitalist societies have been an array of voluntary associations, coming to a political climax in a parliamentary or congressional system. For socialists of almost all varieties, the historic agency has been the working class—and later the peasantry, or parties and unions composed of members of the working class, or (to blur, for now, a great problem) of political parties acting in its name, "representing its interests."

I cannot avoid the view that both these forms of historic agency have either collapsed or become most ambiguous. So far as structural change is concerned, neither seems to be at once available and effective as *our* agency any more. I know this is a debatable point among us, and among many others as well; I am by no means certain about it. But surely, if it is true, it ought not to be taken as an excuse for moaning and withdrawal (as it is by some of those who have become involved with the end-of-ideology); and it ought not to be bypassed (as it is by many Soviet scholars and publicists, who in their reflections upon the course of advanced capitalist societies simply refuse to admit the political condition and attitudes of the working class).

Is anything more certain than that in 1970—indeed, at this time next year—our situation will be quite different, and—the chances are high—decisively so? But of course, that isn't saying much. The seeming collapse of our historic agencies of change ought to be taken as a problem, an issue, a trouble—in fact, as *the* political problem which *we* must turn into issue and trouble.

Second, it is obvious that when we talk about the collapse of agencies of change, we cannot seriously mean that such agencies do not exist. On the contrary, the means of history-making—of decision and of the enforcement of decision—have never in world history been so enlarged and so available to such small circles of men on both sides of The Curtains as they now are. My own conception of the shape of power, the theory of the power elite, I feel no need to argue here. This theory has been fortunate in its critics, from the most diverse political viewpoints, and I have learned from several of these critics. But I have not seen, as of this date, an analysis of the idea that causes me to modify any of its essential features.

The point that is immediately relevant does seem obvious: what is utopian for us, is not at all utopian for the presidium of the Central Committee in Moscow, or the higher circles of the Presidency in Washington, or, recent events make evident, for the men of SAC and CIA. The historic agencies of change that have collapsed are those which were at least thought to be open to *the left* inside the advanced Western nations, to those who have wished for structural changes of these societies. Many things follow from this obvious fact; of many of them, I am sure, we are not yet adequately aware.

Third, what I do not quite understand about some new-left writers is why they cling so mightily to "the working class" of the advanced capitalist societies as *the* historic agency, or even as the most important agency, in the face of the really impressive historical evidence that now stands against this expectation.

Such a labor metaphysic, I think, is a legacy from Victorian Marxism that is now quite unrealistic.

It is an historically specific idea that has been turned into an a-historical and unspecific hope.

The social and historical conditions under which industrial workers tend to become a-class-for-themselves, and a decisive political force, must be fully and precisely elaborated. There have been, there are, there will be such conditions. These conditions vary according to national social structure and the exact phase of their economic and political development. Of course we cannot "write off the working class." But we must *study* all that, and freshly. Where labor exists as an agency, of course we must work with it, but we must not treat it as The Necessary Lever, as nice old Labour Gentlemen in Britian and elsewhere tend to do.

Although I have not yet completed my own comparative studies of working classes, generally it would seem that only at certain (earlier) stages of industrialization, and in a political context of autocracy, *etc.*, do wage workers tend to become a class-for-themselves, *etc.* The *etceteras* mean that I can here merely raise the question.

* * *

It is with this problem of agency in mind that I have been studying, for several years now, the cultural apparatus, the intellectuals, as a possible, immediate, radical agency of change. For a long time, I was not much happier with this idea than were many of you; but it turns out now, at the beginning of the 1960's, that it may be a very relevant idea indeed.

In the first place, is it not clear that if we try to be realistic in our utopianism—and that is no fruitless contradiction—a writer in our countries on the left today *must* begin with the intellectuals? For that is what we are, that is where we stand.

In the second place, the problem of the intelligentsia is an extremely complicated set of problems on which rather little factual work has been done. In doing this work, we must, above all, not confuse the problems of the intellectuals of West Europe and North America with those of the Soviet bloc or with those of the underdeveloped worlds. In each of the three major components of the world's social structure today, the character and the role of the intelligentsia is distinct and historically specific. Only by detailed comparative studies of them in all their human variety can we hope to understand any one of them.

In the third place, who is it that is getting fed up? Who is it that is getting disgusted with what Marx called "all the old crap?" Who is it that is thinking and acting in radical ways? All over the world—in the bloc, and in between—the answer is the same: it is the young intelligentsia.

I cannot resist copying out for you, with a few changes, some materials I recently prepared for a 1960 paperback edition of a book of mine on war:

"In the spring and early summer of 1960, more of the returns from the American decision and default are coming in. In Turkey, after student riots, a military junta takes over the state, of late run by Communist Container Menderes. In South Korea, too, students and others knock over the corrupt American-puppet regime of Syngman Rhee. In Cuba, a genuinely left-wing revolution begins full-scale economic reorganization, without the domination of U. S. corporations. Average age of its leaders: about 30—and certainly a revolution without Labor As Agency. On Taiwan, the eight million Taiwanese under the American-imposed dictatorship of Chiang Kai-shek, with his two million Chinese, grow increasingly restive. On Okinawa, a U.S. military base, the people get their first chance since World War II ended to demonstrate against U.S. seizure of their island; and some students take that chance, snake-dancing and chanting angrily to the visiting President: 'Go home, go home—take away your missiles.' (Don't worry, 12,000 U.S. troops easily handle the generally grateful crowds; also the President is 'spirited out' the rear end of the United States compound—and so by helicopter to the airport.) In Japan, weeks of student rioting succeed in rejecting the President's visit, jeopardizing a new treaty with the U.S.A., and displacing the big-business, pro-American Prime Minister, Kishi. And even in our own pleasant Southland, Negro and white students are—but let us keep that quiet: it really *is* disgraceful.

"That is by no means the complete list; that was yesterday; see today's newspaper. Tomorrow, in varying degree, the returns will be more evident. Will they be evident enough? They will have to be very obvious to attract real American attention: sweet complaints and the voice of reason—these are not enough. In the slum countries of the world today, what are they saying? The rich Americans, they pay attention only to violence—and to money. You don't care what they say, American? Good for you. Still, they may insist; things are no longer under the old control; you're not getting it straight, American: your country—it would seem—may well become the target of a world hatred the like of which the easy-going Americans have never dreamed. Neutralists and Pacifists and Unilateralists and that confusing variety of Leftists around the world—all those tens of millions of people, of course they are misguided, absolutely controlled by small conspiratorial groups of trouble-makers, under direct orders from Moscow and Peking. Diabolically omnipotent, it is *they* who create all this messy unrest. It is *they* who have given the tens of millions the absurd idea that they shouldn't want to remain, or to become, the seat of American nuclear bases—those gay little outposts of American civilization. So now they don't want U-2's on their territory; so now they want to contract out of the American military machine; they want to be neutral among the crazy big antagonists. And they don't want their own societies to be militarized.

"But take heart, American: you won't have time to get really bored with your friends abroad: they won't be your friends much longer. You don't need *them*; it will all go away; don't let them confuse you."

Add to that: In the Soviet bloc, who is it that has been breaking out of apathy? It has been students and young professors and writers; it has been the young intelligentsia of Poland and Hungary, and of Russia, too. Never mind that they have not won; never mind that there are other social and moral types among them. First of all, it has been these types. But the point is clear, isn't it?

That is why we have got to study these new generations of intellectuals around the world as real live agencies of historic change. Forget Victorian Marxism, except when you need it; and read Lenin again (be careful)—Rosa Luxemburg, too.

"But it is just some kind of moral upsurge, isn't it?" Correct. But under it: no apathy. Much of it is direct non-violent action, and it seems to be working, here and there. Now we must learn from the practice of these young intellectuals and with them work out new forms of action.

"But it's all so ambiguous—Cuba, for instance." Of course it is; history-making is always ambiguous. Wait a bit; in the meantime, help them to focus their moral upsurge in less ambiguous political ways. Work out with them the ideologies, the strategies, the theories that will help them consolidate their efforts: new theories of structural changes of and by human societies in our epoch.

"But it is utopian, after all, isn't it?" No, not in the sense you mean. Whatever else it may be, it's not that. Tell it to the students of Japan. Tell it to the Negro sit-ins. Tell it to the Cuban Revolutionaries. Tell it to the people of the Hungry-nation bloc.

The White Negro

Norman Mailer

SUPERFICIAL REFLECTIONS ON THE HIPSTER

Our search for the rebels of the generation led us to the hipster. The hipster is an *enfant terrible* turned inside out. In character with his time, he is trying to get back at the conformists by lying low... You can't interview a hipster because his main goal is to keep out of a society which, he thinks, is trying to make everyone over in its own image. He takes marijuana because it supplies him with experiences that can't be shared with "squares." He may affect a broad-brimmed hat or a zoot suit, but usually he prefers to skulk unmarked. The hipster may be a jazz musician; he is rarely an artist, almost never a writer. He may earn his living as a petty criminal, a hobo, a carnival roustabout or a free-lance moving man in Greenwich Village, but some hipsters have found a safe refuge in the upper income brackets as television comics or movie actors. (The late James Dean, for one, was a hipster hero.)...It is tempting to describe the hipster in psychiatric terms as infantile, but the style of his infantilism is a sign of the times. He does not try to enforce his will on others, Napoleon-fashion, but contents himself with a magical omnipotence never disproved because never tested....As the only extreme nonconformist of his generation, he exercises a

---

Excerpts from Norman Mailer, "The White Negro," *Dissent*, Vol. 4, no. 3, Summer 1957. Reprinted with permission of the author.

powerful if underground appeal for conformists, through newspaper accounts of his delinquencies, his structureless jazz, and his emotive grunt words.

—"Born 1930: The Unlost
Generation" by Caroline Bird
Harper's Bazaar, Feb. 1957

Probably, we will never be able to determine the psychic havoc of the concentration camps and the atom bomb upon the unconscious mind of almost everyone alive in these years. For the first time in civilized history, perhaps for the first time in all of history, we have been forced to live with the suppressed knowledge that the smallest facets of our personality or the most minor projection of our ideas, or indeed the absence of ideas and the absence of personality could mean equally well that we might still be doomed to die as a cipher in some vast statistical operation in which our teeth would be counted, and our hair would be saved, but our death itself would be unknown, unhonored, and unremarked, a death which could not follow with dignity as a possible consequence to serious actions we had chosen, but rather a death by *deus ex machina* in a gas chamber or a radioactive city; and so if in the midst of civilization—that civilization founded upon the Faustian urge to dominate nature by mastering time, mastering the links of social cause and effect—in the middle of an economic civilization founded upon the confidence that time could indeed be subjected to our will, our psyche was subjected itself to the intolerable anxiety that death being causeless, life was causeless as well, and time deprived of cause and effect had come to a stop.

The Second World War presented a mirror to the human conditon which blinded anyone who looked into it. For if tens of millions were killed in concentration camps out of the inexorable agonies and contractions of super-states founded upon the always insoluble contradictions of injustice, one was then obliged also to see that no matter how crippled and perverted an image of man was the society he had created, it was nonetheless his creation, his collective creation (at least his collective creation from the past) and if society was so murderous, then who could ignore the most hideous of questions about his own nature?

Worse. One could hardly maintain the courage to be individual, to speak with one's own voice, for the years in which one could complacently accept oneself as part of an elite by being a radical were forever gone. A man knew that when he dissented, he gave a note upon his life which could be called in any year of overt crisis. No wonder then that these have been the years of conformity and depression. A stench of fear has come out of every pore of American life, and we suffer from a collective failure of nerve. The only courage, with rare exceptions, that we have been witness to, has been the isolated courage of isolated people.

* * *

It is on this bleak scene that a phenomenon had appeared; the American existentialist—the hipster, the man who knows that if our collective condition is to live with instant death by atomic war, relatively quick death by the State as L'univers concentrationnaire, or with a slow death by conformity with every creative and rebellious instict stifled (at what damage to the mind and the heart and the liver and the nerves no research foundation for cancer will discover in a hurry), if the fate of twentieth-century man is to live with death from adolescence to premature senescence, why then the only life-giving answer is to accept the terms of death, to live with death as immediate danger, to divorce oneself from society, to exist without roots, to set out on that uncharted journey with the rebellious imperatives of the self. In short, whether the life is criminal or not, the decision is to encourage the psychopath in oneself, to explore that domain of experience where security is boredom and therefore sickness, and one exists in the present, in that enormous present which is without past or future, memory or planned intention, the life where a man must go until he is beat, where he must gamble with his energies through all those small or large crises of courage and unforeseen situations which beset his day, where he must be with it or doomed not to swing. The unstated essence of Hip, its psychopathic brilliance, quivers with the knowledge that new kinds of victories increase one's power for new kinds of perception; and defeats, the wrong kind of defeats, attack the body and imprison one's energy until one is jailed in the prison air of other people's habits, other people's defeats, boredom, quiet desperation, and muted icy self-destroying rage. One is Hip or one is Square (the alternative which each new generation coming into American life is beginning to feel), one is a rebel or one conforms, one is a frontiersman in the Wild West of American night life, or else a Square cell, trapped in the totalitarian tissues of American society, doomed willy-nilly to conform if one is to succeed.

A totalitarian society makes enormous demands on the courage of men, and a partially totalitarian society makes even greater demands, for the general anxiety is greater. Indeed if one is to be a man, almost any kind of unconventional action often takes disproportionate courage. So it is no accident that the source of Hip is the Negro for he has been living on the margin between totalitarianism and democracy for two centuries. But the presence of Hip as a working philosophy in the sub-worlds of American life is probably due to jazz, and its knifelike entrance into culture, its subtle but so penetrating influence on an avant-garde generation—that postwar generation of adventurers who (some consciously, some by osmosis) had absorbed the lessons of disillusionment and disgust of the twenties, the depression, and the war. Sharing a collective disbelief in the words of men who had too much money and controlled too many things, they knew almost as powerful a disbelief in the socially monolithic ideas of the single mate, the solid family and the respectable love life. If the intellectual antecedents of this generation can be traced to such separate influences as D.H. Lawrence, Henry Miller, and Wilhelm Reich, the viable philosophy of Hemingway fit most of their facts: in a bad world, as he was to say over and over again (while taking time out from his parvenu snobbery and dedicated gourmandize), in a bad world there is no love nor mercy nor charity nor justice unless a man can keep his courage, and this indeed fitted some of the facts. What fitted the need of the adventurer even more precisely was Hemingway's categorical imperative that what made him feel good became therefore The Good.

So no wonder that in certain cities of America, in New York of course, and New Orleans, in Chicago and San Francisco and Los Angeles, in such American cities as Paris and Mexico, D.F., this particular part of a generation was attracted to what the Negro had to offer. In such places as Greenwich Village, a ménage-à-trois was completed—the bohemian and the juvenile delinquent came face-to-face with the Negro, and the hipster was a fact in American life. If marijuana was the wedding ring, the child was the language of Hip for its argot gave expression to abstract states of feeling which all could share, at least all who were Hip. And in this wedding of the white and the black it was the Negro who brought the cultural dowry. Any Negro who wishes to live must live with danger from his first day, and no experience can ever be casual to him, no Negro can saunter down a street with any real certainty that violence will not visit him on his walk. The cameos of security for the average white: mother and the home, job and the family, are not even a mockery to millions of Negroes; they are impossible. The Negro has the simplest of alternatives: live a life of constant humility or ever-threatening danger. In such a pass where paranoia is as vital to survival as blood, the Negro has stayed alive and begun to grow by following the need of his body where he could. Knowing in the cells of his existence that life was war, nothing but war, the Negro (all exceptions admitted) could rarely afford the sophisticated inhibitions of civilization, and so he kept for his survival the art of the primitive, he lived in the enormous present, he subsisted for his Saturday night kicks, relinquishing the pleasures of the mind for the more obligatory pleasures of the body, and in his music he gave voice to the character and quality of his existence, to his rage and the infinite variations of joy, lust, languor, growl, cramp, pinch, scream and despair of his orgasm. For jazz is orgasm, it is the music of orgasm, good orgasm and bad, and so it spoke across a nation, it had the communication of art even where it was watered, perverted, corrupted, and almost killed, it spoke in no matter what laundered popular way of instantaneous existential states to which some whites could respond, it was indeed a communication by art because it said, "I feel this, and now you do too."

So there was a new breed of adventurers, urban adventurers who drifted out at night looking for action with a black man's code to fit their facts. The hipster had absorbed the existentialist synapses of the Negro, and for practical purposes could be considered a white Negro.

To be an existentialist, one must be able to feel oneself—one must know one's desires, one's rages, one's anguish, one must be aware of the character of one's frustration and know what would satisfy it. The overcivilized man can be an existentialist only if it is chic, and deserts it quickly for the next chic. To be a real existentialist (Sartre admittedly to the contrary) one must be religious, one must have one's sense of the "purpose"—whatever the purpose may be—but a life which is directed by one's faith in the necessity of action is a life committed to the notion that the substratum of existence is the search, the end meaningful but mysterious; it is impossible to live such a life unless one's emotions provide their profound conviction. Only the French, alienated beyond alienation from their unconscious could welcome and existential philosphy without ever feeling it at all; indeed only a Frenchman by declaring that the unconscious did not exist could then proceed to explore the delicate involutions of consciousness, the microscopically sensuous and all but ineffable *frissons* of mental becoming, in order finally to create the theology of atheism and so submit that in a world of absurdities the existential absurdity is most coherent.

In the dialogue betwen the atheist and the mystic, the atheist is on the side of life, rational life, undialectical life—since he conceives of death as emptiness, he can, no matter how weary or despairing, wish for nothing but more life; his pride is that he does not transpose his weakness and spiritual fatigue into a romantic longing for death, for such appreciation of death is then all too capable of being elaborated by his imagination into a universe of meaningful structure and moral orchestration.

Yet this masculine argument can mean very little for the mystic. The mystic can accept the atheist's description of his weakness, he can agree that his mysticism was a response to despair. And yet...and yet his argument is that he, the mystic, is the one finally who has chosen to live with death, and so death is his experience and not the atheist's, and the atheist by eschewing the limitless dimensions of profound despair has rendered himself incapable to judge the experience. The real argument which the mystic must always advance is the very intensity of his private vision—his argument depends from the vision precisely because what was felt in the vision is so extraordinary that no rational argument, no hypotheses of "oceanic feelings" and certainly no skeptical reductions can explain away what has become for him the reality more real than the reality of closely reasoned logic. His inner experience of the possibilities within death is his logic. So, too, for the existentialist. And the psychopath. And the saint and the bullfighter and the lover. The common denominator for all of them is their burning consciousness of the present, exactly that incandescent consciousness which the possibilities within death has opened for them. There is a depth of desperation to the condition which enables one to remain in life only by engaging death, but the reward is their knowledge that what is happening at each instant of the electric present is good or bad for them, good or bad for their cause, their love, their action, their need.

It is this knowledge which provides the curious community of feeling in the world of the hipster, a muted cool religious revival to be sure, but the element which is exciting, disturbing, nightmarish perhaps, is that incompatibles have come to bed, the inner life and the violent life, the orgy and the dream of love, the desire to murder and the desire to create, a dialectical conception of existence with a lust for power, a dark, romantic, and yet undeniably dynamic view of existence for it sees every man and woman as moving individually through each moment of life forward into growth or backward into death.

* * *

It is impossible to conceive a new philosophy until one creates a new language, but a new popular language (while it must implicitly contain a new philosophy) does not necessarily present its philosophy overtly. It can be asked then what really is unique in the life-view of Hip which raises its argot above the passing verbal whimsies of the bohemian or the lumpenproletariat.

The answer would be in the psychopathic element of Hip which has almost no interest in viewing human nature, or better, in judging human nature, from a set of standards conceived a priori to the experience, standards inherited from the past. Since Hip sees every answer as posing immediately a new alternative, a new question, its emphasis is on complexity rather than simplicity (such complexity that its language without the illumination of the voice and the articulation of the face and body remains hopelessly incommunicative). Given its emphasis on complexity, Hip abdicates from any conventional moral responsibility because it would argue that the results of our actions are unforeseeable, and so we cannot know if we do good or bad, we cannot even know (in the Joycean sense of the good and the bad) whether we have given energy to another, and indeed if we could, there would still be no idea of what ultimately the other would do with it.

Therefore, men are not seen as good or bad (that they are good-and-bad is taken for granted) but rather each man is glimpsed as a collection of possibilities, some more possible than others (the view of character implicit in Hip) and some humans are considered more capable than others of reaching more possibilities within themselves in less time, provided, and this is the dynamic, provided the particular character can swing at the right time. And here arises the sense of context which differentiates Hip from a Square view of character. Hip sees the context as generally dominating the man, dominating him because his character is less significant than the context in which he must function. Since it is arbitrarily five times more demanding of one's energy to accomplish even an inconsequential action in an unfavorable context than a favorable one, man is then not only his character but his context, since the success or failure of an action in a given context reacts upon the character and therefore affects what the character will be in the next context. What dominates both character and context is the energy available at the moment of intense context.

Character being thus seen as perpetually ambivalent and dynamic enters then into an absolute relativity where there are no truths other than the isolated truths of what each observer feels at each instant of his existence. To take a perhaps unjustified metaphysical extrapolation, it is as if the universe which has usually existed conceptually as a Fact (even if the Fact were Berkeley's God) but a Fact which it was the aim of all science and philosophy to reveal, becomes instead a changing reality whose laws are remade at each instant by everything living, but most particularly man, man raised to a neo-medieval summit where the truth is not what one has felt yesterday or what one expects to feel tomorrow but rather truth is no more nor less than what one feels at each instant in the perpetual climax of the present.

What is consequent therefore is the divorce of man from his values, the liberation of the self from the Super-Ego of society. The only Hip morality (but of course it is an everpresent morality) is to do what one feels whenever and wherever it is possible, and—this is how the war of the Hip and the Square begins—to be engaged in one primal battle: to open the limits of the possible for oneself, for oneself alone, because that is one's need. Yet in widening the arena of the possible, one widens it reciprocally for others as well, so that the nihilistic fulfillment of each man's desire contains its antithesis of human co-operation.

If the ethic reduces to Know Thyself and Be Thyself, what makes it radically different from Socratic moderation with its stern conservative respect for the experience of the past is that the Hip ethic is immoderation, childlike in its adoration of the present (and indeed to respect the past means that one must also respect such ugly consequences of the past as the collective murders of the State). It is this adoration of the present which contains the affirmation of Hip, because its ultimate logic surpasses even the unforgettable solution of the Marquis de Sade to sex, private property, and the family, that all men and women have absolute but temporary rights over the bodies of all other men and women—the nihilism of Hip proposes as its final tendency that every social restraint and category be removed, and the affirmation implicit in the proposal is that man would then prove to be more creative than murderous and so would not destroy himself. Which is exactly what separates Hip from the authoritarian philosophies which now appeal to the conservative and liberal temper—what haunts the middle of the twentieth century is that faith in man has been lost, and the appeal of authority has been that it would restrain us from ourselves. Hip, which would return us to ourselves, at no matter what price in individual violence, is the affirmation of the barbarian, for it requires a primitive passion about human nature to believe that individual acts of violence are always to be preferred to collective violence of the State; it takes literal faith in the creative possibilities of the human being to envisage acts of violence as the catharsis which prepares growth.

Whether the hipster's desire for absolute sexual freedom contains any genuinely radical conception of a different world is of course another matter, and it is possible, since the hipster lives with his hatred, that many of them are the material for an elite of storm troopers ready to follow the first truly magnetic leader whose view of mass murder is phrased in a language which reaches their emotions. But given the desperation of his condition as a psychic outlaw, the hipster is equally a candidate for the most reactionary and most radical of movements, and so it is just as possible that many hipsters will come—if the crisis deepens—to a radical comprehension of the horror of society, for even as the radical has had his incommunicable dissent confirmed in his experience by precisely the frustration, the denied opportunities, and the bitter years which his ideas have cost him, so the sexual adventurer deflected from his goal by the implacable animosity of a society constructed to deny the sexual radical as well, may yet come to an equally bitter comprehension of the slow relentless inhumanity of the conservative power which controls him from without and from within. And in being so controlled, denied, and starved into the attrition of conformity, indeed the hipster may come to see that his condition is no more than an exaggeration of the human condition, and if he would be free, then everyone must be free. Yes, this is possible too, for the heart of Hip is its emphasis upon courage at the moment of crisis, and it is pleasant to think that courage contains within itself (as the explanation of its existence) some glimpse of the necessity of life to become more than it has been.

It is obviously not very possible to speculate with sharp focus on the future of the hipster. Certain possiblities must be evident, however, and the most central is that the organic growth of Hip depends on whether the Negro emerges as a dominating force in American life. Since the Negro knows more about the ugliness and danger of life than the white, it is probable that if the Negro can win his equality, he will possess a potential superiority, a superiority so feared that the fear itself has become the underground drama of domestic politics. Like all conservative political fear it is the fear of unforeseeable consequences, for the Negro's equality would tear a profound shift into the psychology, the sexuality, and the moral imagination of every white alive.

With this possible emergence of the Negro, Hip may erupt as a psychically armed rebellion whose sexual impetus may rebound against the antisexual foundation of every organized power in America, and bring into the air such animosities, antipathies, and new conflicts of interest that the mean empty hypocrisies of mass conformity will no longer work. A time of violence, new hysteria, confusion and rebellion will then be likely to replace the time of conformity. At that time, if the liberal should prove realistic in his belief that there is peaceful room for every tendency in American life, then Hip would end by being absorbed as a colorful figure in the tapestry. But if this is not the reality, and the economic, the social, the psychological, and finally the moral crises accompanying the rise of the Negro should prove insupportable, then a time is coming when every political guidepost will be gone, and millions of liberals will be faced with political dilemmas they have so far succeeded in evading, and with a view of human nature they do not wish to accept. To take the desegregation of the schools in the South as an example, it is quite likely that the reactionary sees the reality more closely than the liberal when he argues that the deeper issue is not desegregation but miscegenation. (As a radical I am of course facing in the opposite direction from the White Citizen's Councils—obviously I believe it is the absolute human right of the Negro to mate with the white, and matings there will undoubtedly be, for there will be Negro high school boys brave enough to chance their lives.) But for the average liberal whose mind has been dulled by the committee-ish cant of the professional liberal, miscegenation is not an issue because he has been told that the Negro does not desire it. So, when it comes, miscegenation will be a terror, comparable perhaps to the derangement of the American Communists when the icons to Stalin came tumbling down. The average American Communist held to the myth of Stalin for reasons which had little to do with the political evidence and everything to do with their psychic necessities. In this sense it is equally a psychic necessity for the liberal to believe that the Negro and even the reactionary Southern white are eventually and fundamentally people like himself, capable of becoming good liberals too if only they can be reached by good liberal reason. What the liberal cannot bear to admit is the hatred beneath the skin of a society so unjust that the amount of collective violence buried in the people is perhaps incapable of being contained, and therefore if one wants a better world one does well to hold one's breath, for a worse world is bound to come first, and the dilemma may well be this: given such hatred, it must either vent itself nihilistically or become turned into the cold murderous liquidations of the totalitarian state.

* * *

No matter what its horrors the twentieth century is a vastly exciting century for its tendency is to reduce all of life to its ultimate alternatives. One can well wonder if the last war of them all will be between the black and the whites, or between the women and the men, or between the beautiful and ugly, the pillagers and managers, or the rebels and the regulators. Which of course is carrying speculation beyond the point where speculation is still serious, and yet depair at the monotony and bleakness of the future have become so engrained in the radical temper that the radical is in danger of abdicating from all imagination. What a man feels is the impulse for his creative effort, and if an alien but nonetheless passionate instinct about the meaning of life has come so unexpectedly from a virtually illiterate people, come out of the most intense conditions of exploitation, cruelty, violence, frustration, and lust, and yet has succeeded as an instict in keeping this tortured people alive, then it is perhaps possible that the Negro holds more of the tail of the expanding elephant of truth than the radical, and if this is so, the radical humanist could do worse than to brood upon the phenomenon. For if a revolutionary time should come again, there would be a crucial difference if someone had already delineated a neo-Marxian calculus aimed at comprehending every circuit and process of society from ukase to kiss as the communications of human energy—a calculus capable of translating the economic relations of man into his psychological relations and then back again, his productive relations thereby embracing his sexual relation as well, until the crises of capitalism in the twentieth century would yet be understood as the unconscious adaptations of a society to solve its economic imbalance at the expense of a new mass psychological imbalance. It is almost beyond the imagination to conceive of a work in which the drama of human energy is engaged, and a theory of its social currents and dissipations, its imprisonments, expressions, and tragic wastes are fitted into some gigantic synthesis of human action where the body of Marxist thought, and particularly the epic grandeur of *Das Kapital* (that first of the major *psychologies* to approach the mystery of social cruelty so simply and practically as to say that we are a collective body of humans whose life-energy is wasted, displaced, and procedurally stolen as it passes from one of us to another)—where particularly the epic grandeur of *Das Kapital* would find its place in an even more God-like view of human justice and injustice, in some more excruciating vision of those intimate and institutional processes which lead to our creation and disasters, our growth, our attrition, and our rebellion.

2 THE CIVIL RIGHTS AND BLACK POWER MOVEMENTS

Dr. Martin Luther King, Jr.'s best selling autobiographical work Stride Toward Freedom offers a vivid portrayal of the 1955-1956 Montgomery bus boycott. The portion reprinted here, "Pilgrimage to Nonviolence," brought to a large audience the challenging idea that it was both desirable and proper to break morally unjust laws by nonviolent means. King's insight was widely employed during the 1960s to sanction the disruptive activities of the civil rights and peace movements.

At its beginning, SNCC affirmed Martin Luther King's philosophy of nonviolent direct action, as evidenced in the organization's founding statement adopted in October 1960. A SNCC position paper "Women in the Movement" was anonymously written in 1964 and circulated by a few female activists. Their straightforward description of male domination in SNCC was an example of feminist values that would increasingly be expressed by the end of the decade. SNCC's position paper of January 1966, "On Vietnam," published in The Movement newspaper, applies the principle of moral law-breaking to draft resistance and shows that SNCC was no longer solely concerned with civil rights issues. The document is also interesting because it equates black struggles in the United States with Thirld World issues. In the winter of 1965–66, SNCC activists wrote "SNCC Speaks for Itself," a document that demonstrates the organization's evolutionary turn to "black power."

SNCC was influenced by the militant nationalism and internationalism of Malcom X. One of Malcom X's most influential speeches was "The Ballot or the Bullet" presented at a meeting of the Congress of Racial Equality on April 3, 1964. While still holding out the hope of a peaceful solution to racial oppression in America, Malcolm X offered a strong rationale for politically motivated violence aimed at achieving black liberation. A recording of this speech was used by later black nationalist and radical organizations to educate their members.

By November 1965, SNCC activists Casey Hayden and Mary King had written "Sex and Caste: A Kind of Memo." This document, published in the respected radical pacifist magazine, Liberation, is an early attempt to develop a personal and theoretical feminist analysis and was widely read in new left organizations.

Stokely Carmichael's polemic "What We Want" appeared in Dissent magazine in the fall of 1966. This piece offers a pragmatic definition of black power which proved attractive to black militants and their white supporters— among them SDS founder Tom Hayden. In Rebellion in Newark, published in 1967, Hayden responds affirmatively to black ghetto riots, adopting an outlook that would soon become popular among many new leftists. Black militant H. Rap Brown, in his book, Die Nigger Die!, completely gives up any hope of a non-violent solution to racism and instead argues for insurrection and clandestine guerrilla war.

The Ten-Point Platform and Program of the Black Panther Party concisely expressed that organization's revolutionary goals and outlook. The platform was used as an organizing tool in black communities across the country, and it inspired many attempts at imitation among militant Hispanics, Asians, senior citizens, and young counterculturalists.

Erika Huggins became a major figure in the Black Panther organization. Her poem For a Woman is dated January 24, 1970 and was written while she was in jail in New Haven, Connecticut, charged with murder. Panther Party cofounder Huey P. Newton's manifesto, Revolutionary Suicide, was written in the early 1970s and is an extreme restatement of the early civil rights imperative to "put your body on the line." Newton believed that the only way for a black person to have a dignified life was to live as a revolutionary, facing death.

Pilgrimage to Nonviolence

Dr. Martin Luther King, Jr.

When I went to Montgomery as a pastor, I had not the slightest idea that I would later become involved in a crisis in which nonviolent resistance would be applicable. I neither started the protest nor suggested it. I simply responded to the call of the people for a spokesman. When the protest began, my mind, consciously or unconsciously, was driven back to the Sermon on the Mount, with its sublime teachings on love, and the Gandhian method of nonviolent resistance. As the days unfolded, I came to see the power of nonviolence more and more. Living through the actual experience of the protest, nonviolence became more than a method to which I gave intellectual assent; it became a commitment to a way of life. Many of the things that I had not cleared up intellectually concerning nonviolence were now solved in the sphere of practical action.

Since the philosophy of nonviolence played such a positive role in the Montgomery Movement, it may be wise to turn to a brief discussion of some basic aspects of this philosophy.

First, it must be emphasized that nonviolent resistance is not a method for cowards; it does resist. If one uses this method because he is afraid or merely because he lacks the instruments of violence, he is not truly nonviolent. This is why Gandhi often said that if cowardice is the only alternative to violence, it is better to fight. He made this statement

Pages 101–107 in *Stride Toward Freedom: The Montgomery Story* by Martin Luther King, Jr. Copyright © 1958 by Martin Luther King, Jr. Reprinted by permission of Harper & Row, Publishers, Inc.

conscious of the fact that there is always another alternative: no individual or group need submit to any wrong, nor need they use violence to right the wrong; there is the way of nonviolent resistance. This is ultimately the way of the strong man. It is not a method of stagnant passivity. The phrase "passive resistance" often gives the false impression that this is a sort of "do-nothing method" in which the resister quietly and passively accepts evil. But nothing is further from the truth. For while the nonviolent resister is passive in the sense that he is not physically aggressive toward his opponent, his mind and emotions are always active, constantly seeking to persuade his opponent that he is wrong. The method is passive physically, but strongly active spiritually. It is not passive nonresistance to evil, it is active nonviolent resistance to evil.

A second basic fact that characterizes nonviolence is that it does not seek to defeat or humiliate the opponent, but to win his friendship and understanding. The nonviolent resister must often express his protest through noncooperation or boycotts, but he realizes that these are not ends themselves; they are merely means to awaken a sense of moral shame in the opponent. The end is redemption and reconciliation. The aftermath of nonviolence is the creation of the beloved community, while the aftermath of violence is tragic bitterness.

A third characteristic of this method is that the attack is directed against forces of evil rather than against persons who happen to be doing the evil. It is evil that the nonviolent resister seeks to defeat, not the persons victimized by evil. If he is opposing racial injustice, the nonviolent resister has the vision to see that the basic tension is not between races. As I like to say to the people in Montgomery: "The tension in this city is not between white people and Negro people. The tension is, at bottom, between justice and injustice, between the forces of light and the forces of darkness. And if there is a victory, it will be a victory not merely for fifty thousand Negroes, but a victory for justice and the forces of light. We are out to defeat injustice and not white persons who may be unjust."

A fourth point that characterizes nonviolent resistance is a willingness to accept suffering without retaliation, to accept blows from the opponent without striking back. "Rivers of blood may have to flow before we gain our freedom, but it must be our blood," Gandhi said to his countrymen. The nonviolent resister is willing to accept violence if necessary, but never to inflict it. He does not seek to dodge jail. If going to jail is necessary, he enters it "as a bridegroom enters the bride's chamber."

One may well ask: "What is the nonviolent resister's justification for this ordeal to which he invites men, for this mass political application of the ancient doctrine of turning the other cheek?" The answer is found in the realization that unearned suffering is redemptive. Suffering, the nonviolent resister realizes, has tremendous educational and transforming possibilities. "Things of fundamental importance to people are not secured by reason alone, but have to be purchased with their suffering," said Gandhi. He continues: "Suffering is infinitely more powerful than the law of the jungle for converting the opponent and opening his ears which are otherwise shut to the voice of reason."

A fifth point concerning nonviolent resistance is that it avoids not only external physical violence but also internal violence of spirit. The nonviolent resister not only refuses to shoot his opponent but he also refuses to hate him. At the center of nonviolence stands the principle of love. The nonviolent resister would contend that in the struggle for human dignity, the oppressed people of the world must not succumb to the temptation of becoming bitter or indulging in hate campaigns. To retaliate in kind would do nothing but intensify the existence of hate in the universe. Along the way of life, someone must have sense enough and morality enough to cut off the chain of hate. This can only be done by projecting the ethic of love to the center of our lives.

In speaking of love at this point, we are not referring to some sentimental or affectionate emotion. It would be nonsense to urge men to love their oppressors in an affectionate sense. Love in this connection means understanding, redemptive good will. Here the Greek language comes to our aid. There are three words for love in the Greek New Testament. First, there is *eros*. In Platonic philosophy *eros* meant the yearning of the soul for the realm of the divine. It has come now to mean a sort of aesthetic or romantic love. Second, there is *philia* which means intimate affection between personal friends. *Philia* denotes a sort of reciprocal love; the person loves because he is loved. When we speak of loving those who oppose us, we refer to neither *eros* nor *philia*; we speak of a love which is expressed in the Greek word *agape*. *Agape* means understanding, redeeming good will for all men. It is an overflowing love which is purely spontaneous, unmotivated, groundless, and creative. It is not set in motion by any quality or function of its object. It is the love of God operating in the human heart.

Agape is disinterested love. It is a love in which the individual seeks not his own good, but the good of his neighbor (I Cor. 10:24). *Agape* does not begin by discriminating between worthy and unworthy people, or any qualities people possess. It begins by loving others *for their sakes.* It is an entirely "neighbor-regarding concern for others," which discovers the neighbor in every man it meets. Therefore, *agape* makes no distinction between friend and enemy; it is directed toward both. If one loves an individual merely on account of his friendliness, he loves him for the sake of the benefits to be gained from the friendship, rather than for the friend's own sake. Consequently, the best way to assure oneself that Love is disinterested is to have love for the enemy-neighbor from whom you can expect no good in return, but only hostility and persecution.

Another basic point about *agape* is that it springs from the *need* of the other person—his need for belonging to the best in the human family. The Samaritan who helped the Jew on the Jericho Road was "good" because he responded to the human need that he was presented with. God's love is eternal and fails not because man needs his love. St. Paul assures us that the loving act of redemption was done "while we were yet sinners"—that is, at the point of our greatest need for love. Since the white man's personality is greatly distorted by segregation, and his soul is greatly scarred, he needs the love of the Negro. The Negro must love the white man, because the white man needs his love to remove his tensions, insecurities, and fears.

Agape is not a weak, passive love. It is love in action. *Agape* is love seeking to preserve and create community. It is insistence on community even when one seeks to break it. *Agape* is a willingness to sacrifice in the interest of mutuality. *Agape* is a willingness to go to any length to restore community. It doesn't stop at the first mile, but it goes the second mile to restore community. It is a willingness to forgive, not seven times, but seventy times seven to restore community. The cross is the eternal expression of the length to which God will go in order to restore broken community. The Holy Spirit is the continuing community creating reality that moves through history. He who works against community is working against the whole of creation. Therefore, if I respond to hate with a reciprocal hate I do nothing but intensify the cleavage in broken community. I can only close the gap in broken community by meeting hate with love. If I meet hate with hate, I become depersonalized, because creation is so designed that my personality can only be fulfilled in the context of community. Booker T. Washington was right: "Let no man pull you so low as to make you hate him." When he pulls you that low he brings you to the point of working against community; he drags you to the point of defying creation, and thereby becoming depersonalized.

In the final analysis, *agape* means a recognition of the fact that all life is interrelated. All humanity is involved in a single process, and all men are brothers. To the degree that I harm my brother, no matter what he is doing to me, to that extent I am harming myself. For example, white men often refuse federal aid to education in order to avoid giving the Negro his rights; but because all men are brothers they cannot deny Negro children without harming their own. They end, all efforts to the contrary, by hurting themselves. Why is this? Because men are brothers. If you harm me, you harm yourself.

Love, *agape*, is the only cement that can hold this broken community together. When I am commanded to love, I am commanded to restore community, to resist injustice, and to meet the needs of my brothers.

A sixth basic fact about nonviolent resistance is that it is based on the conviction that the universe is on the side of justice. Consequently, the believer in nonviolence has deep faith in the future. This faith is another reason why the nonviolent resister can accept suffering without retaliation. For he knows that in his struggle for justice he has cosmic companionship. It is true that there are devout believers in nonviolence who find it difficult to believe in a personal God. But even these persons believe in the existence of some creative force that works for universal wholeness. Whether we call it an unconscious process, an impersonal Brahman, or a Personal Being of matchless power and infinite love, there is a creative force in this universe that works to bring the disconnected aspects of reality into a harmonious whole.

SNCC: Founding Statement

We affirm the philosophical or religious ideal of nonviolence as the foundation of our purpose, the presupposition of our belief, and the manner of our action.

Nonviolence, as it grows from the Judeo-Christian tradition, seeks a social order of justice permeated by love. Integration of human endeavor represents the crucial first step towards such a society.

Through nonviolence, courage displaces fear. Love transcends hate. Acceptance dissipates prejudice; hope ends despair. Faith reconciles doubt. Peace dominates war. Mutual regards cancel enmity. Justice for all overthrows injustice. The redemptive community supersedes immoral social systems.

By appealing to conscience and standing on the moral nature of human existence, nonviolence nurtures the atmosphere in which reconciliation and justice become actual possibilities.

Although each local group in this movement must diligently work out the clear meaning of this statement of purpose, each act or phase of our corporate effort must reflect a genuine spirit of love and good-will.

SNCC Position Paper:
Women in the Movement

1. Staff was involved in crucial constitutional revisions at the Atlanta staff meeting in October. A large committee was appointed to present revisions to the staff. The committee was all men.

2. Two organizers were working together to form a farmers league. Without asking any questions, the male organizer immediately assigned the clerical work to the female organizer although both had had equal experience in organizing campaigns.

3. Although there are women in Mississippi project who have been working as long as some of the men, the leadership group in COFO is all men.

4. A woman in a field office wondered why she was held responsible for day to day decisions, only to find out later that she had been appointed project director but not told.

5. A fall 1964 personnel and resources report on Mississippi projects lists the number of people in each project. The section on Laurel, however, lists not the number of persons, but "three girls."

6. One of SNCC's main administrative officers apologizes for appointment of a woman as interim project director in a key Mississippi project area.

7. A veteran of two years' work for SNCC in two states spends her day typing and doing clerical work for other people in her project.

8. Any woman in SNCC, no matter what her position or experience, has been asked to take minutes in a meeting when she and other women are outnumbered by men.

9. The names of several new attorneys entering a state project this past summer were posted in a central movement office. The first intitial and last name of each lawyer was listed. Next to one name was written: (girl).

10. Capable, responsible, and experienced women who are in leadership positions can expect to have to defer to a man on their project for final decisionmaking.

11. A session at the recent October staff meeting in Atlanta was the first large meeting in the past couple of years where a woman was asked to chair.

Undoubtedly this list will seem strange to some, petty to others, laughable to most. The list could continue as far as there are women in the movement. Except that most women don't talk about these kinds of incidents, because the whole subject is [not] discussable—strange to some, petty to others, laughable to most. The average white person finds it difficult to understand why the Negro resents being called "boy," or being thought of as "musical" and "athletic," because the average white person doesn't realize that *he assumes he is superior.* And naturally he doesn't understand the problem of paternalism. So too the average SNCC worker finds it difficult to discuss the woman problem because of the assumption of male superiority. Assumptions of male superiority are as widespread and deep rooted and every much as crippling to the woman as the assumptions of white supremacy are to the Negro. Consider why it is in SNCC that women who are competent, qualified, and experienced, are automatically assigned to the "female" kinds of jobs such as typing, desk work, telephone work, filing, library work, cooking, and the assistant kind of administrative work but rarely the "executive" kind.

The woman in SNCC is often in the same position as that token Negro hired in a corporation. The management thinks that it has done its bit. Yet, every day the Negro bears an atmosphere, attitudes and actions which are tinged with condescension and paternalism, the most telling of which are when he is not promoted as the equally or less skilled whites are. This paper is anonymous. Think about the kinds of things the author, if made known, would have to suffer because of raising this kind of discussion. Nothing so final as being fired or outright exclusion, but the kinds of things which are killing to the insides—insinuations, ridicule, over-exaggerated compensations.

This paper is presented anyway because it needs to be made know[n] that many women in the movement are not "happy and contented" with their status. It needs to be made known that much talent and experience are being wasted by this movement when women are not given jobs commensurate with their abilities. It needs to be known that just as Negroes were the crucial factor in the economy of the cotton South, so too in SNCC, women are the crucial factor that keeps the movement running on a day-to-day basis. Yet they are not given equal say-so when it comes to day-to-day decisionmaking. What can be done? Probably nothing right away. Most men in this movement are probably too threatened by the possibility of serious discussion on this subject. Perhaps this is because they have recently broken away from a matriarchal framework under which they may have grown up. Then too, many women are as unaware and insensitive to this subject as men, just as there are many Negroes who don't understand they are not free or who want to be part of white America. They don't understand that they have to give up their souls and stay in their place to be accepted. So too, many women, in order to be accepted by men, on men's terms, give themselves up to that caricature of what a woman is—unthinking, pliable, an ornament to please the man.

Maybe the only thing that can come out of this paper is discussion —amidst the laughter—but still discussion. (Those who laugh the hardest are often those who need the crutch of male supremacy the most.) And maybe some women will begin to recognize day-to-day discriminations. And maybe sometime in the future the whole of the women in this movement will become so alert as to force the rest of the movement to stop the discrimination and start the slow process of changing values and ideas so that all of us gradually come to understand that this is no more a man's world than it is a white world.

SNCC Position Paper: Vietnam

"THE U.S. GOVERNMENT HAS DECEIVED US"

The Student Nonviolent Coordinating Committee has a right and a responsibility to dissent with United States foreign policy on any issue when it sees fit. The Student Nonviolent Coordinating Committee now states its opposition to United States' involvement in Vietnam on these grounds:

We believe the United States government has been deceptive in its claims of concern for the freedom of the Vietnamese people, just as the government has been deceptive in claiming concern for the freedom of colored people in such other countries as the Dominican Republic, the Congo, South Africa, Rhodesia, and in the United States itself.

We, the Student Nonviolent Coordinating Committee, have been involved in the black people's struggle for liberation and self-determination in this country for the past five years. Our work, particularly in the South, has taught us that the United States government has never guaranteed the freedom of oppressed citizens, and is not yet truly determined to end the rule of terror and oppression within its own borders.

We ourselves have often been victims of violence and confinement executed by United States governmental officials. We recall the numerous persons who have been murdered in the South because of their efforts to secure their civil and human rights, and whose murderers have been allowed to escape penalty for their crimes.

The murder of Samuel Young in Tuskegee, Alabama, is no different than the murder of peasants in Vietnam, for both Young and the

The Movement, January 1966.

Vietnamese sought, and are seeking, to secure the rights guaranteed them by law. In each case, the United States government bears a great part of the responsibility for these deaths.

Samuel Young was murdered because United States law is not being enforced. Vietnamese are murdered because the United States is pursuing an aggressive policy in violation of international law. The United States is no respecter of persons or law when such persons or laws run counter to its needs or desires.

We recall the indifference, suspicion and outright hostility with which our reports of violence have been met in the past by government officials.

We know that for the most part, elections in this country, in the North as well as the South, are not free. We have seen that the 1965 Voting Rights Act and the 1966 Civil Rights Act have not yet been implemented with full federal power and sincerity.

We question, then, the ability and even the desire of the United States government to guarantee free elections abroad. We maintain that our country's cry of "preserve freedom in the world" is a hypocritical mask behind which it squashes liberation movements which are not bound, and refuse to be bound, by the expediencies of United States cold war policies.

We are in sympathy with, and support, the men in this country who are unwilling to respond to a military draft which would compel them to contribute their lives to United States aggression in Vietnam in the name of the "freedom" we find so false in this country.

We recoil with horror at the inconsistency of a supposedly "free" society where responsibility to freedom is equated with the responsibility to lend oneself to military aggression. We take note of the fact that 16% of the draftees from this country are Negroes called on to stifle the liberation of Vietnam, to preserve a "democracy" which does not exist for them at home.

We ask, where is the draft for the freedom fight in the United States?

We therefore encourage those Americans who prefer to use their energy in building democratic forms within this country. We believe that work in the civil rights movement and with other human relations organizations is a valid alternative to the draft. We urge all Americans to seek this alternative, knowing full well that it may cost them their lives—as painfully as in Vietnam.

SNCC Speaks for Itself

THE BASIS OF BLACK POWER

The myth that the Negro is somehow incapable of liberating himself, is lazy, etc., came out of the American experience. In the books that children read, whites are always "good" (good symbols are white), blacks are "evil" or seen as savages in movies, their language is referred to as a "dialect," and black people in this country are supposedly descended from savages.

Any white person who comes into the movement has these concepts in his mind about black people, if only subconsciously. He cannot escape them because the whole society has geared his subconscious in that direction.

Miss America coming from Mississippi has a chance to represent all of America, but a black person from either Mississippi or New York will never represent America. Thus the white people coming into the movement cannot relate to the black experience, cannot relate to the word "black," cannot relate to the "nitty gritty," cannot relate to the experience that brought such a word into existence, cannot relate to chitterlings, hog's head cheese, pig feet, hamhocks, and cannot relate to slavery, because these things are not a part of their experience. They also cannot relate to the black religious experience, nor to the black church unless, of course, this church has taken on white manifestations.

WHITE POWER

Negroes in this country have never been allowed to organize themselves because of white interference. As a result of this, the stereotype

The Radical Education Project, Ann Arbor, Michigan, n.d.

has been reinforced that blacks cannot organize themselves. The white psychology that blacks have to be watched, also reinforces this stereotype. Blacks, in fact, feel intimidated by the presence of whites, because of their knowledge of the power that whites have over their lives. One white person can come into a meeting of black people and change the complexion of that meeting, whereas one black person would not change the complexion of that meeting until he was an obvious Uncle Tom. People would immediately start talking about "brotherhood," "love," etc.; race would not be discussed.

If people must express themselves freely, there has to be a climate in which they can do this. If blacks feel intimidated by whites, they then are not liable to vent the rage that they feel about whites in the presence of whites—especially not the black people whom we are trying to organize, i.e. the broad masses of black people. A climate has to be created whereby blacks can express themselves. The reason that whites must be excluded is not that one is antiwhite, but because the effects that one is trying to achieve cannot succeed because whites have an intimidating effect. Oftimes the intimidating effect is in direct proportion to the amount of degradation that black people have suffered at the hands of white people.

ROLES OF WHITES AND BLACKS

It must be offered that white people who desire change in this country should go where that problem (racism) is most manifest. The problem is not in the black community. The white people should go into white communities where the whites have created power for the express purpose of denying blacks human dignity and self-determination. Whites, who come into the black community with ideas of change seem to want to absolve the power structure of its responsibility for what it is doing, and saying that change can only come through black unity, which is the worst kind of paternalism. This is not to say that whites have not had an important role in the movement. In the case of Mississippi, their role was very key in that they helped give blacks the right to organize, but that role is now over, and it should be.

People now have the right to picket, the right to give out leaflets, the right to vote, the right to demonstrate, the right to print.

These things which revolve around the right to organize have been accomplished mainly because of the entrance of white people into Mississippi, in the summer of 1964. Since these goals have now been accomplished, whites' role in the movement has now ended. What does it mean if black people, once having the right to organize, are not allowed to organize themselves? It means that blacks' ideas about inferiority are being reinforced. Shouldn't people be able to organize themselves? Blacks should be given this right. Further, white participation means in the eyes of the black community that whites are the "brains" behind the movement, and that blacks cannot function without whites. This only serves to perpetuate existing attitudes within the existing society, i.e. blacks are "dumb," "unable to take care of business," etc. Whites are "smart," the "brains" behind the whole thing.

How do blacks relate to other blacks as such? How do we react to Willie Mays as against Mickey Mantle? What is our response to Mays hitting a home run against Mantle performing the same deed? One has to come to the conclusion that it is because of black participation in baseball. Negroes still identify with the Dodgers because of Jackie Robinson's efforts with the Dodgers. Negroes would instinctively champion all-black teams if they opposed all-white or predominantly white teams. The same principle operates for the movement as it does for baseball: a mystique must be created whereby Negroes can identify with the movement.

Thus an all-black project is needed in order for the people to free themselves. This has to exist from the beginning. This relates to what can be called "coalition politics." There is no doubt in our minds that some whites are just as disgusted with this system as we are. But it is meaningless to talk about coalition if there is no one to align ourselves with, because of the lack of organization in the white communities. There can be no talk of "hooking up" unless black people organize blacks and white people organize whites. If these conditions are met, then perhaps at some later date—and if we are going in the same direction—talks about exchange of personnel, coalition, and other meaningful alliances can be discussed.

In the beginning of the movement, we had fallen into a trap whereby we thought that our problems revolved around the right to eat at certain lunch counters or the right to vote, or to organize our communities. We have seen, however, that the problem is much deeper. The problem of this country, as we had seen it, concerned all blacks and all whites and therefore if decisions were left to the young people, then solutions would be arrived at. But this negates the history of black people and whites. We have dealt stringently with the problem of "Uncle Tom," but we have not yet gotten around to Simon Legree. We must ask ourselves, Who is the real villain—Uncle Tom or Simon

Legree? Everybody knows Uncle Tom, but who knows Simon Legree? So what we have now in SNCC is a closed society, a clique. Black people cannot relate to SNCC because of its unrealistic, nonracial atmosphere; denying their experiences of America as a racist society. In contrast, the Southern Christian Leadership Conference of Martin Luther King, Jr., has a staff that at least maintains a black facade. The front office is virtually all black, but nobody accuses SCLC of being racist.

If we are to proceed toward true liberation, we must cut ourselves off from white people. We must form our own institutions, credit unions, co-ops, political parties, write our own histories.

To proceed further, let us make some comparisons between the Black Movement of the early 1900s and the movement of the 1960s—i.e. compare the National Association of Coloured People with SNCC. Whites subverted the Niagara movement (the forerunner of the NAACP) which, at the outset, was an all-black movement. The name of the new organization was also very revealing, in that it pre-supposed blacks have to be advanced to the level of whites. We are now aware that the NAACP has grown reactionary, is controlled by the black power structure itself, and stands as one of the main roadblocks to black freedom. SNCC, by allowing the whites to remain in the organization, can have its efforts subverted in the same manner, i.e. through having them play important roles such as community organizers, etc. Indigenous leadership cannot be built with whites in the positions they now hold.

These facts do not mean that whites cannot help. They can participate on a voluntary basis. We can contract work out to them, but in no way can they participate on a policy-making level.

BLACK SELF-DETERMINATION

The charge may be made that we are "racists," but whites who are sensitive to our problems will realize that we must determine our own destiny.

In an attempt to find a solution to our dilemma, we propose that our organization (SNCC) should be black-staffed, black-controlled, and black-financed. We do not want to fall into a similar dilemma that other civil rights organizations have fallen into. If we continue to rely upon white financial support we will find ourselves entwined in the tentacles of the white power complex that controls this country. It is also important that a black organization (devoid of cultism) be projected to our people so that it can be demonstrated that such organizations are viable.

More and more we see black people in this country being used as a tool of the white liberal establishment. Liberal whites have not begun to address themselves to the real problem of black people in this country—witness their bewilderment, fear, and anxiety when nationalism is mentioned concerning black people. An analysis of the white liberal's reaction to the word nationalism alone reveals a very meaningful attitude of whites of any ideological persuasion toward blacks in this country. It means previous solutions to black problems in this country have been made in the interests of those whites dealing with these problems and not in the best interests of black people in this country. Whites can only subvert our true search and struggle for self-determination, self-identification, and liberation in this country. Reevaluation of the white and black roles must NOW take place so that whites no longer designate roles that black people play but rather black people define white people's roles.

Too long have we allowed white people to interpret the importance and meaning of the cultural aspects of our society. We have allowed them to tell us what was good about our Afro-American music, art, and literature. How many black critics do we have on the "jazz" scene? How can a white person who is not part of the black psyche (except in the oppressor's role) interpret the meaning of the blues to us who are manifestations of the songs themselves?

It must be pointed out that on whatever level of contact blacks and whites come together, that meeting or confrontation is not on the level of the blacks but always on the level of the whites. This only means that our everyday contact with whites is a reinforcement of the myth of white supremacy. Whites are the ones who must try to raise themselves to our humanistic level. We are not, after all, the ones who are responsible for a genocidal war in Vietnam; we are not the ones who are responsible for neocolonialism in Africa and Latin America; we are not the ones who held a people in animalistic bondage over 400 years. We reject the American dream as defined by white people and must work to construct an American reality defined by Afro-Americans.

WHITE RADICALS

One of the criticisms of white militants and radicals is that when we view the masses of white people we view the over-all reality of America, we view the racism, the bigotry, and the distortion of personality, we view man's inhumanity to man; we view in reality 180 million racists.

The sensitive white intellectual and radical who is fighting to bring about change is conscious of this fact, but does not have the courage to admit this. When he admits this reality, then he must also admit his involvement because he is part of the collective white America. It is only to the extent that he recognizes this that he will be able to change this reality.

Another common concern is, How does the white radical view the black community, and how does he view the poor white community, in terms of organizing? So far, we have found that most white radicals have sought to escape the horrible reality of America by going back into the black community and attempting to organize black people while neglecting the organization of their own people's racist communities. How can one clean up someone else's yard when one's own yard is untidy? Again we feel that SNCC and the civil rights movement in general is in many aspects similar to the anticolonial situations in the African and Asian countries. We have the whites in the movement corresponding to the white civil servants and missionaries in the colonial countries who have worked with the colonial people for a long period of time and have developed a paternalistic attitude toward them. The reality of the colonial people taking over their own lives and controlling their own destiny must be faced. Having to move aside and letting the natural process of growth and development take place must be faced.

These views should not be equated with outside influence or outside agitation but should be viewed as the natural process of growth and development within a movement; so that the move by the black militants and SNCC in this direction should be viewed as a turn toward self-determination.

It is very ironic and curious that aware whites in this country can champion anticolonialism in other countries in Africa, Asia, and Latin America, but when black people move toward similar goals of self-determination in this country they are viewed as racists and anti-white by these same progressive whites. In proceeding further, it can be said that this attitude derives from the overall point of view of the white psyche as it concerns the black people. This attitude stems from the era of the slave revolts when every white man was a potential deputy or sheriff or guardian of the state. Because when black people got together among themselves to work out their problems, it became a threat to white people, because such meetings were potential slave revolts.

It can be maintained that this attitude or way of thinking has perpetuated itself to this current period and that it is part of the psyche of white people in this country whatever their political persuasion might be. It is part of the white fear-guilt complex resulting from the slave revolts. There have been examples of whites who stated that they can deal with black fellows on an individual basis but become threatened or menaced by the presence of groups of blacks. It can be maintained that this attitude is held by the majority of progressive whites in this country.

BLACK IDENTITY

A thorough re-examination must be made by black people concerning the contributions that we have made in shaping this country. If this re-examination and re-evaluation is not made, and black people are not given their proper due and respect, then the antagonisms and contradictions are going to become more and more glaring, more and more intense, until a national explosion may result.

When people attempt to move from these conclusions it would be faulty reasoning to say they are ordered by racism, because, in this country and in the West, racism has functioned as a type of white nationalism when dealing with black people. We all know the habit that this has created throughout the world and particularly among nonwhite people in this country.

Therefore any re-evaluation that we must make will, for the most part, deal with identification. Who are black people, what are black people, what is their relationship to America and the world?

It must be repeated that the whole myth of "Negro citizenship," perpetuated by the white elite, has confused the thinking of radical and progressive blacks and whites in this country. The broad masses of black people react to American society in the same manner as colonial peoples react to the West in Africa, and Latin America, and had the same relationship—that of the colonized toward the colonizer.

The Ballot or the Bullet

Malcolm X

The question tonight, as I understand it, is "The Negro Revolt, and Where Do We Go From Here?" or "What Next?" In my little humble way of understanding it, it points toward either the ballot or the bullet.

* * *

I'm not a politician, not even a student of politics; in fact, I'm not a student of much of anything. I'm not a Democrat, I'm not a Republican, and I don't even consider myself an American. If you and I were Americans, there'd be no problem. Those Hunkies that just got off the boat, they're already Americans; Polacks are already Americans; the Italian refugees are already Americans. Everything that came out of Europe, every blue-eyed thing, is already an American. And as long as you and I have been over here, we aren't Americans yet.

Well, I am one who doesn't believe in deluding myself. I'm not going to sit at your table and watch you eat, with nothing on my plate, and call myself a diner. Sitting at the table doesn't make you a diner, unless you eat some of what's on that plate. Being here in America doesn't make you an American. Why, if birth made you American, you wouldn't need any legislation, you wouldn't need any amendments to the Constitution, you wouldn't be faced with civil-rights filibustering in

Excerpts from Malcolm X, *Malcolm X Speaks*, George Breitman, ed., New York: Pathfinder Press, 1965, pp. 25–26, 34–36, 38–39, 43–44. Reprinted by permission of Pathfinder Press. Copyright © 1965.

Washington, D.C., right now. They don't have to pass civil-rights legislation to make a Polack an American.

No, I'm not an American. I'm one of the 22 million black people who are the victims of Americanism. One of the 22 million black people who are the victims of democracy, nothing but disguised hypocrisy. So, I'm not standing here speaking to you as an American, or a patriot, or a flag-saluter, or a flag-waver—no, not I. I'm speaking as a victim of this American dream system. And I see America through the eyes of the victim. I don't see any American dream; I see an American nightmare.

* * *

When we begin to get in this area, we need new friends, we need new allies. We need to expand the civil-rights struggle to a higher level—to the level of human rights. Whenever you are in a civil-rights struggle, whether you know it or not, you are confining yourself to the jurisdiction of Uncle Sam. No one from the outside world can speak out in your behalf as long as your struggle is a civil-rights struggle. Civil rights comes within the domestic affairs of this country. All of our African brothers and our Asian brothers and our Latin-American brothers cannot open their mouths and interfere in the domestic affairs of the United States. And as long as it's civil rights, this comes under the jurisdiction of Uncle Sam.

But the United Nations has what's known as the charter of human rights, it has a committee that deals in human rights. You may wonder why all of the atrocities that have been committed in Africa and in Hungary and in Asia and in Latin America are brought before the UN, and the Negro problem is never brought before the UN. This is part of the conspiracy. This old, tricky, blue-eyed liberal who is supposed to be your and my friend, supposed to be in our corner, supposed to be subsidizing our struggle, and supposed to be acting in the capacity of an adviser, never tells you anything about human rights. They keep you wrapped up in civil rights. And you spend so much time barking up the civil-rights tree, you don't even know there's a human-rights tree on the same floor.

When you expand the civil-rights struggle to the level of human rights, you can then take the case of the black man in this country before the nations in the UN. You can take it before the General Assembly. You can take Uncle Sam before a world court. But the only level you can do it on is the level of human rights. Civil rights keeps you under his restrictions, under his jurisdiction. Civil rights keeps you in his pocket. Civil rights means you're asking Uncle Sam to treat you right. Human rights are the rights that are recognized by all nations of this earth. And any time any one violates your human rights, you can take them to the world court. Uncle Sam's hands are dripping with blood, dripping with the blood of the black man in this country. He's the earth's number-one hypocrite. He has the audacity—yes, he has—imagine him posing as the leader of the free world. The free world!—and you over here singing "We Shall Overcome." Expand the civil-rights struggle to the level of human rights, take it into the United Nations, where our African brothers can throw their weight on our side, where our Latin-American brothers can throw their weight on our side, and where 800 million Chinamen are sitting there waiting to throw their weight on our side.

Let the world know how bloody his hands are. Let the world know the hypocrisy that's practiced over here. Let it be the ballot or the bullet. Let him know that it must be the ballot or the bullet.

When you take your case to Washington, D.C., you're taking it to the criminal who's responsible; it's like running from the wolf to the fox. They're all in cahoots together. They all work political chicanery and make you look like a chump before the eyes of the world. Here you are walking around in America, getting ready to be drafted and sent abroad, like a tin soldier, and when you get over there, people ask you what you are fighting for, and you have to stick your tongue in your cheek. No, take Uncle Sam to court, take him before the world.

By ballot I only mean freedom. Don't you know—I disagree with Lomax on this issue—that the ballot is more important than the dollar? Can I prove it? Yes. Look in the UN. There are poor nations in the UN; yet those poor nations can get together with their voting power and keep the rich nations from making a move. They have one nation—one vote, everyone has an equal vote. And when those brothers from Asia, and Africa and the darker parts of this earth get together, their voting power is sufficient to hold Sam in check. Or Russia in check. Or some other section of the earth in check. So, the ballot is most important.

Right now, in this country, if you and I, 22 million African-Americans—that's what we are—Africans who are in America. You're nothing but Africans. Nothing but Africans. In fact, you'd get farther calling yourself African instead of Negro. Africans don't catch hell. You're the only one catching hell. They don't have to pass civil-rights bills for Africans. An African can go anywhere he wants right now. All you've got to do is tie your head up. That's right, go anywhere you want.

Just stop being a Negro. Change your name to Hoogagagooba. That'll show you how silly the white man is. You're dealing with a silly man. A friend of mine who's very dark put a turban on his head and went into a restaurant in Atlanta before they called themselves desegregated. He went into a white restaurant, he sat down, they served him, and he said, "What would happen if a Negro came in here?" And there he's sitting, black as night, but because he had his head wrapped up the waitress looked back at him and says, "Why, there wouldn't no nigger dare come in here."

* * *

I would like to say ... a few things concerning the Muslim Mosque, Inc., which we established recently in New York City. It's true we're Muslims and our religion is Islam, but we don't mix our religion with our politics and our economics and our social and civil activities—not any more. We keep our religion in our mosque. After our religious services are over, then as Muslims we become involved in political action, economic action and social and civic action. We become involved with anybody, anywhere, any time and in any manner that's designed to eliminate the evils, the political, economic and social evils that are afflicting the people of our community.

The political philosophy of black nationalism means that the black man should control the politics and the politicians in his own community; no more. The black man in the black community has to be re-educated into the science of politics so he will know what politics is supposed to bring him in return. Don't be throwing out any ballots. A ballot is like a bullet. You don't throw your ballots until you see a target, and if that target is not within your reach, keep your ballot in your pocket. The political philosophy of black nationalism is being taught in the Christian church. It's being taught in the NAACP. It's being taught in CORE meetings. It's being taught in SNCC [Student Nonviolent Coordinating Committee] meetings. It's being taught in Muslim meetings. It's being taught where nothing but atheists and agnostics come together. It's being taught everywhere. Black people are fed up with the dillydallying, pussyfooting, compromising approach that we've been using toward getting our freedom. We want freedom *now*, but we're not going to get it saying "We Shall Overcome." We've got to fight until we overcome.

The economic philosophy of black nationalism is pure and simple. It only means that we should control the economy of our community. Why should white people be running all the stores in our community?

Why should white people be running the banks of our community? Why should the economy of our community be in the hands of the white man? If a black man can't move his store into a white community, you should tell me why a white man should move his store into a black community. The philosophy of black nationalism involves a re-education program in the black community in regards to economics. Our people have to be made to see that any time you take your dollar out of your community and spend it in a community where you don't live, the community where you live will will get poorer and poorer, and the community where you spend your money will get richer and richer. Then you wonder why where you live is always a ghetto or a slum area. And where you and I are concerned, not only do we lose it when we spend it out of the community, but the white man has got all our stores in the community tied up; so that though we spend it in the community, at sundown the man who runs the store takes it over across town somewhere. He's got us in a vise.

So the economic philosophy of black nationalism means in every church, in every civic organization, in every fraternal order, it's time now for our people to become conscious of the importance of controlling the economy of our community. If we own the stores, if we operate the businesses, if we try and establish some industry in our own community, then we're developing to the position where we are creating employment for our own kind. Once you gain control of the economy of your own community, then you don't have to picket and boycott and beg some cracker downtown for a job in his business.

The social philosophy of black nationalism only means that we have to get together and remove the evils, and vices, alcoholism, drug addiction, and other evils that are destroying the moral fiber of our community. We ourselves have to lift the level of our community, the standard of our community to a higher level, make our own society beautiful so that we will be satisfied in our own social circles and won't be running around here trying to knock our way into a social circle where we're not wanted.

* * *

Last but not least, I must say this concerning the great controversy over rifles and shotguns. The only thing that I've ever said is that in areas where the government has proven itself either unwilling or unable to defend the lives and the property of Negroes, it's time for Negroes to defend themselves. Article number two of the constitutional amendments provides you and me the right to own a rifle or a shotgun. It is constitutionally legal to own a shotgun or a rifle. This doesn't mean that you're going to get a rifle and form battalions and go out looking for white folks, although you'd be within your rights—I mean, you'd be justified; but that would be illegal and we don't do anything illegal. If the white man doesn't want the black man buying rifles and shotguns, then let the government do its job. That's all. And don't let the white man come to you and ask you what you think about what Malcolm says—why, you old Uncle Tom. He would never ask you if he thought you were going to say, "Amen!" No, he is making a Tom out of you.

So, this doesn't mean forming rifle clubs and going out looking for people, but it is time, in 1964, if you are a man, to let that man know. If he's not going to do his job in running the government and providing you and me with the protection that our taxes are supposed to be for, since he spends all those billions for his defense budget, he certainly can't begrudge you and me spending $12 or $15 for a single-shot, or double-action. I hope you understand. Don't go out shooting people, but any time, brothers and sisters, and especially the men in this audience—some of you wearing Congressional Medals of Honor, with shoulders this wide, chests this big, muscles that big—any time you and I sit around and read where they bomb a church and murder in cold blood, not some grownups, but four little girls while they were praying to the same god the white man taught them to pray to, and you and I see the government go down and can't find who did it.

Why, this man—he can find Eichmann hiding down in Argentina somewhere. Let two or three American soldiers, who are minding somebody else's business way over in South Vietnam, get killed, and he'll send battleships, sticking his nose in their business. He wanted to send troops down to Cuba and make them have when he calls free elections—this old cracker who doesn't have free elections in his own country. No, if you never see me another time in your life, if I die in the morning, I'll die saying one thing: the ballot or the bullet, the ballot or the bullet.

If a Negro in 1964 has to sit around and wait for some cracker senator to filibuster when it comes to the rights of black people, why, you and I should hang our heads in shame. You talk about a march on Washington in 1963, you haven't seen anything. There's some more going down in '64. And this time they're not going like they went last year. They're not going singing "We Shall Overcome." They're not going with white friends. They're not going with placards already painted for them. They're not going with round-trip tickets. They're going with one-way tickets.

And if they don't want that non-violent army going down there, tell them to bring the filibuster to a halt. The black nationalists aren't going to wait. Lyndon B. Johnson is the head of the Democratic Party. If he's for civil rights, let him go into the Senate next week and declare himself. Let him go in there right now and declare himself. Let him go in there and denounce the Southern branch of his party. Let him go in there right now and take a moral stand—right now, not later. Tell him, don't wait until election time. If he waits too long, brothers and sisters, he will be responsible for letting a condition develop in this country which will create a climate that will bring seeds up out of the ground with vegetation on the end of them looking like something these people never dreamed of. In 1964, it's the ballot or the bullet. Thank you.

Sex and Caste: A Kind of Memo

Casey Hayden and Mary King

A kind of memo from Casey Hayden and
Mary King to a number of other women in the
peace and freedom movements.

November 18, 1965

We've talked a lot, to each other and to some of you, about our own and other women's problems in trying to live in our personal lives and in our work as independent and creative people. In these conversations we've found what seems to be recurrent ideas or themes. Maybe we can look at these things many of us perceive, often as a result of insights learned from the movement:

SEX AND CASTE

There seem to be many parallels that can be drawn between treatment of Negroes and treatment of women in our society as a whole. But in particular, women we've talked to who work in the movement seem to be caught up in a common-law caste system that operates, sometimes subtly, forcing them to work around or outside hierarchical structures of power which may exclude them. Women seem to be placed in the same position of assumed subordination in personal situations too. It is a caste system which, at its worst, uses and exploits women.

Casey Hayden and Mary King, "Sex and Caste: A Kind of Memo," November 1965. Reprinted with permission.

This is complicated by several facts, among them: (1) The caste system is not institutionalized by law (women have the right to vote, to sue for divorce, etc.); (2) Women can't withdraw from the situation (a la nationalism) or overthrow it; (3) There are biological differences (even though those biological differences are usually discussed or accepted without taking present and future technology into account so we probably can't be sure what these differences mean). Many people who are very hip to the implications of the racial caste system, even people in the movement, don't seem to be able to see the sexual caste system and if the question is raised they respond with: "That's the way it's supposed to be. There are biological differences." Or with other statements which recall a white segregationist confronted with integration.

WOMEN AND PROBLEMS OF WORK

The caste system perspective dictates the roles assigned to women in the movement, and certainly even more to women outside the movement. Within the movement, questions arise in situations ranging from relationships of women organizers to men in the community, to who cleans the freedom house, to who holds leadership positions, to who does secretarial work, and who acts as a spokesman for groups. Other problems arise between women with varying degrees of awareness of themselves as being as capable as men but held back from full participation, or between women who see themselves as needing more control of their work than other women demand. And there are problems with relationships between white women and black women.

WOMEN AND PERSONAL RELATIONS WITH MEN

Having learned from the movement to think radically about the personal worth and abilities of people whose role in society had gone unchallenged before, a lot of women in the movement have begun trying to apply those lessons to their own relations with men. Each of us probably has her own story of the various results, and of the internal struggle occasioned by trying to break out of very deeply learned fears, needs, and self-perceptions, and of what happens when we try to replace them with concepts of people and freedom learned from the movement and organizing.

INSTITUTIONS

Nearly everyone has real questions about those institutions which shape perspectives on men and women: marriage, child rearing patterns, women's (and men's) magazines, etc. People are beginning to think about and even to experiment with new forms in these areas.

MEN'S REACTIONS TO THE QUESTIONS RAISED HERE

A very few men seem to feel, when they hear conversations involving these problems, that they have a right to be present and participate in them, since they are so deeply involved. At the same time, very few men can respond non-defensively, since the whole idea is either beyond their comprehension or threatens and exposes them. The usual response is laughter. That inability to see the whole issue as serious, as the strait-jacketing of both sexes, and as societally determined, often shapes our own response so that we learn to think in their terms about ourselves and to feel silly rather than trust our inner feelings. The problems we're listing here, and what others have said about them, are therefore largely drawn from conversations among women only—and that difficulty in establishing dialogue with men is a recurring theme among people we've talked to.

LACK OF COMMUNITY FOR DISCUSSION

Nobody is writing, or organizing or talking publicly about women, in any way that reflects the problems that various women in the movement come across and which we've tried to touch above. Consider this quote from an article in the centennial issue of The Nation:

> However equally we consider men and women, the work plans for husbands and wives cannot be given equal weight. A woman should not aim for "a second-level career" because she is a woman; from girlhood on she should recognize that, if she is also going to be a wife and mother, she will not be able to give as much to her work as she would if single. That is, she should not feel that she cannot aspire to directing the laboratory simply because she is a woman, but rather because she is also a wife and mother; as such, her work as a lab

technician (or the equivalent in another field) should bring both satisfaction and the knowledge that, through it, she is fulfilling an additional role, making an additional contribution.

And that's about as deep as the analysis goes publicly, which is not nearly so deep as we've heard many of you go in chance conversations.

The reason we want to try to open up dialogue is mostly subjective. Working in the movement often intensifies personal problems, especially if we start trying to apply things we're learning there to our personal lives. Perhaps we can start to talk with each other more openly than in the past and create a community of support for each other so we can deal with ourselves and others with integrity and can therefore keep working.

Objectively, the chances seem nil that we could start a movement based on anything as distant to general American thought as a sex-caste system. Therefore, most of us will probably want to work full time on problems such as war, poverty, race. The very fact that the country can't face, much less deal with, the questions we're raising means that the movement is one place to look for some relief. Real efforts at dialogue within the movement and with whatever liberal groups, community women, or students might listen are justified. That is, all the problems between men and women and all the problems of women functioning in society as equal human beings are among the most basic that people face. We've talked in the movement about trying to build a society which would see basic human problems (which are now seen as private troubles) as public problems and would try to shape institutions to meet human needs rather than shaping people to meet the needs of those with power. To raise questions like those above illustrates very directly that society hasn't dealt with some of its deepest problems and opens discussion of why that is so. (In one sense, it is a radicalizing question that can take people beyond legalistic solutions into areas of personal and institutional change.) The second objective reason we'd like to see discussion begin is that we've learned a great deal in the movement and perhaps this is one area where a determined attempt to apply ideas we've learned there can produce some new alternatives.

What We Want

Stokely Carmichael

One of the tragedies of the struggle against racism is that up to now there has been no national organization which could speak to the growing militancy of young black people in the urban ghetto. There has been only a civil rights movement, whose tone of voice was adapted to an audience of liberal whites. It served as a sort of buffer zone between them and angry young blacks. None of its so-called leaders could go into a rioting community and be listened to. In a sense, I blame ourselves— together with the mass media—for what has happened in Watts, Harlem, Chicago, Cleveland, Omaha. Each time the people in those cities saw Martin Luther King get slapped, they became angry; when they saw four little black girls bombed to death, they were angrier; and when nothing happened, they were steaming. We had nothing to offer that they could see, except to go out and be beaten again. We helped to build their frustration.

For too many years, black Americans marched and had their heads broken and got shot. They were saying to the country, "Look, you guys are supposed to be nice guys and we are only going to do what we are supposed to do—why do you beat us up, why don't you give us what we ask, why don't you straighten yourselves out?" After years of this, we are at almost the same point—because we demonstrated from a position of weakness. We cannot be expected any longer to march and have our heads broken in order to say to whites, come on, you're nice guys. For you are not nice guys. We have found you out.

An organization which claims to speak for the needs of a

community—as does the Student Nonviolent Coordinating Committee—
must speak in the tone of that community, not as somebody else's
buffer zone. This is the significance of black power as a slogan. For once,
black people are going to use the words they want to use—not just the
words whites want to hear. And they will do this no matter how often
the press tries to stop the use of the slogan by equating it with racism or
separatism.

An organization which claims to be working for the needs of a
community—as SNCC does—must work to provide that community
with a position of strength from which to make its voice heard. This is
the significance of black power beyond the slogan.

Black power can be clearly defined for those who do not attach the
fears of white America to their questions about it. We should begin
with the basic fact that black Americans have two problems: they are
poor and they are black. All other problems arise from this two-sided
reality: lack of education, the so-called apathy of black men. Any
program to end racism must address itself to that double reality.

Almost from its beginning, SNCC sought to address itself to both
conditions with a program aimed at winning political power for impoverished Southern blacks. We had to begin with politics because black
Americans are a propertyless people in a country where property is
valued above all. We had to work for power, because this country does
not function by morality, love, and nonviolence, but by power. Thus
we determined to win political power, with the idea of moving on from
there into activity that would have economic effects. With power, the
masses could *make* or *participate in making* the decisions which govern
their destinies, and thus create basic change in their day-to-day lives.

But if political power seemed to be the key to self-determination it
was also obvious that the key had been thrown down a deep well many
years earlier. Disenfranchisement, maintained by racist terror, made it
impossible to talk about organizing for political power in 1960. The
right to vote had to be won, and SNCC workers devoted their energies
to this from 1961 to 1965. They set up voter registration drives in the
Deep South. They created pressure for the vote by holding mock
elections in Mississippi in 1963 and by helping to establish the Mississippi
Freedom Democratic Party (MFDP) in 1964. That struggle was eased,
though not won, with the passage of the 1965 Voting Rights Act. SNCC
workers could then address themselves to the question: "Who can we
vote for, to have our needs met—how do we make our vote meaningful?"

* * *

...[T]he concept of "black power" is not a recent or isolated phenomenon: It has grown out of the ferment of agitation and activity by different people and organizations in many black communities over the years. Our last year of work in Alabama added a new concrete possibility. In Lowndes county, for example, black power will mean that if a Negro is elected sheriff, he can end police brutality. If a black man is elected tax assessor, he can collect and channel funds for the building of better roads and schools serving black power—thus advancing the move from political power into the economic arena. In such areas as Lowndes, where black men have a majority, they will attempt to use it to exercise control. This is what they seek: control. Where Negroes lack a majority, black power means proper representation and sharing of control. It means the creation of power bases from which black people can work to change statewide or nationwide patterns of oppression through pressure from strength—instead of weakness. Politically, black power means what it has always meant to SNCC: the coming-together of black people to elect representatives and *to force those representatives to speak to their needs.* It does not mean merely putting black faces into office. A man or woman who is black and from the slums cannot be automatically expected to speak to the needs of black people. Most of the black politicians we see around the country today are not what SNCC means by black power. The power must be that of a community, and emanate from there.

SNCC today is working in both North and South on programs of voter registration and independent political organizing. In some places, such as Alabama, Los Angeles, New York, Philadelphia, and New Jersey, independent organizing under the black panther symbol is in progress. The creation of a national "black panther party" must come about; it will take time to build, and it is much too early to predict its success. We have no infallible master plan and we make no claim to exclusive knowledge of how to end racism; different groups will work in their own different ways. SNCC cannot spell out the full logistics of self-determination but it can address itself to the problem by helping black communities define their needs, realize their strength, and go into action along a variety of lines which they must choose for themselves. Without knowing all the answers, it can address itself to the basic problems of poverty; to the fact that in Lowndes County, 86 white families own 90 percent of the land. What are black people in that county going to do for jobs, where are they going to get money? There must be reallocation of land, of money.

Ultimately, the economic foundations of this country must be shaken if black people are to control their lives. The colonies of the United States—and this includes the black ghettoes within its borders, north and south—must be liberated. For a century, this nation has been like an octopus of exploitation, its tentacles stretching from Mississippi and Harlem to South America, the Middle East, southern Africa, and Vietnam; the form of exploitation varies from area to area but the essential result has been the same—a powerful few have been maintained and enriched at the expense of the poor and voiceless colored masses. This pattern must be broken. As its grip loosens here and there around the world, the hopes of black Americans become more realistic. For racism to die, a totally different America must be born.

This is what the white society does not wish to face; this is why that society prefers to talk about integration. But integration speaks not at all to the problem of poverty, only to the problem of blackness. Integration today means the man who "makes it," leaving his black brothers behind in the ghetto as fast as his new sports car will take him. It has no relevance to the Harlem wino or to the cottonpicker making three dollars a day. As a lady I know in Alabama once said, "The food that Ralph Bunche eats doesn't fill my stomach."

Integration, moreover, speaks to the problem of blackness in a despicable way. As a goal, it has been based on complete acceptance of the fact that in order to have a decent house or education, blacks must move into a white neighborhood or send their children to a white school.

This reinforces, among both black and white, the idea that "white" is automatically better and "black" is by definition inferior. This is why integration is a subterfuge for the maintenance of white supremacy. It allows the nation to focus on a handful of Southern children who get into white schools, at great price, and to ignore the 94 per cent who are left behind in unimproved all-black schools. Such situations will not change until black people have power—to control their own school boards, in this case. Then Negroes become equal in a way that means something, and integration ceases to be a one-way street. Then integration doesn't mean draining skills and energies from the ghetto into white neighborhoods; then it can mean white people moving from Beverly Hills into Watts, white people joining the Lowndes County Freedom Organization. Then integration becomes relevant.

* * *

To most whites, black power seems to mean that the Mau Mau are coming to the suburbs at night. The Mau Mau are coming and whites must stop them. Articles appear about plots to "get Whitey," creating an atmosphere in which "law and order must be maintained." Once again, responsibility is shifted from the oppressor to the oppressed. Other whites chide, "Don't forget—you're only 10 percent of the population; if you get too smart, we'll wipe you out." If they are liberals, they complain, "What about me?—don't you want my help any more?" These are people supposedly concerned about black Americans, but today they think first of themselves, of their feelings of rejection. Or they admonish, "You can't get anywhere without coalitions," when there is in fact no group at present with whom to form a coalition in which blacks will not be absorbed and betrayed. Or they accuse us of "polarizing the races" by our calls for black unity, when the true responsibility for polarization lies with whites who will not accept their responsibility as the majority power for making the democratic process work.

White America will not face the problem of color, the reality of it. The well-intended say: "We're all human, everybody is really decent, we must forget color." But color cannot be "forgotten" until its weight is recognized and dealt with. White America will not acknowledge that the ways in which this country sees itself are contradicted by being black—and always have been. Whereas most of the people who settled this country came here for freedom or for economic opportunity, blacks were brought here to be slaves. When the Lowndes County Freedom Organization chose the black panther as its symbol, it was christened by the press "the Black Panther Party"—but the Alabama Democratic Party, whose symbol is a rooster, has never been called the White Cock Party. No one ever talked about "white power" because power in this country is white. All this adds up to more than merely identifying a group phenomenon by some catchy name or adjective. The furor over that black panther reveals the problems that white America has with color and sex; the furor over "black power" reveals how deep racism runs and the great fear which is attached to it.

Whites will not see that I, for example, as a person oppressed because of my blackness, have common cause with other blacks who are oppressed because of blackness. This is not to say that there are no white people who see things as I do, but that it is black people I must speak to first. It must be the oppressed to whom SNCC addresses itself primarily, not to friends from the oppressing group.

From birth, black people are told a set of lies about themselves. We are told that we are lazy—yet I drive through the Delta area of Mississippi and watch black people picking cotton in the hot sun for fourteen hours. We are told, "If you work hard, you'll succeed"—but if that were true, black people would own this country. We are oppressed because we are black—not because we are ignorant, not because we are lazy, not because we're stupid (and got good rhythm), but because we're black.

I remember that when I was a boy, I used to go to see Tarzan movies on Saturday. White Tarzan used to beat up the black natives. I would sit there yelling, "Kill the beasts, kill the savages, kill 'em." I was saying: Kill me. It was as if a Jewish boy watched Nazis taking Jews off to concentration camps and cheered them on. Today, I want the chief to beat hell out of Tarzan and send him back to Europe. But it takes time to become free of the lies and their shaming effect on black minds. It takes time to reject the most important lie: that black people inherently can't do the same things white people can do, unless white people help them.

The need for psychological equality is the reason why SNCC today believes that blacks must organize in the black community. Only black people can convey the revolutionary idea that black people are able to do things themselves. Only they can help create in the community an aroused and continuing black consciousness that will provide the basis for political strength. In the past, white allies have furthered white supremacy without the whites involved realizing it—or wanting it, I think.

Black people must do things for themselves; they must get poverty money they will control and spend themselves, they must conduct tutorial programs themselves so that black children can identify with black people. This is one reason Africa has such importance: The reality of black men ruling their own nations gives blacks elsewhere a sense of possibility, of power, which they do not now have.

This does not mean we don't welcome help, or friends. But we want the right to decide whether anyone is, in fact, our friend. In the past, black Americans have been almost the only people whom everybody and his momma could jump up and call their friends. We have been tokens, symbols, objects—as I was in high school to many young whites who liked having "a Negro friend." We want to decide who is our friend, and we will not accept someone who comes to us and says: "If you do X, Y, and Z, then I'll help you." We will not be told whom we should choose as allies. We will not be isolated from any group or nation except by our own choice. We cannot have the oppressors telling the oppressed how to rid themselves of the oppressor.

I have said that most liberal whites react to "black power" with the question, What about me?, rather than saying: Tell me what you want me to do and I'll see if I can do it. There are answers to the right question. One of the most disturbing things about almost all white supporters of the movement has been that they are afraid to go into their own communities—which is where the racism exists—and work to get rid of it. They want to run from Berkeley to tell us what to do in Mississippi; let them look instead at Berkeley. They admonish blacks to be nonviolent; let them preach nonviolence in the white community. They come to teach me Negro history; let them go to the suburbs and open up freedom schools for whites. Let them work to stop America's racist foreign policy; let them press this government to cease supporting the economy of South Africa.

There is a vital job to be done among poor whites. We hope to see, eventually, a coalition between poor blacks and poor whites. That is the only coalition which seems acceptable to us, and we see such a coalition as the major internal instrument of change in American society. SNCC has tried several times to organize poor whites; we are trying again now, with an initial training program in Tennessee. It is purely academic today to talk about bringing poor blacks and whites together, but the job of creating a poor-white power bloc must be attempted. The main responsibility for it falls upon whites. Black and white can work together in the white community where possible; it is not possible, however, to go into a poor Southern town and talk about integration. Poor whites everywhere are becoming more hostile—not less—partly because they see the nation's attention focused on black poverty and nobody coming to them. Too many young middle-class Americans, like some sort of Pepsi generation, have wanted to become alive through the black community; they've wanted to be where the action is—and the action has been in the black community.

Black people do not want to "take over" this country. They don't want to "get whitey"; they just want to get him off their backs, as the saying goes. It was for example the exploitation by Jewish landlords and merchants which first created black resentment toward Jews—not Judaism. The white man is irrelevant to blacks, except as an oppressive force. Blacks want to be in his place, yes, but not in order to terrorize and lynch and starve him. They want to be in his place because that is where a decent life can be had.

But our vision is not merely of a society in which all black men have enough to buy the good things of life. When we urge that black money go into black pockets, we mean the communal pocket. We want to see money go back into the community and used to benefit it. We want to see the co-operative concept applied in business and banking. We want to see black ghetto residents demand that an exploiting landlord or store keeper sell them, at minimal cost, a building or a shop that they will own and improve cooperatively; they can back their demand with a rent strike, or a boycott, and a community so unified behind them that no one else will move into the building or buy at the store. The society we seek to build among black people, then, is not a capitalist one. It is a society in which the spirit of community and humanistic love prevail. The word love is suspect; black expectations of what it might produce have been betrayed too often. But those were expectations of a response from the white community, which failed us. The love we seek to encourage is within the black community, the only American community where men call each other "brother" when they meet. We can build a community of love only where we have the ability and power do to so: among blacks.

As for white America, perhaps it can stop crying out against "black supremacy," "black nationalism," "racism in reverse," and begin facing reality. The reality is that this nation, from top to bottom, is racist; that racism is not primarily a problem of "human relations" but of an exploitation maintained—either actively or through silence—by the society as a whole. Camus and Sartre have asked, can a man condemn himself? Can whites, particularly liberal whites, condemn themselves? Can they stop blaming us, and blame their own system? Are they capable of the shame which might become a revolutionary emotion?

We have found that they usually cannot condemn themselves, and so we have done it. But the rebuilding of this society, if at all possible, is basically the responsibility of whites—not blacks. We won't fight to save the present society, in Vietnam or anywhere else. We are just going to work, in the way *we* see fit, and on goals *we* define, not for civil rights but for all our human rights.

Rebellion in Newark

Tom Hayden

FROM RIOT TO REVOLUTION?

This country is experiencing its fourth year of urban revolt, yet the message from Newark is that America has learned almost nothing since Watts.

Of primary importance is the fact that no national program exists to deal with the social and economic questions black people are raising. Despite exhaustive hearings over the last five years on problems of manpower and unemployment, anti-poverty programs and the urban crisis, there is no apparent commitment from national power centers to do something constructive.

During the height of the rioting in Newark and Detroit, Congress discussed gun-control laws, voted down with chuckles a bill for rat extermination, and President Johnson set up a commission to do more investigating of the crisis. The main emphasis of governmental remedial programs seems likely to be on ending the riots rather than dealing with the racial and economic problem. President Johnson made this clear in his televised July 28 address on the "deeper questions" about the riots:

> Explanations may be offered, but nothing can excuse what [the rioters] have done. There will be attempts to interpret the events of the past few days, but when violence strikes, then those in public

Excerpts from *Rebellion in Newark: Official Violence and Ghetto Response*, by Tom Hayden. Copyright © 1967 by Tom Hayden. Reprinted by permission of Random House, Inc.

responsibility have an immediate and a very different job: *not to analyze but to end disorder.*

When it moves past riot-control to discussion of social programs, Congress is likely to lament the failure of past civil rights, welfare, and anti-poverty programs, rather than focus on the need for new ones. As with foreign aid, white politicians (and their voters) tend to view aid to Negroes as a form of "charity" to be trimmed wherever possible, or as a means of eliminating surplus food, or a way to enlarge urban patronage roles. Negroes more than likely will be instructed to "help themselves."

But unlike the Italians, Irish, and Jews, black Americans have always faced a shrinking structure of economic opportunity in which to "help themselves." If sheer effort were the answer, the black people who chopped cotton from dawn to sunset would today be millionaire suburban homeowners. Self-help does not build housing, hospitals, and schools. The cost of making cities livable and institutions responsive is greater than any sum this country has ever been willing to spend on domestic reform. In addition, the very act of spending such money would disrupt much of the status quo. Private interests, from the real estate lobby and the construction unions to the social work profession, would be threatened. Urban political machines would have to make space for black political power. Good intentions tend to collapse when faced with the necessity for massive spending and structural change.

This political bankruptcy leads directly to the use of military force. When citizens have no political way to deal with revolution, they become counter-revolutionary. The race issue becomes defined exclusively as one of maintaining white society. Holding this view forces the white community to adopt the "jungle attitudes" that they fear the Negroes hold. "Go kill them niggers," white crowds shouted to Guardsmen at 7 o'clock Friday morning as they rode into Newark. During the riot, a *New York Times* reporter was stopped at 2:30 A.M. in Mayor Addonizio's west side neighborhood by a pipe-smoking gentleman carrying (illegally) a shotgun. He explained that a protection society was formed in case "they" should come into the neighborhood. Rifle stores in white neighborhoods all over the east coast are selling out. In such way, the society becomes militarized.

A police "takeover" of local government is not necessary to declare war on Negroes. All that is necessary is to instill in the white citizens the idea that only military force stands between them and black savages. The civilians merely turn over the problem to the troops, who define the problem in terms of using arms to maintain the racial status quo. A typical military attitude in the wake of the riots was offered in the July 29th *Times* by the commander of the New York State National Guard, who said that a greater commitment of force might have prevented rioting around the country. He recommended the use of heavy weapons including hand grenades, recoilless rifles and bazookas. He blamed indecisive civilian authority for making National Guard units operate "with one hand behind their backs" in riot areas.

This military orientation means that outright killing of people is condoned where those people cannot accept law and order as defined by the majority. The country is not moved by the deaths of twenty-five Negro "rioters."

News of a Negro's death is received at most as a tragedy, the inevitable result of looting and lawlessness. When a picture appears of a policeman over a fallen victim, the typical reaction is framed in the terms set by the majority: the dead man is a sniper, a looter, a burner, a criminal. If history is any guide, it is a foregone conclusion that no white policeman will be punished for murder in Newark.

Even many white sympathizers with the Negro cause, and Negro leaders themselves, believe that disorder must be stopped so that, in Roy Wilkins' words, "society can proceed." The question they do not ask is: whose society? They say that Negro rioting will create a backlash suppressing the liberties needed to organize for change. But this accurate prediction overlooks the fact that those very civil liberties have meant little protection for civil rights workers and ordinary black people in the South, and nearly as little for people in the ghettoes of the North. The freedom that middle-class people correctly feel are real to themselves have very little day-to-day meaning in the ghetto, which is more like a concentration camp than an open society for a large number of its residents. But in order to protect these liberties, many civil rights leaders take part in condemning the ghetto to brutal occupation. Even where "excessive force" is deplored, as Roy Wilkins deplored it in Newark, the assumption still remains that there is a "proper" degree of force that should be used to maintain the status quo. Top officials welcome this liberal support, and agree that any "excessive" force is regrettable and will be investigated. Thus most of the society becomes involved in organizing and protecting murder.

However, the use of force can do nothing but create a demand for greater force. The Newark riot shows that troops cannot make a people surrender. The police had several advantages over the community, particularly in firepower and mechanical mobility. Their pent-up racism gave them a certain amount of energy and morale as well. But as events in the riot showed, the troops could not apply their methods to urban conditions. The problem of precision shooting—for example, at a sniper in a building with forty windows and escape routes through rooftop, alley, and doorway—is nearly as difficult in the urban jungle as precision bombing is in Vietnam. There is a lack of safe cover. There is no front line and no rear, no way to cordon an area completely. A block that is quiet when the troops are present can be the scene of an outbreak the moment the troops leave.

At the same time, the morale fueled by racism soon turns into anxiety. Because of racism, the troops are unfamiliar with both the people and structure of the ghetto. Patrol duty after dark becomes a frightening and exhausting experience, especially for men who want to return alive to their families and homes. A psychology of desperation leads to careless and indiscriminate violence toward the community, including reprisal killing, which inflames the people whom the troops were sent to pacify.

The situation thus contains certain built-in advantages for black people. The community is theirs. They know faces, corners, rooms, alleys. They know whom to trust and whom not to trust. They can switch in seconds from a fighting to a passive posture. It is impressive that state and local officials could not get takers for their offer of money and clemency to anyone turning in a sniper.

This is not a time for radical illusions about "revolution." Stagnancy and conservatism are essential facts of ghetto life. It undoubtedly is true that most Negroes desire the comforts and security that white people possess. There is little revolutionary consciousness or commitment to violence *per se* in the ghetto. Most people in the Newark riot were afraid, unorganized, and helpless when directly facing the automatic weapons. But the actions of white America toward the ghetto are showing black people, especially the young, that they must prepare to fight back.

The conditions slowly are being created for an American form of guerrilla warfare based in the slums. The riot represents a signal of this fundamental change.

To the conservative mind the riot is essentially revolution against civilization. To the liberal mind it is an expression of helpless frustration. While the conservative is hostile and the liberal generous toward those who riot, both assume that the riot is a form of lawless, mob behavior. The liberal will turn conservative if polite methods fail to stem disorder.

Against these two fundamentally similar concepts, a third one must be asserted, the concept that a riot represents people making history.

The riot is certainly an awkward, even primitive, form of history-making. But if people are barred from using the sophisticated instruments of the established order for their ends, they will find another way. Rocks and bottles are only a beginning, but they cause more attention than all the reports in Washington. To the people involved, the riot is far less lawless and far more representative than the system of arbitrary rules and prescribed channels which they confront every day. The riot is not a beautiful and romantic experience, but neither is the day-to-day slum life from which the riot springs. Riots will not go away if ignored, and will not be cordoned off. They will only disappear when their energy is absorbed into a more decisive and effective form of history-making.

Men are now appearing in the ghettoes who might turn the energy of the riot to a more organized and continuous revolutionary direction. Middle-class Negro intellectuals (especially students) and Negroes of the ghetto are joining forces. They have found channels closed, the rules of the game stacked, and American democracy a system that excludes them. They understand that the institutions of the white community are unreliable in the absence of black community power. They recognize that national civil-rights leaders will not secure the kind of change that is needed. They assume that disobedience, disorder, and even violence must be risked as the only alternative to continuing slavery.

The role of organized violence is now being carefully considered. During a riot, for instance, a conscious guerilla can participate in pulling police away from the path of people engaged in attacking stores. He can create disorder in new areas the police think are secure. He can carry the torch, if not all the people, to white neighborhoods and downtown business districts. If necessary, he can successfully shoot to kill.

The guerrilla can employ violence effectively during times of apparent "peace," too. He can attack, in the suburbs or slums, with paint or bullets, symbols of racial oppression. He can get away with it. If he can force the oppressive power to be passive and defensive at the point where it is administered—by the caseworker, landlord, storeowner, or policeman—he can build people's confidence in their ability to demand change. Persistent, accurately-aimed attacks, which need not be on human life to be effective, might disrupt the administration of the ghetto to a crisis point where a new system would have to be considered.

These tactics of disorder will be defined by the authorities as criminal anarchy. But it may be that disruption will create possibilities of meaningful change. This depends on whether the leaders of ghetto struggles can be more successful in building strong organization than they have been so far. Violence can contribute to shattering the status quo, but only politics and organization can transform it. The ghetto still needs the power to decide its destiny on such matters as urban renewal and housing, social services, policing, and taxation. Tenants still need concrete rights against landlords in public and private housing, or a new system of tenant-controlled living conditions. Welfare clients still need a livable income. Consumers still need to control the quality of merchandise and service in the stores where they shop. Citizens still need effective control over those who police their community. Political structures belonging to the community are needed to bargain for, and maintain control over, funds from government or private sources. In order to build a more decent community while resisting racist power, more than violence is required. People need to create self-government. We are at a point where democracy—the idea and practice of people controlling their lives—is a revolutionary issue in the United States.

Die Nigger Die!

H. Rap Brown

Color is the first thing Black people in america become aware of. You are born into a world that has given color meaning and color becomes the single most determining factor of your existence. Color determines where you live, how you live and, under certain circumstances, if you will live. Color determines your friends, your education, your mother's and father's jobs, where you play, what you play and, more importantly, what you think of yourself.

In and of itself, color has no meaning. But the white world has given it meaning—political, social, economic, historical, physiological and philosophical. Once color has been given meaning, an order is thereby established. If you are born Black in america, you are the last of that order. As kids we learned the formula for the structure of american society:

> If you're white,
> You're all right.
> If you're brown,
> Stick around.
> But if you're black,
> Get back, get back.

Because of the importance assigned to color, negroes choose only to legitimatize two americas: white and negro. When one examines the way in which these two americas are structured, it is obvious that the similarities between them are greater than the differences. The differences exist only in the external control of each and their internal order, which, in turn, create value contradictions. In other words, whites control both white america and negro america for the benefit of whites. And because of this kind of external control by whites in their own self-interest, negroes who structure their communities after those of whites are forced to enforce values of whites. They attempt to explain away their lack of control by saying that they are just members of the larger community of "americans."

A monologue is perpetually expounded by white america which is echoed by negroes afflicted with white patriotism.

white america:
   Think white or I'll kill you.
   And if you think too white, I'll kill you.
negro america:
   Think white or I'll kill you.
   And if you think too white "the man" will kill you.
   So think colored.
   Imitate the white man,
   but not to perfection in front of him.

As Julian Moreau says in his novel, *Black Commandos*:

   Attitudes necessary for survival were vigorously pounded into the wooly heads of black boys and girls by their loving mothers. The boys were reared to be Negroes, not men. A Negro might survive a while, but a black "man" didn't live very long.... A black boy aiming to reach "manhood" rather than "Negro-hood" rarely lived that long.

For 400 years the internal contradictions and inconsistencies of white america have been dealt with through its institutions. In regard to race or color, these contradictions have always been on a national, never a local or individual level. Whites as individuals have always loved to be thought of as superior. They have always known that if they could justify and make their actions legal, either through their religion, their courts or their history (educational system), then it would be unnecessary to actually rectify them because the negro would accept their interpretation. White america's most difficult problem thus becomes how to justify and not rectify national inconsistencies. If white nationalism is disguised as history or religion, then it is irrefutable. White nationalism divides history into two parts, B.C. and A.D.—before the white man's religion and after it. And "progress," of course, is considered to have taken place only after the white man's religion came into being. The implication is evident: God is on the white man's side, for white Jesus was the "son" of God.

White america has used religion and history to its advantage. Thus, the North never really differed from the South for they both taught the same history. Catholics never differed from other religions for they taught from the same text. Republicans are no different from Democrats, as Democrats are no differed from Dixiecrats. As for liberals, Fanon says they are "as much the enemy of oppressed people and Freedom as the self-avowed enemy, because it is impossible to be both a member of the oppressor class and a friend of the oppressed." So we can see that for white america the only real contradictions are those that arise from the Thirteenth, Fourteenth and Fifteenth Amendments of her Constitution. These contradictions give rise to negro america.

Most Black persons of my time were born into negro america. The first thing you learn is that you are different from whites. The next thing you learn is that you are different from each other. You are born into a world of double standards where color is of paramount importance. In your community a color pattern exists which is closely akin to the white man's, and likewise reinforced from both ends of the spectrum. Light-skinned negroes believe they are superior and darker negroes allow them to operate on that belief. Because of the wide color range which exists in negro america, an internal color colony has been created. Dark negroes are taught that they are inferior not only to whites but to lighter-skinned negroes. And lighter-skinned negroes assume a superior attitude.

Negro america is set up the same as white america. The lighter skinned a negro, the more significant a role he can play. (It has always been the one who looked white who made it in negro america. This was the man with the position, the influence, this was the man who usually got the white man's best job.) In between light negro america and Black negro america (in terms of color), there is a special category of people, who are assigned the name of red niggers. These are the people who are light enough to go into light negro america, but do not have caucasian characteristics. They don't have straight hair or white features. So they can go either way, depending on them. They can operate in Black negro america or at the outer fringes of light negro america. Race prejudice in america becomes color prejudice in negro america. That which is cultural prejudice by whites against Blacks becomes class prejudice in negro america. To distinguish themselves, negroes assign class distinctions. Here we find the instituting and substituting of parallel values. Negroes assume that what is good for white america is good for negro america.

Negroes are always confined to what can be called the "shit regiment." I first became acquainted with the shit regiment in the cub scouts. In every parade, we always marched behind the horses, which meant that we always had to march in horseshit. All the way through life there are shit regiments in the negro community and negroes adhere to them. As a matter of fact, negroes will protect these regiments. The debate was never whether or not we had to march, but whether or not the whites were going to put machines down there to wash the horseshit away before we marched in it. There was never any discussion as to whether or not we should march behind the horses. Uh-uh. Everybody accepted that. They just wanted the horseshit washed out of the way before we came through. White america's largest shit regiment is negro america.

Given that negroes are a colonized people, the most important phase of colonization is the sub-cultural phase. In negro america, negroes relate only to negroes of the same educational background. Dr. So-and-So talks only to Dr. So-and-So and the brother on the block better not act like he thinks he can go up to Dr. So-and-So and talk to him man-to-man. To Dr. So-and-So, the brother on the block is nothing but a nigger who's holding the race back. Dr. So-and-So goes to the Episcopal Church, the Presbyterian Church or the Catholic Church. The brother on the block goes to the Baptist Church, the Holy Rollers or the Sanctified Church. And the Methodist Church is in between the two. It ain't as niggerish as the Baptist Church, but it's not as high class as the Episcopal Church. As negroes become more "white-educated," the transition in religion begins. All of a sudden, it's beneath them to go to church and shout and get happy. That's not dignified. As they get more "educated," their religion gets more like the white man's religion as if their heaven will be segregated too. "Education" even extends down to the naming of their children. The more "educated" the negro becomes, the more European names he picks for his children. Michele, Simone, Hubert, Whitney. All of a sudden, Sam and Bertha Lee ain't good enough anymore. In other words, values are assigned to names. Names must now be more than functional.

The poor negro doesn't aspire to be white, he just wants to make it into a negro america. So he works hard all his life and finally rents a little house and puts some furniture in it which he keeps covered with plastic so it won't get dirty. And he gets mad if anybody sits on it, because he's trying to imitate negro america. Once he gets into negro america, he learns of so-called middle-class values, white values. Then he wants to get into white america.

When he tries to enter white america, he is rejected. The doors are shut. Even if he has a big job in some white firm, if he's one of those "only" negroes, he still finds out that he's Black when it's quitting time. The white workers go their way and leave him to go his. They're nice and friendly on the job and all buddy-buddy, but that doesn't go outside the office. They don't want their friends thinking that they're nigger lovers. So this sets up a reaction in the negro. He gets frustrated and tries to live a contradiction and that's why when the rebellions start, he's all for them. He doesn't have the courage to admit it to the white man. When the white folks he works with ask him what he thinks about "the riot," he says it's hurting the cause and all sorts of bull like that. But that night after work, he breaks records getting home to watch it on t.v., cheering like a muthafucka the whole time. Take the Washington, D.C., rebellion, for instance. They arrested something like 3,000 people and when they booked 'em, they found out that the great majority of them worked for the government. Had jobs, making money, still these were the dudes who were out in the street. In Detroit it was the same thing. It wasn't only the unemployed brother. It was the one who was bringing home $110 every Friday. It was the one who had a Thunderbird, and some clean vines. He was the one who had tried to enter white america and had found that no matter what he did, he was still a nigger to the white man.

Those Black people who remain in the Black community, however, remain a viable force. They don't have the frustrations that exist in negro america. In Black america the bonds are tighter. The fight is for freedom, not whiteness.

Negroes have always been treated like wild, caged animals by the white man, and have always felt the passions of caged animals (because they were living in cages), but they would always act civilized with whites, that is, what white people told them was civilized. But inside this "civilized" negro was an undying hate. This hate, however, could only be released in negro america. If it was ever released in white america, it would prove to white people that negroes were savages. That hate became a self-hate. So to preserve their sanity, their humanity and their white civilization, negroes had to hate themselves. And when they hated, they distinguished between those who were most like white people and those who were Black. And they hated Black people and poor negroes. (Poor negroes are those Black people with the values of negro america, but not the means.)

It is clear that the revolution will not come from negro america but from Black america, and Black america is growing. Black america is important because it is here that you will find the self-imposed exiles from both white and negro america. Black america has always offered Black human freedoms—a humanism uncommon to white and negro america. Some enter Black america because negro america rejects darker-skinned negroes, and, of course, if a person is rejected by negro america, he is automatically rejected by white america. Other people enter Black america because of some experience they had in their childhood. Still others, because of something they may have read that was written by someone in Black america. Black america has existed every since the first slave despised the injustice that was done to him and did not seek to accommodate himself to that injustice. Thus, there have always been people who could articulate these injustices and could discuss what the response to these injustices should be. It is self-evident that people always rebel against oppression and there has been one continuous rebellion in Black america since the first slave got here.

* * *

Today I will talk about two things—colonialism and revolution. In other words, sickness and cure. The united states redefined colonialism. It not only went to Africa and exploited the land and its people; it brought back Black people here and continues its exploitation; and it drove the native American Indians by murder and wholesale genocide onto reservations (and now this is romanticized on t.v. as cowboys and Indians). America is the ultimate denial of the theory of man's continuous evolution. This country represents everything that humans have suffered from, their every affliction. The very fact that a place like this can exist appals most of mankind. This country is the world's slop jar. America's very existence offends me. For Black people it is not a question of leaving or separating—given our historical experiences, we know better than anyone that the animal that is america must be destroyed. Through capitalism, this country establishes colonies; but, not colonies in the old sense, but like franchises. The Philippines, Venezuela, Vietnam, Puerto

Rico and other countries are to the united states what dope is to Harlem; bloods use it, but the Mafia owns it. It just goes to show you, you give the cracker an inch, he wants a yard, give him a yard, and he'll BURN A CROSS ON IT, every time. There is no difference between Harlem and Puerto Rico, or Harlem and Vietnam, except that in Vietnam people are fighting for their liberation. (That is, armed struggle.)

Let's examine that war in Vietnam. My position, on that war, is that Black folks ain't got no business shooting other Black folks for white folks. If we must fight, then our war is here at home. We can't let white folks decide for us who our enemy is. We must decide who our enemy is and how to deal with him. Black cats must say that if Lynch'em Burn Johnson can stay here and keep the Vietcong off Ladybird, then we can stay here and keep the crackers off our women. We must refuse to participate in the war of genocide against people of color: a war that also commits genocide against us. Black men are being used on the front lines at a disproportionate rate. Forty-five percent of the casualties are Black. That's genocide! We cannot let our Black brothers fight in Vietnam because we need them here to fight with us. If we can die defending our motherland, we can die defending our mothers. It is the Black man's will to be free that has made him fight for this country, not his love. This same will to be free will make him fight this country. The army is to kill people. We have to decide if we will be killers; when we decide, we have to decide who we are going to kill, and when.

* * *

The question of violence has been cleared up. This country was born of violence. Violence is as american as cherry pie. Black people have always been violent, but our violence has always been directed toward each other. If nonviolence is to be practiced, then it should be practiced in our community and end there. Violence is a necessary part of revolutionary struggle. Nonviolence as it is advocated by negroes is merely a preparation for genocide. Some negroes are so sold on nonviolence that if they received a letter from the White House saying to report to concentration camps, they would not hesitate. They'd be there on time! If we examine what happened to the Jews, we find that it was not the Germans who first began to remove Jews. It was other Jews! We must be prepared to fight anyone who threatens our survival. Black and white. The rebellions taught Blacks the value of retaliatory violence. The most successful rebellion was held in Plainfield. It was successful in the sense that white violence was minimized. The only death that occurred in Plainfield was that of a white racist cop. We know how sensitive america is about the killing of policemen—especially white policemen. But both National Guardsmen and local police were afraid to shoot up the Black community because the brothers had just stolen two crates of guns. Each one of these guns would shoot seven times before you load it, which makes it hard to hold it; eight times fore you cock it, and it takes a man to stop it. The very fact that white folks fear guns shows the value in being armed. Power, indeed, must come from the barrel of a gun.

We can no longer allow threats of death to immobilize us. Death is no stranger to Black folks. We've been dying ever since we got here. To all the brothers and sisters who are here, ours may be to do and die, but for the little brothers and sisters, theirs should be but the reason why. This country has delivered an ultimatum to Black people; america says to Blacks: you either fight to live or you will live to die. I say to america, Fuck It! Freedom or Death.

Power to the People.

The Black Panther Party:
Platform and Program

WHAT WE WANT

WHAT WE BELIEVE

1. We want freedom. We want power to determine the destiny of our Black Community.

We believe that black people will not be free until we are able to determine our destiny.

2. We want full employment for our people.

We believe that the federal government is responsible and obligated to give every man employment or a guaranteed income. We believe that if the white American businessmen will not give full employment, then the means of production should be taken from the businessmen and placed in the community so that the people of the community can organize and employ all of its people and give a high standard of living.

3. We want an end to the robbery by the CAPITALIST of our Black Community.

We believe that this racist government has robbed us and now we are demanding the overdue debt of forty acres and two mules. Forty acres and two mules was promised 100 years ago as restitution for slave

---

Reprinted from *The Black Panther*, July 5, 1969.

What Is A Pig?

"A low natured beast that has no regard for law, justice, or the rights of people; a creature that bites the hand that feeds it; a foul, depraved traducer, usually found masquerading as the victim of an un-provoked attack."

BATTLE FATIGUE

EMORY

labor and mass murder of black people. We will accept the payment in currency which will be distributed to our many communities. The Germans are now aiding the Jews in Israel for the genocide of the Jewish people. The Germans murdered six million Jews. The American racist has taken part in the slaughter of over fifty million black people; therefore, we feel that this is a modest demand that we make.

4. We want decent housing, fit for shelter of human beings.

We believe that if the white landlords will not give decent housing to our black community, then the housing and the land should be made into cooperatives so that our community, with government aid, can build and make decent housing for its people.

5. We want education for our people that exposes the true nature of this decadent American society. We want education that teaches us our true history and our role in the present-day society.

We believe in an educational system that will give to our people a knowledge of self. If a man does not have knowledge of himself and his position in society and the world, then he has little chance to relate to anything else.

6. We want all black men to be exempt from military service.

We believe that Black people should not be forced to fight in the military service to defend a racist government that does not protect us. We will not fight and kill other people of color in the world who, like black people, are being victimized by the white racist government of America. We will protect ourselves from the force and violence of the racist police and the racist military, by whatever means necessary.

7. We want an immediate end to POLICE BRUTAL-ITY and MURDER of black people.

We believe we can end police brutality in our black community by organizing black self-defense groups that are dedicated to defending our black community from racist police oppression and brutality. The Second Amendment to the Constitution of the United States gives a right to bear arms. We therefore believe that all black people should arm themselves for self-defense.

8. We want freedom for all black men held in federal, state, county and city prisons and jails.

We believe that all black people should be released from the many jails and prisons because they have not received a fair and impartial trial.

9. We want all black people when brought to trial to be tried in court by a jury of their peer group or people from their black communities, as defined by the Constitution of the United States.

We believe that the courts should follow the United States Constitution so that black people will receive fair trials. The 14th Amendment of the U.S. Constitution gives a man a right to be tried by his peer group. A peer is a person from a similar economic, social, religious, geographical, environmental, historical and racial background. To do this the court will be forced to select a jury from the black community from which the black defendant came. We have been, and are being, tried by all-white juries that have no understanding of the "average reasoning man" of the black community.

10. We want land, bread, housing, education, clothing, justice and peace. And as our major political objective, a

United Nations-supervised plebiscite to be held throughout the black colony in which only black colonial subjects will be allowed to participate, for the purpose of determining the will of black people as to their national destiny.

When, in the course of human events, it becomes necessary for one people to dissolve the political bands which have connected them with another, and to assume, among the powers of the earth, the separate and equal station to which the laws of nature and nature's God entitle them, a decent respect to the opinions of mankind requires that they should declare the causes which impel them to the separation.

We hold these truths to be self-evident, that all men are created equal; that they are endowed by their Creator with certain unalienable rights; that among these are life, liberty, and the pursuit of happiness. **That, to secure these rights, governments are instituted among men, deriving their just powers from the consent of the governed; that, whenever any form of government becomes destructive of these ends, it is the right of the pople to alter or to abolish it, and to institute a new government, laying its foundation on such principles, and organizing its powers in such form, as to them shall seem most likely to effect their safety and happiness.** Prudence, indeed, will dictate that governments long established should not be changed for light and transient causes; and, accordingly, all experience hath shown, that mankind are more disposed to suffer, while evils are sufferable, than to right themselves by abolishing the forms to which they are accustomed. **But, when a long train of abuses and usurpations, pursuing invariably the same object, evinces a design to reduce them under absolute despotism, it is their right, it is their duty, to throw off such government, and to provide new guards for their future security.**

For a Woman

Erika Huggins

to carry life
to bear it
to be aware of the beauty
of man/to create/is to
become sorrowed by those
who, unaware, kill/exploit/
plunder/dehumanize.

there are times when sorrow
becomes mixed with joy
    tears with smiles
it is then the innocence
of the innocents tears at your soul
                  your mind
carrying a new person, another life
awakens all of you in you—
    the world can be so harsh, so cruel
      and you as a new you,
        a servant of creation, are
           defensive
           afraid

Huey Newton and Erika Huggins, *Insights and Poems*, San Francisco: City Lights Books, 1975, pp. 43–44. Reprinted with permission.

some times alone
even, with many people
you want to protect him/her(the new life)
from society's cruelty—
you will see
you can
not.

Revolutionary Suicide: The Way of Liberation

Huey P. Newton

Let a new earth rise. Let another world be born. Let a
bloody peace be written in the sky. Let a second
generation full of courage issue forth, let a people
loving freedom come to growth, let a beauty full of
healing and a strength of final clenching be the pulsing
in our spirits and our blood. Let the martial songs be
written, let the dirges disappear. Let a race of men
now rise and take control!

Margaret Walker
"For My People"

For twenty-two months in the California Men's Colony at San Luis
Obispo, after my first trial for the death of Patrolman John Frey, I was
almost continually in solitary confinement. There, in a four-by-six cell,
except for books and papers relating to my case, I was allowed no
reading material. Despite the rigid enforcement of this rule, inmates
sometimes slipped magazines under my door when the guards were not

Huey P. Newton, *Revolutionary Suicide,* New York: Harcourt, Brace, Jovanovich,
1973, pp. 3–7. Reprinted with permission of the author.

looking. One that reached me was the May, 1970, issue of *Ebony* magazine. It contained an article written by Lacy Banko summarizing the work of Dr. Herber Hendin, who had done a comparative study on suicide among Black people in the major American cities. Dr. Hendin found that the suicide rate among Black men between the ages of nineteen and thirty-five had doubled in the past ten to fifteen years, surpassing the rate for whites in the same age range. The article had—and still has—a profound effect on me. I have thought long and hard about its implications.

The *Ebony* article brought to mind Durkheim's classic study *Suicide*, a book I had read earlier while studying sociology at Oakland City College. To Durkheim all types of suicide are related to social conditions. He maintains that the primary cause of suicide is not individual temperament but forces in the social environment. In other words, suicide is caused primarily by external factors, not internal ones. As I thought about the conditions of Black people and about Dr. Hendin's study, I began to develop Durkheim's analysis and apply it to the Black experience in the United States. This eventually led to the concept of "revolutionary suicide."

To understand revolutionary suicide it is first necessary to have an idea of reactionary suicide, for the two are very different. Dr. Hendin was describing reactionary suicide: the reaction of a man who takes his own life in response to social conditions that overwhelm him and condemn him to helplessness. The young Black men in his study had been deprived of human dignity, crushed by oppressive forces, and denied their right to live as proud and free human beings.

A section in Dostoevsky's *Crime and Punishment* provides a good analogy. One of the characters, Marmeladov, a very poor man, argues that poverty is not a vice. In poverty, he says, a man can attain the innate nobility of soul that is not possible in beggary; for while society may drive the poor man out with a stick, the beggar will be swept out with a broom. Why? Because the beggar is totally demeaned, his dignity lost. Finally, bereft of self-respect, immobilized by fear and despair, he sinks into self-murder. This is reactionary suicide.

Connected to reactionary suicide, although even more painful and degrading, is a spiritual death that has been the experience of millions of Black people in the United States. This death is found everywhere today in the Black community. Its victims have ceased to fight the forms of oppression that drink their blood. The common attitude has long been: What's the use? If a man rises up against a power as great as the United States, he will not survive. Believing this, many Blacks have been driven to a death of the spirit rather than of the flesh, lapsing into lives of quiet desperation. Yet all the while, in the heart of every Black, there is the hope that life will somehow change in the future.

I do not think that life will change for the better without an assault on the Establishment,* which goes on exploiting the wretched of the earth. This belief lies at the heart of the concept of revolutionary suicide. Thus it is better to oppose the forces that would drive me to self-murder than to endure them. Although I risk the likelihood of death, there is at least the possibility, if not the probability, of changing intolerable conditions. This possibility is important, because much in human existence is based upon hope without any real understanding of the odds. Indeed, we are all—Black and white alike—ill in the same way, mortally ill. But before we die, how shall we live? I say with hope and dignity; and if premature death is the result, that death has a meaning reactionary suicide can never have. It is the price of self-respect.

Revolutionary suicide does not mean that I and my comrades have a death wish; it means just the opposite. We have such a strong desire to live with hope and human dignity that existence without them is impossible. When reactionary forces crush us, we must move against these forces, even at the risk of death. We will have to be driven out with a stick.

Che Guevara said that to a revolutionary death is the reality and victory the dream. Because the revolutionary lives so dangerously, his survival is a miracle. Bakunin, who spoke for the most militant wing of the First International, made a similar statement in his *Revolutionary Catechism*. To him, the first lesson a revolutionary must learn is that he is a doomed man. Unless he understands this, he does not grasp the essential meaning of his life.

When Fidel Castro and his small band were in Mexico preparing for the Cuban Revolution, many of the comrades had little understanding of Bakunin's rule. A few hours before they set sail, Fidel went from man to man asking who should be notified in case of death. Only then did the deadly seriousness of the revolution hit home. Their struggle was no longer romantic. The scene had been exciting and animated; but when the simple, overwhelming question of death arose, everyone fell silent.

Many so-called revolutionaries in this country, Black and white, are not prepared to accept this reality. The Black Panthers are not

*the power structure, based on the economic infrastructure, propped up and reinforced by the media and all the secondary educational and cultural institutions.

suicidal; neither do we romanticize the consequences of revolution in our lifetime. Other so-called revolutionaries cling to an illusion that they might have their revolution and die of old age. That cannot be.

I do not expect to live through our revolution, and most serious comrades probably share my realism. Therefore, the expression "revolution in our lifetime" means something different to me than it does to other people who use it. I think the revolution will grow in my lifetime, but I do not expect it to enjoy its fruits. That would be a contradiction. The reality will be grimmer.

I have no doubt that the revolution will triumph. The people of the world will prevail, seize power, seize the means of production, wipe out racism, capitalism, reactionary intercommunalism—reactionary suicide. The people will win a new world. Yet when I think of individuals in the revolution, I cannot predict their survival. Revolutionaries must accept this fact, especially the Black revolutionaries in America, whose lives are in constant danger from the evils of a colonial society. Considering how we must live, it is not hard to accept the concept of revolutionary suicide. In this we are different from white radicals. They are not faced with genocide.

The greater, more immediate problem is the survival of the entire world. If the world does not change, all its people will be threatened by greed, exploitation, and violence of the power structure in the American empire. The handwriting is on the wall. The United States is jeopardizing its own existence and the existence of all humanity. If Americans knew the disasters that lay ahead, they would transform this society tomorrow for their own preservation. The Black Panther Party is in the vanguard of the revolution that seeks to relieve this country of its crushing burden of guilt. We are determined to establish true equality and the means for creative work.

Some see our struggle as a symbol of the trend toward suicide among Blacks. Scholars and academics, in particular, have been quick to make this accusation. They fail to perceive differences. Jumping off a bridge is not the same as moving to wipe out the overwhelming force of an oppressive army. When scholars call our actions suicidal, they should be logically consistent and describe all historical revolutionary movements in the same way. Thus the American colonists, the French of the late eighteenth century, the Russians of 1917, the Jews of Warsaw, the Cubans, the NLF, the North Vietnamese—any people who struggle against a brutal and powerful force—are suicidal. Also, if the Black Panthers symbolize the suicidal trend among Blacks, then the whole Third World is suicidal, because the Third World fully intends to resist and overcome the ruling class of the United States. If scholars wish to carry their analysis further, they must come to terms with that four-fifths of the world which is bent on wiping out the power of the empire. In those terms the Third World would be transformed from suicidal to homicidal, although homicide is the unlawful taking of life, and the Third World is involved only in defense. Is the coin then turned? Is the government of the United States suicidal? I think so.

With this redefinition, the term "revolutionary suicide" is not as simplistic as it might seem initially. In coining the phrase, I took two knowns and combined them to make an unknown, a neoteric phrase in which the word "revolutionary" transforms the word "suicide" into an idea that has different dimensions and meanings, applicable to a new and complex situation.

My prison experience is a good example of revolutionary suicide in action, for prison is a microcosm of the outside world. From the beginning of my sentence I defied the authorities by refusing to cooperate; as a result, I was confined to "lock-up," a solitary cell. As the months passed and I remained steadfast, they came to regard my behavior as suicidal. I was told that I would crack and break under the strain. I did not break, nor did I retreat from my position. I grew strong.

If I had submitted to their exploitation and done their will, it would have killed my spirit and condemned me to a living death. To cooperate in prison meant reactionary suicide to me. While solitary confinement can be physically and mentally destructive, my actions were taken with an understanding of the risk. I had to suffer through a certain situation; by doing so, my resistance told them that I rejected all they stood for. Even though my struggle might have harmed my health, even killed me, I looked upon it as a way of raising the consciousness of the other inmates, as a contribution to the ongoing revolution. Only resistance can destroy the pressures that cause reactionary suicide.

The concept of revolutionary suicide is not defeatist or fatalistic. On the contrary, it conveys an awareness of reality in combination with the possibility of hope—reality because the revolutionary must always be prepared to face death, and hope because it symbolizes a resolute determination to bring about change. Above all, it demands that the revolutionary see his death and his life as one piece. Chairman Mao says that death comes to all of us, but it varies in its significance: to die for the reactionary is lighter than a feather; to die for the revolution is heavier than Mount Tai.

SDS was the largest, best known, and most effective new left organization of the 1960s. The first document presented here, The Port Huron Statement, was an extremely influential declaration of SDS philosophy. The democratic ideals, values and goals of the 63-page document, published in August 1962, would have a formative impact on social protest during the coming decade.

The Triple Revolution was a 1964 study of the possible political and social effects of automation and computers. It was widely read in SDS, and the group's early organizing projects among poor people were given inpetus by the document's predictions of massive unemployment.

Paul Potter, a national leader of SDS, gave the speech reprinted here to an antiwar rally of 25,000 people on April 17, 1965. The event was organized by SDS and, for the first time, made many Americans aware of an antiwar movement that was strongly opposing President Johnson's foreign policy.

Herbert Marcuse's work, One-Dimensional Man, provided a philosophic rationale for those in SDS who believed that American society was unreformable. Marcuse used a highly sophisticated method of dialectical analysis to question the value of freedom in America. For Marcuse, American society was, in its essence, rigidly authoritarian. The elderly Marcuse was attacked by conservative politicians and the media, who labelled him the "intellectual godfather" of new left activism.

An aspect of the illusory nature of American freedom was explored by two SDS leaders, Naomi Jaffe and Bernardine Dohrn, in their article "The Look Is You." They argued spiritedly against the exploitation of women by consumerist culture.

"Columbia Liberated" offered the student striker's official version of the 1968 campus revolt. The strike's militancy was reflected in the SDS August 1969 pronouncement, "Bring the War Home." Reprinted from the organization's national newspaper, New Left Notes, the pronouncement was SDS's angry call to street confrontation in Chicago during the opening days of the Conspiracy Trial. The phrase "bring the war home" became a popular slogan for the late 1960s antiwar movement. "You Do Need a Weatherman" by Shin'ya Ono is one participant's view of those demonstrations. It reflects the passionate personal commitment to violent revolution which was taking hold of many in SDS.

In 1974 the 150-page book Prairie Fire was published clandistinely by an organization of federal fugitives who were former SDS leaders and activists. In the segment reprinted here, "The 1960s: Achievements/Turning Point," these veteran radicals attempted to evaluate SDS's role in 1960s political protest. Although the book created new interest in the Weather Underground Organization, the group quickly fell apart due to internal political and personal divisions.

The Port Huron Statement

...we seek the establishment of a democracy of individual participation governed by two central aims: that the individual share in those social decisions determining the quality and direction of his life; that society be organized to encourage independence in men and provide the media for their common participation...

Students for a Democratic
Society

INTRODUCTION: AGENDA FOR A GENERATION

We are people of this generation, bred in at least modest comfort, housed now in universities, looking uncomfortably to the world we inherit.

When we were kids the United States was the wealthiest and strongest country in the world; the only one with the atom bomb, the least scarred by modern war, an initiator of the United Nations that we thought would distribute Western influence throughout the world. Freedom and equality for each individual, government of, by, and for the people—these American values we found good, principles by which we could live as men. Many of us began maturing in complacency.

As we grew, however, our comfort was penetrated by events too troubling to dismiss. First, the permeating and victimizing fact of human degradation, symbolized by the Southern struggle against racial bigotry, compelled most of us from silence to activism. Second, the enclosing fact of the Cold War, symbolized by the presence of the Bomb, brought awareness that we ourselves, and our friends, and millions of abstract "others" we knew more directly because of our common peril, might die at any time. We might deliberately ignore, or avoid, or fail to feel all other human problems, but not these two, for these were too immediate and crushing in their impact, too challenging in the demand that we as individuals take the responsibility for encounter and resolution.

While these and other problems either directly oppressed us or rankled our consciences and became our own subjective concerns, we began to see complicated and disturbing paradoxes in our surrounding America. The declaration "all men are created equal..." rang hollow before the facts of Negro life in the South and the big cities of the North. The proclaimed peaceful intentions of the United States contradicted its economic and military investments in the Cold War status quo.

We witnessed, and continue to witness, other paradoxes. With nuclear energy whole cities can easily be powered, yet the dominant nation-states seem more likely to unleash destruction greater than that incurred in all wars of human history. Although our own technology is destroying old and creating new forms of social organization, men still tolerate meaningless work and idleness. While two thirds of mankind suffers undernourishment, our own upper classes revel amidst super-fluous abundance. Although world population is expected to double in forty years, the nations still tolerate anarchy as a major principle of international conduct and uncontrolled exploitation governs the sapping of the earth's physical resources. Although mankind desperately needs revolutionary leadership, America rests in national stalemate, its goals ambiguous and tradition-bound instead of informed and clear, its democratic system apathetic and manipulated rather than "of, by, and for the people."

Not only did tarnish appear on our image of American virtue, not only did disillusion occur when the hypocrisy of American ideals was discovered, but we began to sense that what we had originally seen as the American Golden Age was actually the decline of an era. The worldwide outbreak of revolution against colonialism and imperialism, the entrenchment of totalitarian states, the menace of war, overpopulation, international disorder, supertechnology—these trends were testing the tenacity of our own commitment to democracy and freedom and our abilities to visualize their application to a world in upheaval.

Our work is guided by the sense that we may be the last generation in the experiment with living. But we are a minority—the vast majority of our people regard the temporary equilibriums of our society and world as eternally-functional parts. In this is perhaps the outstanding paradox: we ourselves are imbued with urgency, yet the message of our society is that there is no viable alternative to the present. Beneath the reassuring tones of the politicans, beneath the common opinion that America will "muddle through," beneath the stagnation of those who have closed their minds to the future, is the pervading feeling that there simply are no alternatives, that our times have witnessed the exhaustion not only of Utopias, but of any new departures as well. Feeling the press of complexity upon the emptiness of life, people are fearful of the thought that at any moment things might be thrust out of control. They fear change itself, since change might smash whatever invisible framework seems to hold back chaos for them now. For most Americans, all crusades are suspect, threatening. The fact that each individual sees apathy in his fellows perpetuates the common reluctance to organize for change. The dominant institutions are complex enough to blunt the minds of their potential critics, and entrenched enough to swiftly dissipate or entirely repel the energies of protest and reform, thus limiting human expectancies. Then, too, we are a materially improved society, and by our own improvements we seem to have weakened the case for further change.

Some would have us believe that Americans feel contentment amidst prosperity—but might it not be better called a glaze above deeply-felt anxieties about their role in the new world? And if these anxieties produce a developed indifference to human affairs, do they not as well produce a yearning to believe there is an alternative to the present, that something *can* be done to change circumstances in the school, the workplaces, the bureaucracies, the government? It is to this latter yearning, at once the spark and engine of change, that we direct our present appeal. The search for truly democratic alternatives to the present, and a commitment to social experimentation with them, is a worthy and fulfilling human enterprise, one which moves us and, we hope, others today. On such a basis do we offer this document of our convictions and analysis: as an effort in understanding and changing the conditions of humanity in the late twentieth century, an effort rooted in the ancient, still unfulfilled conception of man attaining determining influence over his circumstances of life.

VALUES

Making values explicit—an initial task in establishing alternatives—is an activity that has been devalued and corrupted. The conventional moral terms of the age, the political moralities—"free world," "people's democracies"—reflect realities poorly, if at all, and seem to function more as ruling myths than as descriptive principles. But neither has our experience in the universities brought us moral enlightenment. Our professors and administrators sacrifice controversy to public relations; their curriculums change more slowly than the living events of the world; their skills and silence are purchased by investors in the arms race; passion is called unscholastic. The questions we might want raised—what is really important? can we live in a different and better way? if we wanted to change society, how would we do it?—are not thought to be questions of a "fruitful, empirical nature," and thus are brushed aside.

Unlike youth in other countries we are used to moral leadership being exercised and moral dimensions being clarified by our elders. But today, for us, not even the liberal and socialist preachments of the past seem adequate to the forms of the present. Consider the old slogans: Capitalism Cannot Reform Itself, United Front Against Fascism, General Strike, All Out on May Day. Or, more recently, No Cooperation with Commies and Fellow Travellers, Ideologies are Exhausted, Bipartisanship, No Utopias. These are incomplete, and there are few new prophets. It has been said that our liberal and socialist predecessors were plagued by vision without program, while our own generation is plagued by program without vision. All around us there is astute grasp of method, technique—the committee, the ad hoc group, the lobbyist, the hard and soft sell, the make, the projected image—but, if pressed critically, such expertise is incompetent to explain its implicit ideals. It is highly fashionable to identify oneself by old categories, or by naming a respected political figure, or by explaining "how we would vote" on various issues.

Theoretic chaos has replaced the idealistic thinking of old—and, unable to reconstitute theoretic order, men have condemned idealism itself. Doubt has replaced hopefulness—and men act out a defeatism that is labelled realistic. The decline of utopia and hope is in fact one of the defining features of social life today. The reasons are various: the dreams of the older left were perverted by Stalinism and never recreated; the congressional stalemate makes men narrow their view of the possible; the specialization of human activity leaves little room for sweeping thought; the horrors of the twentieth century, symbolized in the gas-ovens and concentration camps and atom bombs, have blasted hopefulness. To be idealistic is to be considered apocalyptic, deluded. To have no serious aspirations, on the contrary, is to be "toughminded."

In suggesting social goals and values, therefore, we are aware of entering a sphere of some disrepute. Perhaps matured by the past, we have no sure formulas, no closed theories—but that does not mean values are beyond discussion and tentative determination. A first task of any social movement is to convince people that the search for orienting theories and the creation of human values is complex but worthwhile. We are aware that to avoid platitudes we must analyze the concrete conditions of social order. But to direct such an analysis we must use the guideposts of basic principles. Our own social values involve conceptions of human beings, human relationships, and social systems.

We regard *men* as infinitely precious and possessed of unfulfilled capacities for reason, freedom, and love. In affirming these principles we are aware of countering perhaps the dominant conceptions of man in the twentieth century: that he is a thing to be manipulated, and that he is inherently incapable of directing his own affairs. We oppose the depersonalization that reduces human beings to the status of things—if anything, the brutalities of the twentieth century teach that means and ends are intimately related, that vague appeals to "posterity" cannot justify the mutilations of the present. We oppose, too, the doctrine of human incompetence because it rests essentially on the modern fact that men have been "competently" manipulated into incompetence—we see little reason why men cannot meet with increasing skill the complexities and responsibilities of their situation, if society is organized not for minority, but for majority, participation in decision-making.

Men have unrealized potential for self-evaluation, self-direction, self-understanding, and creativity. It is this potential that we regard as crucial and to which we appeal, not to the human potentiality for violence, unreason, and submission to authority. The goal of man and society should be human independence; a concern not with image of popularity but with finding meaning in life that is personally authentic; a quality of mind not compulsively driven by a sense of powerlessness, nor one which unthinkingly adopts status values, nor one which represses all threats to its habits, but one which has full, spontaneous access to present and past experiences, one which easily unites the fragmented parts of personal history, one which openly faces problems which are troubling and unresolved; one with an intuitive awareness of possibilities, an active sense of curiousity, an ability and willingness to learn.

This kind of independence does not mean egotistic individualism—the object is not to have one's way so much as it is to have a way that is one's own. Nor do we deify man—we merely have faith in his potential.

Human relationships should involve fraternity and honesty. Human interdependence is contemporary fact; human brotherhood must be willed, however, as a condition of future survival and as the most appropriate form of social relations. Personal links between man and man are needed, especially to go beyond the partial and fragmentary bonds of function that bind men only as worker to worker, employer to employee, teacher to student, American to Russian.

Loneliness, estrangement, isolation describe the vast distance between man and man today. These dominant tendencies cannot be overcome by better personnel management, nor by improved gadgets, but only when a love of man overcomes the idolatrous worship of things by man. As the individualism we affirm is not egoism, the selflessness we affirm is not self-elimination. On the contrary, we believe in generosity of a kind that imprints one's unique individual qualities in the relation to other men, and to all human activity. Further, to dislike isolation is not to favor the abolition of privacy; the latter differs from isolation in that it occurs or is abolished according to individual will.

We would replace power rooted in possession, privilege, or circumstance by power and uniqueness rooted in love, reflectiveness, reason, and creativity. As a *social system* we seek the establishment of a democracy of individual participation, governed by two central aims: that the individual share in those social decisions determining the quality and direction of his life; that society be organized to encourage independence in men and provide the media for their common participation.

In a participatory democracy, the political life would be based in several root principles:

that decision-making of basic social consequence be carried on by public groupings;

that politics be seen positively, as the art of collectively creating an acceptable pattern of social relations;

that politics have the function of bringing people out of isolation and into community, thus being a necessary, though not sufficient, means of finding meaning in personal life;

that the political order should serve to clarify problems in a way instrumental to their solution; it should provide outlets for the expression of personal grievance and aspiration; opposing views should be organized so as to illuminate choices and facilitate the attainment of goals; channels should be commonly available to relate men to knowledge and to power so that private problems—from bad recreation facilities to personal alienation—are formulated as general issues.

The economic sphere would have as its basis the principles:

that the economic experience is so personally decisive that the individual must share in its full determination;

that the economy itself is of such social importance that its major resources and means of production should be open to democratic participation and subject to democratic social regulation.

Like the political and economic ones, major social institutions—cultural, educational, rehabilitative, and others—should be generally organized with the well-being and dignity of man as the essential measure of success.

In social change or interchange, we find violence to be abhorrent because it requires generally the transformation of the target, be it a human being or a community of people, into a depersonalized object of hate. It is imperative that the means of violence be abolished and the institutions—local, national, international—that encourage nonviolence as a condition of conflict be developed.

These are our central values, in skeletal form. It remains vital to understand their denial or attainment in the context of the modern world.

THE STUDENTS

In the last few years, thousands of American students demonstrated that they at least felt the urgency of the times. They moved actively and directly against racial injustices, the threat of war, violations of individual rights of conscience and, less frequently, against economic manipulation. They succeeded in restoring a small measure of controversy to the campuses after the stillness of the McCarthy period. They succeeded, too, in gaining some concessions from the people and institutions they opposed, especially in the fight against racial bigotry.

The significance of these scattered movements lies not in their success or failure in gaining objectives—at least not yet. Nor does the significance lie in the intellectual "competence" or "maturity" of the students involved—as some pedantic elders allege. The significance is in the fact the students are breaking the crust of apathy and overcoming the inner alienation that remain the defining characteristics of American college life.

If student movements for change are still rareties on the campus scene, what is commonplace there? The real campus, the familiar campus, is a place of private people, engaged in their notorious "inner emigration." It is a place of commitment to business-as-usual, getting ahead, playing it cool. It is a place of mass affirmation of the Twist, but mass reluctance toward the controversial public stance. Rules are accepted as "inevitable," bureaucracy as "just circumstances," irrelevance as "scholarship," selflessness as "martyrdom," politics as "just another way to make people, and an unprofitable one, too."

Almost no students value activity as citizens. Passive in public, they are hardly more idealistic in arranging their private lives: Gallup concludes they will settle for "low success, and won't risk high failure." There is not much willingness to take risks (not even in business), no setting of dangerous goals, no real conception of personal identity except one manufactured in the image of others, no real urge for personal fulfillment except to be almost as successful as the very successful people. Attention is being paid to social status (the quality of shirt collars, meeting people, getting wives or husbands, making solid contacts for later on); much, too, is paid to academic status (grades, honors, the med school rat race). But neglected generally is real intellectual status, the personal cultivation of the mind.

"Students don't even give a damn about the apathy," one has said. Apathy toward apathy begets a privately-constructed universe, a place of systematic study schedules, two nights each week for beer, a girl or two, and early marriage; a framework infused with personality, warmth, and under control, no matter how unsatisfying otherwise.

Under these conditions university life loses all revelance to some. Four hundred thousand of our classmates leave college every year.

But apathy is not simply an attitude; it is a product of social institutions, and of the structure and organization of higher education itself, The extracurricular life is ordered according to in loco parentis theory which ratifies the Administration as the moral guardian of the young.

The accompanying "let's pretend" theory of student extracurricular affairs validates student government as a training center for those who want to spend their lives in political pretense, and discourages initiative from the more articulate, honest, and sensitive students. The bounds and style of controversy are delimited before controversy begins. The university "prepares" the student for "citizenship" through perpetual rehearsals and, usually, through emasculation of what creative spirit there is in the individual.

The academic life contains reinforcing counterparts to the way in which extracurricular life is organized. The academic world is founded on a teacher-student relation analogous to the parent-child relation which characterizes in loco parentis. Further, academia includes a radical separation of the student from the material of study. That which is studied, the social reality, is "objectified" to sterility, dividing the student from life—just as he is restrained in active involvement by the deans controlling student government. The specialization of function and knowledge, admittedly necessary to our complex technological and social structure, has produced an exaggerated compartmentalization of study and understanding. This has contributed to an overly parochial view, by faculty, of the role of its research and scholarship, to a discontinuous and truncated understanding, by students, of the surrounding social order; and to a loss of personal attachment, by nearly all, to the worth of study as a humanistic enterprise.

There is, finally, the cumbersome academic bureaucracy extending throughout the academic as well as the extracurricular structures, contributing to the sense of outer complexity and inner powerlessness that transforms the honest searching of many students to a ratification of convention and, worse, to a numbness to present and future catastrophes. The size and financing systems of the university enhance the permanent trusteeship of the administrative bureaucracy, their power leading to a shift within the university toward the value standards of business and the administrative mentality. Huge foundations and other private financial interests shape the under-financed colleges and universities, not only making them more commercial, but less disposed to diagnose society critically, less open to dissent. Many social and physical scientists, neglecting the liberating heritage of higher learnings, develop "human relations" or "morale-producing" techniques for the corporate economy, while others exercise their intellectual skills to accelerate the arms race.

Tragically, the university could serve as a significant source of social criticism and an initiator of new modes and molders of attitudes. But the actual intellectual effect of the college experience is hardly distinguishable from that of any other communications channel—say, a television set—passing on the stock truths of the day. Students leave college somewhat more "tolerant" than when they arrived, but basically unchallenged in their values and political orientations. With administrators ordering the institution, and faculty the curriculum, the student learns by his isolation to accept elite rule within the university, which prepares him to accept later forms of minority control. The real function of the educational system—as opposed to its more rhetorical function of "searching for truth"—is to impart the key information and styles that will help the student get by, modestly but comfortably, in the big society beyond.

THE SOCIETY BEYOND

Look beyond the campus, to America itself. That student life is more intellectual, and perhaps more comfortable, does not obscure the fact that the fundamental qualities of life on the campus reflect the habits of society at large. The fraternity president is seen at the junior manager levels; the sorority queen has gone to Grosse Pointe; the serious poet burns for a place, any place, to work; the once-serious and never-serious poets work at the advertising agencies. The desperation of people threatened by forces about which they know little and of which they can say less; the cheerful emptiness of people "giving up" all hope of changing things; the faceless ones polled by Gallup who listed "international affairs" fourteenth on their list of "problems" but who also expected thermonuclear war in the next few years; in these and other forms, Americans are in withdrawal from public life, from any collective effort at directing their own affairs.

Some regard these national doldrums as a sign of healthy approval of the established order—but is it approval by consent or manipulated acquiescence? Others declare that the people are withdrawn because compelling issues are fast disappearing—perhaps there are fewer breadlines in America, but is Jim Crow gone, is there enough work and work more fulfilling, is world war a diminishing threat, and what of the revolutionary new peoples? Still others think the national quietude is a necessary consequence of the need for cities to resolve complex and specialized problems of modern industrial society—but, then, why should *business* elites help decide foreign policy, and who controls the elites anyway, and are they solving mankind's problems? Others, finally, shrug knowingly and announce that full democracy never worked anywhere in the past—but why lump qualitatively different civilizations together, and how can a social order work well if its best thinkers are skeptics, and man is really doomed forever to the domination of today?

There are no convincing apologies for the contemporary malaise. While the world tumbles toward the final war, while men in other nations are trying desperately to alter events, while the very future qua future is uncertain—America is without community, impulse, without the inner momentum necessary for an age when societies cannot successfully perpetuate themselves by their military weapons, when democracy must be viable because of the quality of life, not its quantity of rockets.

The apathy here is, first *subjective*—the felt powerlessness of ordinary people, the resignation before the enormity of events. But subjective apathy is encouraged by the *objective* American situation—the actual structural separation of people from power, from relevant knowledge, from pinnacles of decision-making. Just as the university influences the student way of life, so do major social institutions create the circumstances in which the isolated citizen will try hopelessly to understand his world and himself.

The very isolation of the individual— from power and community and ability to aspire—means the rise of a democracy without publics. With the great mass of people structurally remote and psychologically hesitant with respect to democratic institutions, those institutions themselves attenuate and become, in the fashion of the vicious circle, progressively less accessible to those few who aspire to serious participation in social affairs. The vital democratic connection between community and leadership, between the mass and the several elites, has been so wrenched and perverted that disastrous policies go unchallenged time and again.

* * *

ALTERNATIVES TO HELPLESSNESS

The goals we have set are not realizable next month, or even next election—but that fact justifies neither giving up altogether nor a determination to work only on immediate, direct, tangible problems. Both responses are a sign of helplessness, fearfulness of visions, refusal to hope, and tend to bring on the very conditions to be avoided. Fearing vision, we justify rhetoric or myopia. Fearing hope, we reinforce despair.

The first effort, then, should be to state a vision: what is the perimeter of human possibility in this epoch? This we have tried to do. The second effort, if we are to be politically responsible, is to evaluate the prospects for obtaining at least a substantial part of that vision in our epoch: what are the social forces that exist, or that must exist, if we are to be at all successful? And what role have we ourselves to play as a social force?

1. In exploring the existing social forces, note must be taken of the Southern civil rights movement as the most heartening because of the justice it insists upon, exemplary because it indicates that there can be a passage out of apathy.

This movement, pushed into a brilliant new phase by the Montgomery bus boycott and the subsequent nonviolent action of the sit-ins and Freedom Rides has had three major results: first, a sense of self-determination has been instilled in millions of oppressed Negroes; second, the movement has challenged a few thousand liberals to new social idealism; third, a series of important concessions have been obtained, such as token school desegregation, increased Administration help, new laws, desegregation of some public facilities.

But fundamental social change—that would break the props from under Jim Crow—has not come. Negro employment opportunity, wage levels, housing conditions, educational privileges—these remain deplorable and relatively constant, each deprivation reinforcing the impact of the others. The Southern states, in the meantime, are strengthening the fortresses of the status quo, and are beginning to camouflage the fortresses by guile where open bigotry announced its defiance before. The white-controlled one-party system remains intact; and even where the Republicans are beginning under the pressures of industrialization in the towns and suburbs, to show initiative in fostering a two-party system, all Southern state Republican Committees (save Georgia) have adopted militant segregationist platforms to attract Dixiecrats.

Rural dominance remains a fact in nearly all the Southern states, although the reapportionment decision of the Supreme Court portends future power shifts to the cities. Southern politicians maintain a continuing aversion to the welfare legislation that would aid their people. The reins of the Southern economy are held by conservative businessmen who view human rights as a secondary to property rights. A violent anti-communism is rooting itself in the South, and threatening even moderate voices. Add the militaristic tradition of the South, and its irrational regional mystique and one must conclude that authoritarian and reactionary tendencies are a rising obstacle to the small, voiceless, poor, and isolated democratic movements.

The civil rights struggle thus has come to an impasse. To this impasse, the movement responded this year by entering the sphere of politics, insisting on citizenship rights, specifically the right to vote. The new voter registration stage of protest represents perhaps the first major attempt to exercise the conventional instruments of political democracy in the struggle for racial justice. The vote, if used strategically by the great mass of now-unregistered Negroes theoretically eligible to vote, will be a decisive factor in changing the quality of Southern leadership from low demogoguery to decent statesmanship.

More important, the new emphasis on the vote heralds the use of *political* means to solve the problems of equality in America, and it signals the decline of the shortsighted view that "discrimination" can be isolated from related social problems. Since the moral clarity of the civil rights movement has not always been accompanied by precise political vision, and sometimes not even by a real political consciousness, the new phase is revolutionary in its implications. The intermediate goal of the program is to secure and insure a healthy respect and realization of Constitutional liberties. This is important not only to determine the civil and private abuses which currently characterize the region, but also to prevent the pendulum of oppression from simply swinging to an alternate extreme with a new unsophisticated electorate, after the unhappy example of the last Reconstruction. It is the *ultimate* objectives of the strategy which promise profound change in the politics of the nation. An increased Negro voting rate in and of itself is not going to dislodge racist controls of the Southern power structure; but an accelerating movement through the courts, the ballot boxes, and especially the jails is the most likely means of shattering the crust of political intransigency and creating a semblance of democratic order on local and state levels.

Linked with pressure from Northern liberals to expunge the Dixiecrats from the ranks of the Democratic Party, massive Negro voting in the South could destroy the vise-like grip reactionary Southerners have on the Congressional legislative process.

2. The broadest movement for *peace* in several years emerged in 1961–62. In its political orientation and goals it is much less identifiable than the movement for civil rights: it includes socialists, pacifists, liberals, scholars, militant activists, middle-class women, some profes-

sionals, many students, a few unionists. Some have been emotionally single-issue: Ban the Bomb. Some have been academically obscurantist. Some have rejected the System (sometimes both systems). Some have attempted, also, to "work within" the system. Amidst these conflicting streams of emphasis, however, certain basic qualities appear. The most important is that the "peace movement" has operated almost exclusively through peripheral institutions—almost never through mainstream institutions. Similarly, individuals interested in peace have nonpolitical social roles that cannot be turned to the support of peace activity. Concretely, liberal religious societies, anti-war groups, voluntary associations and ad hoc committees have been the political unit of the peace movement; and its human movers have been students, teachers, housewives, secretaries, lawyers, doctors, clergy. The units have not been located in spots of major social influence; the people have not been able to turn their resources fully to the issues that concern them. The results are political ineffectiveness and personal alienation.

The organizing ability of the peace movement thus is limited to the ability to state and polarize issues. It does not have an institution or a forum in which the conflicting interests can be debated. The debate goes on in corners; it has little connection with the continuing process of determining allocations of resources. This process is not necessarily centralized, however much of the peace movement is estranged from it. National policy, though dominated to a large degree by the "power elites" of the corporations and the military, is still partially founded in consensus. It can be altered when there actually begins a shift in the allocation of resources and the listing of priorities by the people in the institutions which have social influence, e.g., the labor unions and the schools. As long as the debates of the peace movement form only a protest, rather than an opposition viewpoint within the centers of serious decision-making, then it is neither a movement of democratic relevance, nor is it likely to have any effectiveness except in educating more outsiders to the issue. It is vital, to be sure, that this educating go on (a heartening sign is the recent proliferation of books and journals dealing with peace and war from newly-developing countries); the possibilities for making politicians responsible to "peace constituencies" becomes greater.

But in the long interim before the national political climate is more open to deliberate, goal-directed debate about peace issues, the dedicated peace "movement" might well prepare a *local base*, especially by establishing civic committees on the techniques of converting from military to peacetime production. To make war and peace *relevant* to the problems of everyday life, by relating it to the backyard (shelters), the baby (fall-out), the job (military contracts)—and making a turn toward peace seem desirable on these same terms—is a task the peace movement is just beginning and can profitably continue.

3. Central to any analysis of the potential for change must be an appraisal of *organized labor*. It would be ahistorical to disregard the immense influence of labor in making modern America a decent place in which to live. It would be confused to fail to note labor's presence today as the most liberal of mainstream institutions. But it would be irresponsible not to criticize labor for losing much of the idealism that once made it a driving movement. Those who expected a labor upsurge after the 1955 AFL-CIO merger can only be dismayed that one year later, in the Stevenson-Eisenhower campaign, the AFL-CIO Committee on Political Education was able to obtain solicited $1.00 contributions from only one of every 24 unionists, and prompt only 40 percent of the rank-and-file to vote.

As a political force, labor generally has been unsuccessful in the post-war period of prosperity. It has seen the passage of the Taft-Hartley and Landrum-Griffin laws, and while beginning to receive slightly favorable National Labor Relations Board rulings, it has made little progress against right-to-work laws. Furthermore, it has seen less than adequate action on domestic problems, especially unemployment.

This labor "recession" has been only partly due to anti-labor politicians and corporations. Blame should be laid, too, on labor itself for not mounting an adequate movement. Labor has too often seen itself as elitist, rather than mass-oriented, and as a pressure group rather than as an 18-million member body making political demands for all America. In the first instance, the labor bureaucracy tends to be cynical toward, or afraid of, rank-and-file involvement in the work of the union. Resolutions passed at conventions are implemented only by high-level machinations, not by mass mobilization of the unionists. Without a significant base, labor's pressure function is materially reduced since it becomes difficult to hold political figures accountable to a movement that cannot muster a vote from a majority of its members.

There are some indications, however, that labor might regain its missing idealism. First, there are signs within the movement: of worker discontent with their economic progress, of collective bargaining, of occasional splits among union leaders on questions such as nuclear testing or other Cold War issues. Second, and more important, are the social forces which prompt these feelings of unrest. Foremost is the permanence of unemployment, and the threat of automation. But important, too, is the growth of unorganized ranks in white-collar fields. Third, there is the tremendous challenge of the Negro movement for support from organized labor: the alienation from and disgust with labor hypocrisy among Negroes ranging from the NAACP to the Black Muslims (crystallized in the formation of the Negro American Labor Council) indicates that labor must move seriously in its attempts to organize on an interracial basis in the South and in large urban centers. When this task was broached several years ago, "jurisdictional" disputes prevented action. Today, many of these disputes have been settled—and the question of a massive organizing campaign is on the labor agenda again.

These threats and opportunities point to a profound crisis: either labor will continue to decline as a social force, or it must constitute itself as a mass political force demanding not only that society recognize its rights to organize but also a program going beyond desired labor legislation and welfare improvement. It might include greater autonomy and power for political coalitions of the various trade unions in local areas, rather than the more stultifying dominance of the international unions now. It might include reductions in leaders' salaries, or rotation from executive office to shop obligations, as a means of breaking down the hierarchical tendencies which have detached elite from base and made the highest echelons of labor more like businessmen than workers. It would certainly mean an announced independence of the center and Dixiecrat wings of the Democratic Party, and a massive organizing drive, especially in the South to complement the growing Negro political drive there.

A new politics must include a revitalized labor movement: a movement which sees itself, and is regarded by others, as a major leader of the breakthrough to a politics of hope and vision. Labor's role is no less unique or important in the needs of the future than it was in the past; its numbers and potential political strength, its natural interest in the abolition of exploitation, its reach to the grass roots of American society, combine to make it the best candidate for the synthesis of the civil rights, peace, and economic reform movements.

The creation of bridges is made more difficult by the problems left over from the generation of "silence." Middle-class students, still the main actors in the embryonic upsurge, have yet to overcome their ignorance, and even vague hostility, for what they see as "middle class labor" bureaucrats. Students must open the campus to labor through publications, action programs, curricula, while labor opens its house to students through internships, requests for aid (on the picket-line, with handbills, in the public dialogue), and politics. And the organization of the campus can be a beginning—teachers' unions can be advocated as both socially progressive and educationally beneficial; university employees can be organized—and thereby an important element in the education of the student radical.

But the new politics is still contained; it struggles below the surface of apathy, awaiting liberation. Few anticipate the break-through and fewer still exhort labor to begin. Labor continues to be the most liberal—and most frustrated—institution in mainstream America.

4.   Since the Democratic Party sweep in 1958, there have been exaggerated but real efforts to establish a liberal force in Congress, not to balance but to at least voice criticism of the conservative mood. The most notable of these efforts was the Liberal Project begun early in 1959 by Representative Kastenmeier of Wisconsin. The Project was neither disciplined nor very influential but it was concerned at least with confronting basic domestic and foreign problems, in concert with several liberal intellectuals.

In 1960 five members of the Project were defeated at the polls (for reasons other than their membership in the Project). Then followed a "post mortem" publication of *The Liberal Papers*, materials discussed by the Project when it was in existence. Republican leaders called the book "further out than Communism." The New Frontier Administration repudiated any connection with the statements. Some former members of the Project even disclaimed their past roles.

A hopeful beginning came to a shameful end. But during the demise of the Project, a new spirit of Democratic Party reform was occurring: in New York City, Ithaca, Massachusetts, Connecticut, Texas, California, and even in Mississippi and Alabama where Negro candidates for Congress challenged racist political power. Some were for peace, some for the liberal side of the New Frontier, some for realignment of the parties—and in most cases they were supported by students.

Here and there were stirrings of organized discontent with the political stalemate. Americans for Democratic Action and the *New Republic*, pillars of the liberal community, took stands against the President on nuclear testing. A split, extremely slight thus far, developed in organized labor on the same issue. The Rev. Martin Luther King, Jr., preached against the Dixiecrat-Republican coalition across the nation.

5. From 1960 to 1962, the campuses experienced a revival of idealism among an active few. Triggered by the impact of the sit-ins, students began to struggle for integration, civil liberties, student rights, peace, and against the fast-rising right-wing "revolt" as well. The liberal students, too, have felt their urgency thwarted by conventional channels: from student governments to Congressional committees. Out of this alienation from existing channels has come the creation of new ones; the most characteristic forms of liberal-radical student organizations are the dozens of campus political parties, political journals, and peace marches and demonstrations. In only a few cases have students built bridges to power: an occasional election campaign, the sit-ins, Freedom Rides, and voter registration activities; in some relatively large Northern demonstrations for peace and civil rights, and infrequently, through the United States National Student Association whose notable work has not been focused on political change.

These contemporary social movements—for peace, civil liberties, labor—have in common certain values and goals. The fight for peace is one for a stable and racially integrated world; for an end to the inherently volatile exploitation of most of mankind by irresponsible elites, and for freedom of economic, political and cultural organization. The fight for civil rights is also one for social welfare for all Americans; for free speech and the right to protest; for the shield of economic independence and bargaining power; for the reduction of the arms race which takes national attention and resources away from the problems of domestic injustices. Labor's fight for jobs and wages is also one against exploitation of the Negro as a source of cheap labor; for the right of petition and strike; for world industrialization; for the stability of a peacetime economy instead of the instability of a war-time economy; for expansion of the welfare state. The fight for a liberal Congress is a fight for a platform from which these concerns can issue. And the fight for students, for internal democracy in the university, is a fight to gain a forum for the issues.

But these scattered movements have more in common: a need for their concerns to be expressed by a political party responsible to their interests. That they have no political expression, no political channels, can be traced in large measure to the existence of a Democratic Party which tolerates the perverse unity of liberalism and racism, prevents the social change wanted by Negroes, peace protesters, labor unions, students, reform Democrats, and other liberals. Worse, the party stalemate prevents even the raising of controversy—a full Congressional assault on racial discrimination, disengagement in Central Europe, sweeping urban reform, disarmament and inspection, public regulation of major industries; these and other issues are never heard in the body that is supposed to represent the best thoughts and interests of all Americans.

An imperative task for these publicly disinherited groups, then, is to demand a Democratic Party responsible to their interests. They must support Southern voter registration and Negro political candidates and demand that Democratic Party liberals do the same (in the last Congress, Dixicrats split with Northern Democrats on 119 of 300 roll-calls, mostly on civil rights, area redevelopment, and foreign aid bills; the breach was much larger than in the previous several sessions). Labor (either independent or Democratic) should be formed to run against big city regimes on such issues as peace, civil rights, and urban needs. Demonstrations should be held at every Congressional or convention seating of Dixiecrats. A massive publicity and research campaign should be initiated, showing to every housewife, doctor, professor, and worker the damage done to their interests every day a racist occupies a place in the Democratic Party. Where possible, the peace movement should challenge the "peace credentials" of the otherwise-liberals by threatening or actually running candidates against them.

THE UNIVERSITY AND SOCIAL CHANGE

There is perhaps little reason to be optimistic about the above analysis. True, the Dixiecrat-GOP coalition is the weakest point in the dominating complex of corporate, military and political power. But the civil rights, peace, and student movements are too poor and socially slighted, and the labor movement too quiescent, to be counted with enthusiasm. From where else can power and vision be summoned? We believe that the universities are an overlooked seat of influence.

First, the university is located in a permanent position of social influence. Its educational function makes it indispensable and automatically makes it a crucial institution in the formation of social attitudes. Second, in an unbelievably complicated world, it is the central institution for organizing, evaluating, and transmitting knowledge. Third, the extent to which academic resources presently are used to buttress immoral social practice is revealed first, by the extent to which defense contracts make the universities engineers of the arms race. Too, the use of modern social science as a manipulative tool reveals itself in the "human relations" consultants to the modern corporations, who introduce trivial sops to give laborers feelings of "participation" or "belonging," while actually deluding them in order to further exploit their labor. And, of course, the use of motivational research is already infamous as a manipulative aspect of American politics. But these social uses of the universities' resources also demonstrate the unchangeable reliance by men of power on the men and storehouses of knowledge: this makes the university functionally tied to society in new ways, revealing new potentialities, new levers for change. Fourth, the university is the only mainstream institution that is open to participation by individuals of nearly any viewpoint.

These, at least, are facts, no matter how dull the teaching, how paternalistic the rules, how irrelevant the research that goes on. Social relevance, the accessibility to knowledge, and internal openness—these together make the university a potential base and agency in a movement of social change.

1. Any new left in America must be, in large measure, a left with real intellectual skills, committed to deliberativeness, honesty, reflection as working tools. The university permits the political life to be an adjunct to the academic one, and action to be informed by reason.

2. A new left must be distributed in significant social roles throughout the country. The universities are distributed in such a manner.

3. A new left must consist of younger people who matured in the post-war world, and partially be directed to the recruitment of younger people. The university is an obvious beginning point.

4. A new left must include liberals and socialists, the former for their relevance, the latter for their sense of thoroughgoing reforms in the system. The university is a more sensible place than a political party for these two traditions to begin to discuss their differences and look for political synthesis.

5. A new left must start controversy across the land, if national policies and national apathy are to be reversed. The ideal university is a community of controversy, within itself and in its effects on communities beyond.

6. A new left must transform modern complexity into issues that can be understood and felt close-up by every human being. It must give

form to the feelings of helplessness and indifference, so that people may see the political, social, and economic sources of their private troubles and organize to change society. In a time of supposed prosperity, moral complacency, and political manipulation, a new left cannot rely on only aching stomachs to be the engine force of social reform. The case for change, for alternatives that will involve uncomfortable personal efforts, must be argued as never before. The university is a relevant place for all of these activities.

But we need not indulge in illusions: the university system cannot complete a movement of ordinary people making demands for a better life. From its schools and colleges across the nation, a militant left might awaken its allies, and by beginning the process towards peace, civil rights, and labor struggles, reinsert theory and idealism where too often reign confusion and political barter. The power of students and faculty united is not only potential; it has shown its actuality in the South, and in the reform movements of the North.

The bridge to political power, though, will be built through genuine cooperation, locally, nationally, and internationally, between a new left of young people, and an awakening community of allies. In each community we must look within the university and act with confidence that we can be powerful, but we must look outwards to the less exotic but more lasting struggles for justice.

To turn these possibilities into realities will involve national efforts at university reform by an alliance of students and faculty. They must wrest control of the educational process from the administrative bureaucracy. They must make fraternal and functional contact with allies in labor, civil rights, and other liberal forces outside the campus. They must import major public issues into the curriculum—research and teaching on problems of war and peace is an oustanding example. They must make debate and controversy, not dull pedantic cant, the common style for educational life. They must consciously build a base for their assault upon the loci of power.

As students for a democratic society, we are committed to stimulating this kind of social movement, this kind of vision and program in campus and community across the country. If we appear to seek the unattainable, as it has been said, then let it be known that we do so to avoid the unimaginable.

The Triple Revolution

This statement is written in the recognition that mankind is at a historic conjuncture which demands a fundamental reexamination of existing values and institutions. At this time three separate and mutually reinforcing revolutions are taking place.

THE CYBERNATION REVOLUTION

A new era of production has begun. Its principles of organization are as different from those of the industrial era as those of the industrial era were different from the agricultural. The cybernation revolution has been brought about by the combination of the computer and the automated self-regulating machine. This results in a system of almost unlimited productive capacity which requires progressively less human labor. Cybernation is already reorganizing the economic and social system to meet its own needs.

THE WEAPONRY REVOLUTION

New forms of weaponry have been developed which cannot win wars but which can obliterate civilization. We are recognizing only now that the great weapons have eliminated war as a method for resolving international conflicts. The ever-present threat of total destruction is tempered by the knowledge of the final futility of war. The need of a "warless world" is generally recognized, though achieving it will be a long and frustrating process.

Excerpts from W.H. Ferry et al., *The Triple Revolution*, Santa Barbara, Calif.: The Ad Hoc Committee on the Triple Revolution, 1964. Reprinted with permission.

THE HUMAN RIGHTS REVOLUTION

A universal demand for full human rights is now clearly evident. It continues to be demonstrated in the civil rights movement within the United States. But this is only the local manifestation of a worldwide movement toward the establishment of social and political regimes in which every individual will feel valued and none will feel rejected on account of his race.

We are particularly concerned in this statement with the first of these revolutionary phenomena. This is not because we underestimate the significance of the other two. On the contrary, we affirm that it is the simultaneous occurrence and interaction of all three developments which make evident the necessity for radical alterations in attitude and policy. The adoption of just policies for coping with cybernation and for extending rights to all Americans is indispensable to the creation of an atmosphere in the U.S. in which the supreme issue, peace, can be reasonably debated and resolved.

The Negro claims, as a matter of simple justice, his full share in America's economic and social life. He sees adequate employment opportunities as a chief means of attaining this goal: The March on Washington demanded freedom *and* jobs. The Negro's claim to a job is not being met. Negroes are the hardest-hit of the many groups being exiled from the economy by cybernation. Negro unemployment rates cannot be expected to drop substantially. Promises of jobs are a cruel and dangerous hoax on hundreds of thousands of Negroes and whites alike who are especially vulnerable to cybernation because of age or inadequate education.

The demand of the civil rights movement cannot be fulfilled within the present context of society. The Negro is trying to enter a social community and a tradition of work-and-income which are in the process of vanishing even for the hitherto privileged white worker. Jobs are disappearing under the impact of highly efficient, progressively less costly machines.

The U.S. operates on the thesis, set out in the Employment Act of 1964, that every person will be able to obtain a job if he wishes to do so and that this job will provide him with resources adequate to live and maintain a family decently. Thus job-holding is the general mechanism through which economic resources are distributed. Those without work have access only to a minimal income, hardly sufficient to provide the necessities of life, and enabling those receiving it to function as only "minimum consumers." As a result, the goods and services which are needed by these crippled consumers, and which they would buy if they could, are not produced. This in turn deprives other workers of jobs, thus reducing their incomes and consumption.

Present excessive levels of unemployment would be multiplied several times if military and space expenditures did not continue to absorb 10% of the gross national product (i.e., the total goods and services produced). Some 6 to 8 million people are employed as a direct result of purchases for space and military activities. At least an equal number hold their jobs as an indirect result of military or space expenditures. In recent years, the military and space budgets have absorbed a rising proportion of national production and formed a strong support for the economy.

However, these expenditures are coming in for more and more criticism, at least partially in recognition of the fact that nuclear weapons have eliminated war as an acceptable method for resolving international conflicts. Early in 1964 President Johnson ordered a curtailment of certain military expenditures. Defense Secretary McNamara is closing shipyards, airfields, and Army bases, and Congress is pressing the National Space Administration to economize. The future of these strong props to the economy is not as clear today as it was even a year ago.

HOW THE CYBERNATION REVOLUTION SHAPES UP

Cybernation is manifesting the characteristics of a revolution in production. These include the development of radically different techniques and the subsequent appearance of novel principles of the organization of production; a basic reordering of man's relationship to his environment; and a dramatic increase in total available and potential energy.

The major difference between the agricultural, industrial and cybernation revolutions is the speed at which they developed. The agricultural revolution began several thousand years ago in the Middle East. Centuries passed in the shift from a subsistence base of hunting and food-gathering to settled agriculture.

In contrast, it has been less than 200 years since the emergence of the industrial revolution, and direct and accurate knowledge of the new productive techniques has reached most of mankind. This swift dissemination of information is generally held to be the main factor leading to widespread industrialization.

While the major aspects of the cybernation revolution are for the moment restricted to the U.S., its effects are observable almost at once throughout the industrial world and large parts of the non-industrial world. Observation is rapidly followed by analysis and criticism. The problems posed by the cybernation revolution are part of a new era in the history of all mankind but they are first being faced by the people of the U.S. The way Americans cope with cybernation will influence the course of this phenomenon everywhere. This country is the stage on which the machines-and-man drama will first be played for the world to witness.

The fundamental problem posed by the cybernation revolution in the U.S. is that it invalidates the general mechanism so far employed to undergird people's rights as consumers. Up to this time economic resources have been distributed on the basis of contributions to production, with machines and men competing for employment on somewhat equal terms. In the developing cybernated system, potentially unlimited output can be achieved by systems of machines which will require little cooperation from human beings. As machines take over production from men, they absorb an increasing proportion of resources while the men who are displaced become dependent on minimal and unrelated governmental measures—unemployment insurance, social security, welfare payments.

These measures are less and less able to disguise a historic paradox: That a substantial proportion of the population is subsisting on minimal incomes, often below the poverty line, at a time when sufficient productive potential is available to supply the needs of everyone in the U.S.

INDUSTRIAL SYSTEM FAILS TO PROVIDE
FOR ABOLITION OF POVERTY

The existence of this paradox is denied or ignored by conventional economic analysis. The general economic approach argues that potential demand, which if filled would raise the number of jobs and provide incomes to those holding them, is underestimated. Most contemporary economic analysis states that all of the available labor force and industrial capacity is required to meet the needs of consumers and industry and to provide adequate public services: Schools, parks, roads, homes, decent cities, and clean water and air. It is further argued that demand could be increased, by a variety of standard techniques, to any desired extent by providing money and machines to improve the conditions of the billions of impoverished people elsewhere in the world, who need food and shelter, clothes and machinery and everything else the industrial nations take for granted.

There is no question that cybernation does increase the potential for the provision of funds to neglected public sectors. Nor is there any question that cybernation would make possible the abolition of poverty at home and abroad. But the industrial system does not possess any adequate mechanisms to permit these potentials to become realities. The industrial system was designed to produce an ever-increasing quantity of goods as efficiently as possible, and it was assumed that the distribution of the power to purchase these goods would occur almost automatically. The continuance of the income-through-jobs link as the only major mechanism for distributing effective demand—for granting the right to consume—now acts as the main brake on the almost unlimited capacity of a cybernated productive system.

Recent administrations have proposed measures aimed at achieving a better distribution of resources, and at reducing unemployment and underemployment. A few of these proposals have been enacted. More often they have failed to secure congressional support. In every case, many members of Congress have criticized the proposed measures as departing from traditional principles for the allocation of resources and the encouragement of production. Abetted by budget-balancing economists and interest groups they have argued for the maintenance of an economic machine based on ideas of scarcity to deal with the facts of abundance produced by cybernation. This time-consuming criticism has slowed the workings of Congress and has thrown out of focus for that body the inter-related effects of the triple revolution.

An adequate distribution of the potential abundance of goods and services will be achieved only when it is understood that the major economic problem is not how to increase production but how to distribute the abundance that is the great potential of cybernation. There is an urgent need for a fundamental change in the mechanisms employed to insure consumer rights.

* * *

PROPOSAL FOR ACTION

As a first step to a new consensus it is essential to recognize that the traditional link between jobs and incomes is being broken. The economy of abundance can sustain all citizens in comfort and economic security whether or not they engage in what is commonly reckoned as work. Wealth produced by machines rather than by men is still wealth. We urge, therefore, that society, through its appropriate legal and governmental institutions, undertake an unqualified commitment to provide every individual and every family with an adequate income as a matter of right.

This undertaking we consider to be essential to the emerging economic, social and political order in this country. We regard it as the only policy by which the quarter of the nation now dispossessed and soon-to-be dispossessed by lack of employment can be brought within the abundant society. The unqualified right to an income would take the place of the patchwork of welfare measures—from unemployment insurance to relief—designed to ensure that no citizen or resident of the U.S. actually starves.

We do not pretend to visualize all of the consequences of this change in our values. It is clear, however, that the distribution of abundance in a cybernated society must be based on criteria strikingly different from those of an economic system based on scarcity. In retrospect, the establishment of the right to an income will prove to have been only the first step in the reconstruction of the value system of our society brought on by the triple revolution.

The present system encourages activities which can lead to private profit and neglects those activities which can enhance the wealth and the quality of life of our society. Consequently, national policy has hitherto been aimed far more at the welfare of the productive process than at the welfare of people. The era of cybernation can reverse this emphasis. With public policy and research concentrated on people rather than processes we believe that many creative activities and interests commonly thought of as non-economic will absorb the time and the commitment of many of those no longer needed to produce goods and services.

Society as a whole must encourage new modes of constructive, rewarding and ennobling activity. Principal among these are activities such as teaching and learning that relate people to people rather than people to things. Education has never been primarily conducted for profit in our society; it represents the first and most obvious activity inviting the expansion of the public sector to meet the needs of this period of transition.

We are not able to predict the long-run patterns of human activity and commitment in a nation when fewer and fewer people are involved in production of goods and services, nor are we able to forecast the over-all patterns of income distribution that will replace those of the past full employment system. However, these are not speculative and fanciful matters to be contemplated at leisure for a society that may come into existence in three or four generations. The outlines of the future press sharply into the present. The problems of joblessness, inadequate incomes, and frustrated lives confront us now; the American Negro, in his rebellion, asserts the demands—and the rights—of all the disadvantaged. The Negro's is the most insistent voice today, but behind him stand the millions of impoverished who are beginning to understand that cybernation, properly understood and used, is the road out of want and toward a decent life.

THE TRANSITION*

We recognize that the drastic alternations in circumstances and in our way of life ushered in by cybernation and the economy of abundance will not be completed overnight. Left to the ordinary forces of the market such change, however, will involve physical and psychological misery and perhaps political chaos. Such misery is already clearly evident among the unemployed, among relief clients into the third generation and more and more among the young and the old for whom society appears to hold no promise of dignified or even stable livess. We must develop programs for this transition designed to give hope to the

---

*This view of the transitional period is not shared by all the signers. Robert Theobald and James Boggs hold that the two major principles of the transitional period will be (1) that machines rather than men will take up new conventional work openings and (2) that the activity of men will be directed to new forms of "work" and "leisure." Therefore, in their opinion, the specific proposals outlined in this section are more suitable for meeting the problems of the scarcity-economic system than for advancing through the period of transition into the period of abundance.

dispossessed and those cast out by the economic system, and to provide a basis for the rallying of people to bring about those changes in political and social institutions which are essential to the age of technology.

The program here suggested is not intended to be inclusive but rather to indicate its necessary scope. We propose:

1. A massive program to build up our educational system, designed especially with the needs of the chronically under-educated in mind. We estimate that tens of thousands of employment opportunities in such areas as teaching and research and development, particularly for younger people, may thus be created. Federal programs looking to the training of an additional 100,000 teachers annually are needed.

2. Massive public works. The need is to develop and put into effect programs of public works to construct dams, reservoirs, ports, water and air pollution facilities, community recreation facilities. We estimate that for each $1 billion per year spent on public works 150,000 to 200,000 jobs would be created. $2 billion or more a year should be spent in this way, preferably as matching funds aimed at the relief of economically distressed or dislocated areas.

3. A massive program of low-cost housing, to be built both publicly and privately, and aimed at a rate of 700,000-1,000,000 units a year.

4. Development and financing of rapid transit systems, urban and interurban; and other programs to cope with the spreading problems of the great metropolitan centers.

5. A public power system built on the abundance of coal in distressed areas, designed for low-cost power to heavy industrial and residential sections.

6. Rehabilitation of obsolete military bases for community or educational use.

7. A major revision of our tax structure aimed at redistributing income as well as apportioning the costs of the transition period equitably. To this end an expansion of the use of excess profits tax would be important. Subsidies and tax credit plans are required to ease the human suffering involved in the transition of many industries from man power to machine power.

8. The trade unions can play an important and significant role in this period in a number of ways:

    a. Use of collective bargaining to negotiate not only for people at work but also for those thrown out of work by technological change.

b. Bargaining for perquisites such as housing, recreational facilities, and similar programs as they have negotiated health and welfare programs.

c. Obtaining a voice in the investment of the unions' huge pension and welfare funds, and insisting on investment policies which have as their major criteria the social use and function of the enterprise in which the investment is made.

d. Organization of the unemployed so that these voiceless people may once more be given a voice in their own economic destinies, and strengthening of the campaigns to organize white-collar and professional workers.

9. The use of the licensing power of government to regulate the speed and direction of cybernation to minimize hardship; and the use of minimum wage power as well as taxing powers to provide the incentives for moving as rapidly as possible toward the goals indicated by this paper.

These suggestions are in no way intended to be complete or definitively formulated. They contemplate expenditures of several billions more each year than are now being spent for socially rewarding enterprises and a larger role for the government in the economy than it has now or has been given except in times of crisis. In our opinion, this is a time of crisis, the crisis of a triple revolution. Public philosophy for the transition must rest on the conviction that our economic, social and political institutions exist for the use of man and that man does not exist to maintain a particular economic system. This philosophy centers on an understanding that governments are instituted among men for the purpose of making possible life, liberty, and the pursuit of happiness and that government should be a creative and positive instrument toward these ends.

CHANGE MUST BE MANAGED

The historic discovery of the post-World War II years is that the economic destiny of the nation can be managed. Since the debate over the Employment Act of 1946 it has been increasingly understood that the federal government bears primary responsibility for the economic and social well-being of the country. The essence of management is planning. The democratic requirement is planning by public bodies for the general welfare. Planning by private bodies such as corporations for their own welfare does not automatically result in additions to the general welfare, as the impact of cybernation on jobs has already made clear.

The hardships imposed by sudden changes in technology have been acknowledged by Congress in proposals for dealing with the long and short-run "dislocations," in legislation for depressed and "impacted" areas, retraining of workers replaced by machines, and the like. The measures so far proposed have not been "transitional" in conception. Perhaps for this reason they have had little effect on the situations they were designed to alleviate. But the primary weakness of this legislation is not ineffectiveness but incoherence. In no way can these disconnected measures be seen as a plan for remedying deep ailments but only, so to speak, as the superficial treatment of surface wounds.

Planning agencies should constitute the network through which pass the stated needs of the people at every level of society, gradually building into a national inventory of human requirements, arrived at by democratic debate of elected representatives.

The primary tasks of the appropriate planning institutions should be:

• To collect the data necessary to appraise the effects, social and economic, of cybernation at different rates of innovation.

• To recommend ways, by public and private initiative, of encouraging and stimulating cybernation.

• To work toward optimal allocations of human and natural resources in meeting the requirements of society.

• To develop ways to smooth the transition from a society in which the norm is full employment within an economic system based on scarcity, to one in which the norm will be either non-employment in the traditional sense of productive work, or employment on the great variety of socially valuable but "non-productive" tasks made possible by an economy of abundance; to bring about the conditions in which men and women no longer needed to produce goods and services may find their way to a variety of self-fulfilling and socially useful occupations.

• To work out alternatives to defense and related spending that will commend themselves to citizens, entrepreneurs and workers as a more reasonable use of common resources.

• To integrate domestic and international planning. The technological revolution has related virtually every major domestic problem to a world problem. The vast inequities between the industrialized and the underdeveloped countries cannot long be sustained.

The aim throughout will be the conscious and rational direction of economic life by planning institutions under democratic control.

In this changed framework the new planning institutions will operate at every level of government—local, regional and federal—and will be organized to elicit democratic participation in all their proceedings. These bodies will be the means for giving direction and content to the growing demand for improvement in all departments of public life. The planning institutions will show the way to turn the growing protest against ugly cities, polluted air and water, an inadequate educational system, disappearing recreational and material resources, low levels of medical care, and the haphazard economic development into an integrated effort to raise the level of general welfare.

We are encouraged by the record of the planning institutions both of the Common Market and of several European nations and believe that this country can benefit from studying their weaknesses and strengths.

A principal result of planning will be to step up investment in the public sector. Greater investment in this area is advocated because it is overdue, because the needs in this sector comprise a substantial part of the content of the general welfare, and because they can be readily afforded by an abundant society. Given the knowledge that we are now in a period of transition it would be deceptive, in our opinion, to present such activities as likely to produce full employment. The efficiencies of cybernation should be as much sought in the public as in the private sector, and a chief focus of planning would be one means of bringing this about. A central assumption of planning institutions would be the central assumption of this statement, that the nation is moving into a society in which production of goods and services is not the only or perhaps the chief means of distributing income.

THE DEMOCRATIZATION OF CHANGE

The revolution in weaponry gives some dim promise that mankind many finally eliminate institutionalized force as the method of settling international conflict and find for it political and moral equivalents leading to a better world. The Negro revolution signals the ultimate admission of this group to the American community on equal social, political and economic terms. The cybernation revolution proffers an existence qualitatively richer in democratic as well as material values. A social order in which men make the decisions that shape their lives becomes more possible now than ever before; the unshackling of men from the bonds of unfulfilling labor frees them to become citizens, to make themselves and to make their own history.

But these enhanced promises by no means constitute a guarantee. Illuminating and making more possible the "democratic vistas" is one thing; reaching them is quite another, for a vision of democratic life is made real not by technological change but by men consciously moving toward that ideal and creating institutions that will realize and nourish the vision in living form.

Democracy, as we use the term, means a community of men and women who are able to understand, express and determine their lives as dignified human beings. Democracy can only be rooted in a political and economic order in which wealth is distributed by and for people, and used for the widest social benefit. With the emergence of the era of abundance we have the economic base for a true democracy of participation, in which men no longer need to feel themselves prisoners of social forces and decisions beyond their control or comprehension.

One-Dimensional Man

Herbert Marcuse

CONCLUSION

The advancing one-dimensional society alters the relation between the rational and the irrational. Contrasted with the fantastic and insane aspects of its rationality, the realm of the irrational becomes the home of the really rational—of the ideas which may "promote the art of life." If the established society manages all normal communication, validating or invalidating it in accordance with social requirements, then the values alien to these requirements may perhaps have no other medium of communication than the abnormal one of fiction. The aesthetic dimension still retains a freedom of expression which enables the writer and artist to call men and things by their name—to name the otherwise unnameable.

The real face of our time shows in Samuel Beckett's novels; its real history is written in Rolf Hochhut's play *Der Stellvertreter*. It is no longer imagination which speaks here, but Reason, in a reality which justifies everything and absolves everything—except the sin against its spirit. Imagination is abdicating to this reality, which is catching up with and overtaking imagination. Auschwitz continues to haunt, not the memory but the accomplishments of man—the space flights; the rockets and missiles; the "labyrinthine basement under the Snack Bar"; the pretty electronic plants, clean, hygienic and with flower beds; the poison gas which is not really harmful to people; the secrecy in which we all

Herbert Marcuse, *One-Dimensional Man*, Boston: Beacon Press, 1964, pp. 247–57. Reprinted with permission.

participate. This is the setting in which the great human achievements of science, medicine, technology take place; the efforts to save and ameliorate life are the sole promise in the disaster. The willful play with fantastic possibilities, the ability to act with good conscience, *contra naturam*, to experiment with men and things, to convert illusion into reality and fiction into truth, testify to the extent to which Imagination has become an instrument of progress. And it is one which, like others in the established societies, is methodically abused. Setting the pace and style of politics, the power of imagination far exceeds Alice in Wonderland in the manipulation of words, turning sense into nonsense and nonsense into sense.

The formerly antagonistic realms merge on technical and political grounds—magic and science, life and death, joy and misery. Beauty reveals its terror as highly classified nuclear plants and laboratories become "Industrial Parks" in pleasing surroundings; Civil Defense Headquarters display a "deluxe fallout-shelter" with wall-to-wall carpeting ("soft"), lounge chairs, television, and Scrabble, "designed as a combination family room during peacetime (sic!) and family fallout shelter should war break out."[1] If the horror of such realizations does not penetrate into consciousness, if it is readily taken for granted, it is because these achievements are (a) perfectly rational in terms of the existing order, (b) tokens of human ingenuity and power beyond the traditional limits of imagination.

The obscene merger of aesthetics and reality refutes the philosophies which oppose "poetic" imagination to scientific and empirical Reason. Technological progress is accompanied by a progressive rationalization and even realization of the imaginary. The archetypes of horror as well as of joy, of war as well as of peace lose their catastrophic character. Their appearance in the daily life of the individuals is no longer that of irrational forces—their modern avatars are elements of technological domination, and subject to it.

In reducing and even canceling the romantic space of imagination, society has forced the imagination to prove itself on new grounds, on which the images are translated into historical capabilities and projects. The translation will be as bad and distorted as the society which undertakes it. Separated from the realm of material production and material needs, imagination was mere play, invalid in the realm of necessity, and committed only to a fantastic logic and a fantastic truth. When technical progress cancels this separation, it invests the images with its own logic and its own truth; it reduces the free faculty of the mind. But it also reduces the gap between imagination and Reason. The two antagonistic faculties become interdependent on common ground. In the light of the capabilities of advanced industrial civilization, is not all play of the imagination playing with technical possibilities, which can be tested as to their chances of realization? The romantic idea of a "science of the Imagination" seems to assume an ever-more-empirical aspect.

The scientific, rational character of Imagination has long since been recognized in mathematics, in the hypotheses and experiments of the physical sciences. It is likewise recognized in psychoanalysis, which is in theory based on the acceptance of the specific rationality of the irrational; the comprehended imagination becomes, redirected, a therapeutic force. But this therapeutic force may go much further than in the cure of neuroses. It was not a poet but a scientist who has outlined this prospect:

> Toute une psychanalyse matérielle peut... nous aider à guérir de nos images, ou du moins nous aider à limiter l'emprise de nos images. On peut alors espérer... *pouvoir rendre l'imagination heureuse,* autrement dit, pouvoir donner bonne conscience à l'imagination, en lui accordant pleinement tous ses moyens d'expression, toutes les images matérielles qui se produisent dans les *rêves naturels,* dans l'activité onorique normale. Rendre heureuse l'imagination, lui accorder toute son exubérance, c'est précisément donner à l'imagination sa véritable fonction d'entraînement psychique.[2]

Imagination has not remained immune to the process of reification. We are possessed by our images, suffer our own images. Psychoanalysis knew it well, and knew the consequences. However, "to give to the imagination all the means of expression" would be regression. The mutilated individuals (mutilated also in their faculty of imagination) would organize and destroy even more than they are now permitted to do. Such release would be the unmitigated horror—not the catastrophe of culture, but the free sweep of its most repressive tendencies. Rational is the imagination which can become the *a priori* of the reconstruction and redirection of the productive apparatus toward a pacified existence, a life without fear. And this can never be the imagination of those who are possessed by the images of domination and death.

To liberate the imagination so that it can be given all its means of expression presupposes the repression of much that is now free and that perpetuates a repressive society. And such reversal is not a matter of psychology or ethics but of politics, in the sense in which this term has here been used throughout: the practice in which the basic societal institutions are developed, defined, sustained, and changed. It is the practice of individuals, no matter how organized they may be. Thus the question once again must be faced: how can the administered individuals—who have made their mutilation into their own liberties and satisfactions, and thus reproduce it on an enlarged scale—liberate themselves from themselves as well as from their masters? How is it even thinkable that the vicious circle be broken?

Paradoxically, it seems that it is not the notion of the new societal *institutions* which presents the greatest difficulty in the attempt to answer this question. The established societies themselves are changing, or have already changed the basic institutions in the direction of increased planning. Since the development and utilization of all available resources for the universal satisfaction of vital needs is the prerequisite of pacification, it is incompatible with the prevalence of particular interests which stand in the way of attaining this goal. Qualitative change is conditional upon planning for the whole against these interests, and a free and rational society can emerge only on this basis.

The institutions within which pacification can be envisaged thus defy the traditional classification into authoritarian and democratic, centralized and liberal administration. Today, the opposition to central planning in the name of a liberal democracy which is denied in reality serves as an ideological prop for repressive interests. The goal of authentic self-determination by the individuals depends on effective social control over the production and distribution of the necessities (in terms of the achieved level of culture, material and intellectual).

Here, technological rationality, stripped of its exploitative features, is the sole standard and guide in planning and developing the available resources for all. Self-determination in the production and distribution of vital goods and services would be wasteful. The job is a technical one, and as a truly technical job, it makes for the reduction of physical and mental toil. In this realm, centralized control is rational if it establishes the preconditions for meaningful self-determination. The latter can then become effective in its own realm—in the decisions which involve the production and distribution of the economic surplus, and in the individual existence.

In any case, the combination of centralized authority and direct democracy is subject to infinite variations, according to the degree of development. Self-determination will be real to the extent to which the masses have been dissolved into individuals liberated from all propaganda, indoctrination, and manipulation, capable of knowing and comprehending the facts and of evaluating the alternatives. In other words, society would be rational and free to the extent to which it is organized, sustained, and reproduced by an essentially new historical Subject.

At the present stage of development of the advanced industrial societies, the material as well as the cultural system denies this exigency. The power and efficiency of this system, the thorough assimilation of mind with fact, militate against the emergence of a new Subject. They also militate against the notion that the replacement of the prevailing control over the productive process by "control from below" would mean the advent of qualitative change. This notion was valid, and still is valid, where the laborers were, and still are, the living denial and indictment of the established society. However, where these classes have become a prop of the established way of life, their ascent to control would prolong this way in a different setting.

And yet, the facts are all there which validate the critical theory of this society and of its fatal development: the increasing irrationality of the whole; waste and restriction of productivity; the need for aggressive expansion; the constant threat of war; intensified exploitation; dehumanization. And they all point to the historical alternative: the planned utilization of resources for the satisfaction of vital needs with a minimum of toil, the transformation of leisure into free time, the pacification of the struggle for existence.

But the facts and the alternatives are there like fragments which do not connect, or like a world of mute objects without a subject, without the practice which would move these objects in the new direction. Dialetical theory is not refuted, but it cannot offer the remedy. It cannot be positive. To be sure, the dialetical concept, in comprehending the given facts, transcends the given facts. This is the very token of its truth. It defines the historical possibilities, even necessities; but their realization can only be in the practice which responds to the theory, and, at present, the practice gives no such response.

On theoretical as well as empirical grounds, the dialectical concept pronounces its own hopelessness. The human reality is its history and, in it, contradictions do not explode by themselves. The conflict between streamlined, rewarding domination on the one hand, and its achievements that make for self-determination and pacification on the other, may become blatant beyond any possible denial, but it may well continue to be a manageable and even productive conflict, for with the growth in the technological conquest of nature grows the conquest of man by man. And this conquest reduces the freedom which is a necessary *a priori* of liberation. This is freedom of thought in the only sense in which thought can be free in the administered world—as the consciousness of its repressive productivity, and as the absolute need for breaking out of this whole. But precisely this absolute need does not prevail where it could become the driving force of a historical practice, the effective cause of qualitative change. Without this material force, even the most acute consciousness remains powerless.

No matter how obvious the irrational character of the whole may manifest itself and, with it, the necessity of change, insight into necessity has never sufficed for seizing the possible alternatives. Confronted with the omnipresent efficiency of the given system of life, its alternatives have always appeared utopian. And insight into necessity, the consciousness of the evil state, will not suffice even at the stage where the accomplishments of science and the level of productivity have eliminated the utopian features of the alternatives—where the established reality rather than its opposite is utopian.

Does this mean that the critical theory of society abdicates and leaves the field to an empirical sociology which, freed from all theoretical guidance except a methodological one, succumbs to the fallacies of misplaced concreteness, thus performing an ideological service while proclaiming the elimination of value judgments? Or do the dialectical concepts once again testify to their truth—by comprehending their own situation as that of the society which they analyze? A response might suggest itself if one considers the critical theory precisely at the point of its greatest weakness—its ability to demonstrate the liberating tendencies *within* the established society.

The critical theory of society, was, at the time of its origin, confronted with the presence of real forces (objective and subjective) *in* the established society which moved (or could be guided to move) toward more rational and freer institutions by abolishing the existing ones which had become obstacles to progress. These were the empirical grounds on which the theory was erected, and from these empirical grounds derived the idea of the liberation of *inherent* possibilities—the development, otherwise blocked and distorted, of material and intellectual productivity, faculties, and needs. Without the demonstration of such forces, the critique of society would still be valid and rational, but it would be incapable of translating its rationality into terms of historical practice. The conclusion? "Liberation of inherent possibilities" no longer adequately expresses the historical alternative.

The enchained possibilities of advanced industrial societies are: development of the productive forces on an enlarged scale, extension of the conquest of nature, growing satisfaction of needs for a growing number of people, creation of new needs and faculties. But these possibilities are gradually being realized through means and institutions which cancel their liberating potential, and this process affects not only the means but also the ends. The instruments of productivity and progress, organized into a totalitarian system, determine not only the actual but also the possible utilizations.

At its most advanced stage, domination functions as administration, and in the overdeveloped areas of mass consumption, the administered life becomes the good life of the whole, in the defense of which the opposites are united. This is the pure form of domination. Conversely, its negation appears to be the pure form of negation. All content seems reduced to the one abstract demand for the end of domination—the only truly revolutionary exigency, and the event that would validate the achievements of industrial civilization. In the face of its efficient denial by the established system, this negation appears in the politically impotent form of the "absolute refusal"—a refusal which seems the more unreasonable the more the established system develops its productivity and alleviates the burden of life. In the words of Maurice Blanchot:

> "Ce que nous refusons n'est pas sans valeur ni sans importance. C'est bien à cause de cela que le refus est nécessaire. Il y a une raison que nous n'accepterons plus, il y a une apparence de sagesse qui nous fait horreur, il y a une offre d'accord et de conciliation que nous n'entendrons pas. Une rupture s'est produite. Nous avons été ramenés à cette franchise qui ne tolère plus la complicité."[3]

But if the abstract character of the refusal is the result of total reification, then the concrete ground for refusal must still exist, for reification is an illusion. By the same token, the unification of opposites in the medium of technological rationality must be, *in all its reality*, an illusory unification, which eliminates neither the contradiction between the growing productivity and its repressive use, nor the vital need for solving the contradiction.

But the struggle for the solution has outgrown the traditional forms. The totalitarian tendencies of the one-dimensional society render the traditional ways and means of protest ineffective—perhaps even dangerous because they preserve the illusion of popular sovereignty. This illusion contains some truth: "the people," previously the ferment of social change, have "moved up" to become the ferment of social cohesion. Here rather than in the redistribution of wealth and equalization of classes is the new stratification characteristic of advanced industrial society.

However, underneath the conservative popular base is the substratum of the outcasts and outsiders, the exploited and persecuted of other races and other colors, the unemployed and the unemployable. They exist outside the democratic process; their life is the most immediate and the most real need for ending intolerable conditions and institutions. Thus their opposition is revolutionary even if their consciousness is not. Their opposition hits the system from without and is therefore not deflected by the system; it is an elementary force which violates the rules of the game and, in doing so, reveals it as a rigged game. When they get together and go out into the streets, without arms, without protection, in order to ask for the most primitive civil rights, they know that they face dogs, stones, and bombs, jail, concentration camps, even death. Their force is behind every political demonstration for the victims of law and order. The fact that they start refusing to play the game may be the fact which marks the beginning of the end of a period.

Nothing indicates that it will be a good end. The economic and technical capabilities of the established societies are sufficiently vast to allow for adjustments and concessions to the underdog, and their armed forces sufficiently trained and equipped to take care of emergency situations. However, the spectre is there again, inside and outside the frontiers of the advanced societies. The facile historical parallel with the barbarians threatening the empire of civilization prejudges the issue; the second period of barbarism may well be the continued empire of civilization itself. But the chance is that, in this period, the historical extremes may meet again: the most advanced consciousness of humanity, and its most exploited force. It is nothing but a chance. The critical theory of society possesses no concepts which could bridge the gap between the present and its future; holding no promise and showing no success, it remains negative. Thus it wants to remain loyal to those who, without hope, have given and give their life to the Great Refusal.

At the beginning of the fascist era, Walter Benjamin wrote:

Nur um der Hoffnungslosen willen ist uns die Hoffnung gegeben.
It is only for the sake of those without hope that hope is given to us.

NOTES

1.   According to *The New York Times*, November 11, 1960, displayed at the New York City Civil Defense Headquarters, Lexington Ave. and Fifty-fifth Street.

2.   "An entire psychoanalysis of matter can help us to cure us of our images or at least help us to limit the hold of our images on us. One may then hope *to be able to render imagination happy*, to give it good conscience in allowing it fully all its means of expression, all material images which emerge in *natural dreams*, in normal dream activity. To render imagination happy, to allow it all its exuberance, means precisely to grant imagination its true function as psychological impulse and force." Gaston Bachelard, *Le Matérialisme rationnel* (Paris, Presses Universitaires, 1953), p. 18 (Bachelard's emphasis).

3.   "What we refuse is not without value or importance. Precisely because of that, the refusal is necessary. There is a reason which we no longer accept, there is an appearance of wisdom which horrifies us, there is a plea for agreement and conciliation which we will no longer heed. A break has occurred. We have been reduced to that frankness which no longer tolerates complicity." "Le Refus," in *Le 14 Juillet*, no. 2, Paris, Octobre 1958.

Speech to the April 17, 1965 March on Washington

Paul Potter

After two hours of picketing the White House, the president of the Students for a Democratic Society, Paul Potter, closed a meeting in front of the Washington Monument with the following speech:

Most of us grew up thinking that the United States was a strong but humble nation, that involved itself in world affairs only reluctantly, that respected the integrity of other nations and other systems, and that engaged in wars only as a last resort. This was a nation with no large standing army, with no design for external conquest, that sought primarily the opportunity to develop its own resources and its own mode of living. If at some point we began to hear vague and disturbing things about what this country had done in Latin America, China, Spain and other places, we somehow remained confident about the basic integrity of this nation's foreign policy. The Cold War with all of its neat categories and black and white descriptions did much to assure us that what we had been taught to believe was true.

But in recent years, the withdrawal from the hysteria of the Cold War era and the development of a more aggressive, activist foreign policy have done much to force many of us to rethink attitudes that were deep and basic sentiments about our country. The incredible war in Vietnam has provided the razor, the terrifying sharp cutting edge that has finally severed the last vestige of illusion that morality and democracy are the guiding principles of American foreign policy. The saccharine self-righteous moralism that promises the Vietnamese a billion dollars of economic aid at the very moment we are delivering billions for economic and social destruction and political repression is rapidly losing what power it might ever have had to reassure us about the decency of our foreign policy. The further we explore the reality of what this country is doing and planning in Vietnam the more we are driven toward the conclusion of Senator Morse that the United States may well be the greatest threat to peace in the world today. That is a terrible and bitter insight for people who grew up as we did—and our revulsion at that insight, our refusal to accept it as inevitable or necessary, is one of the reasons that so many people have come here today.

The President says that we are defending freedom in Vietnam. Whose freedom? Not the freedom of the Vietnamese. The first act of the first dictator, Diem, the United States installed in Vietnam, was to systematically begin the persecution of all political opposition, non-Communist as well as Communist. The first American military supplies were not used to fight Communist insurgents; they were used to control, imprison or kill any who sought something better for Vietnam than the personal aggrandizement, political corruption and the profiteering of the Diem regime. The elite of the forces that we have trained and equipped are *still* used to control political unrest in Saigon and defend the latest dictator from the people.

And yet in a world where dictatorships are so commonplace and popular control of government so rare, people become callous to the misery that is implied by dictatorial power. The rationalizations that are used to defend political despotism have been drummed into us so long that we have somehow become numb to the possibility that something else might exist. And it is only the kind of terror we see now in Vietnam that awakens conscience and reminds us that there is something deep in us that cries out against dictatorial suppression.

The pattern of repression and destruction that we have developed and justified in the war is so thorough that it can only be called cultural genocide. I am not simply talking about napalm or gas or crop destruction or torture, hurled indiscriminately on women and children, insurgent and neutral, upon the first suspicion of rebel activity. That in itself is horrendous and incredible beyond belief. But it is only part of a larger pattern of destruction to the very fabric of the country. We have uprooted the people from the land and imprisoned them in concentration camps called "sunrise villages." Through conscription and direct political intervention and control, we have destroyed local customs and traditions, trampled upon those things of value which give dignity and purpose to life.

What is left to the people of Vietnam after 20 years of war? What part of themselves and their own lives will those who survive be able to salvage from the wreckage of their country or build on the "peace" and "security" our Great Society offers them in reward for their allegiance? How can anyone be surprised that people who have had total war waged on themselves and their culture rebel in increasing numbers against that tyranny? What other course is available? And still our only response to rebellion is more vigorous repression, more merciless opposition to the social and cultural institutions which sustain dignity and the will to resist.

Not even the President can say that this is a war to defend the freedom of the Vietnamese people. Perhaps what the President means when he speaks of freedom is the freedom of the American people.

What in fact has the war done for freedom in America? It has led to even more vigorous governmental efforts to control information, manipulate the press and pressure and persuade the public through distorted or downright dishonest documents such as the White Paper on Vietnam. It has led to the confiscation of films and other anti-war material and the vigorous harassment by the FBI of some of the people who have been most outspokenly active in their criticism of the war. As the war escalates and the administration seeks more actively to gain suport for any initiative it may choose to take, there has been the beginnings of a war psychology unlike anything that has burdened this country since the 1950s. How much more of Mr. Johnson's freedom can we stand? How much freedom will be left in this country if there is a major war in Asia? By what weird logic can it be said that the freedom of one people can only be maintained by crushing another?

In many ways this is an unusual march because the large majority of people here are not involved in a peace movement as their primary basis of concern. What is exciting about the participants in this march is that so many of us view ourselves consciously as participants as well in a movement to build a more decent society. There are students here who have been involved in protests over the quality and kind of education they are receiving in growingly bureaucratized, depersonalized institutions called universities; there are Negroes from Mississippi and Alabama who are struggling against the tyranny and repression of those states; there are poor people here—Negro and white—from Northern urban areas who are attempting to build movements that abolish poverty and secure democracy; there are faculty who are beginning to question the relevance of their institutions to the critical problems facing the society. Where will these people and the movements they are a part of be if the President is allowed to expand the war in Asia? What happens to the hopeful beginnings of expressed discontent that are trying to shift American attention to long-neglected internal priorities of shared abundance, democracy and decency at home when those priorities have to compete with the all-consuming priorities and psychology of a war against an enemy thousands of miles away?

The President mocks freedom if he insists that the war in Vietnam is a defense of American freedom. Perhaps the only freedom that this war protects is the freedom of the warhawks in the Pentagon and the State Department to experiment with counter-insurgency and guerrilla warfare in Vietnam.

Vietnam, we may say, is a laboratory run by a new breed of gamesmen who approach war as a kind of rational exercise in international power politics. It is the testing ground and staging area for a new American response to the social revolution that is sweeping through the impoverished downtrodden areas of the world. It is the beginning of the American counter-revolution, and so far no one—none of us—not the *N.Y. Times*, nor 17 Neutral Nations, nor dozens of worried allies, nor the United States Congress have been able to interfere with the freedom of the President and the Pentagon to carry out that experiment.

Thus far the war in Vietnam has only dramatized the demand of ordinary people to have some opportunity to make their own lives, and of their unwillingness, even under incredible odds, to give up the struggle against external domination. We are told, however, that the struggle can be legitimately suppressed since it might lead to the development of a Communist system, and before that ultimate menace all criticism is supposed to melt.

This is a critical point and there are several things that must be said here—not by way of celebration, but because I think they are the truth. First, if this country were serious about giving the people of Vietnam some alternative to a Communist social revolution, that opportunity was sacrificed in 1954 when we helped to install Diem and his repression of non-Communist movements. There is no indication that we were serious about that goal—that we were ever willing to contemplate the risks of allowing the Vietnamese to choose their own destinies. Second, those people who insist now that Vietnam can be neutralized are for the most part looking for a sugar coating to cover the bitter pill. We must accept the consequences that calling for an end of the war in Vietnam is in fact allowing for the likelihood that a Vietnam without war will be a self-styled Communist Vietnam. Third, this country must come to understand that creation of a Communist country in the world today is not an ultimate defeat. If people are given the opportunity to choose their own lives it is likely that some of them will choose what we have called "Communist systems." We are not powerless in that situation. Recent years have finally and indisputably broken the myth that the Communist world is monolithic and have conclusively shown that American power can be significant in aiding countries dominated by greater powers to become more independent and self-determined. And yet the war that we are creating and escalating in Southeast Asia is rapidly eroding the base of independence of North Vietnam as it is forced to turn to China and the Soviet Union, involving them in the war and involving itself in the compromises that that implies. Fourth, I must say to you that I would rather see Vietnam Communist than see it under continuous subjugation of the ruin that American domination has brought.

But the war goes on; the freedom to conduct that war depends on the dehumanization not only of Vietnamese people but of Americans as well; it depends on the construction of a system of premises and thinking that insulates the President and his advisors thoroughly and completely from the human consequences of the decisions they make. I do not believe that the President or Mr. Rusk or Mr. McNamara or even McGeorge Bundy are particularly evil men. If asked to throw napalm on the back of a ten-year-old child they would shrink in horror—but their decisions have led to mutilation and death of thousands and thousands of people.

What kind of system is it that allows good men to make those kinds of decisions? What kind of system is it that justifies the United States or any country seizing the destinies of the Vietnamese people and using them callously for its own purpose? What kind of system is it that disenfranchises people in the South, leaves millions upon millions of people throughout the country impoverished and excluded from the mainstream and promise of American society, that creates faceless and terrible bureaucracies and makes those the place where people spend their lives and do their work, that consistently puts material values before human values—and still persists in calling itself free and still persists in finding itself fit to police the world? What place is there for ordinary men in that system and how are they to control it, make it bend itself to their wills rather than bending them to its?

We must name that system. We must name it, describe it, analyze it, understand it and change it. For it is only when that system is changed and brought under control that there can be any hope for stopping the forces that create a war in Vietnam today or a murder in the South tomorrow or all the incalculable, innumerable more subtle atrocities that are worked on people all over—all the time.

How do you stop a war then? If the war has its roots deep in the institutions of American society, how do you stop it? Do you march to Washington? Is that enough? Who will hear us? How can you make the decision makers hear us, insulated as they are, if they cannot hear the screams of a little girl burnt by napalm?

I believe that the administration is serious about expanding the war in Asia. The question is whether the people here are as serious about ending it. I wonder what it means for each of us to say we want to end the war in Vietnam—whether, if we accept the full meaning of that statement and the gravity of the situation, we can simply leave the march and go back to the routines of a society that acts as if it were not in the midst of a grave crisis. Maybe we, like the President, are insulated from the consequences of our own decision to end the war. Maybe we have yet really to listen to the screams of a burning child and decide that we cannot go back to whatever it is we did before today until that war has ended.

There is no simple plan, no scheme or gimmick that can be proposed here. There is no simple way to attack something that is deeply rooted in the society. If the people of this country are to end the war in Vietnam, and to change the institutions which create it, then the people of this country must create a massive social movement—and if that can be built around the issue of Vietnam then that is what we must do.

By a social movement I mean more than petitions or letters of protest, or tacit support of dissident Congressmen; I mean people who are willing to change their lives, who are willing to challenge the system, to take the problem of change seriously. By a social movement I mean an effort that is powerful enough to make the country understand that our problems are not in Vietnam, or China or Brazil or outer space or at the bottom of the ocean, but are here in the United States. What we must do is begin to build a democratic and humane society in which Vietnams are unthinkable, in which human life and initiative are precious. The reason there are twenty thousand people here today and not a hundred or none at all is because five years ago in the South students began to build a social movement to change the system. The reason there are poor people, Negro and white, housewives, faculty members, and many others here in Washington is because that movement has grown and spread and changed and reached out as an expression of the broad concerns of people throughout the society. The reason the war and the system it represents will be stopped, if it is stopped before it destroys all of us, will be because the movement has become strong enough to exact change in the society. Twenty thousand people, the people here, if they were serious, if they were willing to break out of their isolation and to accept the consequences of a decision to end the war and commit themselves to building a movement wherever they are and in whatever way they effectively can, would be, I'm convinced, enough.

To build a movement rather than a protest or some series of protests, to break out of our insulations and accept the consequences of our decisions, in effect to change our lives, means that we can open ourselves to the reactions of a society that believes it is moral and just, that we open ourselves to libeling and persecution, that we dare to be really seen as wrong in a society that doesn't tolerate fundamental challenges.

It means that we desert the security of our riches and reach out to people who are tied to the mythology of American power and make them part of our movement. We must reach out to every organization and individual in the country in the country and make them part of our movement.

But that means that we build a movement that works not simply in Washington but in communities and with the problems that face people throughout the society. That means that we build a movement that understands Vietnam in all its horror as but a symptom of a deeper malaise, that we build a movement that makes possible the implementation of the values that would have prevented Vietnam, a movement based on the integrity of man and a belief in man's capacity to tolerate all the weird formulations of society that men may choose to strive for; a movement that will build on the new and creative forms of protest that are beginning to emerge, such as the teach-in, and extend their efforts and intensify them; that we will build a movement that will find ways to support the increasing numbers of young men who are unwilling to and will not fight in Vietnam; a movement that will not tolerate the escalation or prolongation of this war but will, if necessary, respond to the administration war effort with massive civil disobedience all over the country, that will wrench the country into a confrontation with the issues of the war; a movement that must of necessity reach out to all these people in Vietnam or elsewhere who are struggling to find decency and control for their lives.

For in a strange way the people of Vietnam and the people in this demonstration are united in much more than a common concern that the war be ended. In both countries there are people struggling to build a movement that has the power to change their condition. The system that frustrates these movements is the same. All our lives, our destinies, our very hopes to live, depend on our ability to overcome that system.

An SDS Antiwar Leaflet:
November 27,1965

MARCH ON WASHINGTON

In the name of freedom, America is mutilating Vietnam. In the name of peace, America turns that fertile country into a wasteland. And in the name of democracy, America is burying its own dreams and suffocating its own potential.

Americans who can understand why the Negroes of Watts can rebel should understand too why Vietnamese can rebel. And those who know the American South and the grinding poverty of our Northern cities should understand that our real problems lie not in Vietnam but at home—that the fight we seek is not with Communism but with the social desperation that makes good men violent, both here and abroad.

The War Must Be Stopped

Our aim in Vietnam is the same as our aim in the United States: that oligarchic rule and privileged power be replaced by popular democracy where the people make the decisions which affect their lives and share in the abundance and opportunity that modern technology makes possible. This is the only solution for Vietnam in which Americans can find honor and take pride. Perhaps the war has already so embittered and devastated the Vietnamese that that ideal will require years of rebuilding. But the war cannot achieve it, nor can American military presence, nor our support of repressive unrepresentative governments.

The war must be stopped. There must be an immediate cease fire and demobilization in South Vietnam. There must be a withdrawal of American troops. Political amnesty must be guaranteed. All agreements must be ratified by the partisans of the "other side"—the National Liberation Front and North Vietnam.

We must not deceive ourselves: a negotiated agreement cannot **guarantee** democracy. Only the Vietnamese have the right of nationhood to make their government democratic or not, free or not, neutral or not. It is not America's role to deny them the chance to be what they will make of themselves. **That chance grows more remote with very American bomb that explodes in a Vietnamese village.**

But our hopes extend not only to Vietnam. Our chance is the first in a generation to organize the powerless and the voiceless at home to confront America with its racial injustice, its apathy, and its poverty, and with that same vision we dream for Vietnam: a vision of a society in which all can control their own destinies.

We are convinced that the only way to stop this and future wars is to organize a domestic social movement which challenges the very legitimacy of our foreign policy; this movement must also fight to end racism, to end the paternalism of our welfare system, to guarantee decent incomes for all, and to supplant the authoritarian control of our universities with a community of scholars.

This movement showed its potential when 25,000 people—students, the poverty-stricken, ministers, faculty, unionists, and others—marched on Washington last April. This movement must now show its force. SDS urges everyone who believes that our warmarking must be ended and our democracy-building must begin, **to join in a March on Washington on November 27, at 11 A.M. in front of the White House.**

The Look Is You

Naomi Jaffe and Bernardine Dohrn

Two tits and no head—as the representation, in glossy color, of the Women's Liberation Movement—is an apt example of Ramparts' success in making a commodity out of politics.

Over the past few months, small groups have been coming together in various cities to meet around the realization that as women radicals we are not radical women—that we are unfree within the Movement and in personal relationships, as in the society at large. We realize that women are organized into the Movement by men and continue to relate to it through men. We find that the difficulty women have in taking initiative and in acting and speaking in a political context is the consequence of internalizing the view that men define reality and women are defined in terms of men. We are coming together not in a defensive posture to rage at our exploited status vis a vis men, but rather in the process of developing our own autonomy, to expose the nature of American society in which all people are reified (manipulated as objects). We insist on a recognition of the organic connection of the unfreedom of all groups in society.

The consciousness that our under-developed abilities are not just personal failings but are deeply rooted in this society is an exhilarating and expressive breakthrough. There is the terror of giving up the roles through which we know how to obtain a certain measure of power and security. But again and again there is the rejoicing in the unexplored possibilities of becoming vital potent human beings.

Naomi Jaffe and Bernardine Dohrn, "The Look Is You," *New Left Notes*, March 18, 1968, p. 5.

By refusing to be kept separate from other women by feelings of dislike, jealousy, and competitiveness, we have begun to discuss and research ourselves in our context—to demystify the myth of women by analyzing the forces which have shaped us.

Women suffer only a particular form of the general social oppression, so our struggles to understand and break through society's repressive definitions of us are struggles which have to attack the foundations of that society—its power to define people according to the needs of an economy based on domination.

The dynamic of that economy is a changing technology, which creates an ever-greater scale of production. Lack of social control over this increasing production (the planned use of the productive forces for and by the people of the society) means that the goal of productivity is profit, and profit can only be sustained if markets can be found (or created) to absorb an increasing volume of goods.

This is the dynamic of imperialism—the relentless search for new markets which drains the resources of the Third World and cripples its independent economic development. It is also the dynamic of the domestic imperialism of consumption: the creation of internal markets through a process which defines persons as consumers and cripples their development as free human beings.

Women are the consummate products of that process. We are at the same time the beneficiaries and the victims of the productivity made possible by advanced technology. The innovations that offer us immediate freedom also force us into the service of an overall system of domination and repression. The more we realize ourselves through consumption the greater the power of commodities to define and delimit us. "Women must be liberated to desire new products." (market research executive)

The same new things that allow us to express our new sense of freedom and naturalness and movement—swingy, body-revealing clothing, fun-gimmicky accessories—are also used to force us to be the consumers of the endless flow of products necessary for the perpetuation of a repressive society. Mini-skirts and costume-clothes and high boots and transparent makeup are fun and expressive and pretty; at the same time they are self-expression through things—through acquiring rather than becoming—and it is the expression of all human needs through commodities which sustains an economy that has to produce and sell more and more goods in order to survive.

"But the real point about that swinging 16-to-24 group is not their spending power, but the fact that they have become market leaders. They have created a climate that has enabled fashion to catch on as a new force in the market, driving apparel expenditures higher and higher." (*Fortune*, October 1967)

The same rise in productivity that requires more consumption of more goods also creates more leisure time—so leisure time becomes consumption time, and consumption becomes increasingly a major sphere of life activity. A culture of consumption is created through the mass media, supported by the $16 billion-a-year advertising industry, to channel all potential human development into commodity form.

"Deeply set in human nature is the need to have a meaningful place in a group that strives for meaningful social goals. Whenever this is lacking, the individual becomes restless. Which explains why, as we talk to people across the nation, over and over again, we hear questions like these: 'What does it all mean?' 'Where am I going?' 'Why don't things seem more worthwhile when we all work so hard and have so darn many things to play with?' The question is: Can your product fill this gap?" (from an advertising agency report)

The increased economic importance of consumption is reflected most deeply in the role of women, who are said to make 75% of all family consumption decisions and at whom 75% of all advertising is directed. This consumption culture shapes us as women and as people into an essentially passive mode of being, which in turn enables us to be exploited in the productive sphere in meaningless, low-paying clerical jobs. Women are culturally manipulated to see our work roles as being of secondary importance (since we are defined primarily by our sexual roles); we therefore serve as a reserve army of labor for the lowest-status white-collar jobs, drawn into the labor force when needed, and told to find fulfillment at home when employment is slack.

Or, as in the case of professional and semi-professional women, our very status as "independent women" is the source of our exploitation, forcing us into work and leisure roles which reinforce an illusory image of freedom and creativity. The work-role demands of status and travel open new areas for the creation of commodity "needs," and professional women as consumers are used to create styles and tastes for the larger population.

So our passive roles as producers and consumers reinforce each other, and in turn are reinforced by and perpetuate our passive social-sexual roles. These roles are based on receptivity—being through acquiring objects, rather than becoming through projecting oneself onto the world to change it (active mastery of the world). Real control over one's life is not the same as the illusion deliberately created by commodity culture through a choice of commodities. "Choosing oneself" in commodity form is a choice pre-defined by a repressive system.

The passive-receptive woman role, a product of the structure and development of American society, increasingly defines the culture of that society. Men, too, do not control their environment or project themselves onto it to change it (potency). Although active mastery is still considered a male mode, it is increasingly irrelevant to a society based on the compulsive consumption of commodities. "What is self but a permanent mode of selection?" (advertising executive)

The relationships of a market economy are reflected and reinforced in the dynamic and the forms of human relationships. The real needs of people are translated into a currency of possession, exclusivity, and investment—a language of commodities in which people are the goods. Both men and women are manipulated into functioning within these categories; it is the uniquely visible condition of women as primarily sexual creatures—as decorative, tempting (passive-aggressive), pleasure-giving objects—which exposes the broader framework of social coercion.

Psychology, as a social institution, works in the service of this pacification of human needs and desires. Its categories begin with a historically-bound notion of the restrictive implications of female biology. ("Anatomy is destiny."—Freud) Concepts of women as mutilated men, penis envy, and the electra complex (a mechanical inversion of the oedipal situation) exemplify a society which produces people who are taught to experience themselves as objects. These definitions allow only the possibilities of a passive mode—at best, the liberalism of a "creative" resignation to fulfillment through realizing our feminity. (feminine equals intuitive—unobtrusive—servile—non-castrating—warm—sensitive—cuddly—supportive—rhythmic—good-smelling—sensuous—satisfying—creative, and so forth)

In our social-sexual roles, again, the innovations that offer us immediate freedom also force us into the service of an overall system of domination and repression. Technological emancipation from enslavement to our bodies (for example, The Pill as the Great Liberator) is offered to women as the realization of freedom now. "...almost every aspect of the New Girl's personality reflects her final freedom from the sexual status that was the fate of women in the past." (Playboy, January 1968)

But this greatly expanded area of permissive erotic gratification and personal control occurs inside the context of greater social control and dehumanization. The desublimation is repressive. The liberating potential of expressed sexuality is channeled into mutually exploitative relationships in which people are objects, and into the market economy in which sexuality is a cornerstone. Liberalized sex begins to define the shape and texture of leisure time—in a commodity framework. Again, we are beneficiaries and victims. Thus, a more sexually active role for women actually reinforces a broader passive mode of consumption.

If women are made into objects, the object-relationships between men and women make human communication and community impossible for both; if women are defined by their sexual roles, they are only a paradigm case of the reified role structures that stifle the creative spontaneity of men and women alike.

A strategy for the liberation of women, then, does not demand equal jobs (exploitation), but meaningful creative activity for all; not a larger share of power but the abolition of commodity tyranny; not equally reified sexual roles but an end to sexual objectification and exploitation; not equal aggressive leadership in the Movement, but the initiation of a new style of non-dominating leadership.

Our strategy will focus on the unique quality of our exploitation as women, primarily in our vanguard economic role as consumers. Women Power is the power to destroy a destructive system by refusing to play the part(s) assigned to us by it—by refusing to accept its definition of us as passive consumers, and by actively subverting the institutions which create and enforce that definition.

Columbia Liberated

The Columbia Strike Coordinating Committee

Something is happening here but you don't know
what it is, do you, Mr. Jones?

R. Dylan

"Up against the wall, motherfuckers!"

*Entire Math Commune to several
hundred members of the New
York City Police Dept.'s Tactical
Patrol Force, April 30, 1968.*

THE STRIKE IN CONTEXT

The most important fact about the Columbia strike is that Columbia exists within American society. This statement may appear to be a truism, yet it is a fact too often forgotten by observers, reporters, administrators, faculty members, and even some students. These people attempt to explain the "disturbances" as reaction to an unresponsive and archaic administrative structure, youthful outbursts of unrest much like panty raids, the product of a conspiracy by communist agents in national SDS or a handful of hard-core nihilists ("destroyers") on the campus, or just general student unrest due to the war in Vietnam.

233

But in reality, striking students are responding to the totality of the conditions of our society, not just one small part of it, the university. We are disgusted with the war, with racism, with being a part of a system over which we have no control, a system which demands gross inequalities of wealth and power, a system which denies personal and social freedom and potential, a system which has to manipulate and repress us in order to exist. The university can only be seen as a cog in this machine; or, more accurately, a factory whose product is knowledge and personnel (us) useful to the functioning of the system. The specific problems of university life, its boredom and meaninglessness, help prepare us for boring and meaningless work in the "real" world. And the policies of the university—expansion into the community, exploitation of blacks and Puerto Ricans, support for imperialist wars—also serve the interests of banks, corporations, government, and military represented on the Columbia Board of Trustees and the ruling class of our society. In every way, the university is "society's child." Our attack upon the university is really an attack upon this society and its effects upon us. We have never said otherwise.

The development of the New Left at Columbia represents an organized political response to the society. We see our task, first as identifying for ourselves and for others the nature of our society—who controls it and for what ends—and secondly, developing ways in which to transform it. We understand that only through struggle can we create a free, human society, since the present one is dominated by a small ruling class which exploits, manipulates, and distorts for its own ends— and has shown in countless ways its determination to maintain its position. The Movement at Columbia began years ago agitating and organizing students around issues such as students' power in the university (Action), support of the civil rights movement (CORE), the war in Vietnam (the Independent Committee on Vietnam). Finally, Columbia chapter Students for a Democratic Society initiated actions against many of the above issues as they manifest themselves on campus. Politically speaking, SDS, from its inception on campus in November, 1966, sought to unite issues, "to draw connections," to view this society as a totality. SDS united the two main themes of the movement—opposition to racial oppression and to the imperialist war in Vietnam—with our own sense of frustration, disappointment, and oppression at the quality of our lives in capitalist society.

One of the most important questions raised by the strike was who controls Columbia, and for what ends? SDS pointed to the Board of Trustees as the intersection of various corporate, financial, real-estate, and government interests outside the university which need the products of the university—personnel and knowledge—in order to exist. It is this power which we are fighting when we fight particular policies of the university such as expansion at the expense of poor people or institutional ties to the war-machine. We can hope for and possibly win certain reforms within the university, but the ultimate reforms we need—the elimination of war and exploitation—can only be gained after we over-throw the control of our country by the class of people on Columbia's Board of Trustees. In a sense, Columbia is the place where we received our education—our revolutionary education.

President Emeritus Grayson Kirk, in his 5,000 word "Message to Alumni, Parents, and Other Friends of Columbia," concludes

> the leaders of the SDS—as distinct from an unknown number of their supporters—are concerned with local parochial university issues only as they serve as a means to a larger end.

Though Kirk perceives that we are interested in more than Columbia University, he ignores the fact that the issues we raise are not at all "local parochial university isues," but indeed transcend the physical and class boundary of the university to unite us, the students, with neighborhood people, blacks and Puerto Ricans, and even the Viet-namese, with all the people oppressed by this society.

But why do students, predominantly of the "middle-class," in effect, reject the university designed to integrate them into the system and instead identify with the most oppressed of this country and the world? Why did the gymnasium in Morningside Park become an issue over which Columbia was shut down for seven weeks? Why pictures of Che Guevara, Malcolm X, and red flags in the liberated buildings?

Basically, the sit-ins and strike of April and May gave us a chance to express the extreme dissatisfaction we feel at being *caught in this "system."* We rejected the gap between potential and realization in this society. We rejected our present lives in the university and our future lives in business, government or other universities like this one. In a word, we saw ourselves as oppressed, and began to understand the forces at work which make for our oppression. In turn, we saw these same forces responsible for the oppression and colonization of blacks and Puerto

Ricans in ghettos, and Vietnamese and the people of the third world. By initiating a struggle in support of black and third world liberation, we create the conditions for our own freedom—by building a movement which will someday take power over our society, we will free ourselves.

As the strike and the struggle for our demands progressed, we learned more about the nature of our enemy and his unwillingness to grant any of our demands or concede any of his power. Illusions disappeared: the moral authority of the educator gave way to police violence, the faculty appeared in all its impotent glory. On the other hand, tremendous support came in from community residents, black and white alike, from university employees, from high school students, from people across the country and around the world. Inevitably, we began to re-evaluate our goals and strategy. Chief among the lessons were (1) We cannot possibly win our demands alone: we must unite with other groups in the population; (2) The 6 demands cannot possibly be our ultimate ends: even winning all of them certainly would not go far enough toward the basic reforms we need to live as human beings in this society; (3) "Restructuring" the university, the goal of faculty groups, various "moderate" students, and even the trustees, cannot possibly create a "free" or "democratic" university out of this institution. (First, how can anyone expect any meaningful reforms when even our initial demands have not been met?) Secondly, we realize that the university is entirely synchronized with the society: how can you have a "free", human university in a society such as this? Hence the SDS slogan "A free university in a free society." The converse is equally true.

The basic problem in understanding our strike—our demands, tactics, and history—consists of keeping in mind the social context of the university and of our movement. If you understand that we are the political response to an oppressive and exploitative social and economic system, you will have no difficulty putting together the pieces that follow.

THE ISSUES

From the first afternoon of the demonstrations, back on April 23 the striking students put forward essentially six demands. A joint steering commitee of members of SDS, the Students' Afro-American Society, and unattached liberals created what were to become a cause and an entity unto themselves, the famous "six demands" later ratified by every striking group—from Hamilton Hall through the six thousand eventually represented on the Strike Coordinating Committee.

The six demands:

1) That the administration grant amnesty for the original "IDA 6" and for all those participating in these demonstrations.
2) That construction of the gymnasium in Morningside Park be terminated immediately.
3) That the university sever all ties with the Institute for Defense Analysis and that President Kirk and Trustee Burden resign their positions on the Executive Committee of that institution immediately.
4) That President Kirk's ban on indoor demonstrations be dropped.
5) That all future judicial decisions be made by a student-faculty committee.
6) That the university use its good offices to drop charges against all people arrested in demonstrations at the gym site and on campus.

The first was the precondition for negotiations over the other demands.

As the strike progressed, three main demands emerged: those concerning amnesty, the gymnasium, and IDA. This development was natural and inevitable, due to the fact that these demands represented the three issues uppermost in our minds, namely, racism in our society, the war in Vietnam and the United States' imperialist policies throughout the world, and the attempt for us to take power over the conditions of our lives—at the university and elsewhere. On an intermediate level, these demands were representative of our opposition to a whole series of university policies in support of racism, U.S. imperialism, as well as its own autocratic power for exploiting community residents and employees, and manipulating and controlling students.

After the first bust (April 30), a great cry went up in almost all quarters for "restructuring" of the university. Accordingly, a second precondition was added to the first: recognition of the right of students to participate in restructuring the university (May 3). But since this had already, in fact, been granted, and since "restructuring" seemed to the radical majority of the Strike Coordinating Committee to be merely procedural and empty without the granting of our substantive demands, the original demands and what they stand for continue in the forefront of our attention.

* * *

APRIL 23

Three strains united in the explosive April 23 demonstration: the heightened anti-racist feeling, the almost unanimous hatred for the war in Vietnam, and for the whole imperialist American foreign policy, and opposition to the administration's attempt to repress the Left.

Monday, April 22, the IDA 6 were placed on disciplinary probation. The demonstration organized for the next day drew approximately six hundred supporters around three demands: (1) End all university ties with the Institute for Defense Analyses, (2) End construction of the gym on land stolen from the people of Harlem, and (3) An open hearing, with full rights of due process, for the IDA 6. The intention of the demonstration was to defy the president's ban again with a demonstration in Low Library, but the demonstrators found their way to Low blocked by several hundred counter-demonstrators, and, more important, locked entrances. A proposal from David Truman to sit down with him in McMillan theater to "discuss" the whole matter having been rejected outright, approximately 300 of the demonstrators moved on the gym site in Morningside Park and tore the fence down. One student was busted there. On returning to the campus, the demonstrators decided to take Hamilton Hall as a hostage for the brother busted at the gym; upon taking Hamilton, they discovered that they had not only the building, but also Acting Dean of the College Henry Coleman as hostage.

Immediately, a steering committee for the building was organized, consisting of 3 members of SDS, 4 members of Students' Afro-American Society, and 2 "unaffiliated liberals." This committee's first task was drawing up the original six demands listed above, demands approved by the body of demonstrators later ratified time and again by other groups throughout the campus, as well as community and high school groups throughout the city. Besides solving problems of food, defense, entertainment, and certain political questions, the steering committee also invited community people and other university students to join the occupation of Hamilton Hall, to join the fight against Columbia, in which many had already been involved. Community support was swift and impressive: high school kids, older people from Morningside Heights and Harlem, and from all over the city, were immediately on the scene with food, money, and manpower. It was this moral and material support, continuing throughout the occupation of the buildings and the strike, which was crucial to the strength and growth of the movement.

The feeling of unity in Hamilton Hall began to evaporate as the separate political identities of the black and white demonstrators emerged in a dispute over tactics. The black students, seeing themselves as representatives of the Harlem community and black people everywhere, had as their goal the stopping of gym construction. In order to exercise the rights of black people over this racist institution, they realized that they had to barricade and hold Hamilton Hall—nothing less would force the administration to capitulate. A majority of the white students, on the other hand, saw their task as one of building the radical movement, convincing more and more white students of the relevance of their radical analysis. Accordingly, they believed that to barricade Hamilton would result in confrontation with other students wanting to go to class, rather than with the real enemy, the administration. Also at present in this decision was an element of timidity and lack of understanding of the effects of militancy on "radicalizing" people. In a joint steering committee meeting in the early morning of April 24, the black students asked the whites to leave the building, because they had decided that the only possible tactic was to barricade and hold Hamilton, while the whites were split, disunited, lacked discipline and militancy. It was agreed that the whites would create "diversionary action."

TAKING MORE BUILDINGS

After leaving Hamilton, about 200 white students forced their way into Low Library and President Kirk's' office. As police began arriving on campus, rumors that 40 had been busted in Low Library (though not in Kirk's' office) induced all but about 25 in Low to leave, believing that busts would make no sense toward gaining more support.

The 25 or so who stayed were at that time presented by a professor with the first in a long series of proposals for joint disciplinary boards which were supposed to pacify the strikers and get them to leave the building. This one, like all the others, was rejected.

Many of those who left Low, as well as many who did not enter in the first place, stood in pouring rain as a buffer in front of Hamilton, pledging to pose themselves between the blacks inside and the police. This barrier was maintained throughout the liberation of the buildings, right to the bust of April 30.

In a sense, the flight from Low Library, on Wednesday morning, was the low point of the strike. From there, the students began to learn from their mistakes: they saw that their power was in holding the buildings, that a bust would not mean defeat, that the barricades were a symbol of defiance and a statement of the militancy of those inside, that it was this militancy which won people over. More and more people reentered Low, expanding the number of rooms held. Wednesday evening, the students of the School of Architecture seized Avery Hall. Later that morning, graduate students seized Fayerweather. A meeting of several hundred on Wednesday evening called for a university-wide strike, and, accordingly, pickets went up at all classroom buildings on Thursday.

IN THE COMMUNES

Life within the communes, as the liberated buildings were called, was a totally liberating experience for those inside, the core of the strike. Politics and life were integrated as the communards spent hour after hour discussing policy decisions of the strike, questions of defense, and questions of organization of the commune itself. For many, the communal life within the building represented a break with their individualistic, isolated, fragmented lives as Columbia students: many talked of this as the most important experience of their lives, a new, beautiful high.

The goal of the action was kept in mind at all times—students were not only fighting for significant social (non-student) issues, they were not only uniting with those in the buildings, but with the oppressed of the world.

The best way to understand the sense of common struggle, the awareness of the significance of this struggle, and the sense of liberation gained by those in the buildings is to let the communards speak for themselves. The following are excerpts from a leaflet to "The Brothers and Sisters of Math Commune" by members of Up Against the Wall, Motherfucker chapter of SDS (from the Lower East Side) who were in Math:

> The experience of rebellion has given us five new senses.... We have a sense of brotherhood and love for each other. We have a sense of the enemy. We have a sense of the ongoing struggle created in our own society and isolated territory. And we have a sense of our needs for the future.

We all feel the loss of Math Hall and the life that it provided. But we don't need Math Hall to live.... Wherever we are together is the place. We have lost Math Hall, but we have gained our own environments. Liberated people liberate the air they breathe and the ground they walk upon.... We want it all.

OUTSIDE

While the strikers in the five liberated buildings were forming their communes, the campus outside was a sea of ferment and turbulence with waves of support gradually spreading out from the centers of agitation. People were talking to each other for perhaps the first time in the history of Columbia University; everyone searched his soul to see where he stood. Some joined those in the buildings. Some pledged themselves to support them. Others attempted, futilely, to stand in the middle, while some were so threatened that they found it necessary to oppose the strikers (this last group, however, was the smallest).

A group demanding amnesty for the demonstrators and a peaceful solution to the "troubles" on campus came into being. This was the "green arm-bands," hundreds of whom kept a vigil at the sundial and pledged themselves to protecting the demonstrators in the buildings from the cops. When the bust did come, many were seriously injured.

A group of liberal faculty members met and pledged that they would interpose themselves between the students and the police if the administration called for a bust. Further, they declared that the problem should be settled peacefully, without the use of police. The Ad Hoc Faculty Group began meeting almost around the clock, formulating compromise proposals which would return the university to normalcy. Their position was that of mediator between two sides. Though they for the most part acted conscientiously and in good faith, they were politically naive in not understanding that they had to take a position for or against the strike, that their position "in the middle" supported the administration since they agreed with the administration that amnesty was an "impossible" demand.

The temporary strike committee which had been functioning since Wednesday decided that they should engage in talks with the faculty to clarify the strikers' position and to attempt to win the faculty over to the strike. These talks, however, had two results: first, they convinced the faculty that "progress" was being made and that they should retain their mediator position, not move toward the students, and second, the illusion of progress forestalled a bust.

These forestalling talks were significant the morning of April 26. The first threat of a bust came at 1 A.M., that Friday morning, when Kirk and Truman panicked after Mathematics Hall was liberated by about 30 strikers. Faculty members convinced Kirk and Truman to close school and wait over the weekend while "talks" went on between the occupants of the buildings and the faculty. By then, however, the cop invasion had already resulted in one casualty, French instructor Dick Greeman, who was guarding Low Library.

An organization of right-wing students, calling itself the Majority Coalition, a deliberate misnomer, formed over the weekend. Its main activity was a blockade of Low Library which attempted to keep food and medical supplies from the strikers in Kirk's office. Backing them up was a faculty line which stopped any food going through the "jock" line, claiming they were separating the "jocks" from the strikers inside. Several plainclothesmen were spotted among the faculty cops.

On Friday, the first Strike Coordinating Committee was formed, consisting mostly of representatives from each building except Hamilton. Since each building had to agree before a major policy decision could be made, constant discussion went on in each building, and constant communication ties were set up. The SCC was responsible for policy statements, negotiations, physical arrangements and coordinating activities. A central staff in Ferris Booth Hall kept a flow of press releases, leaflets, information going. It also was responsible for feeding 1,000 people per day. This latter task was accomplished completely through private donations and the help of a few student councils from other schools.

THE BUST

The bust came in the early morning of Tuesday, April 30. 1,500 uniformed and plainclothes cops removed approximately 1,000 people from the five buildings. 720 were arrested on charges ranging from criminal trespass and resisting arrest to incitement to riot. Several hundred people, including numerous faculty, were beaten. Since no demonstrators in any of the buildings resisted arrest or attacked the cops, the violence against the demonstrators was entirely gratuitous and unprovoked. Many people, including certain professors, have reported evidence that the cops also broke furniture, threw ink on walls, and stole and destroyed much property in an effort to discredit the demonstrators as hoodlums.

THE NEW STRIKE COMMITTEE—MASS STRIKE

After the bust, numerous groups rallied to the support of the students—hundreds from other high schools and universities, thousands from the Morningside Heights and Harlem communities, many faculty members, as well as previously uncommitted students. The police attack vindicated the strikers, proving that the administration was more willing to have students arrested and beat-up and to disrupt the university than to stop its policies of exploitation, racism, and support for imperialism, and sacrifice some of its arbitrary power. According to university propaganda, which administrators themselves began to believe, the demonstrations were the work of a handful of hard-core nihilists, not the result of thousands of people's opposition to Columbia's policies. To have forced thousands of people to act against their wills, SDS leaders would have had to be, according to Kirk and Truman's view, the most fantastic hypnotists ever to have lived.

But thousands of people, including a large portion of the faculty, were now quite rationally calling for a strike against the administration. At a meeting of over 1,200 people in Wollman auditorium, the six demands were re-ratified, and a new Strike Coordinating Committee was established on the basis of one vote for every 70 members of a constituent group which pledged to support the strike. Any group in or out of the university could send delegates—students, faculty, employees, community residents, and high school students.

Many of the 6,000 people who eventually sent delegates to the Strike Coordinating Committee were moderates who had been shocked by the police brutality and who also sincerely wanted a reformed university. The majority, however, accepted the view of the radicals that the strike must keep pushing primarily for the original demands—for the content of reform, not the empty formalities. A proposal to demand the resignation of President Grayson Kirk and Vice President David Truman, as well as the Trustees responsible for the bust, was rejected because it emphasized personalities as responsible, not the structure of the system which students oppose.

Later in the strike, approximately 25 of the moderate delegates broke away from the Strike Coordinating Committee, choosing to form a new group, Students for a Restructured University, to concentrate on the work of reforming Columbia. In leaving, however, they pledged to support the original six demands of the strike.

The first day of classes after the bust proved to be almost no classes at all. The College had asked classes to meet, very few, in fact, took place, since most students and faculty respected the picket lines. The strike was approximately 85% effective on the Morningside campus.

The mass meeting which originally established the coalition Strike Coordinating Committee in addition passed a proposal mandating the committee to serve as the provisional government for the university, to get it started again under the people's auspices. One of its primary tasks was the establishment of Liberation Courses, classes in all fields taught by students, faculty, and people from outside Columbia. These classes were designed to experiment in content and teaching form—to break out of the stultification of hierarchical and bourgeois learning traditional at Columbia and other schools. New types of courses appeared—everything from "Alienation from Hegel to Columbia" and "What a university will look like in a liberated society" to "Urban blues" and "Motorcycle mechanics." This was a time of tremendous intellectual excitement, a time in which every traditional concept was re-evaluated. The function of the teacher, the content of courses, people's relationships to each other were all questioned in relation to the struggle in which all were engaged.

COMMUNITY SEIZES A BUILDING

Although various tenant groups on Morningside Heights had for years been fighting Columbia's expansion into the community, the strike gave new impetus to this struggle. A new group of activist Morningside residents, the Community Action Committee, sending delegates to the SCC, was dedicated to organizing the community for its self-preservation. Columbia's' plans call for the eviction of 11,000 more residents (7,500 having already been thrown out), in order to turn Morningside Heights into an upper-middle class institutional enclave with apartments for a few respectable white people. On May 17, approximately 50 members of the Community Action Committee seized two apartments in a partially emptied building owned by Columbia to demand that Columbia's expansion plans be halted as well as the rehabilitation of vacant housing for people's use. Over 1,000 students gathered outside the tenement in support of the comrades inside. That night, as on April 30, the Columbia administration responded in the only way it could—with police power. Forty demonstrators were arrested in the building, along with 100 students and others who had been outside in support of the community people.

THE REPRESSION—HAMILTON II

The administration, determined to punish further those involved in the demonstrations, demanded that four of the original IDA 6, people they considered leaders of the strike, report to Dean Platt's office by Tuesday, May 21. When the four did not appear, but sent 300 supporters instead into Hamilton Hall, they were immediately suspended. While deliberating on the next move, the demonstrators in Hamilton were told by the administration that the police had been called and that any student arrested would also be suspended by the University. After many hours of debate, approximately 120 of those present decided to stay. Seventy of these were students, approximately 20 were faculty members, and the rest were parents, community people, or students from other schools. Their thinking was that they had to show unity with the suspended leaders, that this was the only way the movement could survive.

The administration's reason for using police a third time was given by President Grayson Kirk in a telephone interview with WKCR, the campus radio station: the nihilist-anarchist hard-core inside Hamilton was "exploiting the presence" of "community children" (code name for black kids) for some unstated, dark purpose.

Equally ludicrous was the administration's decision to use 1,000 TPF cops to "clear the campus" after the bust in Hamilton. Students had set up barricades at both ends of college walk to defend the campus, and when the cops attacked, some students defended themselves with bricks. But the police charge was not repulsed and dozens of students were beaten by uniformed and plainclothes cops, including many *inside* dormitory lobbies and corridors....

The felony charges, the beatings, the mass arrests, and the discipline all represent various attempts to repress and kill the student strike. The administration uses the New York City Police Dept. and the courts to stop a political movement under the theory that if you punish people enough, they will be intimidated into submission.... Though the physical power of the administration is strong, they cannot possibly stop the movement at Columbia or the movement for revolutionary change in this society.

June 4, 1968, commencement day at Columbia, saw over 400 graduates walk out of the commencement held in the Cathedral of St. John the Divine, a commencement guarded by close to 1,000 police, including numerous plainclothes cops dressed in academic robes (also used as ringers to fill up the empty seats). The graduates, along with several thousand guests, attended the real commencement of Columbia University, held at the traditional site, Low Plaza, by Students for a Restructured University, and the Strike Coordinating Committee. Following various speeches, approximately 1,000 people attended a rally and picnic at the gym site in Morningside Park. This was, as Erich Fromm noted, a movement for life; the commencement was the festival of life which marked the close of one phase of the struggle.

* * *

As the fall begins, it is clear that Columbia will be the scene of much more radical political action. No demands have yet been met. The university is prosecuting in criminal court close to 1,100 people, most of whom are students. At least 79 students have been suspended, hundreds more placed on probation. Columbia's exploitation of the community and her support for the Government's imperialist policies continue. Most important, people now know that they are fighting the forces behind Columbia, the power of the ruling class in this society, not just the institution. And they have the commitment to keep fighting. The Democratic National Convention killed electoral politics for young people in this country and the Chicago Police Dept. provided an alternative—to fight. So did Columbia in the spring. So does it now, along with every other university in this country. The struggle goes on. Create two, three, many Columbias, that is the watchword!

Bring the War Home

SDS

This is the National Action brochure that the national office has produced. So far they have been going as fast as we can print them. They can be ordered from the n.o. at a price of $5 per thousand.

It will also be printed as a part of the mass newspaper that SDS will have ready within a week. Send in orders for the paper, too, and pass them both out wherever you go.

It has been almost a year since the Democratic Convention, when thousands of young people came together in Chicago and tore up pig city for five days. The action was a response to the crisis this system is facing as a result of the war, the demand by black people for liberation, and the ever-growing reality that this system just can't make it.

This fall, people are coming back to Chicago: more powerful, better organized, and more together than we were last August.

SDS is calling for a National Action in Chicago on October 11. We are coming back to Chicago, and we are going to bring those we left behind last year.

LOOK AT IT: AMERICA, 1969

The war goes on, despite the jive double-talk about troop withdrawals and peace talks. Black people continue to be murdered by agents of the fat cats who run this country, if not in one way, then in another: by the pigs or the courts, by the boss or the welfare department.

New Left Notes, August 1, 1969, pp. 2–3.

Working people face higher taxes, inflation, speed-ups, and the sure knowledge—if it hasn't happened already—that their sons may be shipped off to Vietnam and shipped home in a box. And young people all over the country go to prisons that are called schools, are trained for jobs that don't exist or serve no one's real interest but the boss's, and, to top it all of, get told that Vietnam is the place to defend their "freedom."

None of this is very new. The cities have been falling apart, the schools have been bullshit, the jobs have been rotten and unfulfilling for a long time.

What's new is that today not quite so many people are confused, and a lot more people are angry: angry about the fact that the promises we have heard since first grade are all jive; angry that, when you get down to it, this system is nothing but the total economic and military put-down of the oppressed peoples of the world.

And more: it's a system that steals the goods, the resources, and the labor of poor and working people all over the world in order to fill the pockets and bank accounts of a tiny capitalist class. (Call it imperialism.) It's a system that divides white workers from blacks by offering whites crumbs off the table, and telling them that if they don't stay cool the blacks will move in on their jobs, their homes, and their schools. (Call it white supremacy.) It's a system that divides men from women, forcing women to be subservient to men from childhood, to be slave labor in the home and cheap labor in the factory. (Call it male supremacy.) And it's a system that has colonized whole nations within this country—the nation of black people, the nation of brown people—to enslave, oppress, and ultimately murder the people on whose backs this country was built. (Call it fascism.)

But the lies are catching up to America—and the slick rich people and their agents in the government bureaucracies, the courts, the schools, and the pig stations just can't cut it anymore.

Black and brown people know it.

Young people know it.

More and more white working people know it.

And you know it.

LAST YEAR, THERE WERE ONLY ABOUT 10,000 OF US IN CHICAGO

The press made it look like a massacre. All you could see on TV were shots of the horrors and blood of pig brutality. That was the line that the bald-headed businessmen were trying to run down—"If you mess with us, we'll let you have it." But those who were there tell a different story. We were together and our power was felt. It's true that some of us got hurt, but last summer was a victory for the people in a thousand ways.

Our actions showed the Vietnamese that there were masses of young people in this country facing the same enemy that they faced.

We showed that white people would no longer sit by passively while black communities were being invaded by occupation troops every day.

We showed that the "democratic process" of choosing candidates for a presidential election was nothing more than a hoax, pulled off by the businessmen who really run this country.

And we showed the whole world that in the face of the oppressive and exploitative rulers—and the military might to back them up—thousands of people are willing to fight back.

SDS IS CALLING THE ACTION THIS YEAR

But it will be a different action. An action not only against a single war or a "foreign policy," but against the whole imperialist system that made that war a necessity. An action not only for immediate withdrawal of all U.S. occupation troops, but in support of the heroic fight of the Vietnamese people and the National Liberation Front for freedom and independence. An action not only to bring "peace to Vietnam," but beginning to establish another front against imperialism right here in America—to "bring the war home."

We are demanding that all occupational troops get out of Vietnam and every other place they don't belong. This includes the black and brown communities, the workers' picket lines, the high schools, and the streets of Berkeley. No longer will we tolerate "law and order" backed up by soldiers in Vietnam and pigs in the communities and schools; a "law and order" that serves only the interests of those in power and tries to smash the people down whenever they rise up.

We are demanding the release of all political prisoners who have been victimized by the ever-growing attacks on the black liberation

struggle and the people in general. Especially the leaders of the black liberation struggle like Huey P. Newton, Ahmed Evans, Fred Hampton, and Martin Sostre.

We are expressing total support for the National Liberation Front and the newly-formed Provisional Revolutionary Government of South Vietnam. Throughout the history of the war, the NLF has provided the

political and military leadership to the people of South Vietnam. The Provisional Revolutionary Government, recently formed by the NLF and other groups, has pledged to "mobilize the South Vietnamese armed forces and people" in order to continue the struggle for independence. The PRG also has expressed solidarity with "the just struggle of the Afro-American people for their fundamental national rights," and has pledged to "actively support the national independence movements of Asia, Africa, and Latin America."

We are also expressing total support for the black liberation struggle, part of the same struggle that the Vietnamese are fighting, against the same enemy.

We are demanding independence for Puerto Rico, and an end to the colonial oppression that the Puerto Rican nation faces at the hands of U.S. imperialism.

We are demanding an end to the surtax, a tax taken from the working people of this country and used to kill working people in Vietnam and other places for fun and profit.

We are expressing solidarity with the Conspiracy 8 who led the struggle last summer in Chicago. Our action is planned to roughly coincide with the beginning of their trial.

And we are expressing support for GIs in Vietnam and throughout the world who are being made to fight the battles of the rich, like poor and working people have always been made to do. We support those GIs at Fort Hood, Fort Jackson, and many other army bases who have refused to be cannon fodder in a war against the people of Vietnam.

IT'S ALMOST HARD TO REMEMBER
WHEN THE WAR BEGAN

But, after years of peace marches, petitions, and the gradual realization that this war was no "mistake" at all, one critical fact remains: the war is not just happening in Vietnam.

It is happening in the jungles of Guatemala, Bolivia, Thailand, and all oppressed nations throughout the world.

And it is happening here. In black communities throughout the country. On college campuses. And in the high schools, in the shops, and on the streets.

It is a war in which there are only two sides; a war not for domination but for an end to domination, not for destruction, but for liberation and the unchaining of human freedom.

And it is a war in which we cannot "resist"; it is a war in which we must fight.

On October 11, tens of thousands of people will come to Chicago to bring the war home. Join us.

You Do Need a Weatherman

Shin'ya Ono

In September, I attended the Cleveland Conference on the National Action as an anti-Weatherman representative from the New York Movement for a Democratic Society. A month and a half later, a photograph of me being fucked over by three Chicago pigs appeared on the *Guardian* cover, and I came back with charges amounting to more than ten years. My non-Weatherman comrades ask me: Was it worth it? The answer is yes, yes—wholeheartedly, yes. How I, a firm anti-Weatherman, felt compelled—after a tremendous resistance—to become a Weatherman, is important, but mostly in a personal way. What I would like to go into here is how the Chicago action, and the Weatherman logic behind it, made, and still makes, compelling sense for an old-timer like myself with the usual "credentials."

THE WEATHERMAN PERSPECTIVE

Three key points divide the Weathermen from all other political tendencies:

First: the primacy of confronting national chauvinism and racism among the working class whites; the necessity to turn every issue, problem, and struggle into an anti-imperialist, anti-racist struggle; the assertion that organizing whites primarily around their own perceived

Excerpts from Shin'ya Ono, "You Do Need a Weatherman," *Leviathan*, December 1969, pp. 15–21, 39–43. Reprinted with permission.

oppression (whether it be women's liberation, student power, the draft and the stockades, the crisis of the cities, oppression at the point of production) is bound to lead to a racist and chauvinist direction.

Second: the urgency of preparing for militant, armed struggle now; the necessity of organizing people into a fighting movement, not primarily by critiques, ideas, analyses, or programs, though all these are important, but by actually inflicting material damage to imperialist and racist institutions right now, with whatever forces you've got.

Third: the necessity of building revolutionary collectives that demand total, wholehearted commitment of the individual to struggle against everything that interferes with the revolutionary struggle, and to struggle to transform oneself into a revolutionary and a communist: collectives through which we can forge ourselves into effective "tools of necessity" and through which we can realize, concretely, in our day-to-day lives such well-known Maoist principles as "Politics in command," "Everything for the revolution," "Criticism-self-criticism-transformation."

The Weatherman did not pick up these three points from Mao or the classics abstractly. These points arose out of, and are situated within, a broader revolutionary strategy specific to the conditions prevailing within the imperialist mother country.

* * *

BRING THE WAR HOME!
THE LOGIC OF THE ACTION

The Chicago National Action was conceived by the Weather Bureau as an anti-imperialist action in which a mass of white youths would tear up and smash wide-ranging imperialist targets such as the Conspiracy Trial, high schools, draft boards and induction centers, banks, pig institutes and pigs themselves. The main reason why we chose such a wide range of targets was our desire to project the existence of a fighting force that's out, not primarily to make specific demands, but to totally destroy this imperialist and racist society. Two sets of objectives were stipulated. The first set of objectives arose out of our general strategy. The specific tactic chosen (that is, mass street-fighting attacking imperialist targets) was intended to accomplish several aims to fulfill our strategic goal for the immediate future:

a) To take the first step towards building a new communist party and a red army: the toughening and transformation not only physically and militarily, but also politically and psychologically, of the old cadre; and the recruiting and training of new people as cadres.

b) To compel every youth in the country to become aware of and grapple with the existence of a group of pro-VC and pro-black white youths who effectively fight against imperialism and the pigs, on the basis of their understanding that this country not only needs to be, but can be, brought down. Also, to identify in a dramatic way some of the institutions that oppress these youths.

c) To do material damage so as to help the Viet Cong.

d) To push the entire movement to a new level, to sharpen its "cutting edge," to give militant shape to struggles undertaken by various sectors of the movement in the coming year, so that every struggle and all political work will be defined and judged by what happens in Chicago.

* * *

We frankly told people that, while a massacre was highly unlikely, we expected the actions to be very, very heavy, that hundreds of people might well be arrested and/or hurt, and finally, that a few people might even get killed. We argued that twenty white people (one per cent of the project minimum) getting killed while fighting hard against imperialist targets would not be a defeat, but a political victory, for the same reasons that would make a massacre a politically unacceptable option for the ruling class; that it will hurt the ruling class ten times more than the damage inflicted in an operation with twenty Viet Cong dead. And, finally, not to be willing to risk what were by Third World standards relatively light casualties, when the probable political gains were so clear, was to want to preserve one's white skin privilege, and acquiesce in being a racist. (Some people criticized us for being so frank with people about the heaviness of the actions and possible deaths. We fully realized that we might frighten away some potential fighters, but thought it necessary to psychologically and politically prepare those who came so that we'd be able to fight in a tight, together way. It is politically suicidal to dupe people into very heavy situations.)

The whites in this country are insulated from the world revolution and the Third World liberation struggles because of their access to, and acceptance of, blood-soaked white-skin privileges. In a large measure, this insulation from the struggle holds true for the radicals in the movement. The whole point of the Weatherman politics is to break down this insulation, to bring the war home, to make the coming revolution real. But this breakthrough has to be effected within ourselves before we can work with the masses of white youths. And this was what the Chicago action was all about: bringing the revolution that is already winning in the Third World home, for us radicals as well as for the white youths whom we want to reach and change.

ON TO CHICAGO!

We left for Chicago in two buses with roughly thirty persons in addition to the cadres of our gang. In the last few days of our build-up, we counted two hundred-odd persons from New York who either reserved bus tickets or stated their intention to come. In other words, for every seven persons who promised to come, only one showed up. (Apparently, this ratio roughly held true on a national level, which means that of the three or four thousand expected to come, only six hundred actually showed up.) This extremely small turn-out not only frightened many of us cadres, but also raised some serious questions about our practice for the preceding five weeks.

In the final few days we were expecting a possible mass bust of the leadership and cadres to forestall the national action. We'd recently had a couple of close run-ins with the TPF and the SES (the Special Events Squad of the New York police). So when I saw Inspector Finnegan of SES-Red Squad fame and some of his captains and lieutenants (with whom some of us had been rather rude, so to speak, and had gotten away with it) at the bus assembly point, I expected a bust. But Finnegan merely taunted one of us, saying, "Aren't you scared with so few people in the buses for Chicago?" Obviously, they didn't bust us then, because they wanted to set us up for bigger things to come (federal conspiracy charges, for example). Some of us were compelled to board the bus at another point as a precautionary measure.

As soon as we were on our way, we began our struggle. The internal struggle within the collective involving criticism-self-criticism-transfor mation is in our view just as crucial as the struggle in the streets. Without the former, the latter would be half-hearted and whimpy. Even if the street-fighting were good, without political struggle after- wards, we would learn only a fraction of what we could and must learn from that action. Thus, we looked upon the internal struggles on the buses and in the movement centers as an indispensable part of our battle in Chicago.

We went over the basics of busts and jail. (Don't expect to be bailed out right away; our white-skin privileges are diminishing fast. Be prepared to spend at least a couple of weeks in there. Turn the jail experience into a struggle.) For the eleventh time, we went through first aid. ("For multiple fractures...") In order to get to know each other and learn to move as a group, we divided ourselves into several affinity groups of six or seven persons each and did a couple of tasks together (e.g., preparing food on the bus, shaping up the dilapidated helmet liners into a more or less usable condition with straps and paddings, preparing primitive medical kits). We discussed the functions of the affinity group, what running and fighting together meant, what leadership meant, and why leadership was absolutely necessary in a military situa- tion. The leaders of the affinity groups were appointed, not elected, and we discussed the reasons for that.

* * *

THE FIRST NIGHT

Wednesday night was to be a commemorating rally for Che and Nguyen Van Troi, and a light street march to feel out the city and the pig situation. As soon as we left the movement center, we felt the tense feeling of walking in the midst of the enemy territory. Even though there were more than fifty of us traveling together in full street-fighting gear (helmet, eye-goggles, medical kit, heavy jacket, boots, jocks and cups), many of us were frightened by the heavy pig surveillance. As we approached the rallying point, lit brightly by the bonfire made out of torn park benches, we chatted: "Ho, Ho, Ho Chi Minh, Viet Cong is gonna win. Pick, pick, pick up the gun, the revolution has begun."

The surging fighting spirit within me was immediately dampened when I saw only a few hundred people around the bonfire, many of whom were obviously bystanders. What happened to all those train-loads of kids from Detroit? To the thousand street kids from Chicago? We aren't going to go through with the four-day national action with three hundred people, when the Chicago pigs had prepared to vamp on us weeks in advance?! I could hardly concentrate on any of the speeches. Sudenly I heard Marion Delgado announce: "We are going to see Judge Hoffman. Let's go!" Before the absurdity of going through with the action sank in my head fully, three or four hundred people started running towards the park's exit. Having lost the New York leadership group, I led ten people under my leadership (four cadres and six new people, divided into two separate affinity groups) into the running mob. Within a minute or two, right in front of my eyes, I saw and felt the transformation of the mob into a battalion of three hundred revolutionary fighters.

We passed by a group of more than a hundred pigs outside of the park who were taken by surprise. (We learned later that there were more than two thousand pigs in the general area specifically mobilized for us.) Windows were smashed; Rolls Royces and Cadillacs and every other car in this ruling class neighborhood were smashed; small groups of ten, fifteen pigs on the way were taken by surprise and were totally powerless against the surging battalion. Some pigs were overpowered and vamped on severely. Within a few minutes all of us lost whatever fear and doubts we had before. Yes, we were out to smash the totality of this imperialist social order; we were really out to fight. Each one of us felt the soldier in us.

It took the pigs twenty minutes to regain their sense and to counter-attack. The leadership up front broke through, but the rear sections turned to another street. One of the cadres in my group sprained his ankle, and I told him to drop out with another cadre to look out for him. We couldn't have anyone drag the group back. Another intersection, another confrontation, another turn. Pigs were vamped on by some people here and there. I saw two completely bloodied pigs in a badly smashed-up pig car, but continued on. (Fear of winning?) At a third (or was it fourth?) intersection, we confronted a large group of pigs. Crack, crack, and streams of bright light. Tear grenades? "Who has the medical kit? Two persons have been shot." Shotguns. (Later it turned out that ten persons received shotgun wounds and one cadre was hit fairly seriously with pistol bullets). Some people panicked, but most turned back in a quick but orderly retreat. We were blocked by a large group of pigs at the next corner, so we turned around again, and found that intersection also heavily blocked by pigs. The two groups of pigs triumphantly moved on us to trap what was left of our rear group (by now about a hundred persons). Luckily, we found a long, narrow alleyway and went through it, heading back to Lincoln Park. (We did so without any good reason; there was not a single person in the group who knew the streets of Chicago.)

By this time, we had been on the streets for a good forty-five minutes, running and jogging most of that time, and many people were slowing down. I also noticed that there were no national or regional leaders in our group (they were either busted or fighting in another section of the area). People were screaming: "Where is the leadership?" "What's our goal now?" "Let's split!" I saw the necessity of my seizing the leadership, but was afraid of doing so because I knew that there were undercover pigs in the crowd, and taking leadership would make me much more visible and vulnerable, so I merely shouted at the people who were slowing down or thinking of splitting. "Don't split until we are so instructed." "Come on! We're in the red army, right? We've got to run much faster and tighter!" I pushed and shoved people to move ahead. After turning away from the park to avoid being trapped in it, a few regional leaders rejoined our ranks, and we kept on running for twenty more minutes. When the regional leader shouted, "Everyone on his own; split in any way you can!," I led my group into an alleyway and hid in the back yard of a house for about an hour before taking a cab back to the movement center. While we were waiting, we debated whether we should ditch our defense gear so as to make ourselves less visible, but I decided that we should keep our gear since it would be needed in the three remaining days of the national action.

At several points in the hour-and-twenty-minute street fight I was sure that we would get busted. In fact, a couple of times, the pigs were so close upon us that I almost ordered my group to give ourselves up. But we got away free by persisting and persevering. This fact had a tremendous impact on me. Now I understood why some comrades in the New York collective were criticized for their defeatism because of the way they were busted several times in a month and a half—that is, for not having the spirit of fighting through to the end which in many cases means doing your best to get away instead of giving up after a half-hearted effort. It was also amazing that only thirty out of three hundred cadres were busted that night (along with forty-odd freaks who were mistaken for us). It was absolutely amazing that three hundred of us were able to go on a rampage for more than one hour, smashing windows, cars, and pigs, when there were two thousand supposedly well-prepared pigs concentrated in that small area. Without any doubt, on a military and tactical level, Wednesday night was a clear victory.

* * *

A VICTORY/A PRESENCE

Two hundred fifty arrests and several serious injuries; at least forty out of three hundred cadres with very heavy felony charges. More than $1,500,000 ($150,000 cash) in bail money. That was the cost of the four-day national action. Are these costs justified by the results? In other words, did we win a victory in Chicago? This was the question on everyone's mind in the aftermath. Some non-Weatherman radicals say that since the Weathermen feel so high about themselves and about Chicago, our evaluation of it must be strictly "internal" and subjective. Let me then summarize my own evaluation of the action in as objective a way as possible:

1. Militarily and tactically, it was a victory. Fifty-seven pigs were hospitalized, including a few who almost got killed, while we ourselves suffered many fewer physical casualties. On both Wednesday and Thursday, three hundred Weathermen moved on the streets in a together, military manner. This was a great accomplishment, given the over-

whelming numerical superiority of the pig forces. We inflicted more than $1 million of damage on a ruling class neighborhood. And our actions apparently inspired some people to blow up a couple of induction centers early Saturday morning. To balance against this, we suffered tremendously heavy legal casualties. In addition to the forty felonies and several attempted murder charges, we expect even heavier federal charges to come down on us soon. While all this was anticipated, the level of repression is nevertheless extremely heavy by white-radical standards. So, over-all, what we did in Chicago confirmed J.J.'s statement that mass street action is a necessary, but a losing, tactic.

2. Politically, we did establish our presence as a white fighting force in a dramatic way in Chicago and in the surrounding areas. As a result, millions of kids are grappling for the first time with the existence of a pro-black pro-VC white fighting force that understands that this social order can be, and is going to be, brought down. As to how much we polarized their consciousness and shook up their defeatist-chauvinist presumption of the permanence of this social order, that can only be judged and verified by our follow-up work and actions in that area. Because of the smallness of our numbers, our actions did not have much impact on the youths outside the Chicago area.

3. In terms of its impact on the movement, the indications are that the Weathermen in general and the Chicago action in particular (after initially pushing people to the right) are now helping many people to re-examine the nature of their revolutionary commitment, to push out their own politics more, and to struggle harder....

4. As for the development of the cadre, Chicago was an unqualified success. The Chicago action, its various "personal" consequences, and the heavy criticism sessions afterwards, are transforming us into revolutionaries. Turning jail and court experiences into full-fledged Weatherman actions also played an important part in this process of self-transformation. In the Cook County Jail, we organized ourselves into affinity groups, chose our leadership, and carried on full, disciplined political lives: political education, karate and physical exercises, criticism sessions, general political meetings, doing the housekeeping chores in a collective way, carrying on political struggle in alliance with other inmates, etc. In the courtroom, we have turned the usually intimidating, atomizing, and mystifying legal process into collective political struggles. We march one hundred strong into the courthouse, chanting "Ho, Ho, Ho Chi Minh, Viet Cong is gonna win." Most of us wear our usual street-fighting clothes and boots; we defend ourselves, and demand an

immediate jury trial. We're pushing through a political offensive as avowed Weathermen, as open communists. One judge after one session with us cried out in dismay: "I feel like I'm in a mob action right now." All this is not only to expose and fuck over the courts as a major oppressive institution, but also to ensure that our cadres stay together and grow politically. By pushing out the struggle to the very limit, even in the constrained tactical situation of a courtroom, by regarding every word, every gesture, every motion and every moment as the realm of power struggle between the revolution and the imperialist state, we can take the sting out of the intended intimidation which is the core of the bourgeois court system.

Weatherman is going through a difficult period at the present time, primarily because of the repression unleashed by the enemy, and secondarily, because of the shortcomings in its past practice. I am confident though, that in the near future, it will overcome all the difficulties and shortcomings, and will come to occupy a widely recognized position as the revolutionary vanguard of the entire movement in the white mother country. This will occur even if the majority of the Weatherman leadership and cadres are wiped out in the coming waves of repression.

The 1960s: Achievements/Turning Point

The Weather Underground Organization

THE SIXTIES

Denunciations of the struggles of the sixties as a failure do the enemy's work. These surrenders are a live burial of our people's great moments, and weaken the future by poisoning the lessons of the past. The movement produced some of the highest expressions of international solidarity and commitment in an oppressor nation. Weaknesses there were plenty. We cannot evade them, ignore them nor be reluctant to learn from them. But the lessons won't be drawn apart from the context—where we were coming from and how far we still have to go to revolutionize ourselves and society.

Achievements

The struggles of the 60's changed everything, and we strongly affirm the general thrust and direction of the politics and movements of the last decade. The achievements only represent beginnings, but they are not small:

Desanctification of the Empire. The lesson that the US imperial system is not permanently superior, not invincible even at the height of

---

Excerpts from Weather Underground, *Prairie Fire: The Politics of Revolutionary Anti-Imperialism*, 1974.

its power, not loved by the people of the world, and not satisfying the needs of the great majority of the US people—this is of incalculable importance to the awakening of consciousness. In this year of cynicism about the US rulers it is hard to remember the power of the myths of US invincibility and democracy which governed our people at the beginning of the 60's. Although US global aims had already been rocked by the success of the Chinese Revolution in 1949, the struggles for African independence through the 1950's and the failure to win in Korea, the implications of all this were not known by the US people. The forces unleashed at Little Rock and Montgomery and the triumph of the Cuban Revolution were already burrowing away at the edifice of US superiority, yet we were still asleep.

People now see that imperialism is warlike, with an economy based on the arms race, defense spending and a need to support expansion with the bloodiest interventions in history. People understand corporate greed: the criminal policies of ITT, United Fruit, Standard Oil, Gulf Oil, Dow Chemical, Chase Manhattan, Safeway, and Honeywell. People can now see the hypocrisy of US freedom, justice and democracy—high sounding words masking the fact of US exploitation, aggression and counter-revolution.

Material Contribution to Vietnamese Victory. The anti-war movement made a significant contribution toward forcing the US government to withdraw troops from Vietnam. As part of the worldwide united front against imperialism our movement helped prevent the use of nuclear weapons against Vietnam, a major assault on the dike system, or an invasion of the North. The ruling class is not restrained by scruples—only by their estimation of the political consequences of their actions. The imperial army became an unreliable tool of domination. There were serious interruptions in the functioning of the draft. In addition, part of the anti-war movement saw through the blinders of national chauvinism and brought a glimpse to the US people of the righteousness and humanity of the so-called **"enemy."**

Opposition to Racism. The spirit of resistance inside the US was rekindled by Black people. The power and strategy of the civil rights movement, SNCC, Malcom X, and the Black Panther Party affected all other rebellion. They created a form of struggle called direct action; awoke a common identity, history and dignity for Black people as a colonized and oppressed people within the US; drew out and revealed the enemy through a series of just and undeniable demands such as the vote, equal education, the right to self-defense, and an end to Jim Crow. The police, the troops, the sheriffs, the mass arrests and assassinations were the official response. The Black movement was pushed forward into a revolutionary movement for political power, open rebellion and confrontation with the racism of white people and the racism of institutions.

Growth of Insurgent Cultures. Young women and men fighting to be human beings in the midst of disgusting and crushing social forms found ourselves in opposition to empire. Since World War II imperialism sought to tame its youth thru tracked education, the draft, the oppression of women. These conditions produced a profound alienation in work, school, family, and an openness to revolutionary alternative. The youth revolt and the women's movement moved practically an entire generation on one level or another. This means a substantial sector was torn away from sexist and competitive culture and gave birth to new cultures, fragile but real—cultures in opposition to the system. The overthrowing of rotten values of male supremacy, consumerism, passivity, respectability and the rat race, was a wonderful advance. For women working, for women forced into the marriage marketplace, trapped in oppressive relationships, raising children alone, the women's movement brought a new sense of self-worth and dignity; it explained the conditions of women's oppression. We began to create solidarity among women.

Challenge To Inaction. We inherited a deadening ideology of conformity and gradualism. Our first protests were law-abiding and peaceful. But the treacherous nature of US power was revealed as we began to comprehend Hiroshima, napalm, slavery, lynching, capital punishment, rape, Indian reservations. We came to see that change is violently opposed every step of the way. We stood up and defied propriety, the state and the law, in street demonstrations and outrageous actions. Militant confrontation politics transformed us, we broke with a powerless past. We saw popular uprisings, armed revolution, people's war, and guerrilla combat around the world. We realized the power of armed self-defense, mass rebellion and revolutionary violence in the Black movement. As our own protest elicited teargas, prison and bullets, we recognized the need to fight and the terrible cost of not doing all we possibly can.

Turning Point

The year 1968 was a high point and a turning point. It is not surprising that the maturing of the movement took place at a time when the world was in flames. 500,000 US troops were dealt a staggering blow by the Vietnamese popular forces during Tet. Armed struggle raged throughout Latin America and the Palestinian liberation forces emerged in the Mideast. Student movements in France and throughout the industrialized world were in full revolt, challenging their own governments and demonstrating open solidarity with the people of the world. The Chinese Cultural Revolution was unleashing a new dimension to class struggle.

The movement emerged with a growing revolutionary consciousness that it was involved in a battle for power. This grew out of experience. Black Power had become the slogan for the Black liberation movement, and its political thrust transformed the civil rights movement. Black power was applied in persistent struggles for community control of schools, in rebellions in 60 cities following the assassination of Martin Luther King, by Black students occupying universities, sometimes with arms, and in the emergence of the Black Panther Party.

We also came to recognize that issues which once seemed separate had a relationship to one another. Imperialism was **"discovered"** as a whole, one system. This was a tremendous political breakthrough—it made sense of the world and our own experience. The same school which tracked students by sex, race and class into the appropriate niche, turned out to own slums in the Black community and to develop anti-personnel weapons and strategies against revolution—to be in fact a tool of the corporations and the military.

We were up against a ruling class, and it made no sense to ask them to reform themselves. Our rebellion had led us to revolution—a long and many-sided struggle for power.

SDS was a leading anti-imperialist organization in this movement. Historically, students play an advanced and militant role in anti-imperialist struggle, opposing war and racial injustice. The revolt at Columbia University was a catalyst which exploded the previous era of resistance into a popular revolutionary movement of students and young people. The street battles at the Democratic National Convention in Chicago several months later led to further occupations and demonstrations involving hundreds of thousands of militants. The demonstrations built on each other; each struggle was unique and beautiful. The vitality of SDS was rooted in its local experiences and the application of national programs to different regions and conditions—applying the lessons of Columbia, films on Cuba, building alliances with a Black Student Union. The taste of liberation, the intense struggles, transformed our identifications, our lives.

At this point, some new contradictions appeared.

The state set into motion a plan to discredit, divide and set back the movement. The May 1968 J. Edgar Hoover counterinsurgency memo reveals a national plan to **"expose, disrupt, and otherwise neutralize the activities of the various New Left organizations, their leadership and adherents."** Infiltration and sabotage were carried out by a variety of police agents, including the FBI, the Nixon-Mitchell team, military intelligence, and local red squads. As always the attack was focused on the Black liberation movement and included violent assaults against Black communities and leaders, particularly the Black Panther Party.

With enormous growth of membership, militancy and consciousness after the 1968 demonstrations in Chicago, SDS was faced with several urgent necessities: to draw broader masses of people into the struggle, and also to organize our cadre and transform ourselves into a force which could eventually contend for power. These necessities coexisted uneasily. What were the roads taken at this juncture?

Our strategy was the Revolutionary Youth Movement (RYM). It was aimed at extending the movement among young people—to expand its base and class character, to mobilize those affected by the draft, the army, unemployment, schools, prisons, into anti-imperialist struggle. RYM was a transitional strategy to maintain the militant mass base on the campuses, while we deepened our base among the working class. Young people's openness and consciousness/identification with militant anti-imperialism was a strategic strength. This movement continued to grow spontaneously even after the decline of SDS.

This politics was opposed by an opportunist politics that took the form of economism. Economism appears in every revolutionary movement as the reduction of revolution to a struggle for purely economic gains. Economism has many masks. It was then expressed in a leftish form of **"going to the workers,"** not by creating revolutionary consciousness and action but by sacrificing principle in the hope of gaining a place in the labor movement. This is a corrupt politics, proven bankrupt again and again. In the US, where many of the people who are exploited by imperialism also receive benefits from the super-exploitation of the colonies, economism feeds the idea that people here can be free while other oppressed people are still under the yoke of US imperialism.

Our deep political concern was the historic tendency of the white left to abandon militant anti-imperialism and anti-racism—principled support for Third World struggle—in search of easy integration with the masses. It is difficult to synthesize militant anti-imperialism with a mass base among oppressor-nation people because of the whole fabric of relative social/material white-skin privilege. Much of the movement resolved this contradiction in the direction of opportunism around race. This was the main error of the period, deeply rooted in US radical history.

A comparable example was the student power movement. Some argued that the demand for student's rights and power would become revolutionary in and of itself. This is not true. The chauvinism of **"student power"** demands by white students ignored the claims of university workers, the community, and the Third World people who would be the victims of university-researched weapons and programs. This demand encouraged narrow concern for a relatively privileged sector at the expense of the more oppressed. But when the student revolts actively allied with other movements in the interests of the most oppressed peoples against the common enemy, they became a serious threat to the empire. When each movement only sees its own claims and interests in isolation from other movements, they play themselves out, one after the other.

Another major factor at this point was the rebellion of women against sexism in the society and in the left. The left is not immune from the sexism which pervades US society: the oppressor culture persists and must be opposed and fought again and again. This requires an active commitment to anti-sexism. In the late sixties and early seventies many women left the anti-imperialist movement and built a separate women's movement. Sisters inside—and now outside—the anti-imperialist movement began to force men to deal with their sexist practice. These were absolutely necessary advances. The struggles against sexism did not only mean criticism and change of individual practice, they also transformed the overall analysis of the left. The contradiction was that the women's movement, rejecting sexist and authoritarian leadership, raised blanket challenges to **all** forms of leadership and organization in the movement, good and bad, and failed at that point to build lasting organizations to carry on the task of strong determined anti-imperialist struggle.

SDS was torn by these internal and external dynamics. It was becoming an organization of revolutionaries, anti-imperialist activists. This was recognized by the state which moved to disrupt it. Major ideological struggles about the correct path to transforming SDS into a broader mass organization polarized rapidly, while simultaneously the urgent necessity to join the struggle against imperialism in a serious and armed way was heightened by the Vietnam War and the liberation movement of Black people. Things were in great turmoil and a continuous process of change.

4   THE ANTIWAR MOVEMENT

Robert Scheer's 80-page pamphlet, How the United States Got Involved in Vietnam, was published in July 1965 and distributed in large numbers on college campuses. Because of the pamphlet's thorough documentation, well informed arguments, and reasonable style, many of its readers became persuaded that America's involvement in Vietnam was unjust and immoral.

Master Sergeant Donald Duncan was among the earliest of the antiwar Vietnam veterans. His exposé "The Whole Thing Was a Lie" was published in Ramparts magazine in 1966. Duncan was a decorated war hero whose denunciations of the Vietnam conflict at antiwar rallies helped spark a peace movement among American soldiers. The 1966 court martial of three GI's who refused to go to Vietnam was widely publicized and demonstrated that antiwar sentiment was spreading within the armed forces.

In July 1967 the prestigious Wall Street Journal published an antiwar editorial, "Nightmares of Empire." The article reflected a growing fear in the business community that America might be overreaching in its role as an imperial superpower and convinced many antiwar activists that they were beginning to have an effect on public opinion.

Ho Chi Minh's naturalistic poetry and personal statements to the peace movement made Vietnam's revolutionary leader a popular figure among many new leftists and served to counter the American government's portrayal of him as a fanatical idealogue. Former SDS President Carl Oglesby's existential account of what goes into making someone a revolutionary demonstrated that by 1967 increasingly militant new leftists were finding their heroes among Third World guerilla fighters.

The belief that the United States might be committing genocide in Vietnam became a major motivating force among antiwar activists. Dave Dellinger, a well-known pacifist and leader of the antiwar movement, authored "Unmasking Genocide" upon his return from an International War Crimes Tribunal held in Denmark in 1967. The article appeared in Liberation magazine.

Opposition to the war spread as the body count of U.S. casualties rose and increasing numbers of Americans were affected as family and friends were killed or wounded in Vietnam. Lee Felsenstein's 1968 article "No Door to Tomorrow" was published in The Berkeley Barb.

The Chicago Conspiracy Trial of 1969 was the most important legal confrontation between the antiwar movement and the U.S. government. The flagrant denial of Black Panther leader Bobby Seale's right to counsel and the sight of him bound to a chair in an American courtroom received extensive and embarrassing media coverage. "The Chaining and Gagging of Bobby Seale" is reprinted here verbatim from the trial transcript.

By 1969 many young people were abandoning moderate views and coming to believe that America was a dangerously violent country. The testimony of a young woman radical at the Conspiracy Trial shows her evolution from pacifism to a belief in armed self-defense.

Diane DiPrima's poems caught the inner spiritual experience of someone making a commitment to revolution. Her work was regularly reprinted in the underground press.

Frustration at failing to end the war and the belief that violent confrontation was futile caused many protesters to develop nonviolent and highly original approaches to antiwar activities. Phil Ochs, who organized "The War is Over" march in November 1967 and wrote a song of the same name, was one of the decade's most popular protest singers. His article "Have you Heard? The War is Over" was originally published in the Village Voice.

How the United States Got Involved in Vietnam

Robert Scheer

On June 27, 1950, President Truman announced that he had "directed acceleration in the furnishing of military assistance to the forces of France and the Associated States in Indochina and the dispatch of a military mission to provide close working relations with those forces." This step-up came after the start of the war in Korea and was undoubtedly viewed by the Administration as an operation, on another flank, against the same enemy.

Between 1950 and 1954, the United States sent $2.6 billion worth of military and economic aid to the French in Vietnam (80 per cent of the cost of the war)—$800 million during 1950–52 but $1.8 billion in 1953 and 1954 in response to the imminent French collapse. Senator Mansfield's Subcommittee on State Department Organization and Public Affairs reported in 1954 that French forces outnumbered those of the Viet Minh by a factor of 5 to 3 and "as a result largely of American assistance...the non-Communist forces possessed great superiority— estimated as high as 10-1 in armaments, and the flow of American aid was constant and increasingly heavy."

Why, then, did the French lose the war? The right wing in America has suggested that it was lost because the Administration was not fully

Excerpts from Robert Scheer, *How the United States Got Involved in Vietnam*, Santa Barbara, Calif.: The Center for the Study of Democratic Institutions, 1965, pp. 10–46. Reprinted with permission.

committed to a "win" policy. According to this view, "winning" required a show of strength to the Kremlin with the full commitment of American power in men and weapons.

The idea of a mass attack had been entertained. "Operation Vulture," a joint French-American plan, called for the obliteration of the Viet Minh through the onslaught of 300 carrier-based fighter bombers and sixty heavy bombers from the Philippines. At the request of the U.S. Joint Chiefs of Staff, U.S. aircraft carriers had been sent to the Indochinese coast. Two of the aircraft were rumored at the time to be loaded with atomic bombs, and Secretary of State Dulles is reported to have hinted in Paris that the United States might launch an atomic attack.

President Eisenhower, however, was reluctant to allow Americans to be dragged further into the war. This was due in part to the opposition of our allies, particularly England, and to American exhaustion with war following Korea. But there was also the President's belief that a military victory was not possible because of the political situation: the people supported the Viet Minh and identified Ho Chi Minh as the leader of their independence movement. As Eisenhower stated some years later in his memoirs, *Mandate for Change,*

> The enemy had much popular sympathy, and many civilians aided them by providing both shelter and information. The French still had sufficient forces to win if they could induce the regular Vietnamese soldiers to fight vigorously with them and the populace to support them. But guerrilla warfare cannot work two ways; normally only one side can enjoy reliable citizen help.

In other words, Bao Dai, the anti-Communist nationalist alternative, whom the Truman and Eisenhower Administrations had backed, had failed to undercut the appeal of the Viet Minh. Eisenhower was

> convinced that the French could not win the war because the internal political situation in Vietnam, weak and confused, badly weakened their military position. I have never talked or corresponded with a person knowledgeable in Indochinese affairs who did not agree that had elections been held as of the time of the fighting, possibly 80% of the populace would have voted for the Communist Ho Chi Minh as their leader rather than Chief of State Bao Dai. As one Frenchman said to me, "What Vietnam needs is another Syngman Rhee, regard-

less of all the difficulties the presence of such a personality would entail."

The fact that the United States declined to be involved further at this point undercut that minority of French leaders who wanted to continue a war that the majority of the French population had opposed for years. With the decisive defeat at Dien Bien Phu, the French sued for peace at a conference in Geneva in the spring of 1954.

The negotiations began on May 8, 1954, one day after the fall of Dien Bien Phu, and were concluded on July 21. With hindsight, the meetings at Geneva form a remarkable interlude in the cold war. England, China, and the Soviet Union were a strange group of "peace-makers" urging conciliation on the part of the "belligerents"—France and the Viet Minh. The United States was off to the side, being "handled" by the English and French as a powerful, though not always wise, party that could easily upset the delicate negotiations. Dulles did not approve of their drift and withdrew from the conference, leaving his Under-Secretary, Walter Bedell Smith, a leader of the U.S. delegation. It seemed that the price of peace would involve surrendering control of some portion of the country to the Communists, and the United States was not able to oppose this since it was not willing to become any more deeply involved.

However, although resigned to a military settlement that would concede territory to the Viet Minh, the United States was far from willing to accept the decisions of the conference as determining factors in the ultimate *political* solution for Vietnam. Instead, the United States was soon to place its hope for a favorable political outcome on "a new anti-Communist nationalist alternative." Bao Dai was, by now, unacceptable; American policy came to center around a man whom Bao Dai, then in Paris, had chosen as his new Premier, Ngo Dinh Diem.

* * *

The settlement at Geneva in July, 1954, did three things: (1) it ended the war; (2) it divided Vietnam in half "temporarily"; and (3) it set up an apparatus for "ensuring" the peace and reunification of the country. The basic agreement was drawn up and signed by the representatives of the Viet Minh and the French, the real contestants in Vietnam. The most specific provisions concerned the disengagement of the rival armies and their withdrawal into two "regrouping" zones. The agreement prohibited "reinforcements in the form of all types of arms, munitions and other war materiel" and specified that "the establishment of new military bases is prohibited throughout Viet-Nam territory."

* * *

The basic agreement was then "noted" by the full nine-nation meeting in Geneva. The conference routinely recorded its approval of most of the clauses of the basic agreement but chose to amplify the meaning of the basic political settlement. Since this paragraph has been so often mangled in "interpretations," it is worth recording here:

> The Conference declares that, so far as Viet-Nam is concerned, the settlement of political problems, effected on the basis of respect for the principles of independence, unity and territorial integrity, shall permit the Viet-Namese people to enjoy the fundamental freedoms, guaranteed by democratic institutions established as a result of free general elections by secret ballot. In order to ensure that sufficient progress in the restoration of peace has been made, and that all the necessary conditions obtain for the free expression of the national will, general elections shall be held in July 1956, under the supervision of an international commission composed of representatives of the Member States of the International Supervisory Commission, referred to in the agreement on the cessation of hostilities. Consultations will be held on this subject between the competent representative authorities of the two zones from 20 July 1955 onwards.

This "Declaration of Geneva Conference" was issued in the name of the conference and approved by eight of the nine nations. In a separate statement the United States declared:

> The Government of the United States being resolved to devote its efforts to the strengthening of peace in accordance with the principles and purposes of the United Nations takes note of the agreements concluded at Geneva...[and] it would view any renewal of the aggression in violation of the aforesaid agreements with grave concern...we shall continue to seek to achieve unity through free elections supervised by the United Nations...the United States reiterates its traditional position that peoples are entitled to determine their own future....

The United States and the Diem government were later to claim that they were not bound by the agreement because they had not signed it. However, the United States, for its part, had implied approval when it returned Walter Bedell Smith to the conference, from which he had earlier been withdrawn, at the insistence of the English and the French. Eisenhower acknowledged in his *Mandate for Change:* "Our direct interest in these negotiations arose out of the assumption that the United States would be expected to act as one of the guarantors of whatever agreement should be achieved." He also wrote: "By and large, the settlement obtained by the French Union at Geneva in 1954 was the best it could get under the circumstances."

In any event, the French had signed an agreement with the Viet Minh wherein the latter exchanged a favorable military situation for one in which it could pursue its goals through elections—the culmination of ten years of bloody fighting. Three days after the French and Viet Minh signed their agreement at Geneva, John Foster Dulles entered a demurrer on the part of the United States. He seemed to accept the military solution while rejecting the political implications. At a news conference on July 23, 1954, Dulles said:

> The Geneva negotiations reflected the military developments in Indochina. After nearly eight years of war the forces of the French Union had lost control of nearly one-half of Viet-Nam, their hold on the balance was precarious, and the French people did not desire to prolong the war.... Since this was so, and since the United States itself was neither a belligerent in Indochina nor subject to compulsions which applied to others, we did not become a party to the conference results. We merely noted them and said that, in accordance with the United Nations Charter, we would not seek by force to overthrow the settlement.... The important thing for now is not to mourn the past but to seize the future opportunity to prevent the loss in northern Viet-Nam from leading to the extension of Communism throughout Southeast Asia.... One lesson is that resistance to Communism needs popular support, and this in turn means that the people should feel that they are defending their own national institutions....

This recognition of the pragmatic value of freedom—"resistance to Communism needs popular support"—was to become a keystone of U.S. policy in Vietnam. The French colonial puppet regime must be replaced by a "new," "independent" regime, which could then set about to win the support of people who now backed the Viet Minh. Dulles stated that the new government would be protected by collective security arrangements under the Southeast Asia Treaty Organization (SEATO) "to promote the security of the free peoples...[against] Communist subversion...." If 80 per cent of the people supported Ho, as Eisenhower was to state later in his memoirs, the threat to the Diem government would presumably come from the people themselves, and free world support of the Diem government would mean frustrating the popular will. But, as the U.S. view had it, the people chose Ho because they had not yet been offered a better way. The U.S.-supported Diem government would become the alternative.

* * *

The installation of Diem as the Premier of Vietnam helped focus U.S. policy in Southeast Asia. Diem was committed to the re-making of Vietnamese society according to a not always lucid, but always anti-Communist and anti-French, model that required for its enactment the concentration of total power in the hands of a small trusted group. According to Bernard Fall, in *The Two Vietnams*, Diem, unlike some of his advisers, never had any doubts about the necessity for tight central control to divert the nationalist revolution from Communist objectives. Ho and Giap, the Communist leaders of the Viet Minh, were heroes of the resistance to the French. Diem understood that changing the course of their revolution required the liquidation of the Viet Minh and the "re-education" of the majority of the population that supported the movement. It was a formidable task for a regime that had arisen late in the day and by grace of a foreign power.

Diem in his first year in office moved to consolidate his control by crushing all sources of opposition—the religious sects and nationalist but anti-Diem politicians, along with the cadres left behind by the Viet Minh. These came to be called the Viet Cong. It was soon clear that Diem would refuse to provide for the popular mandate called for in the Geneva agreements. Each step to that end required American support and conflicted with the interests of the French, who wanted to limit Diem's power, keep the situation fluid, and maintain whatever influence they could.

Eisenhower was sympathetic to the French position, as his later writings make clear. He recognized not only Ho's popularity but the high cost of any effort to crush his movement. He resisted grandiose

schemes for building up Diem's regime as a Western-style alternative to
the Viet Minh, and the man he chose as his Special Ambassador to
Vietnam, General Lawton Collins, shared these sentiments. But the
Eisenhower Administration was particularly vulnerable to political
pressure, and it was during this unsettled period that Diem's pre-Geneva
lobbying began to bear fruit.

One of the first voices raised publicly on behalf of a "hard line" of
all-out support for Diem was that of Cardinal Spellman. In a speech
before the American Legion Convention on August 31, 1954, he was
quoted by The New York Times:

> If Geneva and what was agreed upon there means anything at all, it
> means...Taps for the buried hopes of freedom in Southeast Asia!
> Taps for the newly betrayed millions of Indochinese who must now
> learn the awful facts of slavery from their eager Communist masters!
> Now the devilish techniques of brainwashing, forced confessions
> and rigged trials have a new locale for their exercise.

Spellman emphasized the essential theses of the cold war containment
policy: "...Communism has a world plan and it has been following a
carefully set-up time table for the achievement of that plan..." "...the
infamies and agonies inflicted upon the hapless victims of Red Russia's
bestial tyranny...." A show of strength was required, "...else we shall
risk bartering our liberties for lunacies, betraying the sacred trust of our
forefathers, becoming serfs and slaves to Red rulers' godless goons."
The danger lay in the illusion of peace with the Communists:

> Americans must not be lulled into sleep by indifference nor be
> beguiled by the prospect of peaceful coexistence with Communists.
> How can there be peaceful coexistence between two parties if one of
> them is continually clawing at the throat of the other...? Do you
> peacefully coexist with men who thus would train the youth of their
> godless, Red world...?

The Cardinal demonstrated his support of Diem by going to
Vietnam to deliver personally the first check for Catholic Relief Services
funds spent in Vietnam. Others of Diem's early supporters followed
suit. Wesley Fishel, the Michigan State University professor who had
originally induced Diem to come to the United States, turned up in
Vietnam as one of his chief advisers, with residence in the presidential

palace. Another American inhabitant of the palace was Wolf Ladejinsky, a New Dealer who had stayed on in the Department of Agriculture only to be fired under pressure from Senator Joseph McCarthy for alleged (but never proved) radical connections. Ladejinsky had worked on the Japanese land reform program, and Diem hired him to work on land problems in Vietnam—proof to many American liberals of Diem's commitment to serious social reform.

Another visitor to Diem was Leo Cherne, who had helped to found the Research Institute of America, one of the first of the management-research firms designed to help American corporations cope with the expanding government of the post-1930's. It also supplied its 30,000 business clients with general political information. Cherne was also president of the International Rescue Committee, an organization aimed at helping refugees from communism.

Cherne went to Vietnam in September of 1954 and spent two and a half weeks there, becoming very interested in Diem's potentialities as a democratic, nationalist alternative to the Communists. In a cable he sent back to the subscribers to his Research Institute he reported:

> ... have been talking intimately with American officials here, including Ambassador Heath. Conferred at length yesterday with Vietnam Premier Ngo Dinh Diem... success of effort to hold Vietnam from Communists depends on whether all non-Communist Vietnamese can unite for struggle. U.S. Embassy, strongly supporting Diem, views him as key to the whole situation. Political and financial instability... unless Vietnamese Government can organize important forces and U.S. continues pouring in substantial help and money.... If free elections held today all agree privately Communists would win... situation not hopeless... future depends on organizing all resources to resettle refugees, sustain new bankrupt government, give people something to fight for and unite them to resist Communism.... West can't afford to lose from now on.

Upon returning to the United States, Cherne sent his second-in-command in the International Rescue Committee, Joseph Buttinger, to set up an office in Vietnam. At this time Buttinger was involved in Socialist politics as an editor of *Dissent* magazine; during the mid-Thirties, under the name of Gustave Richter, he had been the leader of the underground Social Democratic Party in Austria. This had been a bitter experience. His one accomplishment, as he writes about it in his memoirs, *In the Twilight of Socialism*, had been to stop the growth of the Communists.

A year after this book was published, a C.I.A. agent named Edward Lansdale introduced Buttinger to the men around Ngo Dinh Diem, and after some three months in Vietnam Buttinger believed Diem to be the answer to the Communist revolution. As Buttinger remarked to this author, "He was strong and shrewd and determined to stay in power and would stay in power."

During the late fall of 1954, while Buttinger was in Vietnam, a serious split was developing among Americans concerned with Vietnam. As Cherne's telegram indicated, U.S. missions in Saigon were strongly backing Diem. For example, an abrupt halt was called to the revolt of General Hinh, the head of the Vietnamese army and an officer in the French army as well. When General Collins arrived in mid-November of 1954, as Eisenhower's Special Ambassador, he made it clear that the United States would not pay the army if Diem was overthrown. In a matter of days Hinh was sent out of the country and dismissed as head of the army.

However, from the very beginning Diem displayed that tendency toward autocracy and family rule for which the mass media of the United States would belatedly condemn his administration eight years later. In early 1955, when he moved to crush the religious sects, whose military forces rivaled his power, some influential Americans began to side with the French against him. The most important of these was General Collins, and his view was shared by other American observers. Among them was the newspaper columnist Joseph Alsop, who contended that Diem's base of support was too narrow to rival that of the Viet Minh. (Both men were later to renew their support of Diem after he defeated the sects.)

At this juncture, when it looked as if the United States might dispose of Diem, his reservoir of support, his "lobby," proved decisive. In the ensuing struggle the curious alliance of Lansdale, the C.I.A. agent, Buttinger, the ex-Austrian Socialist, and Cardinal Spellman won the day.

On the official level, Lansdale convinced his Director, Allen Dulles, of Diem's efficiency, and the latter convinced his brother, who, as Secretary of State, talked with the President. The recent book on the C.I.A., *The Invisible Government*, by David Wise and Thomas B. Ross, places the total responsibility for swinging U.S. support to Diem at this stage on Lansdale, but the private political pressures were important. Buttinger returned from Vietnam excited about Diem but fearful that the United States was not totally committed to him. He turned to the group around the International Rescue Committee, one of the most useful of them being the public relations counsel for the organization, Harold Oram. Oram knew the head of the Catholic Relief Services in Washington and that gentleman introduced Buttinger to Cardinal Spellman. The Cardinal was still an enthusiastic believer in Diem, and Buttinger alerted him to the impending crises in Diem's fortunes.

Spellman sent Buttinger back to Washington to meet with Joseph P. Kennedy and finally, according to Buttinger in an interview with this author, these two powerful men, in a long-distance telephone conversation, decided to whom Buttinger should tell his story. In Washington, Kennedy introduced him to Senator Mike Mansfield and to Kenneth Young of the State Department. John F. Kennedy was in California at the time but Buttinger had a long conversation with his administrative assistant.

Meanwhile, Cardinal Spellman had arranged meetings with the editorial board of the New York *Herald Tribune*, the chief editors of *Life* and *Time*, and several editors of *The New York Times*. On January 29, 1955, two days after Buttinger's visit to the *Times*, that paper carried an editorial which closely paralleled Buttinger's arguments on Diem's behalf. Buttinger also elaborated his position in *The Reporter* of January 27, 1955, and *The New Republic* of February 28, 1955.

From the Spring of 1955 on, the U.S. commitment to Diem was complete. This meant that the United States would ignore any French protestations and the Geneva Accords—including the provisions calling for reunification through free elections, which, as even Diem's most ardent supporters conceded, would bring the Communist-oriented Viet Minh to power. A Cardinal, a C.I.A. agent and an ex-Austrian Socialist seemed to have carried the day against the instincts of a General turned President.

* * *

Between 1954 and 1958 Diem's government did attain a degree of stable rule over parts of South Vietnam. But it is clear now that it was not evolving toward a free society. Indeed the essential condition of its stability was the absence of political freedom. From the very beginning the Diem regime showed no reluctance to utilize political terror to strengthen and maintain its rule. During this period the United States set out to ensure the loyalty of the army to Diem, as the Michigan State professors had done in the course of training the secret police and the

Palace Guard. Colonel Lansdale of the C.I.A. also was concerned with winning over the peasants and toward that end organized Civic Action teams which roamed the countryside with megaphones and film projectors extolling the virtues of the Diem regime. The M.S.U. group later took over this project, but it was able to report only limited success. It was difficult to recruit members for the teams and they were forced to rely heavily on refugees from the North loyal to Diem. As John D. Montgomery reported in his book, *The Politics of Foreign Aid,*

> The villagers who were the project's beneficiaries sometimes resented the visiting teams because they were staffed with refugees from the north—strangers who spoke a different dialect and practiced a different religion. Almost all refugees from the Communist regime in North Viet-Nam were Roman Catholics, and the government's costly program for them, together with the policy of using such strong anti-Communists as Civic Action leaders, stimulated much envy and resentment.

The Diem government's contribution to the idea of civic action was to unleash a reign of terror upon the countryside. There were massive anti-Communist renunciation campaigns. Thousands of people suspected of sympathizing with the Viet Minh were sent to re-education centers. Those thought to be active Viet Cong agents were jailed or shot. Prizes were offered for turning in one's parents or relatives, and detailed statistics were compiled on the number who confessed and were re-educated.

Article 14c of the Geneva Accords had protected the rights of those sympathetic to the belligerents in the war, but the Diem government did not permit the International Control Commission to investigate charges of violation of these provisions. It was the the view of the Commission that because of the obstruction of the Diem government, "The Commission is therefore no longer able to supervise the implementation of this article by the Government of the Republic of South Vietnam."

The Accords embodied concepts ostensibly cherished by the "free world," and it was these provisions the Diem government refused to uphold. For example, the Sixth Interim Report of the International Control Commission reported that the Viet Minh offered "to have complete freedom of movement between the two zones" making an "iron" or "bamboo" curtain impossible, but the forces in the South rejected this. During the summer of 1955, demonstrations in Saigon against the Geneva Accords had resulted in the burning of the hotel that housed the Control Commission.

The Viet Minh, on the other hand, was more respectful of the Accord because they were counting on the Commission's carrying out the elections. The Sixth Interim Report of the unanimous finding of the Commission stated: "...the degree of cooperation given by the two parties has not been the same. While the Commission has experienced difficulties in North Vietnam, the major part of its difficulties has arisen in South Vietnam."

These reports indicate that the apparent political stability of the Diem regime in those first five years was due primarily to the Viet Minh willingness to withhold pressure in view of its virtually certain victory at the polls under the Geneva Accords. This is conceded in the account of that period offered in the U.S. State Department's White Paper of October, 1961:

> It was the Communists' calculation that nationwide elections scheduled in the accords for 1956 would turn all of Viet-Nam over to them.... The primary focus of the Communists' activity during the post-Geneva period was on political action...the refusal [to hold elections] came as a sharp disappointment to Hanoi, whose political program for two years had been aimed at precisely that goal. The failure of 1956 was a severe blow to the morale of the Viet Cong organization in the South.... The period of 1956–58 was one of rebuilding and reorganization for the Viet Cong.

By 1959, the Viet Minh had finally written off the possibility of elections and turned to military means. Thus ended the illusory stability of the Diem regime.

The Whole Thing Was a Lie!

Don Duncan

When I was drafted into the Army, ten years ago, I was a militant anti-Communist. Like most Americans, I couldn't conceive of anybody choosing communism over democracy. The depths of my aversion to this ideology was, I suppose, due in part to my being Roman Catholic, in part to the stories in the news media about communism, and in part to the fact that my stepfather was born in Budapest, Hungary. Although he had come to the United States as a young man, most of his family had stayed in Europe. From time to time, I would be given examples of the horrors of life under communism. Shortly after Basic Training, I was sent to Germany. I was there at the time of the Soviet suppression of the Hungarian revolt. Everything I had heard about communism was verified. Like my fellow soldiers I felt frustrated and cheated that the United States would not go to the aid of the Hungarians. Angrily, I followed the action of the brute force being used against people who were armed with sticks, stolen weapons, and a desire for independence.

While serving in Germany, I ran across the Special Forces. I was so impressed by their dedication and élan that I decided to volunteer for duty with this group. By 1959 I had been accepted into the Special Forces and underwent training at Fort Bragg. I was soon to learn much about the outfit and the men in it. A good percentage of them were Lodge Act people—men who had come out from Iron Curtain countries. Their anti-communism bordered on fanaticism. Many of them who, like me, had joined Special Forces to do something positive, were to leave because "things" weren't happening fast enough. They were to

Excerpts from Don Duncan, "The Whole Thing Was a Lie!," *Ramparts*, February 1966. Reprinted with permission.

show up later in Africa and Latin America in the employ of others or as independent agents for the CIA.

Initially, training was aimed at having United States teams organize guerrilla movements in foreign countries. Emphasis was placed on the fact that guerrillas can't take prisoners. We were continuously told, "You don't have to kill them yourself—let your indigenous counterpart do that." In a course entitled, "Countermeasures to Hostile Interrogation," we were taught NKVD (Soviet Security) methods of torture to extract information. It became obvious that the title was only camouflage for teaching us "other" means of interrogation when time did not permit more sophisticated methods, for example, the old cold water-hot water treatment, or the delicate operation of lowering a man's testicles into a jeweler's vise. When we asked directly if we were being told to use these methods the answer was, "We can't tell you that. The Mothers of America wouldn't approve." This sarcastic hypocrisy was greeted with laughs. Our own military teaches these and even worse things to American soldiers. They then condemn the Viet Cong guerrilla for supposedly doing those very things. I was later to witness firsthand the practice of turning prisoners over to ARVN for "interrogation" and the atrocities which ensued.

Throughout the training there was an exciting aura of mystery. Hints were continually being dropped that "at this very moment" Special Forces men were in various Latin American and Asian countries on secret missions. The anti-Communist theme was woven throughout. Recommended reading would invariably turn out to be books on "brainwashing" and atrocity tales—life under communism. The enemy was THE ENEMY. There was no doubt that THE ENEMY was communism and Communist countries. There never was a suggestion that Special Forces would be used to set up guerilla warfare against the government in a Fascist-controlled country.

It would be a long time before I would look back and realize that this conditioning about the Communist conspiracy and THE ENEMY was taking place. Like most of the men who volunteered for Special Forces, I wasn't hard to sell. We were ready for it. Artur Fisers, my classmate and roommate, was living for the day when he would "lead the first 'stick' of the first team to go into Latvia." "How about Vietnam, Art?" "To hell with Vietnam. I wouldn't blend. There are not many blue-eyed gooks." This was to be only the first of many contradictions of the theory that special Forces men cannot be prejudiced about the color or religion of other people.

After graduation, I was chosen to be a Procurement NCO for Special Forces in California. The joke was made that I was now a procurer. After seeing how we were prostituted, the analogy doesn't seem a bad one. General Yarborough's instructions were simple: "I want good, dedicated men who will graduate. If you want him, take him. Just remember, he may be on your team someday." Our final instructions from the captain directly in charge of the program had some succinct points. I stood in shocked disbelief to hear, "Don't send me any niggers. Be careful, however, not to give the impression that we are prejudiced in Special Forces. You won't find it hard to find an excuse to reject them. Most will be too dumb to pass the written test. If they luck out on that and get by the physical testing, you'll find that they have some sort of a criminal record." The third man I sent to Fort Bragg was a "nigger." And I didn't forget that someday he might be on my team.

My first impressions of Vietnam were gained from the window of the jet while flying over Saigon and its outlying areas. As I looked down I thought, "Why, those could be farms anywhere and that could be a city anywhere." The ride from Tan Son Nhut to the center of town destroyed the initial illusion.

My impressions weren't unique for a new arrival in Saigon. I was appalled by the heat and humidity which made my worsted uniform feel like a fur coat. Smells. Exhaust fumes from the hundreds of blue and white Renault taxis and military vehicles. Human excrement; the foul, stagnant, black mud and water as we passed over the river on Cong Ly Street; and overriding all the others, the very pungent and rancid smell of what I later found out was *nuoc mam*, a sauce made much in the same manner as sauerkraut, with fish substituted for cabbage. No Vietnamese meal is complete without it. People—masses of them! The smallest children, with the dirty faces of all children of their age, standing on the sidewalk unshod and with no clothing other than a shirtwaist that never quite reached the navel on the protruding belly. Those a little older wearing overall-type trousers with the crotch seam torn out—a practical alteration that eliminates the need for diapers. Young grade school girls in their blue butterfly sun hats, and boys of the same age with hands out saying, "OK—Salem," thereby exhausting their English vocabulary. The women in *ao dais* of all colors, all looking beautiful and graceful. The slim, hipless men, many walking hand-in-hand with other men, and so misunderstood by the newcomer. Old men with straggly Fu Man Chu beards staring impassively, wearing wide-legged, pajama-like trousers.

Bars by the hundreds—with American-style names (Playboy,

Hungry i, Flamingo) and faced with grenade-proof screening. Houses made from packing cases, accommodating three or four families, stand alongside spacious villas complete with military guard. American GI's abound in sport shirts, slacks, and cameras; motorcycles, screaming to make room for a speeding official in a large, shiny sedan, pass over an intersection that has hundreds of horseshoes impressed in the soft asphalt tar. Confusion, noise, smells, people—almost overwhelming.

My initial assignment was in Saigon as an Area Specialist for III and IV Corps Tactical Zone in the Special Forces Tactical Operations Center. And my education began here. The officers and NCO's were unanimous in their contempt of the Vietnamese.

There was a continual put-down of Saigon officials, the Saigon government, ARVN (Army Republic of Vietnam), the LLDB (Luc Luong Dac Biet—Vietnamese Special Forces) and the Vietnamese man-in-the-street. The government was rotten, the officials corrupt, ARVN cowardly, the LLDB all three, and the man-in-the-street an ignorant thief. (LLDB also qualified under "thief.")

I was shocked. I was working with what were probably some of the most dedicated Americans in Vietnam. They were supposedly in Vietnam to help "our Vietnamese friends" in their fight for a democratic way of life. Obviously, the attitude didn't fit.

It occurred to me that if the people on "our side" were all these things, why were we then supporting them and spending $1.5 million dollars a day in their country? The answer was always the same: "They are anti-Communists," and this was supposed to explain everything.

As a result of this insulation, my initial observations of everything and everyone Vietnamese were colored. I almost fell into the habit, or mental laziness, of evaluating Vietnam not on the basis of what I saw and heard, but on what I was told by other biased Americans. When you see something contradictory, there is always a fellow countryman willing to interpret the significance of it, and it won't be favorable to the Vietnamese. This is due partially to the type of Vietnamese that the typical American meets, coupled with typical American prejudices. During his working hours, the American soldier deals primarily with the Vietnamese military. Many (or most) of the higher-ranking officers attained their status through family position, as a reward for political assistance, and through wealth. Most of the ranking civilians attained their positions in the same manner. They use their offices primarily as a means of adding to their personal wealth. There is hardly any social rapport between GI Joe and his Vietnamese counterpart.

Most contact between Americans and Vietnamese civilians is restricted to taxi drivers, laborers, secretaries, contractors, and bar girls. All these people have one thing in common: they are dependent on Americans for a living. The last three have something else in common. In addition to speaking varying degrees of English, they will tell Americans anything they want to hear as long as the money rolls in. Neither the civilian nor military with whom the American usually has contact is representative of the Vietnamese people.

Many of our military, officers and enlisted, have exported the color prejudice, referring to Vietnamese as "slopes" and "gooks"—two words of endearment left over from Korea. Other fine examples of American Democracy in action are the segregated bars. Although there are exceptions, in Saigon, Nha Trang, and Da Nang and some of the other larger towns, Negroes do not go into white bars except at the risk of being ejected. I have seen more than one incident where a Negro newcomer has made a "mistake" and walked into the wrong bar. If insulting catcalls weren't enough to make him leave, he was thrown out bodily. There are cases where this sort of thing has led to near-riots.

It is obvious that the Vietnamese resent us as well. We are making many of the same mistakes that the French did, and in some instances our mistakes are worse. Arrogance, disrespect, rudeness, prejudice, and our own special brand of ignorance, are not designed to win friends. This resentment runs all the way from stiff politeness to obvious hatred. It is so common that if a Vietnamese working with or for Americans is found to be sincerely cooperative, energetic, conscientious, and honest, it automatically makes him suspect as a Viet Cong agent.

After my initial assignment in Saigon, which lasted two and one-half months, I volunteered for a new program called Project Delta. This was a classified project wherein specially selected men in Special Forces were to train and organize small teams to be infiltrated into Laos. The primary purpose of dropping these teams into Laos was to try and find the Ho Chi Minh trail and gather information on traffic, troops, weapons, etc....

* * *

...Toward this end we sent people on a mission that had little or no chance of success. It became apparent that we were not interested in the welfare of the Vietnamese but, rather, in how we could best promote our own interests. We sent 40 men who had become our friends. These were exceptionally dedicated people, all volunteers, and their CO showed up drunk at the plane to bid the troops farewell—just all boozed up. Six returned, the rest were killed or captured.

* * *

To many in Vietnam this mission confirmed that the Ho Chi Minh trail, so called, and the traffic on it, was grossly exaggerated, and that the Viet Cong were getting the bulk of their weapons from ARVN and by sea. It also was one more piece of evidence that the Viet Cong were primarily South Vietnamese, not imported troops from the North. One more thing was added to my growing lists of doubts of the "official" stories about Vietnam.

When the project shifted to in-country operations Americans went on drops throughout the Viet Cong-held areas of South Vietnam. One such trip was into War Zone D north of Dong Xoi, near the Michelin plantation. There is no such thing as a typical mission. Each one is different. But this one revealed some startling things. Later I was to brief Secretary of Defense McNamara and General Westmoreland on the limited military value of the bombing, as witnessed on this mission.

As usual we went in at dusk—this time in a heavy rain squall. We moved only a nominal distance, perhaps 300 meters, through the thick, tangled growth and stopped. Without moonlight we were making too much noise. It rained all night so we had to wait until first light to move without crashing around. Moving very cautiously for about an hour, we discovered a deserted company headquarters position, complete with crude tables, stools, and sleeping racks. After reporting this by radio, we continued on our way. The area was crisscrossed with well-traveled trails under the canopy. A few hours later we reached the edge of a large rubber plantation, we skirted the perimeter. We discovered that it was completely surrounded by deserted gun positions and fox holes, all with beautiful fields-of-fire down the even rows of rubber trees. None gave evidence of having been occupied for at least three or four days. We transmitted this information to the Tactical Operations Center (TOC) and then the team proceeded across the plantation, heading for the headquarters and housing area in the center.

When we arrived at a point 100 meters from our destination, the team leader and I went forward, leaving the team in a covering position. As we got closer, we could hear sounds from the houses, but assumed

292 / THE ANTIWAR MOVEMENT

these were only workers. The briefing had neglected to tell us that the plantation was supposed to be deserted. Crawling, we stopped about 25 meters from the first line of houses. Lifting our heads, we received a rude shock. These weren't plantation workers. These were Viet Cong soldiers, complete with blue uniforms, webbing, and many with the new Soviet bloc weapons. The atmosphere seemed to be one of relaxation. We could even hear a transistor radio playing music. After 30 or 40 minutes we drew back to the team position. We reported our find to the TOC and estimated the number of Viet cong to be at least one company. The whole team then retraced the two kilometers to the jungle and moved into it. Crawling into the thickest part, we settled down just as darkness and the rain closed in on us.

Underneath ponchos, to prevent light from our flashlights escaping, the Vietnamese team leader and I, after closely poring over our maps, drafted a detailed message for TOC. In the morning we sent the message, which gave map coordinates of a number of small Landing Zones (LZs) around the area. We also gave them a plan for exploiting our find. It was fairly simple. Make simultaneous landings at all LZs and have the troops move quickly to the deserted Viet Cong gun positions and man them. At the sight of bombers approaching, the Viet Cong would leave the housing area for the jungle. This would involve them having to travel across two kilometers of open plantation into prepared positions. We told TOC that we were going to try and get back to the housing area so we could tell them if the Viet Cong were still there. If they didn't hear from us on the next scheduled contact, they were to assume that we had been hit and hadn't made it. If this occurred it would be verification of the Viet Cong presence and they were to follow through with the plan. We would stay in the area and join the Rangers when they came in.

This time, we were more cautious in our trip across the plantation. On the way, we found a gasoline cache of 55-gallon drums. We took pictures and proceeded. Again the Vietnamese team leader and I crawled forward to within 25 meters of the houses. It was unbelievable. There they were and still with no perimeter security. Now, however, there was much activity and what seemed like more of them. We inched our way around the house area. This wasn't a company. There were at least 300 armed men in front of us. We had found a battalion, and all in one tight spot—unique in itself. We got back to the team, made our radio contact, and asked if the submitted plan would be implemented. We were told, yes, and that we were to move back to the edge of the jungle. There would be a small delay while coordination was made to get the troops and helicopters. At 1000 hours (10:00 a.m.) planes of all descriptions started crisscrossing this small area. I contacted one plane (there were so many I couldn't tell which one) on the Prick 10 (AN/PRC-10 transmitter-receiver for air-ground communications). I was told that they were reconning the area for an operation. What stupidity. No less than 40 overflights in 45 minutes. As usual, we were alerting the Viet Cong of impending action by letting all the armchair commandos take a look-see. For about 30 minutes all was quiet, and then we started to notice movement. The Viet Cong were moving out from the center of the plantation. Where were the troops? At 1400 hours Skyraiders showed up and started bombing the center of the plantation. Was it possible that the troops had moved in without our knowing it? TOC wouldn't tell us anything. The bombing continued throughout the afternoon with never more than a 15-minute letup. Now we had much company in the jungle with us. Everywhere we turned there were Viet Cong. I had to agree that, in spite of the rain, it was a much better place to be than in the housing center. Why didn't we hear our troops firing?

Finally the bombing ended with the daylight, and we crouched in the wet darkness within hearing distance of Viet Cong elements. Darkness was our fortress. About 2030 (8:30 p.m.) we heard the drone of a heavy aircraft in the rainy sky. We paid little attention to it. Then, without warning, the whole world lit up, leaving us feeling exposed and naked. Two huge flares were swinging gently to earth on their parachutes, one on each side of us. At about the same time, our radio contact plane could be heard above the clouds. I grabbed the radio and demanded to know, "Who the hell is calling for those flares and why?"

"What flares?"

"Damn it, find out what flares and tell whoever is calling for them that they're putting us in bad trouble." I could hear the operator trying to call the TOC. I figured that friendly troops in the area had called for the flares to light their perimeter. Crack—crump. I was lifted from the ground, only to be slammed down again. I broke in on the radio. "Forget that transmission. I know why the flares are being dropped."

"Why?"

"They're being used as markers for jets dropping what sounds like 750-pounders. Tell TOC thanks for the warning. Also tell them two of the markers bracketed our position. I hope to hell they knew where we are." A long pause.

"TOC says they don't know anything about flares or jet bombers."

Another screwup. "Well how about somebody finding out something and when they find out, how about telling us unimportant folks? In the meantime, I hope that 'gooniebird' (C-47 plane) has its running lights on."

"Why?"

"Because any moment now the pilot is going to find he is dawdling around in a bomb run pattern. Come back early in the morning and give me the hot skinny."

"Roger—we're leaving—out."

I was mad, a pretty good sign that I was scared. The bombing continued through the night. Sometimes it was "crump" and sometimes it was "crack," depending on how close the bombs fell. When it finally stopped sometime before dawn, I realized that it was a dazzling exhibition of flying—worthless—but impressive. The flare ship had to fly so low becaue of the cloud cover that its flares were burning out on the ground instead of in the air. The orbiting jets would then dive down through the clouds, break through, spot the markers, make split-second corrections, and release their bombs. However, while it was going on, considering what a small error became at jet speeds, a small error would wipe us out. Should this happen, I could see a bad case of "C'est la guerre" next day at air operations. I couldn't help wondering also how "Charlie" was feeling about all this—specifically the ones only 25 or 30 meters away. It didn't seem possible, but I wondered if the shrapnel tearing through the tree tops was terrifying him as much as us.

First thing in the morning, my Vietnamese counterpart made contact on the big radio (HC-162D). After some talk into the mike, he turned to me with a helpless look:

"They say we must cross plantation to housing area again."

"What? It's impossible—tell them so."

More talk. "They say we must go. They want to talk to you."

When the hollow voice came through on the side band, I couldn't believe it—it was the same order. I told them it was impossible and that we were not going to go.

"You must go. That is an order from way up."

That figures. The Saigon wheels smelling glory have taken over our TOC. "My answer is, Will Not Comply; I say again, Will Not Comply. Tell those people to stop trying to outguess the man on the ground. If they want someone to assess damage on the housing area send a plane with a camera. Better yet, have the Rangers look at it, there's more of them.''

"There are no other friendly troops in the area. You are the only ones that can do it. You must go. There will be a plane in your area shortly. Out.''

Up to this point we had assumed friendly troops were in the area and that if we got in trouble, maybe we could hold out until they could help us. No troops. Little wonder the Viet Cong are roaming all over the place not caring who hears them.

Soon a plane arrived and I received: "We must know how many Viet Cong are still in the housing area. You must go and look. It is imperative. The whole success of this mission depends on your report. Over.''

"I say again, Will Not Comply. Over.'' (Hello court martial.) I looked at the Vietnamese team leader. He was tense and grim, but silently cheering me on. While waiting for the plane I asked him what he was going to do. He replied:

"We go, we die. Order say we must go, so we go. We will die.''

Tell me Vietnamese have no guts. Another transmission from the plane:

"Why won't you comply? Over.''

These type questions aren't normally answered. I knew, however, that the poor bastard up there had to take an answer back to the wheels. Well, he got one: "Because we can't. One step out of this jungle and it's all over. I'm not going to have this team wiped out for nothing. There are no Viet Cong in the village; not since 1400 yesterday. The mission was screwed up when you started the bombing without sending in troops yesterday. As for the mission depending on us, you should have thought of that yesterday before you scrapped the plans and didn't bother to tell us. Over.''

"Where are the Viet Cong now? Over.''

"Which ones? The ones 25 meters from us, or the ones 35 meters from us? They're in the jungle all around us. Over.''

"Roger. Understand Viet Cong have left houses—now in jungle— have information necessary—you do not have to go across plantation.''

This was unbelievable. On TV it would be a comedy—a bad one.

Shortly after this uplifting exchange, the bombers returned, and we spent the remainder of the day moving from one Viet Cong group to another. We would come upon them, pull back, and then an A1-E (bomber) would come whining down, machine-gunning or dropping bombs.

I discovered that the old prop fighter bombers were more terrifying than the jets. The jets came in so fast that the man on the ground couldn't hear them until the bombs were dropped and they were climbing away. The props were something else. First the droning noise while in orbit. Then they would peel off and the drone would change to a growl, increasing steadily in pitch until they were a screaming whine. Under the jungle canopy, this noise grabbed at the heart of every man. And every man knew that the plane was pointed directly at him. The crack of the bomb exploding was almost a relief. Many of these bombs landed 25 to 35 meters from where we were lying on the ground. The closest any of us came to being hurt was when a glowing piece of shrapnel lodged in the pack on my back. I couldn't help thinking, "These are our planes. They know where we are. What must it be like for a woman or child to hear that inhuman, impersonal whine directed at them in their open villages? How they must hate us!" I looked around at my team. Others were thinking. Each of us died a little that day in the jungle.

At 1730 (5:30 p.m.) the last bomb was dropped. A great day for humanity. Almost 28 hours of bombing in this small area with barely a break.

On the next afternoon we were told by radio to quickly find an LZ and prepare to leave the area. We knew of only one within reasonable distance and headed for it. A short distance from the LZ we could hear voices. Viet Cong around the opening. We were now an equal distance between two groups of the Viet Cong.

Finally they allowed the pick-up ship to come in. Just as the plane touched down and we started toward it, two machine gun positions opened up—one from each side of the clearing. The bullets sounded like gravel hitting the aluminum skin of the chopper. My American assistant took one position under fire and I started firing at the other. Our backs were to the aircraft and our eyes on the jungle. The rest of the team started climbing aboard. The machine guns were still firing, but we had made them less accurate. I was still firing when two strong hands picked me up and plumped me on the floor of the plane. Maximum power and we still couldn't make the trees at the end of the clearing, but had to make a half-circle over the machine guns. All of a sudden something slapped me in the buttock, lifting me from the floor. A bullet came through the bottom of the plane, through the gas tank and the floor. When it ripped through the floor it turned sideways. The slug left an eight-inch bruise but did not penetrate. Through some miracle, we were on our way to base—all of us. We would get drunk tonight. It was the only way we would sleep without reliving the past days. It would be at least three days before anybody would unwind. That much is typical.

I had seen the effect of the bombing at close range. These bombs would land and go for about 15 yards and tear off a lot of foliage from the trees, but that was it. Unless you drop these things in somebody's hip pocket they don't do any good. For 28 hours they bombed that area. And it was rather amusing because, when I came out, it was estimated that they had killed about 250 Viet Cong in the first day. They asked me how many Viet Cong did I think they had killed and I said maybe six, and I was giving them the benefit of the doubt at that. The bombing had no real military significance. It would only work if aimed at concentrated targets such as villages.

One of the first axioms one learns about unconventional warfare is that no insurgent or guerrilla movement can endure without the support of the people....

We were still being told, both by our own government and the Saigon government, that the vast majority of the people of South Vietnam were opposed to the Viet Cong. When I questioned this contradiction, I was always told that the people only helped the Viet Cong through fear. Supposedly, the Viet Cong held the people in the grip of terror by assassination and torture. This argument was also against doctrine. Special Forces are taught that reliable support can be gained only through friendship and trust. History denied the "terror" argument. The people feared and hated the French, and they rose up against them. It became quite obvious that a minority movement could not keep tabs on a hostile majority. South Vietnam is a relatively small country, dotted with thousands of small villages. In this very restricted area companies and battalions of Viet Cong can maneuver and live under the very noses of government troops; but the people don't betray these movements, even though it is a relatively simple thing to pass the word. On the other hand, government troop movements are always reported....

* * *

I know a couple of cases where it was suggested by Special Forces officers that Viet Cong prisoners be killed. In one case in which I was involved, we had picked up prisoners in the valley around Kai. We didn't want the prisoners, but they walked into our hands. We were supposed to stay in the area four more days, and there were only eight of us and four of them, and we didn't know what the hell to do with them. You can't carry them. Food is limited, and the way the transmission went with the base camp you knew what they wanted you to do—get rid of them. I wouldn't do that, and when I got back to operation base a major told me, "You know we almost told you right over the phone to do them in." I said that I was glad he didn't, because it would have been embarrassing to refuse to do it. I knew goddamn well I wasn't going to kill them. In a fight it's one thing, but with guys with their hands bound it's another. And I wouldn't have been able to shoot them because of the noise. It would have had to be a very personal thing, like sticking a knife into them. The major said, "Oh, you wouldn't have had to do it; all you had to do was give them over to the Vietnamese." Of course, this is supposed to absolve you of any responsibility. This is the general attitude. It's really a left-handed morality. Very few of the Special Forces guys had any qualms about this. Damn few.

Little by little, as all these facts made their impact on me, I had to accept the fact that, Communist or not, the vast majority of the people were pro-Viet Cong and anti-Saigon. I had to accept also that the position, "We are in Vietnam because we are in sympathy with the aspirations and desires of the Vietnamese people," was a lie. If this is a lie, how many others are there?

* * *

...[W]henever anybody questioned our being in Vietnam—in light of the facts—the old rationale was always presented: "We have to stop the spread of communism somewhere...if we don't fight the commies here, we'll have to fight them at home...if we pull out, the rest of Asia will go Red...these are uneducated people who have been duped; they don't understand the difference between democracy and communism...."

Being extremely anti-Communist myself, these "arguments" satisfied me for a long time. In fact, I guess it was saying these very same things to myself over and over again that made it possible for me to participate in the things I did in Vietnam. But were we stopping communism? Even during the short period I had been in Vietnam, the Viet Cong had obviously gained in strength; the government controlled less and less of the country every day. The more troops and money we poured in, the more people hated us. Countries all over the world were losing sympathy with our stand in Vietnam. Countries which up to now had preserved a neutral position were becoming vehemently anti-American. A village near Tay Ninh in which I had slept in safety six months earlier was the center of a Viet Cong operation that cost the lives of two American friends. A Special Forces team operating in the area was almost decimated over a period of four months. United States Operations Mission (USOM), civilian representatives, who had been able to travel by vehicle in relative safety throughout the countryside, were being kidnapped and killed. Like the military, they now had to travel by air.

The real question was, whether communism is spreading in spite of our involvement or because of it.

The attitude that the uneducated peasant lacked the political maturity to decide between communism and democracy and " ... we are only doing this for your own good," although it had a familiar colonialistic ring, at first seemed to have merit. Then I remembered that most of the villages would be under Viet Cong control for some of the time and under government control at other times. How many Americans had such a close look at both sides of the cloth? The more often government troops passed through an area, the more surely it would become sympathetic to the Viet Cong. The Viet Cong might sleep in the houses, but the government troops ransacked them. More often than not, the Viet Cong helped plant and harvest the crops; but invariably government troops in an area razed them. Rape is severely punished among the Viet Cong. It is so common among the ARVN that it is seldom reported for fear of even worse atrocities.

I saw the Airborne brigade come into Nha Trang. Nha Trang is a government town and the Vietnamese Airborne brigade are government troops. They were originally, in fact, trained by Special Forces, and they actually had the town in a grip of terror for three days. Merchants were collecting money to get them out of town; cafes and bars shut down.

The troops were accosting women on the streets. They would go into a place—a bar or cafe—and order varieties of food. When the checks came they wouldn't pay them. Instead they would simply wreck the place, dumping over the tables and smashing dishes. While these men were accosting women, the police would just stand by, powerless or unwilling to help. In fact, the situation is so difficult that American troops, if in town at the same time as the Vietnamese Airborne brigade, are told to stay off the streets at night to avoid coming to harm.

The whole thing was a lie. *We weren't preserving freedom in South Vietnam. There was no freedom to preserve. To voice opposition to the government meant jail or death.* Neutralism was forbidden and punished. Newspapers that didn't say the right thing were closed down. People are not even free to leave and Vietnam is one of those rare countries that doesn't fill its American visa quota. It's all there to see once the Red film is removed from the eyes. We aren't the freedom fighters. We are the Russian tanks blasting the hopes of an Asian Hungary.

It's not democracy we brought to Vietnam—it's anti-communism. This is the only choice the people in the village have. This is why most of them have embraced the Viet Cong and shunned the alternative....

* * *

It had taken a long time and a mountain of evidence but I had finally found some truths. The world is not just good guys and bad guys. Anti-communism is a lousy substitute for democracy. I know now that there are many types of communism but there are none that appeal to me. In the long run, I don't think Vietnam will be better off under Ho's brand of communism. But it's not for me or my government to decide. That decision is for the Vietnamese. I also know that we have allowed the creation of a military monster that will lie to our elected officials; and that both of them will lie to the American people.

* * *

When I returned from Vietnam I was asked, "Do you resent young people who have never been in Vietnam, or in any war, protesting it?" On the contrary, I am relieved. I think they should be commended. I had to wait until I was 35 years old, after spending 10 years in the Army and 18 months personally witnessing the stupidity of the war, before I could figure it out. That these young people were able to figure it out so quickly and so accurately is not only a credit to their intelligence but a great personal triumph over a lifetime of conditioning and indoctrination. I only hope that the picture I have tried to create will help other people come to the truth without wasting 10 years. Those people protesting the war in Vietnam are not against our boys in Vietnam. On the contrary. What they are against is our boys *being* in Vietnam. They are not unpatriotic. Again the opposite is true. They are opposed to people, our own and others, dying for a lie, thereby corrupting the very word democracy.

The Fort Hood Three: The Case of the Three GIs Who Said "No" to the War in Vietnam—Three Speeches

Pvt. Dennis Mora
Pvt. David Samas
and PFC James Johnson

JOINT STATEMENT BY FORT HOOD THREE

The following statement was read to over 40 cameramen, reporters, and antiwar fighters at a press conference in New York on June 30th. The statement was prepared jointly and read by Pvt. Dennis Mora.

We are Pfc. James Johnson, Pvt. David Samas, and Pvt. Dennis Mora, three soldiers formerly stationed at Fort Hood, Texas in the same company of the 142 Signal Battalion, 2nd Armored Division. We have received orders to report on the 13th of July at Oakland Army Terminal in California for final processing and shipment to Vietnam.

We have decided to take a stand against this war, which we consider immoral, illegal and unjust. We are initiating today, through our attorneys, Stanley Faulkner of New York and Mrs. Selma Samols of Washington, D.C. an action in the courts to enjoin the Secretary of

The Fort Hood Three Defense Committee, *The Fort Hood Three*, New York: The Fort Hood Three Defense Committee, July 1966, pp. 9–11, 14–20.

Defense and the Secretary of the Army from sending us to Vietnam. We intend to report as ordered to the Oakland Army Terminal, but under no circumstances will we board ship for Vietnam. We are prepared to face Court Martial if necessary.

We represent in our backgrounds a cross section of the Army and of America. James Johnson is a Negro, David Samas is of Lithuanian and Italian parents, Dennis Mora is a Puerto Rican. We speak as American soldiers.

We have been in the army long enough to know that we are not the only G.I.'s who feel as we do. Large numbers of men in the service either do not understand this war or are against it.

When we entered the army Vietnam was for us only a newspaper box score of G.I.'s and Viet Cong killed or wounded. We were all against it in one way or another, but we were willing to "go along with the program," believing that we would not be sent to Vietnam.

We were told from the very first day of our induction that we were headed for Vietnam. During basic training it was repeated often by sergeants and officers, and soon it became another meaningless threat that was used to make us take our training seriously.

But later on Vietnam became a fact of life when some one you knew wondered how he could break the news to his girl, wife, or family that he was being sent there. After he solved that problem, he had to find a reason that would satisfy him. The reasons were many—"Somebody's got to do it," "When your number's up, your number's up," "The pay is good," and "You've got to stop them someplace" were phrases heard in the barracks and mess hall, and used by soldiers to encourage each other to accept the war as their own. Besides, what could be done about it anyway? Orders are orders.

As we saw more and more of this, the war became the one thing we talked about most and the one point we all agreed upon. No one wanted to go and more than that, there was no reason for anyone to go.

The Viet Cong obviously had the moral and physical support of most of the peasantry who were fighting for their independence. We were told that you couldn't tell them apart—that they looked like any other skinny peasant.

Our man or our men in Saigon has and have always been brutal dictators, since Diem first violated the 1954 Geneva promise of free elections in 1956.

The Buddhist and military revolt in all the major cities proves that the people of the cities also want an end to Ky and U.S. support for him.

The Saigon Army has become the advisor to American G.I.'s who have to take over the fighting.

No one used the word "winning" anymore because in Vietnam it has no meaning. Our officers just talk about five and ten more years of war with at least ½ million of our boys thrown into the grinder. We have been told that many times we may face a Vietnamese woman or child and that we will have to kill them. We will never go there—to do that—for Ky!

We know that Negroes and Puerto Ricans are being drafted and end up in the worst of the fighting all out of proportion to their numbers in the population; and we have first hand knowledge that these are the ones who have been deprived of decent education and jobs at home.

The three of us, while stationed together, talked a lot and found we thought alike on one over-riding issue—the war in Vietnam must be stopped. It was all talk and we had no intentions of getting into trouble by making waves at that stage.

Once back in Texas we were told that we were on levy to Vietnam. All we had discussed and thought about now was real. It was time for us to quit talking and decide. Go to Vietnam and ignore the truth or stand and fight for what we know is right.

We have made our decision. We will not be a part of this unjust, immoral, and illegal war. We want no part of a war of extermination. We oppose the criminal waste of American lives and resources. We refuse to go to Vietnam!!!!!!

STATEMENT BY DENNIS MORA

Besides the joint statement that was presented at the June 30th press conference, each of the three men presented individual statements. The following statement was prepared and read by Pvt. Dennis Mora.

I was active in the peace movement before I was drafted. The Army knew this and took me anyway. My opposition to this criminal war of aggression has become stronger while I have been in the Army. The decision as to what I will give my life for remains mine and mine alone.

Contrary to what the Pentagon believes, cannon-fodder can talk. It is saying that we are not fighting for "freedom" in South Vietnam, but supporting a Hitler-loving dictator. It is saying that it will not accept as a rationale for exterminating a whole people, theories of dominoes, Chinese "aggression" or arguments of "appeasement." It further says that the only foreign power in Vietnam today is the United States and that the Vietcong is an indigenous force which has the support of most of the people and is in control of 80% of the country.

It is a war of genocide. A genocide which has at its disposal the technology of a military chamber of horrors from bomblets to napalm, gas and defoliants. The American people are victims of their war in a very real sense. Apart from the tragedy of losing American boys in a war we cannot win, the war is a colossal waste of resources which are urgently needed here at home. The hypocrisy of a war on poverty is clear. It is all guns and no butter. The war has created inflation and the chief sufferer is the working man. Corporate profits soar and union men are told to hold to 3.2 wage increase in the "national interest." Free lunch programs are cut by 80%. Are we now ready to accept, in the national interest of course, the malnutrition of our children in order to incinerate Vietnamese children? This is the price we must pay for military miracles.

As a Puerto Rican the first war I knew was against the poverty of Spanish Harlem. My mother worked for $35 a week to help make ends meet and we seldom saw her. I went to school where teachers counseled Puerto Ricans to forget plans for higher education because they were Puerto Ricans and therefore somehow inferior.

The first uniform I knew was that of the cop on the corner. He was there to let you know that you could only look at the clean world outside as a prisoner looks from his cell. The billy clubs told us to keep our place.

The first casualties I knew in this war were two childhood buddies who became drug addicts. They died trying to escape a world which held no jobs or education for them, and where they were made to feel ashamed of their color, language and culture.

This is the war we must fight. The billions for slaughter must be invested in the reconstruction of our country's ghettoes and the meeting of our social and educational needs. This is the only battle which makes sense and which can truly honor the U.S.

There must be jobs provided for all youth—White, Negro, Puerto Rican and Mexican-American.

Our leaders have just brought us knowingly another step closer to an all out land war in Asia with the attacks on Hanoi and Haiphong. Will this mean war for generations to come?

I will not fight for the blood money of war industries nor will I give my life so that U.S. corporations can claim as their property the people and resources of Vietnam.

SPEECH BY DAVID SAMAS

The following speech was prepared by Pvt. David Samas for the July 7th meeting. When he was seized by military police minutes before the meeting, his wife, Marlene Samas, read the speech.

Thank you. I was asked to read my husband's speech tonight, since I guess you already know he's unable to be here. This is a rough draft actually because he intended to proofread it on the way down here, but circumstances have prevented that, so bear with me.

I've been in the army since December 1965 and my feelings about the Vietnam situation have always been as they are now. I've been opposed to American participation in Vietnam from the very beginning but have never until a few days ago made my feelings public. Last Thursday afternoon we held a press conference in this same church and announced our refusal to participate in any way in the Vietnam war. Since that time we have been plagued by federal agents and what can only be called hired thugs.

I kept my whereabouts secret from the press and the police and only my parents and a very few people knew where I was living. The Modesto city police visited my parents in California saying they had been sent by some "higher authorities" but were not able to reveal those authorities. An officer who my father happened to know approached him in a friendly manner saying he came to help the family. My parents live three thousand miles away in California and it is not easy to remain in close and constant contact with them, so they don't realize the actual circumstances that exist here in New York. And they are not familiar with any of the peace groups—either here or on the West Coast. It didn't prove hard for the police to persuade my parents into believing I was being used as a tool of the Communists. They were told that I was in serious trouble and that the only way for them to help was to reveal my address to the police so that the authorities in New York might get in contact with me and try to help and protect me. My father became terribly upset, fearing for my safety, and gave the police my address in New York. He immediately sent me a telegram urging me to call home as soon as possible.

I called and found my parents very upset and they told me what the police had said to them. Although they have absolutely no authority the Modesto city police had offered me a deal. They had told my father that if I would retract my statement and withdraw completely from the civil action now in progress that I would receive a discharge from the army and no serious repercussions would result. In their concern for me my parents believed this fantastic story.

The next morning, when we left our apartment we were followed by three men in their early twenties who made no attempt to be discreet about tailing us. They remained within twenty feet of us all day long and when approached would deny any connection with us. Since then there have at all times been at least two men parked in front of our apartment. Undoubtedly they are present now. They have attempted to intimidate the three of us in one way or another and have approached all of our parents in different ways.

But we have not been scared. We have not been in the least shaken from our paths. And we will not be, even if physical violence is used. We are not pacifists. We are not non-violent, and if the need arises we will fight back.

I have never been involved with any of the peace groups until a few weeks ago when we approached the Parade Committee for help. As a civilian I was interested and extremely concerned, but I neglected to show my concern. In a great way I too am responsible for the boys who already are in Vietnam.

But even as an unaffiliated civilian, I was closer to the peace movement than most soldiers are now. To me the peace movement always looked like concerned students and citizens trying to protect their country from war and nuclear devastation. To a soldier the movement appears very differently. The soldier is very far indeed from the outside world and the normal news media do not usually reach him. News of the free world reaches him through letters from home, or through his buddies. It often seems that the peace groups are united against the soldier, and that forces the soldiers to cling together and

ignore the real issues made public by the peace movement. The stories that reach the soldiers usually show that the peace movement is backing their enemies, and is against the Army, and against the individual soldiers. Upon too many occasions groups have offered aid to the Viet Cong and too few times have they approached the G.I.'s with help.

The G.I. should be reached somehow. He doesn't want to fight. He has no reasons to risk his life. Yet he doesn't realize that the peace movement is dedicated to his safety. Give the G.I. something to believe and and he will fight for that belief. Let them know in Vietnam that you want them home, let them know that you are concerned about their lives also. Tell them you want them to live, not die. Bring home our men in Vietnam!

The three of us here, James, Dennis, and I came to the movement for help and we received help. We asked for support in our stand and we received that support. We asked for money for the case and have gotten some. The legal aspects of our case are numerous and complex, but we cannot depend alone upon our legal stand. The war in Vietnam cannot be stopped just by legal action. The war can only be stopped by the efforts of the movement with the sympathy of the public.

In the end we depend entirely upon the public. We have placed ourselves in the hands of the people of the United States, and all of our hopes lie with them. We win or lose depending upon how the people respond. We risk our futures and maybe our lives on the hopes of the American public. We need your help.

SPEECH BY JAMES JOHNSON

The following speech was to be given by PFC James Johnson to a public meeting in New York at the Community Church on July 7th. On the way to the meeting Johnson and the other two G.I.'s were seized and taken to Fort Dix for "investigative detention." Darwin Johnson, James' brother, read the speech in his place.

I was with Jimmy when he got arrested today. Just like Dave and Dennis he didn't finish his speech either, so this is just a rough draft of his speech but I'll do my best to see how it comes out. Okay?

On December 6, 1965, I entered the Army reluctantly. Although I did not voice my opposition I was opposed to the war in Vietnam. But like most of the other G.I.'s I was inducted and went along with the program. After basic training I began to seriously consider the prospect of Vietnam. I devoted much of my free time to reading, listening, and discussing America's role in Vietnam. I felt that I had been following blindly too long in the Army. A soldier is taught not to question, not to think, just to do what he is told. Are your convictions and your conscience supposed to be left at home, or on the block? I had to take a stand.

I once told a Colonel about my opposition to the war. I was told that I was being paid to be a soldier not a politician. Should I let the Pentagon decide whether I should live or die? After studying the situation in Vietnam, I learned that the government was not being honest with the American people. The government tells us that the United States is in Vietnam at the request of the Vietnamese government in Saigon. They fail to tell us, though, that the Saigon government was not elected by the people. There have never been free elections there. In fact the U.S. government installed a regime of its own choosing, headed by Diem, in 1954. Since then there has been a succession of military dictators. All supported at our expense. Not one of these governments was worth the support of the people. They were supported by our army.

The government also tells us that we are spending our men and money to preserve freedom in Vietnam. Yet the current dictator, General Ky, declared that Adolf Hitler is his hero. Like Hitler he uses extreme brutality to crush any opposition that may arise. President Johnson tells us that he is trying to bring about discussions for peace in Vietnam. Yet peace offers were made by North Vietnam last spring. But they were rejected by our government and the American people were not told about them.

Is the U.S. afraid of losing Asia to the Communists? I read a statement by Senator Church which said, "We cannot lose what we never owned. We cannot force everyone to adopt our way of life. We must escape the trap of becoming so preoccupied with communism that we dissipate our strength in a vain attempt to force local quarantine against it."

Now there is a direct relationship between the peace movement and the civil rights movement. The South Vietnamese are fighting for representation, like we ourselves. The South Vietnamese just want a voice in the government, nothing else. Therefore the Negro in Vietnam is just helping to defeat what his black brother is fighting for in the United States. When the Negro soldier returns, he still will not be able to ride in Mississippi or walk down a certain street in Alabama. There will still be proportionately twice as many Negroes as whites in Vietnam. Those Negroes that die for their country still cannot be assured of a burial place which their family feels is suitable for them. His children will still receive an inferior education and he will still live in a ghetto. Although he bears the brunt of the war he will reap no benefits.

It is time that the Negro realizes that his strength can be put to much better use right here at home. This is where his strength lies. We can gain absolutely nothing in Vietnam. All this is lending to the decision I have made. I know it is my right to make this decision.

This is what my brother was going to say, but they wouldn't let him speak. They just wouldn't give him a chance.

Nightmares of Empire

The following is an editorial that appeared in *The Wall Street Journal* in July 1967.

It is becoming fashionable to talk of the American "empire." The term has a certain validity, but it is misleading; the real point, it seems to us, is not imperialism but interventionism.

One observer, former Foreign Service officer Ronald Steel, calls it an accidental empire. In his new book *Pax Americana* (Viking) he explains as follows:

> Nobody planned our empire. In fact nobody even wanted it. We are a people whom the mantle of empire fits uneasily, who are not particularly adept at running colonies. Yet, by any conventional standards for judging such things, we are indeed an imperial power, possessed of an empire on which the sun truly never sets, a benevolent empire that embraces the entire western hemisphere, the world's two great oceans, and virtually all of the Eurasian land mass that is not in Communist hands.

All true enough if one is merely suggesting the scope of American involvement. The trouble with that word empire, though, is that it connotes physical possession, more or less autocratic rule and profit from the imperial holdings.

By those criteria the U.S. "empire" doesn't qualify. In particular, it is unbelievably costly to the U.S.; at the same time U.S. influence in various parts of the world is visibly diminishing. Rather than an empire in the traditional sense, what the U.S. has is a foreign policy of global interventionism.

Once the semantic hurdle is passed, much of what Mr. Steel says strikes us as sound. It is in fact similar to what we and a good many others have been contending for some time: The U.S. is overcommitted around the world, perhaps dangerously so, and the main reason is its obsession with opposing communism.

We think Mr. Steel underestimates the seriousness of the Communist threat, but unquestionably its nature has changed since 1945. There are now several varieties of communism. In most Red lands nationalism is a stronger force than communism. Not every Communist state is automatically a threat to U.S. security. It follows that a policy of global interventionism risks undertaking the wrong kind of intervention.

Vietnam is of course a classic case of questionable intervention. By itself it posed no security threat, although it is true the U.S. thought it important to try to contain Red China in this way. South Vietnam is a nation with little feeling of nationhood. It has an unrepresentative government. In terms of terrain it is a poor choice for a fight. It cannot seem to muster sufficient will for the struggle.

That last point is tragically dramatized in the fact that U.S. casualties now exceed those of the South Vietnamese army, which in any event is a largely ineffective fighting force. The Vietnam war has turned into what everyone in Washington and elsewhere always said it must never become—an almost completely American war.

While the very depth of the U.S. involvement makes it extremely difficult to get out of it, we find this an inexcusable exercise in foreign policy: That the Government has finally got the country into a situation where American boys are bearing the brunt of the struggle, even as South Vietnamese units frequently refuse to fight.

Turning to the larger question, if global interventionism is an unsatisfactory policy, what is the alternative? It cannot be the opposite extreme, literal isolationism, for that would simply be to invite the Soviet Union to take over much of the world.

What is needed is a more modest and limited policy carefully tuned to the national interest. As Mr. Steel writes, the issue "is not isolationism.... The task now is to strike a balance among competing interests, to determine which involvements are crucial to American security and which are peripheral, to exercise responsibility toward states with which we share common values and to show an enlightened restraint toward those which make unjustified claims upon us."

Admittedly easier said than done. Yet the evidence is that it was not done in Vietnam, and the result is about as ugly as can be imagined. If caution and selectivity are not brought back to policymaking, if the U.S. permits more and more Vietnam-type involvements, it may end up not as an empire but as a nation on the decline.

Prison Poem

Ho Chi Minh

囚人出去或為國
患過頭時始見忠
人有憂愁優點大
籠開竹門出真龍

拆字

Ho Chi Minh, *Prison Diary*, Hanoi: Foreign Languages Publishing House, 1972, pp. 10, 134.

WORD-PLAY

I

Take away the sign 人 *(man)* from the sign 囚 for *prison,*
Add to it 或 *(probability)* that makes the word 國 *(nation)*
Take the head-particle from the sign 患 for misfortune:
That gives the word 忠 *(fidelity),*
Add the sign 亻 for *man* (standing) to the sign 憂 for *worry*
That gives the word 優 *(quality).*
Take away the *bamboo* top 竹 from the sign 籠 for *prison,*
That gives you 龍 *(dragon).*

II

People who come out of prison can build up the
                              country.
Misfortune is a test of people's fidelity.
Those who protest at injustice are people of true merit.
When the prison-doors are opened, the real dragon
                              will fly out.

We Shall Win and So Will You

Ho Chi Minh

NEW YEAR MESSAGE OF PRESIDENT HO CHI MINH*

This Spring far surpasses the previous ones.
Happy news of victory comes from all over the country.
Let South and North vie with each other in fighting the U.S. aggressors!
Forward!

                    Total victory shall be ours.

                                        HO CHI MINH

I send you, friends, my best wishes for the New Year 1968.

As you all know, no Vietnamese has ever come to make trouble in the United States. Yet, half a million U.S. troops have been sent to South Viet Nam who, together with over 700,000 puppet and satellite troops, are daily massacring Vietnamese people and burning and demolishing Vietnamese towns and villages.

In North Viet Nam, thousands of U.S. planes have dropped over 800,000 tons of bombs, destroying schools, churches, hospitals, dykes and densely populated areas.

The U.S. government has caused hundreds of thousands of U.S. youths to die or to be wounded in vain on Viet Nam battlefields.

Ho Chi Minh, "We Shall Win and So Will You," *The Berkeley Barb*, February 16–22, 1968, p. 5.

*From Viet Nam Courier, Hanoi and "Bohemia," Havana (UPS)

Each year, the U.S. government spends tens of billions of dollars, the fruit of American people's sweat and toil, to wage war on Viet Nam.

In a word, the U.S. aggressors have not only committed crimes against Viet Nam, they have also wasted U.S. lives and riches, and stained the honour of the United States.

Friends, in struggling hard to make the U.S. government stop its aggression in Viet Nam, you are defending justice and, at the same time, you are giving us support.

To ensure our Fatherland's independence, freedom and unity, with the desire to live in peace and friendship with all peoples the world over, including the American people, the entire Vietnamese people, united and of one mind, are determined to fight against the U.S. imperialist aggressors. We enjoy the support of brothers and friends in the five continents. We shall win and so will you.

Thank you for your support for the Vietnamese people.

Best wishes to you all,

HO CHI MINH

The Revolted

Carl Oglesby

Killing is evil.... All countries are different and
progress should be achieved by peaceful means
wherever possible.

—Che Guevara[1]

The young men joining them [the NLF] have been
attracted by the excitement of the guerrilla life.

—Robert S. McNamara[2]

Everyone in the rich world has heard that there is another world
out there, almost out of sight, where two thirds of all of us are living,
where misery and violence are routine, where Mozart has not been
widely heard nor Plato and Shakespeare much studied.

There is a world, that is, which, according to the mainstream
intuitions of mainstream middle-class America, must be somebody's
exaggeration, a world which is fundamentally implausible. For the most
part, we really believe in it, this poor world, only to the extent that we
have it to blame for certain of our troubles. It is the "breeding ground,"

Carl Oglesby and Richard Schaull, *Containment and Change*, New York: The
Macmillan Company, 1967, pp. 140–156. Reprinted with permission of the author.

we say (a favorite term, packed with connotations of the plague), of those discontents which harass us. Most ordinary rich-world people would much prefer never even to have heard of Vietnam or Mozambique, not to mention the nearly thirty other states of the world where long-term insurgencies are under way.

The main fact about the revolutionary is that he demands total change. The corresponding fact about most Americans is that they are insulted by that demand. But what of that demand's moral force? When the statistics of world poverty reach us, as they now and then do, we can respond in several characteristic ways. Sometimes we cluck our tongues, shake our heads, and send a check off to CARE. Sometimes we tell tales about brave missionaries of either the Baptist or the AID persuasion. Someone might name the Alliance for Progress. And someone else might cough. When the statistics are voiced by the poor man's machine-gun fire, we are more decisive. While waiting for our bombers to warm up, we develop our poor-devils theory, according to which the wretched have been duped by Communist con men. It is a bad thing to be hungry; we can see that. But it is better to be hungry and patient than hungry and Red, for to be Red proves to us that all this hunger was really just a trick. It is probably the case that a Communist *has* no hunger.

In the land of remote-controlled adventure, the office-dwelling frontiersman, the automated pioneer—how can matters be seen otherwise?

Middle-class America is the nation to which the forthcoming obsolescence of the moral choice has been revealed.

Middle-class America is the condition of mind which supposes that a new, plastic Eden has been descried upon a calm sea, off our bow. A point here and there, a firm rudder, a smart following breeze, a bit of pluck, and we shall make port any time now in this "American Century."

Middle-class America regards itself as the Final Solution. Its most intense desire is not to be bothered by fools who disagree about that.

What must be difficult for any nation seems out of the question for us: To imagine that we may from time to time be the enemies of men who are just, smart, honest, courageous, and *correct*— Who could think such a thing? Since we love rose arbors and pretty girls, our enemies must be unjust, stupid, dishonest, craven, and *wrong*.

Such conceptions are sometimes shaken. After the 1965 battle of Plei Me, Special Forces Major Charles Beckwith described NLF guerrilla fighters as "the finest soldiers I have ever seen in the world except

Americans. I wish we could recruit them." After the same battle, another American said of a captured Viet Cong, "We ought to put this guy on the north wall and throw out these Government troops. He could probably hold it alone. If we could get two more, we would have all the walls [of the triangular camp] taken care of." Major Beckwith was intrigued with the "high motivation" and "high dedication" of this enemy force and suggested an explanation: "I wish I knew what they were drugging them with to make them fight like that."[3]

That curiosity, at least, is good. Why do men rebel? Let us try to find out what could possibly be so wrong with so many of the world's men and women that they should fight so hard to stay outside the Eden we think we are offering them.

I make three assumptions. First, everyone who is now a rebel *became* a rebel; he was once upon a time a child who spoke no politics. The rebel is someone who has changed.

Second, men do not imperil their own and others' lives for unimpressive reasons. They are sharp accountants on the subject of staying alive. When they do something dangerous, they have been convinced that not to do it was more dangerous. There are always a few who can evidently be persuaded by some combination of statistics and principles to put their lives on the line. Lenin, for example, did not materially *need* the Russian Revolution. His commitment was principled and it originated from a basic detachment. But I am not trying to describe the Lenins. I am after those nameless ones but for whom the Lenins would have remained only philosophers, those who (as Brecht put it) grasp revolution first in the hand and only later in the mind.

Third, I assume that the rebel is much like myself, someone whom I can understand. He is politically extraordinary. That does not mean that he is psychologically so. My assumption is that what would not move me to the act of rebellion would not move another man.

It is safe to say first that revolutionary potential exists only in societies where material human misery is the denominating term in most social relationships. No one thinks that bankers are going to make disturbances in the streets. Less obviously, this also implies that privation can be political only if it is not universal. The peasant who compares his poverty to someone else's richness is able to conceive that his poverty is special, a social identity. To say that hunger does not become a rebellious sensation until it coexists with food is to say that rebellion has less to do with scarcity than with maldistribution. This states a central theme:

revolutionary anger is not produced by privation, but by understood injustice.

But the self-recognized victim is not at once his own avenger. He is first of all a man who simply wants to reject his humiliation. He will therefore recreate his world via social pantomines which transfigure or otherwise discharge that humiliation. "They whipped Him up the hill," sang the black slave, "and He never said a mumbling word." That divine reticence is clearly supposed to set an example. But it also does much more. In such a song, the slave plays the role of himself and thus avoids himself, puts his realities at the distance of a pretense which differs from the realities only to the extent that it *is* a pretense. The slave creates for the master's inspection an exact replica of himself, of that slave which he is; and even as the master looks, the slave escapes behind the image. It is not that he pretends to be other than a slave. Such an act would be quickly punished. He instead pretends to be what he knows himself to be, acts out the role of the suffering and humiliated, in order to place a psychic foil between himself and the eyes of others. The American Negro's older Steppinfetchit disguise, or the acutely ritualized violence of ghetto gangs: these are intentional lies which intentionally tell the truth. The victim-liar's inner reality, his demand for freedom, precludes telling the truth. His outer reality, his victimhood, precludes telling a lie. Therefore he *pretends* the truth, pretends to hold that truth in his hand and to pass judgment on it. And by choosing to enact what he *is* he disguises from himself the fact that he had no choice.

A crucial moment comes when something ruptures this thin membrane of pretense. What can do that? A glimpse of weakness in his master sometimes; sometimes the accidental discovery of some unsuspected strength in himself. More often it will be the master's heightened violence that confronts the slave with the incorrigible authenticity of his slave act. A black man sings blues about his powerlessness, his loneliness; he has taken refuge behind that perfect image of himself. The white master, for no reason, in mid-song, takes the guitar away, breaks it, awaits the slave's reaction. The slave is at that moment forced into his self-image space, is psychologically fused with this truth-telling pretense of his: He *is* powerless; he *is* lonely. He cannot now enact himself; he must *be* the man of whom he had tried to sing. This encounter strips life of its formality and returns it to pure, primitive substance. For the victim, there is no longer even the fragile, rare escape of the simultaneous re-enactment of reality. He lives wholly now in his victim space, without manners, not even allowed to mimic the horror of victimhood in the same gesture that expresses it. He is nothing now but the locus of injustice.

Grown less random, injustice becomes more coherent. Confronted at every instant by that coherence, the victim may find that it is no longer so easy to avoid the truth that his suffering is *caused*, that it is not just an accident that there are so many differences between his life and the life of the round, white-suited man in the big hillside house. He begins to feel singled out. He rediscovers the idea of the system of power.

And at that same moment he discovers that he also may accuse. When the victim sees that what had seemed universal is local, that what had seemed God-given is man-made, that what had seemed quality is mere condition—his permanent immobility permanently disappears. Being for the first time in possession of the stark idea that his life could be different were it not for others, he is for the first time someone who might move. His vision of change will at this point be narrow and mundane, his politics naive: Maybe he only wants a different landlord, a different mayor, a different sheriff. The important element is not the scope or complexity of his vision but the sheer existence of the idea that change can happen.

Then who is to be the agent of this change? Surely not the victim himself. He has already seen enough proof of his impotence, and knows better than anyone else that he is an unimportant person. What compels him to hope nevertheless is the vague notion that his tormentor is answerable to a higher and fairer authority. This sheriff's outrageous conduct, that is, belongs strictly to this particular sheriff, not to sheriffness. Further, this sheriff represents only a local derangement within a system which the victim barely perceives and certainly does not yet accuse, a hardship which High Authority did not intend to inflict, does not need, and will not allow. (Once Robin Hood meets King Richard, the Sheriff of Nottingham is done for.)

We meet in this the politics of the appeal to higher power, which has led to some poignant moments in history. It is the same thing as prayer. Its prayerfulness remains basic even as it is elaborated into the seemingly more politically aggressive mass petition to the king, a main assumption of which is that the king is not bad, only uninformed. This way of thinking brought the peasants and priests to their massacre at Kremlin Square in 1905. It prompted the so-called Manifesto of the Eighteen which leading Vietnamese intellectuals published in 1960. It rationalized the 1963 March on Washington for Jobs and Freedom. The Freedom Rides, the nonviolent sit-ins, and the various Deep South marches were rooted in the same belief: that there was indeed a higher power which was responsive and decent.*

Sometimes mass-based secular prayer has resulted in change. But more often it has only shown the victim-petitioners that the problem is graver and change harder to get than they had imagined. The bad sheriffs turn out to be everywhere; indeed, there seems to be no other kind. It turns out that the king is on their side, that the state's administrative and coercive-punitive machinery exists precisely to serve the landlords. It turns out that the powerful know perfectly well who their victims are and why there should be victims, and that they have no intention of changing anything. This recognition is momentous, no doubt the spiritual low point of the emergent revolutionary's education. He finds that the enemy is not a few men but a whole system whose agents saturate the society, occupying and fiercely protecting its control centers. He is diverted by a most realistic despair.

But this despair contains within itself the omen of that final shattering reconstitution of the spirit which will prepare the malcontent, the fighter, the wino, the criminal for the shift to insurgency, rebellion, revolution. He had entertained certain hopes about the powerful: They can tell justice from injustice, they support the first, they are open to change. He is now instructed that these hopes are whimsical. At the heart of his despair lies the new certainty that there will be no change which he does not produce by himself.

The man who believes that change can only come from his own initiative will be disinclined to believe that change can be less than total. Before he could see matters otherwise, he would have to accept on some terms, however revised, the power which he now opposes. The com-

---

*What was new was the way these forms enlarged the concept of petition. Instead of merely writing down the tale of grievance, they reproduced the grievance itself in settings that forced everyone to behold it, tzar included, and to respond. The Vietnam war protest demonstrations are no different. The speeches they occasion may sometimes seem especially pugnacious. But inasmuch as the antiwar movement has never been able to dream up a threat which it might really make good, this fiercer face-making has remained basically a kind of entertainment. The main idea has always been to persuade higher authority—Congress, the UN, Bobby Kennedy—to do something. Far from calling higher authority into question, these wildly militant demonstrations actually dramatize and even exaggerate its power.

promises which will actually be made will be arranged by his quietly "realistic" leaders and will be presented to him as a total victory. He himself is immoderate and unconciliatory. But the more important, more elusive feature of this immoderation is that he may be powerless to change it. He could only compromise with rebelled-against authority if he were in possession of specific "solutions" to those "problems" that finally drove him to revolt. Otherwise there is nothing to discuss. But the leap into revolution has left these "solutions" behind because it has collapsed and wholly redefined the "problems" to which they referred. The rebel is an incorrigible absolutist who has replaced all "problems" with the one grand claim that the entire system is an error, all "solutions" with the single irreducible demand that change shall be total, all diagnoses of disease with one final certificate of death. To him, total change means only that those who now have all power shall no longer have any, and that those who have none—the people, the victimized—shall have all. Then what can it mean to speak of compromise? Compromise is whatever absolves and reprieves an enemy who has already been sentenced. It explicitly restores the legitimacy of the very authority which the rebel defines himself by repudiating. This repudiation being total, it leaves exactly no motive—again, not even the motive—for creating that fund of specific proposals, that *conversation*, without a compromise is not even *technically* possible.

"What do you want?" asks the worried, perhaps intimidated master. "What can I give you?" he inquires, hoping to have found in this rebel a responsible, realistic person, a man of the world like himself. But the rebel does not fail to see the real meaning of this word *give*. Therefore he answers, "I cannot be purchased." The answer is meant mainly to break off the conference. But at one level, it is a completely substantive comment, not at all just a bolt of pride. It informs the master that he no longer exists, not even in part.

At another level, however, this answer is nothing but an evasion. The master seems to have solicited the rebel's views on the revolutionized, good society. The rebel would be embarrassed to confess the truth: that he has no such views. Industry? Agriculture? Foreign trade? It is not such matters that drive and preoccupy him. The victorious future is at the moment any society in which certain individuals no longer have power, no longer exist. The rebel fights for something that will not be like *this*. He cannot answer the question about the future because that is not his question. It is not the future that is victimizing him. It is the present. It is not an anticipated Utopia which moves him to risk his life. It is pain. "Turn it over!" he cries, because he can no longer bear it as it is. The revolutionary is not *by type* a Lenin, a Mao, a Castro, least of all a Brezhnev. He is neither an economist nor a politician nor a social philosopher. He may become these; ultimately he must. But his motivating vision of change is at root a vision of something absent—not of something that *will* be there, but of something that will be there *no longer*. His good future world is elementally described by its empty spaces: a missing landlord, a missing mine owner, a missing sheriff. Who or what will replace landlord, owner, sheriff? Never mind, says the revolutionary, glancing over his shoulder. Something better. If he is there-upon warned that this undefined "something" may turn out to make things worse than ever, his response is a plain one: "Then we should have to continue the revolution."

The fundamental revolutionary motive is not to construct a Paradise but to destroy an Inferno. In time, Utopian ideas will appear. Because the world now has a revolutionary past, it may seem that they appear at the same moment as destructive anger, or even that they precede and activate or even cause it. This is always an illusion produced by the predictive social analytic which revolutionist intellectuals claim to have borrowed from history. We may be sure that the people have not said:

Here is a plan for a better life—socialism, Montes called it. He has proved to us that it is good. In its behalf, we shall throw everything to the wind and risk our necks. Rather, they have said: What we have here in the way of life cannot be put up with anymore. Therefore, we must defend ourselves.

It happens that at least the spirit of socialism will be implied by the inner dynamics of mass revolt: What was collectively won should be collectively owned. But it cannot be too much emphasized that the interest in developing other social forms, however acute it will become, follows, *does not precede*, the soul-basic explosion against injustice which is the one redemption of the damned. When Turcois takes his rebel band to a Guatemalan village for "armed propaganda," there is no need to talk of classless societies. Someone kneels in the center of the circle and begins to speak of his life, the few cents pay for a hard day's labor, the high prices, the arrogance of the *patrón*, the coffins of the children. It is this talk—very old talk, unfortunately always new—which finally sets the circle ringing with the defiant cry, *"Sí, es cierto!"* Yes, it is true. Something will have to be done.

Revolutionary consciousness exists for the first time when the victim elaborates his experience of injustice into an inclusive definition of the society in which he lives. *The rebel is someone for whom injustice and society are only different words for the same thing.* Nothing in the social world of the master is spared the contempt of this definition, which, as soon as it exists, absorbs everything in sight. No public door is marked overnight with a device that permits its survival. The loanshark's corner office and the Chase Manhattan Bank, Coney Island and Lincoln Center, look very much the same from 137th Street. They are all owned by someone else.

Everywhere he looks the man-who-is-being-revolted sees something which is not his. The good land which the *campesino* works belongs to the *hacienda*. That belongs to the *patrón*. As often as not, the *patrón* belongs to the United Fruit Company. And that prime mover unmoved belongs to nothing. It can only be for a brief moment that the *campesino* gazes with unashamed wonder at these skyscrapers. For all the justice they promise him, they might as well be so many rocks. He is soon unimpressed and grows apathetic toward Western grandeur. *The rebel is someone who has no stakes.* He is an unnecessary number, a drifter into a life that will be memorable chiefly for its humiliations. No use talking to him about the need to sustain traditions and preserve institutions or to help society evolve in an orderly way toward something better bit by bit. He very well knows that it is not in his name that the virtue of this orderliness is being proved. *The rebel is an irresponsible man whose irresponsibility has been decreed by others.* It is no doing of his own that his fantasy is now filled with explosions and burning Spanish lace.

But this new consciousness, this radical alienation from past and present authority, does not lead straightway to political action. A commitment to violence has only just become possible at this point. We have a man who certainly will not intervene in a streetcorner incident in behalf of the "law and order" of which he considers himself the main victim. He will even betray a government troop movement or shelter an "outlaw." But he may also find a tactical rationale for joining a "moderate" march or applauding a "reasonable" speech or doing nothing at all. At odd moments, he will abide talk of reform. Maybe things left to themselves will get better. He will keep the conversation open and the switchblade closed.

What is wrong with this man who thinks things can change without being changed? Who knows everything and does nothing?

Nothing is wrong with him but the fact that he is a human being. All these excuses, these cautions and carefully rationalized delays, add up to one thing: *He wants to be free.* He therefore temporizes with freedom. His desire for an independent private life has been intensified everywhere by the conditions that prohibit it. He has understood his situation and the demands it makes. He knows he is being asked to become a historical object. But he seems to recognize in this demand an old familiar presence. He has been drafted before by this history, has he not? Is the new allurement of rebellion really so different at bottom from the old coercion of slavery? Are his privacy and freedom not pre-empted equally by both? Is the rebel anything more than the same unfree object in a different costume, playing a new role? When the slave kills the master, argues Sartre, two men die. He meant that the slave dies too and the free man materializes in his place. Very well, the image is nearly overwhelming. But where is the freedom of this ex-slave who, instead of cutting cane, is now sharpening knives? That he has removed himself from one discipline to another does not hide the fact that he remains under discipline. It will be said that he at least chose the new one. But that does not diminish the servitude. When the slave conceives rebellion and remains a slave, one may say that he has chosen his slavery. That makes him no less a slave, no more a free man. In fact, the free man was glimpsed only in the moment at which he said: *I can! I may!* At that moment, the whole world shook with his exhilaration. Everywhere, he saw commotion and uncertainty where there had been only stillness and routine before. He stops at the window of a firearms dealer. He does not go in. He proceeds to the window of an agency of escape. This is not irresolution; it is freedom, the liquidity of choice. When he changes I may into I will, when he has taken the rifle and changed I will into I am, this man who was for one moment a profuse blur of possibilities, a fleeting freedom, has disappeared into another pose, has transformed himself into another image: that of the rebel.

Of all people, Sartre should have been distant enough from his partisanship to see that in this case freedom was only the possibility of transition from one binding contract to another—and therefore not freedom. As the slave found himself isolated from freedom by the master's power, so the rebel finds himself isolated from it by the decision which his life has forced upon him not merely to be a slave no longer, but to be this rebel. Once again, he is not his own man. Once again his future, which was for one moment molten, has hardened into a specific object.

Do not be deceived by the high-mindedness of these concepts. Freedom is not an ecstasy reserved for enlightened Europeans. It is not as if its subtleties confine their influence to the bourgeois radicals who anatomize and name them. The psychiatric appendices to Fanon's The Wretched of the Earth often read like case-study illustrations for Sartre's Being and Nothingness. Drop-outs on Lexington Avenue are jangling and illumined with this torment. Freedom is not something which only certain men will discover only under certain conditions, and its goodness is not limited by the well-known fact that there are better and worse, nobler and baser ways in which it can be lost. We must not get it into our heads that the rebel wants to be a rebel. We must not think that he hurls his Molotov cocktails with a howl of glee, much less with a smirk on his face. We have to catch the wince, the flinch, those moments when he unaccountably turns aside. For the slave, there is simply no way to put an end to his current servitude except to exchange it for another. He is not at liberty to be just a nonslave. He is only free to choose between two hard masters. He will struggle to escape this fork, to liberate himself from these titles, to balance on the peak between them. But always he is about to be blown off on one side or the other. For him, it is a clear case of either/or.

I think Camus misses this. I cannot otherwise understand how he could believe himself to be making a useful, relevant moral point when he affirms that men should be "neither victims nor executioners." This is excellent advice for the executioner. It is less illuminating for the victim, perhaps even beyond his depth. The victim does not belong to that category of men for whom action can be regulated by such advice. This does *not* mean that he will recognize himself as the object of Camus's brilliant epithet, "privileged executioner," much less that he somehow prefers to be such a thing. What is so poignant about the victim, in fact, is the desperation with which he seeks to *enter* that category, to become *available* to Camus, for that is the category of free men. It is ruthless to assume that not ourselves but others are so appallingly strange as to choose shattered lives—as if pursuit, revenge, estrangement made up a career.

On the contrary. The rebel will have resisted his rebellion fiercely. The same inner agility that guarded his spirit from his body's subjugation, the same good guile that kept him from becoming for himself that slave which he could not help being for others-this talent for inner survival now stands up to ward off the new version of the old threat. At the moment at which he is most accelerated by his revulsion, he may also be most alarmed to see that he is about to be *reduced* to that revulsion, that he is in danger of becoming it—of becoming a revolted one, a revolutionary. He will for a long time affect a kind of reserve; he will not permit the loss of what Harlem has named his "cool," a word which could only be translated into the languages of oppressed people—"native tongues." To be cool is to float upon one's decisions, to remain positioned just barely beyond the reach of one's commitments. To be cool is to act freedom out without quite denying that there is a hoax involved. It is to tantalize oneself with the possibility that one may do *nothing*, at the same time never letting anyone forget the *fatefulness* of one's situation. Since he wants to be free, the slave cannot renounce rebellion. Since he cannot renounce rebellion, he craves freedom all the more hungrily. That tension can only be controlled by irony: The slave-rebel evades both captivities by refusing to destroy either.

But the evasion is only a more precarious form of the older ritualized self-enacting, and it dooms itself. As soon as the slave defines himself as *other* than the slave, he has already defined himself as the rebel, since the slave is precisely that person who cannot otherwise define himself without committing the act of rebellion.

How can he be said to make a choice when to choose anything at all is already to stand in rebellion?

This man's predicament can almost be touched with the hands. He wants nothing but freedom. That simple demand pits him against the injustice of being defined by the master. It also pits him against the internal and external forces that pressure him to define himself. The choice seems to lie between submitting to murder and committing suicide. Freedom is always escaping him in the direction of his anger or his fatigue. Desiring only that his objective life can have some of the variousness and elasticity of his subjective life, he is always rediscovering that this will be possible only if he forgoes variousness for concentration, elasticity for discipline. *The revolutionary is someone who is nothing else in order to be everything else.*

"We have come to the point," writes someone from the Brazilian underground, "of making a rigorous distinction between being leftist—even radically leftist—and being revolutionary. In the critical situation through which we are now living, there is all the difference in the world between the two. We are in dead earnest. At stake is the humanity of man."

Anyone who wants to know where revolution's strange capacity for terror and innocence comes from will find the answer vibrating between these last two sentences. How can ordinary men be at once warm enough to want what revolutionaries say they want (humanity), cold enough to do without remorse what they are capable of doing (cutting throats), and poised enough in the turbulence of their lives to keep the aspiration and the act both integrated and distinct? How is it that one of these passions does not invade and devour the other? How is it that the knife that is still wet from a second person's blood and a third person's tears can be raised in an intimate salute to "humanity"?

Thus the rebel's picture of himself: a dead-earnest soldier for the humanity of man. If we join him in accepting that picture, if we take the rebel's *machismo* as offered, then we shall probably convince ourselves that he is trapped in a deadly moral contradiction which can be resolved in only one of two ways. Most sympathetically, stressing his aspirations, we should then decide that he is *tragic*, someone driven to disfigure what he most highly prizes. Least sympathetically, stressing his actions, we should find in him the hypocrite *criminal* who cynically pretends that death is only relatively evil.

Both views are wrong. When the "criminal" affirms that he is "in dead earnest," his tone of voice attributes to himself a decision that has originated elsewhere. "In dead earnest" is a euphemism for "desperate." When the "tragic" figure affirms that his cause is "the humanity of man," he has either forgotten the way he came or he has failed to see that negating one thing is not the same as affirming its opposite. "The humanity of man" is a euphemism for "survival."

This abstract man has come through a good many changes. From one whose reaction to his own victimhood was resignation and ritual flight, he has become a self-conscious victim who understands that no one will change things for him, that he may himself take action, and that there is such a thing as revolution. Wretched man has come to the edge of violence. But he is not yet revolutionary man. He may very well piece together an entire habit of life out of hesitation, ambiguity, reserve. He is oblique, ironic, elegant, and cool, someone whose detachment tries not to become treachery, whose sympathy tries not to become irreversible involvement.

What drives him over the divide? What is the difference between the Guatemalan, Mozambiquan, Brazilian farmers who have joined Turcios, Mondlane, Alepio in the mountains, and those likeminded ones who have remained onlookers in the villages? What is the difference between the "revolutionary" and the "radical leftist" which the Brazilian informs us is so critical?

If I am correct in assuming that men resist danger and want freedom from *all* servitudes, then it follows that rebellion does not take place until it has become compulsory. The rebel is someone who is no longer free to chose even his own docile servitude. He has been driven to the wall. Somebody is even trying to pound him through it. He has been reduced from the slave to the prisoner, from the prisoner to the condemned. It is no longer a matter of standing before two objects and choosing which he shall be. Totally possessed by his predicament, and therefore in its command, he is no longer able to make even a subjective distinction between that predicament and himself. His anger, like his previous humiliation, was for awhile still something which he could set beside himself and contemplate or enact: his *situation,* not his *person.* But this changes. In spite of himself, he is pushed into the same space which he formerly quarantined off for his anger. He is fused with it—with the poverty, estrangement, futurelessness which gave it its murderous content. He is turned into the venom from which he has tried to stand apart. Except for rebellion, there is nothing. The strange apparent freedom of the rebel, and hence that pride of his which is so enormous when it arrives as to dwarf everything else, a psychic flood which sweeps everything before it, lie in his having finally affirmed the only life that is available to him: *The rebel is someone who has accepted death.*

It is this deprivation of choice that makes the difference between the "revolutionary," who may not be at all "radical" and the "radical," who may never become "revolutionary."

Who determined that this most severe and absolute of reductions should have taken place? We contented Westerners prefer to think that it was the rebel himself. This gives us the right to treat him as though he were a criminal. This is what allows us to single out for pity those "innocent women and children" whom our bombs also destroy, as if there is nothing wrong in killing adult male rebels. But this distinction, because it presupposes that the rebel has had a choice, obliges us to concoct a whole new second definition of man, a definition to place beside the one which we reserve for ourselves. The rebel will in that case be for us the very astounding slave who found it in his power to walk away from his slavery.

There is a more mundane explanation.

Here is someone who was lucky. He was *educated*. It was systematically driven into his head that justice is such and such, truth this, honor that. One day he surfaced from his education. Powerless not to do so, he observed his world. Having no measures other than those that had been nailed into his brain, and unable to detach them, he found himself possessed by certain conclusions: There is no justice here. Innocently, meaning no harm, he spoke the names of the guilty. No doubt he vaguely expected to be thanked for this, congratulated for having entered the camp of Socrates and Bruno. Matters were otherwise and now he is in prison making plans. This happened.

Here is another, a humbler person. Belly rumbling but hat in hand, he goes before the mighty; does not accuse them of being mighty, far from it; points out politely that there is unused grain in the silos, and untilled land; makes a modest suggestion. His son is dragged from bed the following dawn to see someone whipped for having dangerous ideas. This happened.

A third spoke of a union. He survived the bomb that destroyed his family, but it appears that no one will accept his apologies.

Another who joined a freedom march believing that men were good; he saw an old black man fall in the heat, where he was at once surrounded by white men who said, "Watch him wiggle. Let him die." This is memorable.

A quiet one who spoke for peace between the city and the countryside. It is whispered to him that he must hide; the police have his name; he has committed the crime of neutralism. Where shall this quiet one go now that he is a criminal?

A scholar speculates in a public article that aspects of his nation's foreign-trade system are disadvantageous to development. A week later he hears that his name has been linked with the names of certain enemies of society. Another week, and he finds that he may no longer teach.

One day someone's telephone develops a peculiar click.

Two bombs go off in San Francisco. No clues are found. Two pacifists are shot in Richmond. The police are baffled. Gang beatings of a political nature occur in New York. There are no arrests. The murder toll in Dixie mounts year by year. There are no convictions. One group proposes to rethink the idea of nonviolence. Its supporters are alarmed. Another group arms itself. Its supporters disaffiliate.

Stability, after all, must be ensured. The *peace* must be kept.

But the master seems to grow less and less confident with each of his victories. Now he requires the slave to affirm his happiness. Suspicion of unhappiness in the slave becomes ground for his detention; proved unhappiness constitutes a criminal assault upon the peace. The master is unsure of something. He wants to see the slave embracing his chains.

Trying only to reduce his pain for a moment, the slave forces his body to fade away. The backward faction acquires hard proof from this that its assessment of the situation has been correct. "See this docility? After all, the whip is the best pacifier."

Exasperated, the slave spits out a curse. Shocked to discover that a slave can have learned to curse, the advanced faction hastens forward with a principled rebuke: "Bad tactics! No way to change the hearts of men!"

It is almost comic. As though he were really trying to produce the angry backlash, the master grinds the slave's face deeper and deeper into the realities of his situation. Yet the master must be blameless, for he is only trying to satisfy his now insatiable appetite for security, an appetite which has actually become an addiction. He only wants to know that he is still respected, if not loved, that matters stand as matters should, and that no threat to the peace is being incubated here. "I love you, master," whispers the slave, squinting up between the two huge boots, thinking to steal a moment's relief. To no one's real surprise, he is promptly shot. The master's explanation rings true: "He was a liar. He *must* have been. Liars are untrustworthy and dangerous."

The rebel is the man for whom it has been decreed that there is only one way out.

The rebel is also the man whom America has called "the Communist" and taken as her enemy. The man whom American now claims the right to kill.

NOTES

1.   John Gerassi, *The Great Fear in Latin America*, The Macmillan Company (Collier Book), New York, 1965, p. 45.

2.   Robert S. McNamara, "Response to Aggression" (address delivered March 26, 1964), in Marcus G. Raskin and Bernard B. Fall, Random House (Vintage Book), New York, 1965, p. 201.

3.   *New York Times*, October 28, 1965.

Unmasking Genocide

Dave Dellinger

There is no possibility of summing up the evidence presented at the second session of the International War Crimes Tribunal, held at Roskilde, Denmark, from November 20 to December 1, 1967. For much of the time I sat numbed by the accumulation of horrors, convinced intellectually of the reality of the events being described but too limited emotionally to be able to grasp them.

I doubt if Americans will ever be able to comprehend the depravity represented by United States actions in Vietnam or the nightmare of Vietnamese suffering, as both were revealed at the Tribunal. Most Germans have never come to grips with Dachau and Buchenwald and most Communists, in and out of the Soviet Union, are as yet unable to grasp the reality of Stalin's purges and death camps. Still, neither German nor Stalinist atrocities were adequately documented while they were taking place, though of course there were rumors and some evidence. The Tribunal performed an historic task by gathering and sifting volumes of evidence while the crimes are still being enacted and in the very midst of the denials and justifications of their perpetrators. We owe a debt of gratitude to Bertrand Russell for launching the Tribunal and to the investigators who risked their lives and their Western "careers" by gathering the information.

No matter that the U.S. press chose to ignore most of the evidence. (The New York *Times* correspondent did not attend on the days that ex-G.I.'s Peter Martinsen and David Tuck gave their testimony of G.I.

Dave Dellinger, "Unmasking Genocide," *Liberation*, December 1967/January 1968, pp. 3–13. Reprinted with permission.

tortures of prisoners, though he was in town and forewarned.) Anyone who reads the documents reproduced in this issue will realize that this dereliction condemns the mass media and seriously handicaps the developing American conscience but does not nullify the work of the Tribunal, which will out in the end.

Read the statements by Martinsen, Tuck and former Green Beret Sergeant Donald Duncan (who placed the events described by the other two in the context of the world-wide counterinsurgency apparatus and of the United States) and consider that hardly a mumbling word of this reached the American public. Yet every pious assertion of U.S. idealism by President Johnson, Secretary Rusk and General Westmoreland is trumpeted to our attention, overshadowed only by the commercials and the trivia. We are misled by the fact that opposition is reported and a certain amount of muckraking takes place. We congratulate ourselves on the contrast with the one-party press of most Communist countries and forget that this is one of the worst aspects of those regimes. Erroneously we conclude that the Free World's press is indeed significantly free and the truth available to those who have the wit to discern it. So the slaughter continues and we are not really aware of its extent or of what it portends, for our society and for the human race.

At the opening sessions of the Tribunal, we learned that the pattern of psychosocial targeting that had been exposed at Stockholm has been extended and intensified during the last few months. According to the U.S. Air Force Manual, "Fundamentals of Aerospace Weapons," the purpose of "attacking a nation's psychosocial structure" is "to create unrest, ... to cause strikes, sabotage, riots, fear, panic, hunger and passive resistance to the government and to create a general feeling that the war should be terminated." Under psychosocial targeting, known Catholic areas have become prime targets in Vietnam, apparently on the somewhat plausible assumption that the loyalty of the Catholic minority to the Vietnamese culture and government is less than that of Buddhists. As with so many of the Pentagon's schemes, however, bombing of Catholic areas has backfired because the generals forgot that bombing does not endear the assailant to his victim.

In April, at Stockholm, we had learned that eighty Catholic churches had been destroyed from the air in North Vietnam during the twenty-three months of 1965 and 1966 in which bombing took place, as against thirty Buddhist pagodas. At Roskilde we learned that during the first ten months of 1967, an additional 227 Catholic churches were destroyed and 86 Buddhist pagodas. Thus there was a major increase in the number of attacks on religious institutions and the concentration continued to be on the Catholic institutions. In Vietnam the Catholic churches are big and easily identifiable, usually sitting in somewhat isolated splendor in the midst of extensive church properties.

SCHOOLS AND HOSPITALS

In addition to churches, key psychosocial targets in Vietnam are schools and hospitals, livestock and agriculture, civilian housing and whatever people live in the N.L.F. areas of the South or in North Vietnam. Frank Harvey, who is not a Tribunal witness but a military specialist chosen by the Air Force to write an authoritative report on the air war, gives the feeling, from within the master race, of the bombing of houses and people. Harvey writes:

> A pilot going into combat for the first time is a bit like a swimmer about to dive into an icy lake. He likes to get his big toes wet and then wade around a little before leaping off the high board into the numbing depths. So it was fortunate that young pilots could get their first taste of combat under the direction of a forward air controller over a flat country in bright sunshine where nobody was shooting back with high-powered ack-ack. *He learned how it feels to drop bombs on human beings and watch huts go up in a boil of orange flame when his aluminum napalm tanks tumble into them. He gets hardened to pressing the fire button and cutting people down like little cloth dummies, as they sprint frantically under him.* He gets his sword bloodied [in the South] for the rougher things to come [in the North, where there are antiaircraft defenses]. (*The Air War— Vietnam*, Bantam Books; emphasis added)

The Tribunal was impatient with reports of devastation in the North, since the pattern of the bombing had already been established at Stockholm. It cut short all such reports and moved on to new matters, most notably the types of weapons and patterns of attack in the South, the destruction of villages and herding of the surviving population into concentration camps, the treatment of prisoners and the drastic escalation of attacks on Laos. First though, it took note of recent "improvements" in the dreaded C.B.U.'s, the antipersonnel bombs which scatter a deadly broadside of steel pellets so tiny that they are useless against military installations, structures of any kind (except straw huts), railroads, truck convoys, etc., though they are deadly against human flesh. In one raid, it was estimated that over three million of these pellets saturated an area of approximately one and a half square kilometers. (A kilometer is .62 miles.)

In recent months, many of the baseball-size secondary bombs (guavas), each of which holds approximately three hundred pellets, have been equipped with timing devices and other mechanisms for delaying firing of the lethal pellets until hours or days after the attack or until they are set off by activity in the area. In this way, vast areas are turned into death traps for rescue workers, people emerging from their shelters, peasants returning to the fields, children going to school. A second recent "improvement" is the development of a model in which "flechettes" or barbed steel splinters, the thickness of a needle, are substituted for the rounded, pea-sized pellets. Currently this type is being manufactured near San Jose, California. (One ironic result of the Tribunal's earlier work is that the Pentagon has declassified the original pellet bombs, whose use it denied from their first employment on February 8, 1965 until after they had been exhibited and analyzed by weapons experts at the Tribunal's first session in April of 1967. Now it has released the design for competitive bidding and has openly contracted for their delivery.)

A PATTERN OF GENOCIDE

As the Tribunal moved its searchlight from North to South Vietnam and on to Laos, Thailand and Cambodia, there emerged a pattern of gradually escalating contempt for Asian life and dignity and a resulting scale of death and destruction that stuns the imagination and legitimizes—nay requires—use of the term genocide. Significantly, former G.I.'s Martinsen and Tuck indicated that they were content to kill "Communists" in Vietnam but that their disillusionment began when they discovered that the entire Vietnamese population was subject to attack unless they left their native homesteads and moved into the U.S.-occupied areas.

A team of three French investigators traveled for three weeks through an N.L.F. zone. They reported:

> During those three weeks we have not seen a single hamlet, a single house which was spared by bombings or strafing....
>
> For two months, the whole Tay Ninh province was particularly well combed by "search and destroy" teams. All the hamlets were razed, all the rice plantations poisoned by chemical products, samples of which we have brought back. The grain reserves were annihilated and the civilians discovered were deported to concentration camp zones....
>
> Many peasants we talked with had escaped from concentration camps, many others had fled from the advancing U.S. troops or simply hid in the forest and escaped the tank columns.
>
> Civilians are now forced to lie in hiding in the forests. They build miserable huts... Each family has dug an underground shelter, they live like primitive men to avoid being located.
>
> The so-called "white" or "free-fire" zone is now declared by the Americans as totally "Vietcong," where all signs of life must be systematically extinguished. From the military bases...the American artillery shoots at random to maintain a constant state of anxiety and insecurity. [The U.S. military admits to this practice and calls it "H & I," or harassment and interdiction.]
>
> The reconnaissance planes fly methodically over the whole zone in large concentric circles. As soon as some movement appears as a sign of human presence, as soon as a field appears to be cultivated, orders are given for a concentrated artillery attack. The least sign of life located by reconnaissance planes is immediately followed by an attack of fighter-bombers which fire rockets, drop fragmentation bombs, napalm and phosphorus bombs....
>
> If we believe the reports of the...officials, since the beginning of...the policy of attack on "everything that moves" [February, 1967], the average expended ordinance is two tons of projectiles per inhabitant and one killed or wounded in every eight persons.... Peasants are obliged to cultivate by night tiny kitchen gardens and the rice paddies on the fringe of the forests. Otherwise any rice patch slightly showing cultivation would be automatically destroyed by defoliants dropped from planes or helicopters. We saw a number of metallic drums dropped on rice paddies and then shot full of holes by the same planes in order to permit the chemical products to dissolve into the water or the rice field and to pollute and contaminate the produce.

TOTAL DESTRUCTION

Particularly shocking to me were reports from Laos of a parallel policy of total destruction of all life in the Pathet Lao districts. One of the Tribunal investigators reported that he walked more than 300 kilometers zig-zig through that part of Laos and did not see a single village that has not been destroyed. Here too the entire surviving population is forced to live in caves, underground shelters or as nomads in the forests. The only agriculture that is possible is the cultivation of tiny patches deep in the forest at night. According to Tribunal witnesses, an estimated one thousand Laotian villages had been destroyed by November 1, 1967. When I was in Vientiane, Laos, in May 1967, numerous clean-cut, well-dressed, pleasant Americans dominated the airport. Some of them joked about the daily bombing run which was launched at 5 p.m. Sure enough, at 5 p.m. I watched twenty-four small planes take off, each with two bombs on the wings. A few minutes later, Nick Egleson and I finished our beer and boarded the International Control Commission plane for Hanoi and took off on the same runway previously used by the bombers. As happens to American TV viewers who sit in security and see war scenes on their screens, sandwiched in between the luxuriant commercials, it was hard for me to realize the significance of what I was seeing. The Tribunal was told that bombers also take off daily for Laos from Thailand.

Facts such as these render obsolete the present level of debate and oppostion in the Western World. Given the systematic destruction of people, habitations and countryside about which there can be no question for those interested enough to find out, Johnson's talk about North Vietnamese aggression becomes both as fanciful and irrelevant as Hitler's catalog of Jewish crimes against Germany. One would have to think less of the North Vietnamese if they failed to help their South Vietnamese brothers—not just because Vietnam is one country, as guaranteed by the Geneva accords and violated by the United States under Eisenhower, Kennedy and Johnson, but because elementary human solidarity requires standing together. And the frequent claim that the war should be ended by mutual concessions and compromise rather than by U.S. withdrawal becomes like arguing, as many Germans did in the thirties, that you are against Hitler's excesses but would not dream of calling for an end to his political program. What reciprocal acts should the Jews have offered in return for a suspension of cremations?

VIETNAMESE GESTAPO*

On April 18, 1960 at 8 P.M., right in the streets of Saigon, the U.S.-Diemist security police arrested me because of my patriotic activities. I was taken to the Commando Post Number 1, the Ba Hoa Post at Cho Lon. The commandant himself directed the interrogation, which started immediately after my arrest. He put questions about my activities with the patriots. I did not reply to these questions, so they started to torture me. Reeking with alcohol, the "commandos" as the Vietnamese call them, started beating me, shouting with rage. The commandos are a sort of Vietnamese Gestapo.

They tied my two arms behind my back, then hauled me up to the ceiling by strong cords attached to my wrists. They beat me with sticks, stopping only when I fainted. Then they let me down, throwing cold water over my face. Little by little I recovered consciousness. More questions. Silence. Furious, they hung me up again. This was repeated I don't know how many times. They called this operation: "ride in a Dakota."

My body was covered with wounds and was most painfully swollen. I suffered atrociously—the slightest movement and I thought I would faint with pain.

After a moment's rest, they applied the "ride in a submarine." They undressed me and tied me, face upward, to a plank. A towel was used to tie my head to the plank; a rubber tube led from a 200-liter barrel, fixed to a stand. The water fell drop by drop onto the towel, soon flooding my face. To breathe, I sucked in water through my nose and mouth. I was suffocating, my stomach started to swell like a balloon. I could no longer breathe and I fainted. When I regained consciousness, I suffered unimaginable pains. I opened my eyes and saw two commandos called Duc and Danh, and nick-named the "Gray Tigers" because of their blood-curdling exploits, stamping on my chest and stomach to get the water out of me. I vomited through my mouth and nose, water mixed with blood pouring out. This was repeated several times. I suffered atrociously in my chest and in my stomach; it was as if someone was twisting my entrails.

"Serve her another dish" the commander said to his agents. The latter formed a square and with myself in the center, they beat me with sticks. They pushed me from one to another as if I were a ping-pong ball, shouting and hurling insults at me. I was seriously

---

*Tribunal statement of Mrs. Pham Thi Yen, member of the N.L.F. delegation, prisoner for seven years.

342 / *THE ANTIWAR MOVEMENT*

wounded in the head, blood trickled down. They stopped beating me and started to shave my head, to bandage it.

They started to lull me with doubtful promises mixed with threats—

Talk, and you can rejoin your children. If not, you will die and your children will be orphans.

Talk, and you can keep your pharmacy, your possessions. Otherwise we will ruin you.

Talk, or we will torture you to death and even if you survive you'll be useless, without strength to brush a fly away.

Neither their sickening promises nor their threats had any effect. Screaming with rage, they threw my face down on the floor, a huge brute squatting on my back, two others holding my feet with the soles turned upwards. Using police truncheons they beat the soles of my feet with all their strength. My feet and legs swelled up visibly as they struck. I felt as if my skin was going to burst.

Afterward they hung me by my wrists, this time attached to the iron bars of a window with handcuffs, my arms crossed and at a height at which I could only stand on the tips of my toes. My arms and legs hurt terribly. They started to hammer my arms against the bars. My arms became numb. Seeing this had no effect, the untied me and kicked me on to the floor again. They started to kick me. Blood was running all over the place. I fainted.

Again there were promises, threats and insults. Tired themselves, they called other prisoners and tried to force them to beat me. They all refused, so the prisoners were furiously beaten. In that place there was no room for any human sentiments at all.

Just before dawn they said they would serve me a "sensational dish." They attached me to a kaki tree in the garden near a cage where two tigers were ferociously roaring. In South Vietnam, kaki trees, which produce very sweet fruit, are always covered with yellow ants. If a single ant stings you, you'll yell with pain. And the spot where you are stung will swell up immediately with the effect of the poison. This tree was just of this species—its branches full of yellow ants...

The tigers continued roaring, the torturers were shouting with rage. It was a frightful and at the same time terribly sinister experience. But all this also had no effect. My feelings were entirely concentrated on the little ants, their stings were so painful.

The torturers threatened me: "If you don't talk, your children will be tortured in front of your eyes; your parents, your brothers and sisters will be imprisoned. Your family will be destroyed, your pharmacy seized..."

At 6 o'clock in the morning, after ten hours of torture, they threw me into a cell. I could hardly stand up, I had to lie down on the cold floor....

DIEM'S PRISONS*

...In March 1957, I was transferred from Thu Dau Mot prison to that of Gia Dinh and the following month I was sent to Poulo Condore. There were four hundred prisoners on our boat, including twenty-four women, of whom two were over 60, and two babies of one year and six months. The total number of prisoners on the island while I was there ranged from four thousand to eight thousand, including common-law offenders, about one hundred women and four children under one year.

At the time I arrived in Poulo Condore, prisoners were gradually being killed off. They were not being killed outright, but the treatment was so terrible, with not enough food or water, not even enough air because of the frightful overcrowding in the cells, and with no medical care at all, prisoners were just dying of exhaustion and disease.

For the first two days after my arrival, I was detained in a fairly large room with enough food and water. On the third day, Captain Nam, deputy head at Poulo Condore, explained the prison regime. He said:

In Poulo Condore, the number killed equals the number of bricks used in building the prison. This island is far from the mainland, far from your friends. There's nobody here to protect you. Poulo Condore prison applies U.S. policy to gradually kill all those who refuse to denounce Communism, who refuse to respect President Ngo Dinh Diem, who refuse to learn how to denounce Communists and who oppose U.S. presence in South Vietnam. There are thousands of sick, already dying, prisoners here. I advise you not to follow their road.

That evening Captain Nam gave each of us a prepared statement of our willingness to break with Communism and tried to compel us to sign them. We refused and were beaten up and then taken to our

*Tribunal statement of Mrs. Nguyen Thi Tho, member of the N.L.F. delegation, prisoner for four years.

cells, four to each cell. These latter were built by the French colonial-ists to hold one person each in solitary confinement. On three sides are stone-and-concrete walls about eighteen inches thick with a concrete roof. There was a two-and-a-half-inch thick door with a small air hole in it of about an inch in diameter. Above the door was another hole about two feet long and a foot wide, covered with an iron grill, hermetically closed when we arrived. There was another small hole connecting the cell to an outside latrine. The cell itself was about six feet square with a bench five feet long and a little over one foot wide, where one person could lie down. There was no lighting at all and all ventilation was blocked except for the hole leading to the outside latrine. The warders brought in a two-gallon-sized latrine bucket which was emptied once a week.

After fifteen minutes in the cell, it was impossible to breathe. The fetid stench from the latrine was stifling. Drops of water stood out on the black stone walls. The heat was terrible, sweat poured down our bodies. We soon had to take off our clothes and cut our long hair, but even so the heat was unendurable.

At first we were four in our cell, then eight and finally twelve in this same tiny cell. There were many cases of asphyxiation. We waged a struggle for more air, shouting and screaming until the warders had to open the door. Within three minutes those that had fainted came to again.

Our daily ration was two bowls of rice, of which about a third was unhusked, two spoonfuls of salted water and just under half a pint of drinking water. There was no water at all for washing.

In front of the door passed a foul-smelling canal leading from the latrine. The rice was set down alongside this canal before being given to us, and we watched the flies and blowflies crawling over it before we had to eat it. We never once saw real white rice. It was impossible not to vomit after getting it down. There were cases of cholera and dysentery.

For four months we were never allowed to wash or bathe. We were filthy. During menstruation we could only stand against the wall and let the blood flow out, sometimes collapsing into our own blood.

We suffered like this in the cell for ten months. Everybody became weak and exhausted, our skins grew pallid. Some of the women could not move their legs, we were suffering from intestinal and nervous ailments, from malarian ulcers, inflammation of the uterus...we looked like skeletons. Some of us were at death's door when people on the mainland started a campaign protesting the detention of women in Poulo Condore, demanding that the U.S.-Diem clique bring us back to the mainland. As a result we were transferred to a building known as "Death Prison" where we were given better food for two months and then shipped back to the mainland.

As far as the regular prisoners at Poulo Condore are concerned, about two hundred are detained in one room which was so cramped that for every four inmates there was an average of ten square feet in which to sit or lie down. Prisoners were detained for years on end under such conditions. Food and water supply was the same as I mentioned above. Usually after one year of this, prisoners die from exhaustion, malnutrition and disease. Once a year they are allowed to bathe in the sea, most of them so weak when they move out that they looked like skeletons, hardly able to drag themselves along....

LIMITS OF UNDERSTANDING

Our capacity to comprehend evils as great as those taking place in Southeast Asia may be limited but within the normal limits of human understanding one can react by refusal and resistance. The Vietnamese have made this clear. In fact, the ability of resisters like Mrs. Pham Thi Yen and Mrs. Nguyen Thi Tho to undergo the tortures described in their testimony without yielding is almost as incomprehensible to most of us as the ability of their torturers to continue to inflict such barbarities month after month. Apparently each course of action has its own internal momentum which carries its practitioners far beyond the realms of ordinary human behavior—though in opposite directions. Thus ex-G.I. Peter Martinse, whose job was to interrogate prisoners of war, testifies:

None of us ever thought we would actually torture or even beat a prisoner...until after members of the detachment were killed.... Then you realize that everyone participates in the torture, unless we have a special group of sadists working as interrogators, which I don't believe. I believe that they are just normal people....

It's so horrifying to recall an interrogation where you beat the fellow to get an effect [i.e., information] and then you beat him out of anger and then you beat him out of pleasure.

On the other hand it is doubtful if anyone, including Mrs. Yen or Mrs. Tho themselves, would have been able to predict in advance of their ordeal that these women could stand up to the treatment they received. Perhaps the first lesson in all this is that we must do everything in our power to stop society from putting ourselves or others in Peter Martinsen's predicament—and that we should not be deterred in our resistance by fear of ending up in Mrs. Yen's or Mrs. Tho's situation. That sounds far braver than I feel or than I imagine most people will feel after reading the documents, but can we do less without suffering moral deterioration?

MORE THAN ORDINARY

In any event, no one listening to Mrs. Yen or Mrs. Tho could believe that they were "ordinary persons" any longer, after their ordeal and triumphs. On the other hand the preponderance of evidence from Vietnam, not just at the Tribunal but from a variety of sources, including statements by American fighting men, indicates that otherwise "ordinary" Vietnamese take on extraordinary powers of resistance to hardship and suffering in the ranks of the Viet Cong. By contrast, of course, the complaint about the Vietnamese who side with the United States is just the opposite—that they won't fight; that they lack motivation, etc. Notice the testimony of former G.I. David Tuck:

> Our officers told us...that the only good Vietnamese was a dead Vietnamese, that they were no good, that they would not fight.

But describing acts of torture against a captured V.C., he says,

> They had the man tied on the ground, he was spread-eagled. They were using a knife to sort of pry under his toenails and the soles of his feet. When this got no results they went on to other more sensitive parts of the body. Well this still got no results, because evidently this man was, as we say in America, a tough nut to crack. So then...they put the knife under his eyeball...and he still would not talk.

The behavior of both torturers and the tortured goes so far beyond our normal experience that any isolated account automatically arouses our suspicions, or alternatively makes us think in terms of an occasional sadist or heroine. But Martinsen makes it clear that he participated in "several hundred formal interrogations" and that

> I cannot think of an interrogation that I saw in Vietnam during which a war crime, as defined by the Geneva Convention, was not committed. I cannot think of one without harrassment or coercion.

Reading testimonies like that of Mrs. Yen and Mrs. Tho in N.L.F. literature in the past, I have found myself automatically discounting them, wondering if they were not exaggerated in places to make propaganda. But it is the war itself which offends credibility and I don't believe that anyone who listened to Mrs. Yen or Mrs. Tho in person doubted a syllable that they uttered. I say this not to make their printed statements more credible to the reader but to indicate the problem we all face at a time when our country has passed the normal limits of human morality.

After the Tribunal's first session in Stockholm, in April 1966, an American TV and radio tycoon who had attended some of the sessions (Gordon McLendon who is currently hoping to run for governor in Texas) held a press conference in New York at which he attacked the Tribunal by repeating some of the evidence it had listened to—evidence that the United States had deliberately attacked a Vietnamese leprosorium on thirty-nine separate occasions. Undoubtedly Mr. McLendon had a sound sense of public credibility and succeeded in discrediting the Tribunal. The sad reality is that the leprosorium had indeed been attacked in the manner described.

A CREDIBILITY PROBLEM

Thus an honest investigatory body like the Tribunal—or the aggrieved victims of genocide, the Vietnamese, who have no need to exaggerate—are confronted with a credibility problem far more serious than that faced by President Johnson. Most everyone knows that the government lies regularly about what it is doing in Vietnam. Its lies have been exposed time after time. But even knowing this, the nature of our daily lives and the handling of the war by the mass media makes it easier for us to believe the government's version of what is happening in Vietnam, give or take a few details, than to accept that of the Tribunal or of the Vietnamese. The reality is too far-fetched, but we ignore it at our peril.

At Roskilde I was convinced of the authenticity and pervasiveness of the atrocities because the same incredible pattern was described to us by the victims and the practitioners, by independent nonpolitical observers and by committed partisans on both sides, by journalists who lived and traveled with the Americans and journalists who lived and traveled with the Vietnamese. We heard descriptions of what goes on in Vietnam and we saw it in photographs and films and in the seared flesh and mutilated bodies of the Vietnamese witnesses. We saw it in sample weapons brought from the battlefields and it was confirmed in the testimony of doctors, chemists, weapons analysts, historians, lawyers and social scientists.

On the last day of testimony, Erich Wulff, a West German doctor who had served on the Faculty of Medicine and in the hospitals of Hue for six years (from September 1961 to November 20, 1967), flew into Copenhagen to report on what he had seen in this American-occupied Vietnamese city. Without much idea of what the American G.I.'s, the Vietnamese victims or the other witnesses had said, he supported their evidence by delineating the same realities. Six years ago he was an anti-Communist humanitarian who went to Vietnam to supplement U.S. efforts to aid the Vietnamese. He said that step by step the war in Vietnam has become a war against the whole population. A profoundly fair man, he argued that the average American official in Vietnam successfully shielded himself from perceiving this reality but that the primitive understanding of the less sophisticated Marine—that he must kill every "gook"—comes closer to the actuality of the present U.S. policy than the rationalizations of the officials.

Let me conclude by summarizing one example of the concatenation of evidence from diverse sources—the use and effects of poison gas. All quotations, including statements by U.S. officials, which appeared first in American periodicals, are taken from documents that were presented to the Tribunal.

NO COMPREHENSION

There can be no doubt that certain types of gas are used by the United States in South Vietnam. The only argument is about whether or not the effects are lethal. Here again we have a typical situation in which most Americans are vaguely aware that gas is being used—and are even proud that their democratic government and "free press" have not concealed this fact from them—but have absolutely no comprehension of the realities. In trying to present itself in the most favorable light, the United States has officially taken a position which is scientifically untenable: it describes the supposed effects of the gases it uses without describing the concentrations employed or the conditions under which they are used. Referring to occasions when mild doses of the same gases are used outside Vietnam without killing anyone, it argues that the employment of gas in Vietnam is clearly nonlethal. It is as if the murderer claimed that his victim could not possibly have died from an overdose of some barbiturate because the substance is widely used to combat insomnia.

Secretary of Defense Robert McNamara in a U.S.I.S. bulletin of March 24, 1965, described three "tear gases" in use in Vietnam, CN, CS, and DM. He stated that CN on the average makes the victim helpless "for a period of three minutes," CS "on the average makes one incapable of resistance for about 5 to 15 minutes," and DM incapacitates the victim during "a period of from half an hour to two hours."

For United States consumption, an article in the New York Times of March 23, 1965, reported that

The United States disclosed today that it was giving the South Vietnamese some temporarily disabling "types of tear gas" for combat use.... [A] statement was also distributed by the Defense Department. It said: "In tactical situations in which the Vietcong intermingle with or take refuge among non-combatants, rather than use artillery or air-bombardment, Vietnamese troops have used a type of tear gas. It is a non-lethal gas which disables temporarily, making the enemy incapable of fighting. Its use in such situations is no different than the use of disabling gases in riot control."

Unfortunately these explanations were more effective in lulling public indignation in the West than in saving the lives of the Vietnamese. The reasons can be found in the following analysis by the Tribunal's Scientific Commission, which describes the chemical properties of the gases far more scientifically than Secretary McNamara did, for all his computers and university research teams:

CN (choloracetopheneone) in air suspension produces a temporary irritation of the cornea and the appearance of tears at the weak concentration of 1/10,000 mg. per litre of air; a serious irritation of the eyes and of the respiratory tracts at a concentration of 2/10,000 mg. per litre; and death, through acute pulmonary edema at strong concentrations of 10 to 15 mg. per litre of air.

Secretary McNamara admits that both CS and DM are significantly stronger in their effects than CN. The scientists who testified before the Tribunal pointed out that as with CN their effects vary in accord with the degree of concentration, with both becoming lethal in milder concentrations than CN. In laboratory tests conducted in Tokyo, Tribunal scientists found that when they exploded a single small grenade, captured in Vietnam, in an underground shelter measuring 50 square feet, the resulting concentration of gas was sufficient to kill a healthy monkey or cat within a few minutes.

AMERICAN EFFICIENCY

At the Tribunal we saw captured U.S. films which showed gas being sprayed into underground tunnels and American soldiers pulling out the dead bodies of Vietnamese, including women and children. The spraying is carried out with typical American technological efficiency. The gas is forced into the tunnels by "'Mighty Mite,' an air pump which sends out a jet of gas at about 200 m.p.h." (A.P. dispatch from Saigon, Le Monde, Paris, January 5, 1966) The same dispatch mentions "cylindrical grenades thrown by hand or fired from rifles." Sample grenades were presented in evidence at the Tribunal, together with the powder inside which turns into a highly concentrated gas when the grenade explodes. The use of the powder and grenades is not accidental. Brig. Gen. Gacquard Rothschild explains in his book Tomorrow's Weapons that higher concentrations of gas are achieved through the explosion of powder.

The Wall Street Journal reports:

Most peasant houses have underground shelters designed to protect residents from typhoons and wars. Now when American troops are entering South Vietnamese villages, they generally throw grenades in the shelters. Of course there are innocent victims. (January 5, 1966)

In more concrete terms, Dr. A. Behar reported to the Tribunal that on the 5th of September, 1965, in the village of Vinh Quang (Binh Dinh province),

> The spraying of 48 toxic gas containers into the shelters resulted in the death of 35 persons and seriously poisoned 25 others. (Out of the total of 60 it should be mentioned that 28 were children and 26 women.)

Ex-G.I. Peter Martinsen, relating his experiences as a prisoner interrogator, testified as follows:

> There were some people in a tunnel, and the Americans found the tunnel entrance. They looked inside the tunnel and found it was occupied. They immediately gassed the tunnel with tear gas. It might have been "antiriot" gas.... The people came out the other end of the tunnel badly gassed and coughing. All of them sounded like they had serious damage to their lungs. The prisoners were brought in to us.... Four or five of the prisoners were girls between the ages of 16 and 20.... They were coughing, wheezing and gasping.... I took one look and called the doctor [who] gave them all injections of dosages of adrenalin.... One girl grew more ill.... The doctor said "No, no, she'll get better," and she was growing worse.

Later she was evacuated to a field hospital where she died.

* * *

EXECUTIONER FALLS VICTIM

Despite precautions, even the executioner sometimes falls victim. On January 13, 1966, the Brisbane (Australia) *Courier Mail* reported that an Australian corporal, Robert William Botwell, 24, *who was wearing a gas mask,* "died of asphyxiation" when he was trapped in a tunnel into which the Australian forces had thrown "tear-gas grenades" and smoke bombs.

> Two other Australian soldiers were overcome by the gas when they attempted to rescue Botwell...; four Australian engineers were

overcome by carbon monoxide poisoning during the same operation. Army dogs brought in to help in the tunnel were also overcome.

In addition to inundating shelters and tunnels, as we have seen, the U.S. forces drop the gas wholesale on enemy troops and suspected V.C. areas. The *New York Times* of February 23, 1966 prints a dispatch from Saigon which states that

> Before the bombers struck the area, 12 miles southwest of Bongson, hundreds of tear-gas grenades were dropped from helicopters. The first soldiers to enter the area wore gas masks.

On August, 17, 1967, a UPI dispatch from Danang said that

> Marine helicopter gunships dropped thousands of gallons of combination tear-nausea gas on a suspected Communist position last Thursday, the first use of gas this way in Vietnam. (*Asahi Evening News*, Tokyo, August 18, 1967)

To add a footnote to the above, Dr. Wulff told of treating patients in the Hue hospital who were suffering from "vast burnings of a great degree, cramps and vomiting" after having been exposed to "tear gas" in the open air in the suppression of Buddhist demonstrations. "The South Vietnamese authorities themselves told me that the gas used was tear gas," he testified. "In a slight concentration it is tear gas, but in greater degrees of concentration it is lethal."

* * *

I have mentioned the impossibility of summing up the *evidence* given at Roskilde...but it has been possible to sum up the *findings* and to spell out some of their implications for mankind. It was to this last task that I devoted the closing speech of the session, and I shall end here with some words from this "appeal of the Tribunal to world and American public opinion":

> The Nuremberg Tribunal asked for and secured the punishment of individuals. The International War Crimes Tribunal is asking the peoples of the world, the masses, to take action to stop the crimes. At Nuremberg the accused rested safely in jail, and the main focus was on the past; our Tribunal is quite different. Unless the masses act, and act successfully, we stand only at the beginning of war

crimes and genocide—genocide that could bring down the cities and destroy the populations of the world....

Let us remind you that the history of the war in Vietnam is a history of continuous escalation. When the United States has found that it cannot defeat the enemy of the moment at the level of warfare of the moment, it continually redefines the enemy and expands the form of its aggression. I will not go into the history of this expansion, but I will remind you that it began with diplomatic warfare at Geneva and elsewhere; it went through the stages of political infiltration, the training of puppets, the organizing of counterinsurgency, the training and leading of massive Saigon troops and, finally, the commitment of masses of U.S. troops.

A State of Mind

As the United States loses in its battle with one enemy, it takes on new enemies. And as it escalates its enemies, it escalates the weapons.... The state of mind that affirms napalm and pellet bombs and poison gases as weapons is the state of mind that can affirm nuclear warfare.

Many people in the countries of the world, especially the Western countries, are watching from the sidelines, as they watched Hitler. In the time of Hitler they said, "It can't happen here." And in the time of the U.S. aggression in Vietnam they are saying, "It can't happen to our cities; it can't happen to our populations." But already their countries are subjected to the diplomatic warfare that began the attack on Vietnam. They are subject to pressures on their governments and their economies. The U.S. Special Forces are scattered throughout the world. The Vietnamese know that they have no choice, except to resist. In many other countries, particularly the Western countries, people think that they have a choice still. But they have none; they must resist.

Democracy and Genocide

Paradoxically, if Hitler announced his intention to wipe out the Jews, the photos and the reports of the atrocities did not appear in the daily newspapers or go into the living rooms on television. And if the democratic facade in the United States has prevented the American generals and presidents from announcing their intentions, perhaps even from comprehending them in their full intensity themselves, the same democratic facade allows some of the reports and some of the photos to appear in the American mass media.... And at a certain stage, the psychology becomes: because we admit that we are doing these things, we are not really doing them at all. In other words, they do not call them by their proper name, and they do not present them in their proper perspective or intensity. But a democratic society *can* commit genocide, as is illustrated by the history of the United States. I need only remind you of what happened to the American Indians and the black people.

If the people in the Western countries in particular underestimate the total and genocidal nature of the United States' aggression, there is something else which they underestimate also. And that is the ability of the Vietnamese people to resist. If they underestimate the inhuman nature of U.S. actions, they also underestimate the human nature of the Vietnamese resistance.

The legitimacy of the Tribunal has sometimes been questioned. Its legitimacy will be determined by the answer given to its findings by the people of the world. The people of the world must refuse to commit the crimes that have been documented here. They must refuse to be accomplices in these crimes. But it is not enough to stop there. In addition they must take positive action to stop the crimes. The Tribunal appeals to the people of the United States to stop the monstrous aggression of the United States at its source. It appeals to the people of the United States to put an end to U.S. genocide. And finally, the Tribunal appeals to all the peoples of the world to act in the name of humanity and the name of solidarity with our Vietnamese brothers and with all other peoples whose lives and honor and integrity are threatened.

A SOLDIER'S STORY

The following is a report to the Tribunal by one of its investigative teams, which on September 11, 1967 questioned a soldier at the Phnom Parh [?] base in Takeo province, Cambodia, where he had arrived the previous day.

Cambodian officials introduced him as a Khmer soldier from the American-South Vietnamese army who had given himself up with his weapons to the Cambodian authorities. He was middle-aged, with the physical characteristics of the Khmer ethnic group (dark skinned) and was wearing camouflage uniform. On his cap there was a badge showing two wings. He was carrying a Colt AR-5* 5.56 mm. automatic rifle equipped with a 40 mm. grenade thrower plus ammunition—registration number of rifle: 134 053. He spoke neither

---

*This is apparently a misprint for AR-15, an earlier name for what today is better known as the M-16.

French nor English. We questioned him with the assistance of the governor of the region of Takeo, who acted as our interpreter.

What is your name?
Muong Ponn.
How old are you?
Thirty-nine.
How long have you been in the army?
I have been in the army for nineteen years. At first I was in an infantry battalion of the French Army of the Far East. When the French left they handed me over to the South Vietnamese government. I have been in the intervention forces since 1957. I am a master sergeant.
What was your last unit?
I was in a helicopter unit, known as the "MY" or "Mail Force," stationed to the north of Saigon.
What are the functions of this unit?
It has to carry out "mopping-up" operations in the villages.
How many men are in the unit? Who is its commanding officer?
There are five hundred men—Koreans, Chinese, and Khmers. The commanding officer is an American.
So there are no Vietnamese in it?
No, there are none.
Who are the Chinese you mentioned?
They speak Vietnamese. I think they are Chinese from South Vietnam who support Taiwan. There are 180 of them.
What was the unit doing in the region?
It was taking part in an operation to rescue five Americans who were thought to be prisoners on a nearby hill.
Why have you come to Cambodia?
I was disgusted with the massacres of Khmer villages and the Khmer population in villages we had to "mop up."
What is meant by "mopping up"?
We were dropped by helicopters, we fired at everything and killed everyone.
Had orders been given to [do] that?
Yes.
Who gave the orders?
The Americans.
Can you describe a recent operation against a Khmer village?
Yes. On 12th April of this year we took part in an operation against a village, at Phum Oc Yum. First of all the F-105's bombed it. Then we were dropped by parachute. There was a terrible massacre, mostly women and children. There were only a few men, apart from

the very old ones. Our instructions were to shoot at everything that moved.

Did Americans take part?

Yes. The commanding officer in charge of the operation was an American, Major Marchand (or Marchett).

What kind of village was it?

It was almost entirely Khmer. It was after this operation that I decided to leave.

Can you tell me other cases of this kind?

There was an operation on My Da [My Tho—?] village in the province [environs—?] of Moc Hoa. Sixty people were killed, nearly all of them women and children. It was a mixed village of Vietnamese and Khmers. We had been given orders to wipe out the whole village. There were practically only women and children. They were the only ones to stay. I was disgusted.

(The Khmer officer from the 2nd Bureau later added that the man had told him that a group of women and children had been lined up and the American officer gave the order to fire. The Khmer soldiers refused and it was the Americans who did the shooting.)

Have you used gas grenades in these villages in the course of operations?

No.

Were there other operations of the same kind against villages?

Yes.

Were there other Khmer soldiers in your unit?

Yes, many.

What was your pay?

Eight thousand nine hundred Veitnamese dongs* a month, plus combat rations.

Did you have other reasons for coming to Cambodia?

Yes, I have had enough of being a soldier. I want to have a quiet life. The Americans despised us. We had to salute them whatever their grade. They isolated us. When we returned from an operation we had to stay within barracks. We wouldn't have any contacts with civilians.

Is that all?

No, I couldn't bear to kill my own people, the Khmers. Fortunately, the present operation took us close to the Cambodian border. (At one moment we were transported in a hydroglider.) Then there is the fact that I'm a Bhuddist. They refused to let me practice my religion. I had to hide this (he pulled out of his jacket a fairly bulky statuette which he was wearing round his neck on a ribbon). I couldn't go on accepting that.

F. KAHN, W. BURCHETT, R. PIC and MME CUKIER-KAHN.

---

* Popular word for piastres; the sum is not entirely clear in the text and might be "eight to nine hundred." Piastres are quoted at $.0085 in New York City.

No Door to Tomorrow

Lee Felsenstein

I've had a dead man with me this past week.

Bud Anello was killed last May in Vietnam. He would have been twenty one by now. I got to know him from the letters his older brother Don showed me.

Bud was a kid who went along with the system. It chewed him up and spat him out Dead.

Bud spent a few months in Berkeley; the summer of 1966. He was just beginning to explore the freedom he had gained by leaving his father to stay with his brother.

He was outgoing and almost excessively humorous, according to his brother. He was probably trying to cover his feelings. He kept a list of cues to his repertoire of jokes and routines with him.

His brother turned Bud on when he got out here, and that gave him a lot to think about. He was good at music and drawing, but he didn't know what he wanted to do with his life.

His letters convey the feeling that he was confused, searching for something. Halfway through his tour of Vietnam he began sending back poetry, much to his brothers' surprise.

An excerpt...

The scared have no thoughts
Nor a right nor a wrong
Just self-defence

Lee Felsenstein, "No Door to Tomorrow," *The Berkeley Barb*, December 20–26, 1968, p. 11.

as the eyes of the victim
say a last prayer.
It all smells so bad
It all feels nothing
And there is no door to
walk into tomorrow.

Bud, like all of his brothers, was raised in the Milton Hershey School in Pennsylvania; an orphanage. His mother died bearing her fourth son.

"He was used to institutions," his brother told me, "he figured he could goof off and get through by taking the path of least resistance."

It didn't work. The Army is not an orphanage.

Bud found the way back to base for his platoon once during maneuvers. They put him into jungle training school and a speeded-up NCO training course.

The machine was desperate for raw material. Quotas weren't being met. So Bud Anello found himself with sergeant's stripes and an M-16 in someone else's country.

"Today there was a suspected V.C. in a village, but by the time we surrounded it everybody left," he wrote. "So the platoon sergeant said tear it down, let them know we were here. It really made me sick. For no

reason guys were burning down some poor farmers hooch. Tramping down his garden. Ripping his only tools apart.

"I got so sick I told one dude I hope some neighbor smashes his TV tube and breaks all his windows while he's over here. And see if he still remains friends with him. Some felt the way I did, so we went around screaming on them to give them a bad conscience at least. A lot were so hard ass ignorant they just told us to go to hell.

"It really brought me down to an all time low. So I slung my weapon on my shoulder, put my hands in my pockets, went down the trail kicken up stones. Your mind is free at least."

Bud should have realized the meaning of the old army saying, "you're not required to like it, just to eat it."

Bud ate what he was required to, bummed off whenever possible, got stoned occasionally and drew his trademark cartoon on every letter he sent back to his brother. It was the little medieval foot soldier from the comic strip "Wizard of Id" and he titled it "The Pawn."

His letters constantly talked about going home. He was planning to take a motorcycle trip across country when he got out.

" ...It makes you feel so good inside," he wrote of a flight to Taipei for leave. "I thought, some day brother, some day soon, I'm going to be walking on those clouds, skipen' along all that softness, laughen' hard and my heart's gonna be singen' loud, cause someday, someday soon brother, I'm coming home too!"

He came home in an aluminum box. His patrol had been ambushed and totally wiped out. He caught six rounds and fell back into a ditch. They didn't find him for several days.

So now all that's left of Bud are his letters and drawings and photos. His humor and his hopes—and his experience; these can be passed on.

The lesson is simple. You can get people to walk into the gas chambers by seeing that at every decision point the alternative courses seem unreasonable. They'll go unwillingly and under protest, but most will go.

Most, not all. Perhaps there are some of us who have learned.

In my own case it remains to be seen. I am due for an induction notice any day now.

The Conspiracy Trial:
The Chaining and Gagging
of Bobby Seale[1]

October 28, 1969

THE CLERK: There is a motion on behalf of the defendant Seale.

MR. SEALE: I have another written motion respect to—

THE COURT: I can't hear you, sir. When I say I can't hear you, I hear you but I am not permitted under the law to hear you make a motion. You have a lawyer of record here. But I tell you that I have read your motion carefully, considered it, and I deny it.

MR. SEALE: You don't want to hear me read the motion?

THE COURT: I read it. I am the one that has to read it.

MR. SEALE: I want it for the court record. I will present it myself in behalf of myself in my own defense.

THE COURT: It will be of record.

I direct the clerk to file it.

MR. KUNSTLER: Your Honor, I have three applications which I would like to make. One is on behalf of all defendants except Mr. Seale. I move for a mistrial on the basis of your Honor's persistent refusal to allow Mr. Seale to defend himself. The defendants take the position that this being a conspiracy trial, that this adversely affects all defendants in this trial and therefore for all of the reasons that have been stated

Excerpts from Judy Clavir and John Spitzer, *The Conspiracy Trial* (New York: Bobbs-Merrill, 1970) pp. 147–171. Reprinted with permission.

to your Honor before we feel that there should be a mistrial in this case because of your Honor's refusal to permit Mr. Seale to have the constitutional right to defend himself as his attorney as he has expressed to your Honor on numerous occasions.

That is my first application.

THE COURT: I will deny the motion.

What is your next motion?

MR. KUNSTLER: Your Honor, I am moving for a one-day adjournment of this trial so that Mr. Weinglass and I can consult with Mr. Garry in San Francisco. There is other legal action contemplated in an effort to obtain for Mr. Seale his right to be able to represent himself in this action, and Mr. Garry has indicated that he would very much like to consult with Mr. Weinglass and myself because of our intimate knowledge of what has gone on in this courtroom.

Mr Garry is confined to his home. I spoke to him last night and he has not been to his office since the operation and cannot travel to Chicago. Therefore we would have to travel to him. I would request your Honor's permission to grant such a motion for tomorrow morning.

THE COURT: I deny the motion.

MR. KUNSTLER: Now that it has been denied, I would ask your Honor to grant permission for one of co-counsel here, Mr. Weinglass or myself, to be absent tomorrow to consult with Mr. Garry.

THE COURT: Only on these conditions, Mr. Kunstler; that first each and every defendant in this case stand up at his place at the defense table and agree that either you or Mr. Fineglass look after his interests.

MR. KUNSTLER: Weinglass, your Honor.

THE COURT: Mr. Weinglass. I will begin over again.

Only under these conditions: That each and every defendant consent to the absence of either yourself or Mr. Weinglass, and on this further condition, that you live up to your oral and written representation to me that you represent Mr. Seale.

MR. SEALE: Since you say each and every defendant, I ain't going for it no way. He ain't my lawyer so—

MR. KUNSTLER: Your Honor, I don't think I could even ask the defendants to make any comment on that. I know what their reaction would be.

THE COURT: If you know, the motion will be denied.

(jury enters)

* * *

October 29, 1969

THE COURT: Mr. Marshal, bring in the jury.

ABBIE HOFFMAN: There are twenty-five marshals in here now, and they all got guns. There's two practically sitting in the jury box.

MR. WEINGLASS: If the Court please, within observation of your Honor is a phalanx of marshals literally. I believe there are ten standing in the narrow aisles leading to the doorway of this courtroom. There are three more standing at another door, one more standing at another door.

Now, the jury is about to be brought in. They will enter from that door. The first thing that they will see as they walk into this room is a group of twenty marshals standing in a very ominous posture, and I cannot begin my cross-examination of a witness. The jury cannot sit here unmoved by that.

THE COURT: If you don't want to cross-examine, that is up to you, sir.

Bring in the jury.

MR. KUNSTLER: Your Honor, we are objecting to this armed camp aspect that is going on since the beginning of this trial.

THE COURT: This is not an armed camp.

MR. SCHULTZ: If the Court please, before you came into this courtroom, if the Court please, Bobby Seale stood up and addressed this group.

MR. SEALE: That's right, brother. I spoke on behalf of my constitutional rights. I have a right to speak on behalf of my constitutional rights. That's right.

MR. SCHULTZ: And he told those people in the audience, if the

	Court please—and I want this on the record. It happened this morning—that if he's attacked, they know what to do. He was talking to these people about an attack by them.
MR. SEALE:	You're lying. Dirty liar. I told them to defend themselves. You are a rotten racist pig, fascist liar, that's what you are. You're a rotten liar. You are a fascist pig liar.
	I said they had a right to defend themselves if they are attacked, and I hope that the record carries that, and I hope the record shows that tricky Dick Schultz, working for Richard Nixon and administration all understand that tricky Dick Schultz is a liar, and we have a right to defend ourselves, and if you attack me I will defend myself.
SPECTATORS:	Right on.
MR. SCHULTZ:	If the Court please, that is what he said, just as he related it. In terms of a physical attack by the people in this—
MR. SEALE:	A physical attack by those damned marshals, that's what I said.
THE COURT:	Let—
MR. SEALE:	And if they attack any people, they have a right to defend themselves, you lying pig.
THE COURT:	Let the record show the tone of Mr. Seale's voice was one shrieking and pounding on the table and shouting. That will be dealt with appropriately at some time in the future.
MR. KUNSTLER:	Your Honor, the record should indicate that Mr. Schultz shouted—went up here in a very loud shouting voice and stood at this lectern and shouted quite loudly in the courtroom.
THE COURT:	Yes, he raised his voice and I think he raised his voice—if what he said was the truth, I can't blame him for raising his voice.
MR. SCHULTZ:	If the Court please, just for the purposes of the record, the people who are on the right, most of them, responded to Mr. Seale's remarks before the Court came in with "Right on" and the rest of whatever it is they say.

MR. SEALE: Will you please tell the Court I told them to keep their cool because I didn't want a spontaneous response to any kind of activity that might go on? Would you please tell the court I said to keep cool?

MR. HAYDEN: They did nothing when Bobby Seale was physically attacked. They did nothing.

THE COURT: Will you remain silent, you defendants, please? You have a lawyer.

MR. HAYDEN: Just as he ordered them to.

THE COURT: Mr. Marshal, bring in the jury.

MR. KUNSTLER: I want to indicate Mr. Seale was attacked in the courtroom by the marshals, thrown out of his chair on the ground, and I think the record must indicate that.

MR. FORAN: Your Honor, in response to Mr. Kunstler's usual misrepresentation, Mr. Seale was not thrown out of his chair on the ground. He was placed in his chair while he was standing screaming at—

MR. SEALE: I wasn't placed in my chair. I was shoved in my chair.

MR. FORAN: —and pounding on the desk, and he was put forcibly in his chair in an attempt by the marshals to keep order in this courtroom.

MR. KUNSTLER: Your Honor, I observed what I observed, and Mr. Seale was thrown into the chair and the chair was tipped over backwards.

THE COURT: I saw it. I will make my findings in due course.
Ladies and gentlemen of the jury, good morning.

MR. SEALE: Good morning, ladies and gentlemen of the jury.

MR. DELLINGER: Good morning.

THE COURT: The witness will please resume the stand.

MR. SEALE: I would like to request the right again to cross-examine this witness because my lawyer, Charles R. Garry, is not here and because I have also been denied my rights to defend myself in this courtroom. I am requesting and demanding, in fact, that I have a right to cross-examine this witness, sir, at this trial.

THE COURT: Mr. Marshal, take the jury out.

MR. DELLINGER: And all the defendants support Bobby Seale's right to have a counsel of his choice here and affirm that he has been denied that right.

MR. SEALE: Why don't you recognize my constitutional rights—

THE COURT: I have recognized every constitutional right you have.

MR. SEALE: I want to cross-examine. You have not. You have not recognized any constitutional rights of mine.

THE COURT: All I want to tell you is this: if you speak once again while the jury is in the box and I have to send them out, we will take such steps as are indicated in the circumstances.

Bring in the jury, Mr. Marshal.

MR. SEALE: If a witness is on the stand and testifies against me and I stand up and speak out in behalf of my right to have my lawyer and to defend myself and you deny me that, I have a right to make those requests. I have a constitutional right to speak, and if you try to suppress my constitutional right to speak out in behalf of my constitutional rights, then I can only see you as a bigot, a racist, and a fascist, as I said before and clearly indicated on the record.

Good morning, ladies and gentlemen of the jury.

THE COURT: Mr. Weinglass, will you please continue with the cross-examination of this witness if you desire to?

MR. WEINGLASS: Now, during the period of time that you were acting as an undercover agent in the month of August 1968, did you see karate training sessions being held in Lincoln Park?

THE WITNESS*: I saw karate demonstrated, sir.

MR. WEINGLASS: In watching it, was your impression that the instructor was actually attempting to give instruction in karate or was it all just a staged affair for camera?

MR. FORAN: Objection.

THE COURT: Sustained.

---

*William Frapolly.

MR. WEINGLASS: When the karate instruction was being given, did you hear people laugh?

THE WITNESS: I think there might have been some people laughing, sir.

MR. WEINGLASS: Was the atmosphere in the area of the exercise one of frivolity, playfulness?

MR. FORAN: Objection.

THE COURT: Sustain the objection.

MR. WEINGLASS: I have nothing further.

THE COURT: Is there any redirect examination?

MR. SEALE: Before the redirect, I would like to request again—demand—that I be able to cross-examine the witness. My lawyer is not here. I think I have a right to defend myself in this courtroom.

THE COURT: Take the jury out.

MR. SEALE: You have George Washington and Benjamin Franklin sitting in a picture behind you, and they was slave owners. That's what they were. They owned slaves. You are acting in the same manner, denying me my constitutional rights being able to cross-examine this witness.

THE COURT: Mr. Seale, I have admonished you previously—

MR. SEALE: I have a right to cross-examine the witness.

THE COURT: —what might happen to you if you keep on talking.
        We are going to recess now, young man. If you keep this up—

MR. SEALE: Look, old man, if you keep denying me my constitutional rights, you are being exposed to the public and the world that you do not care about people's constitutional rights to defend themselves.

THE COURT: I will tell you that what I indicated yesterday might happen to you—

MR. SEALE: Happen to me? What can happen to me more than what Benjamin Franklin and George Washington did to black people in slavery? What can happen to me more than that?

THE COURT: And I might add since it has been said here that all of the defendants support you in your position that I might conclude that they are bad risks for bail, and I

	say that to you, Mr. Kunstler, that if you can't control your client—
MR. SEALE:	I still demand my constitutional rights as a defendant in this case to defend myself. I demand the right to be able to cross-examine this witness. He has made statements against me and I want my right to—
THE COURT:	Have him sit down, Mr. Marshal.
MR. SEALE:	I want my constitutional rights. I want to have my constitutional rights. How come you won't recognize it? How come you won't recognize my constitutional rights? I want to have the right to cross-examine that witness.
MR. SCHULTZ:	May the record show, if the Court please, that while the marshals were seating Bobby Seale, pushing him in the chair, the defendant Dellinger physically attempted to interfere with the marshals by pushing them out of the way.
THE COURT:	I tell you that Mr. Dellinger—if that is his name—has said here that they support the performances of this man, the statements of this man.
MR. KUNSTLER:	They support his right to have a lawyer or to defend himself.
THE COURT:	You told me you were his lawyer.
MR. KUNSTLER:	Your Honor—
MR. SEALE:	He is not my lawyer.
THE COURT:	I have the transcript right here.
MR. KUNSTLER:	You Honor, we have gone over that.
MR. SEALE:	I told you I fired him before the trial began.
THE COURT:	You haven't explained—
MR. KUNSTLER:	I have explained it fully. I have been discharged—
THE COURT:	No, you haven't, and you will.
MR. KUNSTLER:	I told you on the twenty-seventh and I told you on the thirtieth.
THE COURT:	I tell you some day you will have to explain it.
MR. KUNSTLER:	That is another threat to the lawyers, your Honor. We have had so many that—
THE COURT:	Now, Mr. Kunstler, I will tell you this, that since it has been said here that all of the defendants support this man in what he is doing, I over the noon hour will reflect on whether they are good risks for bail

and I shall give serious consideration to the termination of their bail if you can't control your clients, and you couldn't yesterday afternoon.

MR. SEALE: I am not—I am not a defendant—he is not my lawyer. I want my right to defend myself.

MR. KUNSTLER: Your Honor, they said they supported fully his right to defend himself or have his lawyer of choice, and if that is the price of their bail, then I guess that will have to be the price of their bail.

MR. SEALE: I have a right to defend myself. That's what you—

THE COURT: Will, you, Mr. Marshal, have that man sit down?

MR. SEALE: You trying to make jive bargaining operations and that's different from the right I have.

I have a right to defend myself. I still have a right to defend myself whether you sit me down or not. I got a right to speak on behalf of my defense, and you know it. You know it. Why don't you recognize my right to defend myself?

MR. SCHULTZ: May the record show that the defendant Dellinger did the same thing just now?

THE COURT: I saw it myself.

MR. KUNSTLER: Your Honor, he is trying to see what is happening.

THE COURT: Mr. Marshal, we will recess.

Mr. Kunstler, will you ask your clients to rise?

MR. KUNSTLER: If you will direct me, your Honor, I will ask them to rise.

THE COURT: I direct you to ask your clients to rise and I tell you that I will not retain on bail in this court men who defy the United States District Court and I will give them the noon hour, the noon recess, to think about it.

MR. KUNSTLER: They are protesting, your Honor, and I think that is protective of the First Amendment.

THE COURT: They will have to obey the law in the process of protesting, sir. Now if they prefer to sleep in the county jail, let them reflect on it.

MR. KUNSTLER: I have passed your direction on.

THE MARSHAL: This honorable court will take a brief recess.

* * *

MR. KUNSTLER: Your Honor, at the close of the session this morning you asked the defendants, as I recall, to reflect upon their support of the right of Bobby Seale to assert his constitutional right to defend himself or to have a lawyer of his choice in this courtroom, and I want to report back to you that they have reflected as follows:

They want to point out to the Court that from the very beginning of this trial they feel that their constitutional rights have been infringed upon by the Court in the following circumstances.

First of all, your Honor ordered the arrest of their pretrial attorneys which ultimately resulted in two of them being incarcerated at the very beginning of this trial. Following that your Honor told me in open court that the keys to the jailhouse were in the defendant's hands; that if they waived their right to counsel argument with reference to Mr. Garry, then the jailhouse would open for these attorneys.

Since that time there has been a constant rain from the bench of threats of contempt over both attorneys and clients in this case....

When Mr. Weinglass attempted his opening statement, again a threat was expressed that he would be in essence dealt with later. During one of his cross-examinations this was also done, again another threat on the record to intimidate and deter this attorney.

In essence, almost any remark that the Court has not liked has in some way found itself embodied in language which a reasonable person could interpret as a threat of future action.

When laughter has occurred in the courtroom spontaneously, the same type of approach has been met from the bench.

Just this morning when I indicated again my status in this case with reference to Mr. Seale, I was informed by your Honor that this was something that I would meet again at some future time.

This what we consider to be a blanket and overall umbrella of intimidation has surrounded this trial from its very beginning and we think has not only infringed upon the right of counsel in this case but has been attempted to intimidate and deter defendants and their counsel from a vigorous defense to these charges.

Furthermore, there has been an attempt to make the defendant Seale waive his right to counsel argument as the price of the visit of an attorney from this trial to Mr. Garry in San Francisco.

We finally come to today, to a threat to revoke bail of the defendants who dare to support Mr. Seale's position that he wants to assert his constitutional right to defend himself in this court if he cannot have his counsel of choice.

Now I might indicate in passing on the bail question that the defendants have always been present in court, that none of them have ever had a default in bail, and that their action in this court of protesting the treatment of Bobby Seale, has never been disruptive of this courtroom, and has not been done during any ongoing business of the court that has been going on and been disrupted.

Then lastly, your Honor, the armed camp atmosphere which we have objected to here. We have counted nineteen marshals in the courtroom this afternoon alone. There is no space in the aisle for anyone to stand because of the profusion of marshals presently standing there.

We hold, your Honor, with the Supreme Court language in Morre vs. Dempsey that the armed camp atmosphere which is easily seen by every juror as he comes in is denying these defendants any chance of a fair trial.

The defendants want me to say that under no circumstances will they let their liberty stand in the way of the assertion of the constitutional rights of Bobby Seale to defend himself, and if the price of those rights is that they must remain in jail, then that will have to be the price that is paid. Many have paid much greater prices in the past for the defense and assertion of constitutional rights.

MR. FORAN: Your Honor, after listening to Mr. Kunstler's statement, I must say that sometimes I feel like one of the characters in Alice in Wonderland that just went through the looking glass.

I have never, your Honor, in twenty years of practice, heard attorneys like Mr. Kunstler and Mr. Weinglass refuse to direct their clients to conduct themselves with decency and courtesy in a courtroom....

Your Honor, I felt it necessary to reply to Mr. Kunstler because I considered that the grossest type of misrepresentation by an officer of the court that I have ever heard. It is my belief that a lawyer who is a professional need not say whatever his client asks him to say, that in fact on many occasions a lawyer in his honor to the law and in his honor to his own profession would say, "Forget it. I wouldn't make any such comment."

It seems to me that many of the people who do attend this court, these courtroom sessions, with an interest in the law itself, should know that we, as lawyers, that our major obligation above all others is our oath to uphold the law, and that if the law is to be changed, that this Government, the only one in the world, provides for an opportunity to change law by law and not by disruptive tactics and not by the grossest kind of attack on the very values of the law itself.

MR. SEALE: Since he made all of these statements, can I say something to the Court?

THE COURT: No, thank you.

MR. SEALE: Why not?

THE COURT: Because you have a lawyer and I am not going to go through that again.

MR. SEALE: He is not my lawyer. How come I can't say nothing? He had distorted everything, and it relates to the fact I have a right to defend myself.

THE COURT: Well, I have been called a racist, a fascist—he has pointed to the picture of George Washington behind me and called him a slave owner and—

MR. SEALE: They were slave owners. Look at history.

THE COURT: As though I had anything to do with that.

MR. SEALE: They were slave owners. You got them up there.

THE COURT: He has been known as the father of this country, and I would think that it is a pretty good picture to have in the United States District Court.

MR. KUNSTLER: We all share a common guilt, your Honor.

THE COURT: I didn't think I would ever live to sit on a bench or be in a courtroom where George Washington was assailed by a defendant in a criminal case and a judge was criticized for having his portrait on the wall.

MR. KUNSTLER: Your Honor, I am just saying that the defendants are not for disruption. They are for peace. The judge of the court sits there and won't let a codefendant have his attorney of record or defend himself.

Then I have nothing further to say, your Honor.

THE COURT: Bring in the jury please.

MR. SEALE: What about Section 1982, Title 42 of the Code where it says the black man cannot be discriminated against in my legal defense in any court in America?

THE COURT: Mr. Seale, you do know what is going to happen to you—

MR. SEALE: You just got through saying you observed the laws. That law protects my right not to be discriminated against in my legal defense. Why don't you recognize that? It's a form of racism, racism is what stopped my argument.

THE COURT: Hold the jury, Mr. Marshal.

Mr. Seale, do you want to stop or do you want me to direct the marshal—

MR. SEALE: I want to argue the point about this so you can get an understanding of the fact I have a right to defend myself.

THE COURT: We will take a recess.

Take that defendant into the room in there and deal with him as he should be dealt with in this circumstance.

MR. SEALE: I still want to be represented. I want to represent myself.

THE MARSHAL: Mr. Kunstler, will you instruct the defendants, sir,

	that is the order of the Court that they will arise upon recess?
MR. KUNSTLER:	If that is direction of the Court, I certainly will pass it on.
THE COURT:	Let the record show none of the defendants have stood at this recess in response to the Marshal's request.
	The court will be in recess for a few minutes.
MR. SEALE:	Let the record show that—
THE COURT:	This court will take a brief recess.
MR. SEALE:	Let the record show—

(brief recess)

MR. FORAN:	Your Honor, if Mr. Seale would express to the Court his willingness to be quiet, would the Court entertain the possibility under those circumstances of Mr. Seale being unbound and ungagged?
THE COURT:	I have tried so hard, with all my heart, to get him to sit in this court and be tried fairly and impartially, and I have been greeted on every occasion with all sort of vicious invective.
	Mr. Seale, not only Sixth Amendment rights, but all of your constitutional and statutory rights have been and will be preserved in this trial. I want you to conduct yourself in a manner that is gentlemanly and hear the evidence of the witnesses as it is given from the witness stand. I assure you that if you have any evidence when the time comes, we will listen attentively, and all we want is you to be respectful to the Court. If you will assure the Court that you will be respectful and not cause the disorder and commotion that you have up to now, I am willing that you resume your former place at the table along with the other defendants and the lawyers. Will you, sir?
MR. SEALE:	[*gagged*] I can't speak. I have a right to speak. I have a right to speak and be heard for myself and my constitutional rights.
THE COURT:	Will you give me your assurance, sir? If you will give

me your assurance, will you please indicate by raising your head up and down.

MR. SEALE: [*gagged*] Give me your assurance that you will let me defend myself.

THE COURT: I can't understand you, sir.

MR. SEALE: [*gagged*] I want to defend myself. I have a right to speak in behalf of my constitutional rights, and you just violated my constitutional rights to speak on behalf of my constitutional rights.

THE COURT: Mr. Marshal.

Well, Mr. Foran, I tried to do what you suggested. Is there anything you want to say in the light of my questioning of Mr. Seale?

MR. FORAN: No, your Honor. I would also like the record to show, your Honor, that just prior to Mr. Seale speaking through his gag, the defendant Davis was whispering to him.

THE COURT: Did you want to say something, sir?

MR. KUNSTLER: I wanted to say the record should indicate that Mr. Seale is seated on a metal chair, each hand handcuffed to the leg of the chair on both the right and left sides so he cannot raise his hands, and a gag is tightly pressed into his mouth and tied at the rear, and that when he attempts to speak, a muffled sound comes out.

MR. SEALE: [*gagged*] You don't represent me. Sit down, Kunstler.

THE COURT: Mr. Marshal, I don't think you have accomplished your purpose by that kind of a contrivance. We will have to take another recess.

Let the record show again that the defendants have not risen.

(*short recess*)

MR. KUNSTLER: Your Honor, for the record, I would like to indicate that their codefendant is handcuffed and legcuffed to a metal chair with a gag deep in his mouth consisting of a cloth and covered with layers of adhesive tape. I also want the record to indicate that he has passed a note across the table in which he indicates that the handcuffs and leg irons are stopping his blood circulation and he wants this brought to the Court's attention.

I might also indicate, your Honor, that the remarks of Mr. Foran that Mr. Seale was being spoken to prior by one of the other defendants, the implication being that he was being told what to do, and so on, is a thoroughly racist remark. Mr. Seale is a black man who is not told what to do by white people. He makes his own decisions. I think the record ought to clearly indicate that.

(jury enters)

THE COURT: Ladies and gentlemen of the jury, I must tell you that in a trial by jury in a Federal court in the United States, the judge is not a mere moderator under the law but is the governor of the trial for the purpose of assuring its proper conduct, and fairness, and for the purpose of determining such questions of law. The law requires that the judge maintain order and to take such steps as in the discretion of the judge are warranted, and, accordingly the marshals have endeavored to maintain order in the manner that you see here in the courtroom.

Mr. Weinglass, do you wish to cross-examine this witness?

MR. KUNSTLER: Your Honor, before Mr. Foran proceeds, I just want to move for the other seven defendants other than Mr. Seale for the removal of the irons and the gag on the ground that he was attempting only to assert his right to self-defense under the Constitution and I move on behalf of the other seven defendants for the immediate removal of the gag and the arm and leg cuffs.

THE COURT: Mr. Kunstler has made a motion in behalf of the seven other defendants.

I direct you, ladies and gentlemen of the jury, to not hold it against any of the seven other defendants when these measures are taken with respect to the defendant Mr. Seale. These measures indicate no evidence of his guilt or lack of guilt of the charges contained in the indictment. These measures have been taken only, as I say, to ensure the proper conduct of this trial which I am obligated to do under the law.

The motion of Mr. Kunstler will be denied.

* * *

(*jury enters*)

THE COURT: Ladies and gentlemen of the jury, I must repeat in substance some of the observations I made to you yesterday about the unusual and extraordinary things that occurred in this court.

These incidents are not to be considered by you in determining the guilt or innocence of any of the defendants and I order you to disregard the incidents as you saw them and as you heard them.

Mr. Seale, I will ask you to refrain from making those noises. I order you to refrain from making those noises.

MR. DAVIS: Ladies and gentlemen of the jury, he was being tortured while you were out of this room by these marshals. They come and torture him while you are out of the room. It is terrible what is happening. It is terrible what is happening.

MR. FORAN: That is Mr. Davis, your Honor.

THE COURT: Ladies and gentlemen of the jury, my usual order—

(*jury excused*)

Who is that man who was talking?

A DEFENDANT: Your Honor, he is being choked to death—tortured—

MR. SEALE: The Judge is not—he is not trying to give you no fair trial. That's what you are. You are lying. You know exactly what you are.

MR. HAYDEN: Now they are going to beat him, they are going to beat him.

ABBIE HOFFMAN: You may as well kill him if you are going to gag him. It seems that way, doesn't it?

THE COURT: You are not permitted to address the Court, Mr. Hoffman. You have a lawyer.

ABBIE HOFFMAN: This isn't a court. This is a neon oven.

MR. FORAN: That was the defendant Hoffman who spoke.

MR. SCHULTZ: Prior to that it was Mr. Hayden who was addressing the jury while they were walking out of here.

MR. HAYDEN: I was not addressing the jury. I was trying to protect Mr. Seale. A man is supposed to be silent when he sees another man's nose being smashed?

ABBIE HOFFMAN: The disruption started when these guys got into overkill. It is the same thing as last year in Chicago, the same exact thing.

THE COURT: Mr. Hoffman, you are directed to refrain from speaking. You are ordered to refrain from speaking.

It is clear after this morning that I think we cannot go ahead. I would be glad to entertain first suggestions from the Government and then from the defense as to whether or not this trial shouldn't be recessed until two o'clock.

MR. FORAN: Your Honor, I would like to see if we couldn't continue.

THE COURT: All right. Then we will take a brief recess.

MR. HAYDEN: I thought you were going to ask the defendants.

MR. WEINGLASS: We are part—weren't we being invited to participate in the dialogue between the—

MR. SCHULTZ: It is they who are disrupting this trial and now they want to make the decision as to whether or not we should proceed. It is incredible. It is they who are fostering this and they want to advise the Court—

THE COURT: I have ordered a recess.

THE MARSHAL: Everyone please rise.

MR. HAYDEN: Stand up. Stand up. Don't let them have any pretext.

THE COURT: Let the record show that Mr. Hayden asked the people—

MR. HAYDEN: I ask the people here to do what they were told and they did it.

THE COURT: Mr. Hayden, do not try to fill out my sentences for me, and you are not permitted to speak except as you may come to be a witness in this case. You are not permitted to speak out loud. You may, of course, consult with your lawyer.

MR. SCHULTZ: There are three defendants who have not risen, Mr. Dillinger, Mr. Rubin, and Mr. Hoffman.

THE COURT: Mr. Seale, do you mind looking over here? Can you look over here? All right. I will talk to you even though you don't.

Mr. Seale, I would like to get your assurance that there will be no repetition of the conduct engaged in by you this morning and on occasions prior to this morning.

You have—you are on trial here under an indictment to which you have pleaded not guilty. The burden is on the Government to prove you guilty; you do not have any burden whatsoever. All you have to do here is to sit in your chair and listen.

I would like to get from you, sir, your assurance as an American citizen that you will not be guilty of any disruptive act during the continuance of this trial.

May I have that assurance? You know that if you continue to be disruptive the Court will have to deal appropriately with such conduct.

May I have that assurance? And if you can't speak I would like to have you raise your head up and down, or if you refuse to give me that assurance, please shake your head from the left to the right and the right to the left.

Mr. Marshal, bring in the jury and let the record show that the defendant did not reply in the manner—

MR. WEINGLASS: If your Honor please, Mr. Seale, while the Court was addressing him, was endeavoring to answer the court by writing in spite of his hands being manacled to the chair.

Of course, he can't answer the Court verbally since he is also gagged and so I would like to read and then offer into the record as an exhibit the following note which Mr. Seale has written.

"I want and demand my right to defend myself, to be able to object acting as my own defense counsel, to be able to continue to argue my motions and requests as any defendant or citizen of America."

And the note is not complete since the Court has indicated the jury would be brought it. I would like to have it marked as an exhibit.

MR. SCHULTZ: If the Court please, before the jury is brought in here, we have one brief motion.

Yesterday when Mr. Seale was manacled and the jury was in the courtroom the young lady sitting next to him was holding his hand as tenderly as she possibly could.

I would ask that this display not be permitted in front of the jury.

THE COURT: I do not know the lady.

MR. WEINGLASS: She has been introduced in the court the first day of the trial. She is one of the four legal people of our staff, Mickey Leaner.

THE COURT: In view of the statement of the United States Attorney, I do not wish her to be close to the defendant Seale.

MISS LEANER: I would like to say, your Honor, this statement is not true.

THE COURT: I have indicated, young lady, that I will not hear from you.

I will instruct the marshal now sitting there not to permit this lady—what is your name?

MISS LEANER: Marie—Jean Marie Leaner.

THE COURT: —not to have any physical contact with the defendant. Bring in the jury.

Please call your next witness, Mr. Foran or Mr. Schultz.

NOTE

1. Judy Clavir and John Spitzer, The Conspiracy Trial (New York: Bobbs-Merrill, 1970) pp. 147–171.

The Conspiracy Trial: A Witness's Testimony[1]

December 16, 1969

THE COURT: Call your next witness, please.

MR. KUNSTLER: Would you state your full name?

THE WITNESS: Linda Hager Morse.

MR. KUNSTLER: Can you indicate something of your background and education?

THE WITNESS: I was born in Philadelphia, Pennsylvania. I went to high school there. While in high school I was a Merit Scholarship semifinalist. I won the Juvenile Decency Award from the Kiwanis Club, one of thirteen high school students in Philadelphia that year. I went to the University of New Hampshire after graduating from high school. Then I left college and went back to Philadelphia and worked for several years in a community organizing project for a nonviolent pacifist group. Then I went to New York City and started working for the Fifth Avenue Vietnam Peace Parade Committee in 1965.

MR. KUNSTLER: Now, Miss Morse, I call your attention to July 25, 1968, and particularly in the area of 8:00 P.M. of that day, and ask you to tell the Court and jury if you can recall where you were.

THE WITNESS: I was at the Hotel Diplomat in New York City.

MR. KUNSTLER: And at that time, what was going on?

Excerpts from Judy Clavir and John Spitzer, *The Conspiracy Trial* (New York: Bobbs-Merrill, 1970) pp. 147–171. Reprinted with permission.

THE WITNESS: The Parade Committee, for which I worked at that point, had organized a public meeting. The speakers included Mrs. Cora Weiss, Mrs. Beulah Sanders and Mr. Tom Hayden.

MR. KUNSTLER: What did Mr. Hayden say as you recall it?

THE WITNESS: He went through a whole analysis of United States policy in Vietnam starting out with the reasons for President Johnson's March 31 speech. He said that CBS had sent a reporter to North Vietnam to interview the North Vietnamese and the reporter learned that the North Vietnamese were about to make a major concession to the United States with regard to peace talks.

So the reporter sent back word to President Johnson that this was to occur and because of the crisis at home, because of the growing antiwar movement, because of the crisis with the dollar, and because of the crisis internationally with countries being opposed to United States policy against the war, President Johnson felt that he had to make some move to undercut the upcoming North Vietnamese move. So he made his March 31 speech where he withdrew from the race and where he called for a partial deescalation of bombing.

Tom said that this would be a seeming concession to peace to the United States people and to the Vietnamese and to the world, but that in reality it would enable the United States which was short on bomber pilots, short on planes and short on bombs at that point to concentrate its energies on the bombing of one section.

Then Mr. Hayden went into a whole long discussion of what the Vietnamese were feeling at this point to the effect, in essence, that the Vietnamese felt that they had won the war militarily and politically and that it was a matter that there was nothing to negotiate except for the easiest way for the United States to withdraw from Vietnam, and that these phony "concessions" would not do any good, and that the Vietnamese just felt that they had to continue, you know, keeping up the pressure, continue fighting and—until the Americans got out.

At that point he said that the United States had only two alternatives, you know, since it couldn't win militarily by conventional means: it had either the alternative of withdrawing or of genocide. He stated that this was a different form of colonialism nowadays, and that Vietnam would be as useful to the United States with no people in it as it would be populated by the Vietnamese, and that the United States could afford to kill off the Vietnamese.

Tom said that he thought that the United States was seriously considering nuclear weapons in Vietnam and that one nuclear bomb placed in the right place would destroy three million Vietnamese people, and that he didn't think they could stand up under that; that they had done fantastically in standing up under the bombing and the troops so far, but that they couldn't stand up under that, and that was a real alternative to the United States at this point: it could bomb Vietnam into a dust heap. Therefore, it was the duty of every American to protest, you know, what was happening by any means possible, because it was going to be genocide in Vietnam in a short period of time otherwise.

MR. KUNSTLER: Did he explain how he had gotten some of the information about the Vietnamese?

THE WITNESS: He had just returned from Paris a week or two before that where he had been negotiating the release of three American prisoners of war, and he had successfully negotiated that release. He had spoken to both Harriman and to the North Vietnamese in Paris.

MR. KUNSTLER: In the speech was there any mention made of the forthcoming Democratic National Convention?

THE WITNESS: Yes. It was mentioned in two sentences. It was something like, you know, "we must protest the war whenever possible, you know, on our campuses, in the streets of Chicago," you know, so forth and so on.

MR. KUNSTLER: Calling your attention to Friday, August 23, do you know what you did on that particular day?

THE WITNESS: I went down to the Mobilization office and met Dave Dellinger down there.

MR. KUNSTLER: Will you state to the Court and jury what you said to Dave Dellinger, and what he said to you?

THE WITNESS: He asked me to come with him for a permit negotiation meeting, and the reason for that was they had just learned that the courts had overturned an injunction that the Mobilization had put into the court asking for permits, and therefore there were no permits for the upcoming march the next week. And so, David asked me to come along, because I had had a lot of experience in negotiating for permits, for this emergency meeting down at City Hall where they were going to ask to see Mayor Daley.

MR. KUNSTLER: As a result of this conversation, did you and Mr. Dellinger do anything?

THE WITNESS: Yes. We went down to City Hall. We went into an anteroom or waiting room outside of the mayor's offices and sat around for quite a long time asking to see Mayor Daley. There were press people down there with us from various TV stations and newspapers who had followed us down there. Finally, a man came out, a city official, and spoke to us and said that Mayor Daley would not see us and that the matter was closed at this point.

So that was the end of that.

MR. KUNSTLER: Now, I call your attention to Sunday, August 25, approximately 10:30, in Lincoln Park. Can you describe the scene when you arrived?

THE WITNESS: Some people were sitting around, singing or talking, other people were walking around. It was just kind of an ordinary park scene with a little bit of excitement.

MR. KUNSTLER: Did there come a time when you saw some policemen in the park?

THE WITNESS: Oh, yes. There was a little house in the middle of the park, and at one point a group of policemen moved in front of the house, and stood with their backs up against the house, just standing there in formation.

I went over with a group of people to see what they were doing, and there was some chanting and stuff at them. I thought it was funny—we were teasing—

MR. KUNSTLER: Did you see anything thrown?

THE WITNESS: No.

MR. KUNSTLER: Did you see Jerry Rubin at all at this time?

THE WITNESS: No.

MR. KUNSTLER: Do you know Jerry Rubin?

THE WITNESS: Yes, I have known him since 1967.

MR. KUNSTLER: Now, Miss Morse, I call your attention to Wednesday, August 28, and particularly to the time between 12:30 and 1:00 P.M. Do you know where you were then?

THE WITNESS: That is the time that I arrived at Grant Park, the Bandshell.

MR. KUNSTLER: What happened after that?

THE WITNESS: I went with the people who were going to march.

MR. KUNSTLER: Can you tell the Court and jury where, if any place, the line moved to?

THE WITNESS: It moved about a block and a half or two blocks, and then we were stopped by policemen, a large group of them.

MR. KUNSTLER: After the march had been stopped by the police what happened to the demonstrators?

THE WITNESS: People got up slowly at first in small groups, couples, you know, twos and threes, and walked away from the march and across the first park toward the bridges to get across to the second park to the Hilton.

MR. KUNSTLER: Now, did you do this yourself?

THE WITNESS: I went through the first park and came up to the first bridge. It was blocked off by National Guardsmen, and I got very frightened because we were trapped.

MR. SCHULTZ: Objection, if the Court please.

THE COURT: "I got very frightened"—those words may go out and the jury is directed to disregard them.

MR. KUNSTLER: Did you have a conversation with Dave Dellinger?

THE WITNESS: Yes, I did. I told him that I was afraid that we were encircled by the National Guardsmen and the police, and that if we attempted to march that we would be beaten and arrested, and that I thought that it was too great a risk, and we had to call off the march and go back in front of the Conrad Hilton where I thought we would be safe.

MR. KUNSTLER: Did Dave Dellinger respond to the suggestion?

THE WITNESS: He told me that he felt we had to try to march; that Vietnamese and GI's were dying and this was least we could do, was to attempt to protest the war, and we had to follow through with it.

MR. KUNSTLER: Did you cross over the first bridge?

THE WITNESS: There was a row of Guardsmen in front and some trucks behind them and they were standing there with guns and tear gas masks, and one of the trucks had some weird kind of gun mounted on it. I don't know whether it was a machine gun or to shoot tear gas or what.

MR. KUNSTLER: When you couldn't get across the first bridge, what did you do?

THE WITNESS: Went up to the second bridge which was further north, I guess. We started to trot at this point and we came up to the bridge and the Guardsmen saw us coming and they shot tear gas at us. After that tear gassing we had to go and wash our eyes out in a fountain because it was really bad. Then we ran up to the last bridge, you know, and just made it across the last bridge as a group of Guardsmen were coming up.

MR. KUNSTLER: Where did you go?

THE WITNESS: We ran across the park and then back down that big street towards the Conrad Hilton. It was dark or late dusk by this time and there were really brilliant lights shining on the crowd and people were chanting. I remember hearing, "The whole world is watching. The whole world is watching. Flash your lights. Flash your lights."

They were referring to the buildings and asking people in the buildings who were watching if they were sympathetic to us to flash their lights and there were lots of lights flashing. And people were standing around in that area and sitting on the side resting.

MR. KUNSTLER: Then what did you do yourself?

THE WITNESS: I sat there for a little while and I was exhausted and frightened and I just went home after that.

MR. KUNSTLER: I show you D-112 for identification and ask you if you can identify what is in that picture.

THE WITNESS: Yes, this is one of the bridges with Guardsmen blocking it off. And they have guns.

MR. KUNSTLER: Did you see any of that equipment before?

THE WITNESS: Yes, that gun.

MR. KUNSTLER: What type of gun is that?

THE WITNESS: Machine gun is what it looks like to me.

MR. KUNSTLER: I have no further questions, your Honor.

MR. SCHULTZ: You saw one of the machine guns in the picture; you don't know what caliber it is, do you?

THE WITNESS: No.

MR. SCHULTZ: You practice shooting an M-1 yourself, don't you?

THE WITNESS: Yes, I do.

MR. SCHULTZ: You also practice karate, don't you?

THE WITNESS: Yes, I do.

MR. SCHULTZ: That is for the revolution, isn't it?

THE WITNESS: After Chicago I changed from being a pacifist to the realization we had to defend ourselves. A nonviolent revolution was impossible. I desperately wish it was possible.

MR. SCHULTZ: And the only way you can change this country, is it not, is by a violent revolution, isn't that your thought?

THE WITNESS: I believe we have to have a revolution that changes the society into a good society, and to a society that meets the ideals that the country was founded on years ago which it hasn't met since then, and I think that we have the right to defend ourselves. The Minutemen in New York City were arrested with bazookas. Housewives in suburban areas have guns.

MR. SCHULTZ: And the way you are going to change this country is by violent revolution, isn't that right, Miss Morse?

THE WITNESS: The way we are going to change this country is by political revolution, sir.

MR. SCHULTZ: And is it a fact that you believe that the revolution will be gradual, and you and your people will gain control of the cities of the United States just like the guerrillas of the National Liberation Front are gaining control of the cities in Vietnam?

THE WITNESS: I believe that the people of the United States will regain control of their own cities just like the Vietnamese people are regaining control of their country.

MR. SCHULTZ: Isn't it a fact that you believe that the United States Government will control sections of its cities while the fighting rages in other sections of the cities not controlled by the Government of the United States?

THE WITNESS: The Government of the United States has lost its credibility today; there is fighting going on in cities in this country today. People's Park in Berkeley, the policemen shot at us when people were unarmed, were fighting with rocks, the policemen used double-buckshot and rifles and pistols against unarmed demonstrators.

That is fighting. OK. People are fighting to regain their liberty, fighting to regain their freedom, fighting for a totally different society, people in the black community, people in the Puerto Rican community, people in the Mexican-American community and people in the white communities. They are fighting by political means as well as defending themselves.

MR. SCHULTZ: Your Honor, I move to strike that as nonresponsive.

MR. KUNSTLER: Your Honor, they are intensely political questions and she is trying to give a political answer to a political question.

THE COURT: This is not a political case as far as I am concerned. This is a criminal case. I can't go into politics here in this court.

MR. KUNSTLER: Your Honor, Jesus was accused criminally, too, and we understand really that was not truly a criminal case in the sense that it is just an ordinary—

THE COURT: I didn't live at that time. I don't know. Some people think I go back that far, but I really didn't.

MR. KUNSTLER: Well, I was assuming your Honor had read of the incident.

THE COURT: We are dealing with a cross-examination of a witness, and I direct you to answer the question.

MR. SCHULTZ: Gradually the Government of the United States will be taken over by this revolution?

THE WITNESS: Yes.

MR. SCHULTZ: And that your ultimate goal is to create a nation with this revolutionary party?

THE WITNESS: Revolutionary party? My ultimate goal is to create a society that is a free society; that is a joyous society where everyone is fed, where everyone is educated, where everyone has a job, where everyone has a chance to express himself artistically or politically, or spiritually, or religiously.

MR. SCHULTZ: With regard to the revolution that we are talking about, you are prepared, aren't you, both to die and to kill for it, isn't that right?

THE WITNESS: Yes, in self-defense.

MR. SCHULTZ: And further, because the educational system is so rotten, that if you cannot change it you will attempt to totally destroy it in the United States, isn't that right?

THE WITNESS: The educational system in the United States right now is destroying millions of people in Vietnam and around the world. The aerosol bombs that are used in Vietnam, or are being prepared to be used in Vietnam for CBW warfare were prepared right in Berkeley, California, where I live, and the educational system in the country is used currently to destroy people, not to create life. I believe we have to stop the murder of people around the world and in the United States and when the educational system of this country participates in it technologically, yes, we have to put our bodies in the way and stop that process.

MR. SCHULTZ: That is part of the reason why you are learning how to shoot your M-1 rifle?

THE WITNESS: I am learning how to shoot my M-1 rifle for two reasons, sir. One of them is to protect myself from situations that I was in in Berkeley some time back where I was grabbed by two young men and taken off to the hills and molested, and housewives all over the country have guns in their houses for that very purpose. The other thing is the fact that every time I walk on the street in Berkeley and pass a police car, the policemen look out their windows and make snide comments and say, "Hi, Linda, how are you doing? You better watch out. Hi, Linda, you better be careful," and it seems like every single policeman in Berkeley knows who I am, and when policemen start doing things like what they have been doing lately, killing Fred Hampton, attacking the Black Panther office in Los Angeles, shooting people in People's Park and in Chicago, then I believe we have the right to defend ourselves.

MR. SCHULTZ: One of the reasons further for your revolution is your opposition to capitalism and imperialism, isn't that right?

THE WITNESS: That's right.

MR. SCHULTZ: And the more you realize our system is sick, the more you want to tear it limb to limb, isn't that right?

THE WITNESS: The more that I see the horrors that are perpetrated by this Government, the more that I read about things like troop trains full of nerve gas traveling across the country where one accident could wipe out thousands and thousands of people, the more that I see things like companies just pouring waste into lakes and into rivers and just destroying them, the more I see things like the oil fields in the ocean off Santa Barbara coast where the Secretary of the Interior and the oil companies got together and agreed to continue producing oil from those off-shore oil fields and ruined a whole section of the coast; the more I see things like an educational system which teaches black people and Puerto Rican people and Mexican-Americans that they are only fit to be domestics and dishwashers, if that; the more that I see a system that teaches middle class whites like me that we are supposed to be techno-logical brains to continue producing CBW warfare, to continue working on computers and things like that to learn how to kill people better, to learn how to control people better, yes, the more I want to see that system torn down and replaced by a totally different one, one that cares about people learning; that cares about children being fed breakfast before they go to school; one that cares about people learning real things, one that cares about people going to college for free; one that cares about people living adult lives that are responsible, fulfilled adult lives, not just drudgery, day after day after day of going to a job; one that gives people a chance to express themselves artistically and politically, and religiously and philosophically. That is the kind of system I want to see in its stead.

MR. SCHULTZ: Now, isn't it a fact, Miss Morse, that your learning your karate and your other skill is to use these skills in revolutionary guerrilla warfare on the streets of the American cities?

THE WITNESS: I still don't know whether I could ever kill anyone, Mr. Schultz. I haven't reached that point yet.

MR. SCHULTZ: I have no further questions on the examination.

THE COURT: All right. Does the defense want to conduct a redirect examination?

MR. KUNSTLER: Can you state to the jury what your views were about the United States and the world prior to the Democratic National Convention in 1968?

THE WITNESS: Prior to the Democratic Convention I had believed that the United States system had to be changed, but the way to bring about that change was through nonviolent means, through nonviolent action, and through political organizing. I felt that we could reach policemen, that we could reach the Government of the United States by holding nonviolent sit-ins and nonviolent demonstrations, by putting our bodies on the line and allowing ourselves to be beaten if they choose to do that.

MR. KUNSTLER: Can you explain to the jury why your attitude toward your country and the world changed because of the Democratic Convention week?

THE WITNESS: The specific things that made me change my attitude were the actions on Mayor Daley's part in refusing to give us permits, in violating completely as far as I was concerned, the Constitution which allows you the right to march and demonstrate, the actions on the part of the policemen and some of the National Guardsmen in beating demonstrators horribly, and what I saw on television of what was going on inside the Convention which convinced me that the democratic process, political process, had fallen apart; that the police state that existed outside the convention also existed inside the Convention and that nonviolent methods would not work to change that; that we had to defend ourselves or we would be wiped out.

MR. KUNSTLER: By the way, how old are you?

THE WITNESS: Twenty-six years old. Just twenty-six.

MR. KUNSTLER: That is all.

THE COURT: Please call your next witness.

NOTE

1.   Judy Clavir and John Spitzer, *The Conspiracy Trial* (New York: Bobbs-Merrill, 1970) pp. 147–171.

Revolutionary Letter #7

Diane DiPrima

there are those who can tell you
how to make molotov cocktails, flamethrowers,
bombs whatever
you might be needing
find them and learn, define
your aim clearly, choose your ammo
with that in mind

it is not a good idea to tote a gun
or knife
unless you are proficient in its use
all swords are two-edged, can be used against you
by anyone who can get 'em away from you

it is
possible even on the east coast
to find an isolated place for target practice
success
will depend mostly on your state of mind:
meditate, pray, make love, be prepared
at any time, to die

Diane DiPrima, *Revolutionary Letters*, San Francisco: City Lights Books, 1971, pp. 15–16. © 1971 by Diane DiPrima. Reprinted by permission of CITY LIGHTS BOOKS.

but don't get uptight: the guns
will not win this one, they are
an incidental part of the action
which we better damn well be good at,
what will win
is mantras, the sustenance we give each other,
the energy we plug into
    (the fact that we touch
    share food)
the buddha nature
of everyone, friend and foe, like a million earthworms
tunnelling under this structure
till it falls

NOTE

1. Judy Clavir and John Spitzer, *The Conspiracy Trial* (New York: Bobbs-Merrill, 1970) pp. 147–171.

Revolutionary Letter #34

Diane DiPrima

hey man let's make a revolution, let's give
every man a thunderbird
color TV, a refrigerator, free
antibiotics, let's build
apartments with a separate bedroom for every child
inflatable plastic sofas, vitamin pills
with all our daily requirements that come in the mail
free gas & electric & telephone &
no rent. why not?

hey man, let's make a revolution, let's
turn off the power, turn on the
stars at night, put metal
back in the earth, or at least not take it out
anymore, make lots of guitars and flutes, teach the chicks
how to heal with herbs, let's learn
to live with each other in a smaller space, and build
hogans, and domes and teepees all over the place
BLOW UP THE PETROLEUM LINES, make the cars
into flower pots or sculptures or live
in the bigger ones, why not?

Diane DiPrima, *Revolutionary Letters*, San Francisco: City Lights Books, 1971, p. 48. © 1971 by Diane DiPrima. Reprinted by permission of CITY LIGHTS BOOKS.

396

The War Is Over!

Phil Ochs

Does protesting the war leave you tired and upset? Does civil disobedience leave you nervous and irritable? Does defending liberalism leave you feeling friendless and perhaps wondering about your breath? Does defending the need of repelling communist aggression leave you exhausted and give you that generation gap feeling?

On the other hand, are you tired of taking drugs to avoid the crushing responsibilities of a sober world? Do you want to do something about the war and yet refuse to bring yourself down to the low level of current demonstrations?

Is everybody sick of this stinking war?

In that case, friends, do what I and thousands of other Americans have done—declare the war over.

That's right, I said declare the war over from the bottom up.

This simple remedy has provided relief for countless frustrated citizens and has been overlooked for an amazingly long time, perhaps because it is so obvious. After all, this is our country, our taxes, our war. We pay for it, we die for it, we curiously watch it on television—we should at least have the right to end it.

Now I enjoy violence as much as the next guy, but enough is enough. Five seasons is plenty for the most exciting of series.

On Saturday, November 25, we are going to declare the war over and celebrate the end of the war in Washington Square Park at 1 p.m.

Phil Ochs, "Have You Heard? The War is Over!," *The Village Voice*, November 23, 1967. Reprinted with permission.

For one day only, you and your family can achieve that moment you've all been waiting for. Ludicrous as this may appear, it is certainly far less so than the war itself. I am not recommending this as a substitute for other actions; it is merely an attack of mental disobedience on an obediently insane society.

This is the sin of sins against an awkward power structure, the refusal to take it seriously. If you are surprised the war is over, imagine the incredulity of this administration when they hear about it.

Two or three years ago the morality of this war was argued, and those who said the war was indecent and ineffectual were proven correct. And if you feel you have been living in an unreal world for the last last couple of years, it is partially because this power structure has refused to listen to reason, or to recognize that they've lost their argument. But like all bullies and empires gone mad, they will not give in simply because they are stronger.

By this time it must be apparent that Johnson is more absurd than wrong. The very word "wrong" has more connotations than immorality. There is no dialogue on this war, only the repetition of cliches from outworn arguments. Logic repeated too many times becomes ineffectual boredom, and Washington is numbing us with the rules of longevity. Step outside the guidelines of the official umpires and make your own rules and your own reality. One outrage must answer another; only absurdity can deal with absurdity.

Demonstrations should turn people on, not off. The spiritually depraved American public has shown it won't stand for the blunt truth served on a negative platter, which it always defensively assumes is insult. Demonstrations should satisfy the demands of this electronic and cinematic age. A protest demonstration can become one act of negation against another, canceling each other out. We need a newer and more positive approach, a pro-life, joyful, energized, magnificently absurd demonstration against the sucking vacuum of war.

More militant action could follow from this living theatre piece. You could refuse to go for a physical on the ground that there is no war. And suppose 20 or 30 million people signed a petition declaring the war over—the war which, by the way, has yet to be declared. What could be more democratic?

Think of that for a moment. How embarassing can it get, to have an entire nation mobilized for war, to have the propaganda mills running full blast, to have half a million men near the field of battle, and this young country, so corrupt, so frightened, so sterile as to even avoid the minimum of ritual, to justify the travesty of their own self-destined down-fall. If they don't have the courage of their reality to declare this war on, we should at least have the courage of our imagination to declare it over.

Everyone who comes should try to do something creative on his own—make up a few signs like "God Bless you Lyndon for Ending the War," wear clothes appropriate to the re-enactment of VE day, wave a flag and mean it, invite a soldier along, form a brass band to play "When Johnnie Comes Marching Home," bring extra noisemakers and confetti, drink beer, kiss girls, and give thanks this weekend that the war is over.

There will be songs, dancing, music, flowers, and hundreds of celebrities will be there, people like Ho Chi Minh, Betty Grable, Lyndon Johnson, Regis Toomey, and John Wayne.

The war in Vietnam is an amphetamine trip, a reflection of the spiritual disease that has gripped this country and distorted every principle on which it was built. This generation must make a choice between the total rejection of the country and the decision to regain a spiritual balance. I believe there is still something inherent in the fibre of America worth saving, and that the fortunes of the entire world may well ride on the ability of young America to face the responsibilities of an old American gone mad.

Old America has proven herself decadent enough to be willing to sacrifice one of her finest generations into the garbage truck of cold war propaganda. What kind of depths have they sunk into to dishonor the very meaning of the word "honor" by asking you men to die for nothing? This is not my America, this is not my war; if there is going to be an America, there is no war—la guerre est finie!

The criminal patriotism of today demands the corruption of every citizen, and now we pay the consequences—not only in the jungles of Asia, but in the materialist ravaged cities of America. Now we are the lost patrol who chase their chartered souls like old whores following tired armies.

Have you heard? The war is over!

5 THE COUNTERCULTURE

Keith Lampe's article, "On making a Perfect Mess," first appeared in The Mobilizer, an official publication of the antiwar National Mobilization Coalition in September 1967. This tongue-in-cheek essay scandalized many members of that peace group, and the article was quickly withdrawn from circulation. Lampe would later become a prominent activist in the ecology movement and change his name to Ponderosa Pine.

Judith Melina and Julian Beck were founders of the "Living Theatre," a group that was critically praised for their successful blending of dramatic performance, experimental technique, and political agitation. The June 1968 selection, "Notes Toward a Statement on Anarchism and Theatre," is taken from Beck's book The Life of the Theatre and is typical of the group's radical aesthetics.

Paul Krassner was the founder and editor of The Realist, a pioneer underground magazine that linked fifties gallows humor with sixties rebellion. His article, "The Birth of the Yippie Conspiracy," initally appeared in January 1968. Revolution for the Hell of It by Abbie Hoffman was the original Yippie book. It presented a unique approach to theatrical politics and attracted many young people to countercultural forms of political protest. Poet and musician Ed Sanders was a member of a rock group, The Fugs. His scenario for the Festival of Life reveals what the Yippies dreamed of doing in Chicago during the 1968 Democratic National Convention.

Gary Snyder became a hero to the fifties "beat generation" as a major fictional character in Jack Kerouac's novel The Dharma Bums. His later poetry and essays, such as "Buddhism and the Coming Revolution," written in November 1968, kept him popular throughout the 1960s.

Stew Albert, who ran for sheriff as a Yippie candidate in Alameda County in 1970, wrote "People's Park: Free for All" in the spring of 1969. The article first appeared in The Berkeley Barb and inspired many to work in the park. F.J. Bardacke's leaflet "Who owns the Park?" helped mobilize opposition to the University of California by eloquently questioning that institution's claim to the land.

Do It! was written by Yippie Jerry Rubin while he was on trial in Chicago in 1969. The book had worldwide sales of 250,000, and its title came to be used as a militant political slogan. Konstantin Berlandt was one of the original founders of the gay liberation movement. He wrote "Been down So Long it Looks Like Up to Me" in September 1969 for The Berkeley Tribe. The article represented a turn in gay politics away from demands for civil rights toward a positive assertion that homosexual lifestyles were liberating and worthy of emulation.

Joy Marcus was a founder of the "radical therapy" movement, which emerged in 1969 and linked psychological liberation with social revolution. Its practitioners helped popularize therapeutic ideas among many activists. By the mid-1970s, however, this new movement was overwhelmed by therapists who took an assertively apolitical approach.

Revolutionary Letter #4

Diane DiPrima

Left to themselves people
grow their hair.
Left to themselves they
take off their shoes.
Left to themselves they make love
sleep easily
share blankets, dope & children
they are not lazy or afraid
they plant seeds, they smile, they
speak to one another. The word
coming into its own: touch of love
on the brain, the ear.

We return with the sea, the tides
we return as often as leaves, as numerous
as grass, gentle, insistent, we remember
the way,
our babes toddle barefoot thru the cities of the universe.

Diane DiPrima, *Revolutionary Letters*, San Francisco: City Lights Books, 1971, p. 11. ©1971 by Diane DiPrima. Reprinted by permission of CITY LIGHTS BOOKS.

On Making a Perfect Mess

Keith Lampe

A good new feeling in the streets of America. Feels like there's going to be a white rebellion too. The work of the black men of Newark and Detroit has freed us honkies (beep! beep!) of a few more scholarly hangups and we're getting down into it now.

Now, at last, we're getting past the talk and the analysis and the petitions and the protests—past the cunning white logic of the universities—and we're heading back down into ourselves. The worst trip of all finally coming to an end: "Either A or not—A" and "Men have souls, animals don't" kept us freaked out for 2500 years.

Gary Snyder says it's the neolithic that's coming to an end. He says man is transferring his best attention from objects to states of mind.

In any case, we emancipated primitives of the coming culture are free to do what we *feel* now because we understand that logic and proportion and consistency and often even perspective are part of the old control system and we're done with the old control systems.

Among the honkies the Diggers probably best understand this and they've been helpful dragging us kicking and screaming into the last third of the century.

Psychic guerrilla warfare now. Diggers raining dollar bills to the floor of the stock exchange in gleeful exorcism. Sgt. Pepper's Lonely Hearts Club Hate Parade down Wall Street to hold up a mirror to the studious monkeys: Kill a Commie for Christ, Commie a Christ for Killer, Christ a Killer for Commie.

Keith Lampe, "On Making a Perfect Mess," *The Mobilizer*, September 1, 1967, p. 3.

Seventy-six point two per cent of the following gigs will hit Washington last half this October:

1.   Ten thousand exuberant people will clog the Pentagon and close it down. Later they'll jam the jails, take them over and turn them into communities.

2.   A thousand children will stage Loot-Ins at department stores to strike at the property fetish that underlies genocidal war.

3.   A hundred professors will use their bodies to close down the induction center.

4.   Seven tailored fraternity boys will wrestle LBJ to the ground and take his pants down. Fotos of the fleshy seat of the government will circulate freely.

5.   Hey, who defoliated the White House lawn?

6.   Two authentic D.C. cop impersonators will take twelve peace demonstrators to jail and the charges later will poof as the impersonators evaporate into the populace.

7.   Country Joe and the Fish will make music.

8.   A single elderly shaman, intoning in his belly, will drive 2600 evil spirits shrieking from the Pentagon. Fourteen key colonels will defect to the Diggers and get $42,000 from *Life* for a piece on their earlier karmas.

9.   Eight thousand hippies will panhandle at embassies to create a certain international embarrassment for U.S. imagers.

10.   A large black truck containing mysterious electronic equipment will move slowly through the streets of the city. Rumors of a Martian flag flying above the FBI building.

11.   Hippie chemists will experiment nonviolently on police with anti-riot control agents. "It just makes them feel lazy, that's all."

12.   Fifteen hundred mothers will hold a Smoke-In in Lafayette Park and the sweet scent in the evening air will cause Lady Bird to sigh in her sleep.

13.   Nineteen thousand hippies will jam the banks, paralyze them, and proclaim the death of money.

14.   As the network cameras wheel in for classic counter-demonstrator footage, the BOMB PEKING picket signs will be flipped to say, "Does LBJ suck?"

15.   Forty bearded ghosts from the last revolution will rise from

Arlington cemetery and scramble the Pentagon's radar system.

16. Alices' Air Force will provide mobile civil-disobedience units anyplace in Washington within 45 seconds.

17. Hey, who kidnapped the guard at the Tomb of the Unknown Soldier?

18. During a block party in front of the White House a lad of nine will climb the fence and piss, piss.

19. And, of course, there will be God's Intergalactic Light Show over all.

Most of these things are patiently waiting for people to do them. If you don't dig any of them, do *your* thing.

Afterwards, in November, how many kids will go back to school? The universities are cultural lag areas now—and in most cases it's no longer possible to advise a bright young person to pass time at one.

Jails should become voluntary. This places the government into the monastery or retreat business and we win the simple right to be fed and housed austerely in a nonsectarian environment whenever we feel like meditating. Since the blacks emphatically are in no mood to meditate this season, let them out, get them out, immediately.

Because as a honkie I have a bully heritage, I dig nonviolence as my best expression. But I know nonviolence is a faith—not a demonstrable truth—and, being ecumenically inclined, I have no desire to impose it on anybody else.

Up-to-the minute progress reports on all Washington activities can be had at any hour from (202) LI 5-6700. Call collect only.

Notes Toward a Statement on Anarchism and Theatre

Julian Beck

The purpose of the theatre is to serve the needs of the people.
    The people have no servants. The people serve themselves.
The people need revolution, to change the world, life itself.
    Because the way we are living is too full of pain
    and dissatisfaction. Fatally painful for too many people.
    For all of us.
This is a period of emergency. Therefore emergency theatre is the
    theatre of awareness.
The first thing is to feed everybody, to stop the violence, and
    free us all. This is what anarchism means in our time.
The theatre of anarchism is the theatre of action.
The slavery to money has to end. Which means that the entire
    money system has to end. A society of free goods, freely
    produced, freely distributed. You take what you need, you give
    what you can. The world is yours to love and work for. No state,
    no police, no money, no barter, no borders, no property. Time
    and disposition to seek good, seek one another, to take trips
    deep into the mind, and to feel, to find out what it is to have
    a body, and to begin to use and make joy with it.

Julian Beck, "Notes Toward a Statement on Anarchism and Theatre," *The Life of the Theatre*, San Francisco: City Lights Books, 1972. Copyright © 1972 by Julian Beck. Reprinted by permission of CITY LIGHTS BOOKS.

The theatre has to work with the people to destroy the systems of
civilization that prohibit the development of body and brain.
In order to work in most factories you have to stop the mind
from working lest it die of pain and injury. You have to stop
the body from feeling lest it wince consciously thru the day.
This is the work of the theatre.
Theatre has to stop being a product bought and paid for by the
bourgeoisie. The whole age of buying and selling has to end.
Theatre has to stop being the servant of a system in which the
only people who go to the theatre are those who can pay for it.
The poor are disinherited. Well, activist artists are going to play
in the streets,
we are going to tell what's going on, how bad it is,
and what the people can do to change things,
and what the destination—the objective of the revolution—is,
and ways to get there:
how to make the revolution, to bring it into being, and what to
do when we have it, and how to carry it further.
The revolutionary artist will seek ways to drench the people in
such beauty that they tear down the flags and subvert the armies,
form communes and cells and a society in which there is a
possibility of being.
Because bourgeois society doesn't tell the people what beauty is.
The secrets have been appropriated by the rich with their
exclusive education and avidity, and the people are poisoned
by the mercury in the mass media.
The working people are going to take over the means of production,
occupy the places of industry and turn them all into factories
of food clothing shelter heat love and the extended mind.
It is going to happen.
And we are going to do this by exorcising all violence, and the cause
of violence, the need for violence, violence in all its forms,
violence of hands, teeth, bombs, police, army, state, law, land,
real estate, property, education, social, political,
moral and sexual.
This is the work of the world.
And this work of the world is the only work of the theatre:
because the theatre principally is the dancing place of the
people

and therefore the dancing place of the gods who dance in ecstasy
    only amid the people
And therefore we aim this theatre at God
and the people
who are the destination of the most holy
holy holy revolution

Avignon, France. 7 June 1968.

The Birth of the Yippie Conspiracy

Paul Krassner

Now that Lynda Bird Johnson has publicly revealed in *McCall's* magazine the occasional bedroom togetherness of her parents, the slogan *Make Love, Not War* can no longer be thought of as necessarily requiring a choice between those two alternatives.

Of course, that has to apply to us Good Guys as well as them Bad Guys. So, first, picture W.C. Fields announcing: "You don't *decide* something is absurd— you *recognize* it!" And then come share with me the perspective of this unforgiving minute.

I'm writing here on a tiny island off the coast of Florida. There are four of us: Abbie Hoffman and his wife, Anita; me, and my temporary soulmate. Yesterday we all took a li'l ol' LSD tripereeno, and either it was very powerful acid or else there was an actual hurricane. What was it Tim Leary said about the importance of proper set and setting?

It was also the day Stokely Carmichael came home. We might have been at the airport cheering for him had we been in New York. For Stokely had said in Paris that we don't want peace in Vietnam, we want a Vietnamese victory over the United States. Yet I only began to really understand the impact of his statement here in this context while listening to unbelievably *schmaltzy* music coming in over Radio Free Havana.

I was in Cuba on the first anniversary of the revolution. I had always been Against Violence. But as I learned what total inhumanity my own country had fostered there, I realized that there would be no

---

Paul Krassner, "The Birth of the Yippie Conspiracy," *The Realist*, January 1968, pp. 15–21.

alternative *but* a violent revolution to overthrow the Batista regime. Now the same total inhumanity is taking place in Vietnam and, with Marshall McLuhan's blessing, even Bob Dylan knows it's happening.

A few of us had been interviewed for the Walter Cronkite version of the news— you have to think of the news as a *gift* bestowed upon you each evening by the professionals in whose care it has been placed— because he wanted to know who was behind the cow's blood thrown in Dean Rusk's honor as Janis Ian sang *Society's Child* at his daughter's wedding.

We wouldn't tell. The *Village Voice* has since revealed that it was Protestors, Troublemakers and Anarchists (PTA). Abbie did tell the CBS interviewer that he was prepared to win or die. Well, they didn't exactly leave *that* on. And when I was asked about future plans, I could only smile and say, "You think I'm going to tell you?" I went on to suggest that we were going to put truth serum in reporters' drinks, but they left that out.

I remember a press conference in Cuba held by a group of visiting professors. I watched how correspondents took notes on negative aspects of the revolution but kept their pencils poised during the exposition of positive accomplishments. There were no memos from any publishers. It wasn't necessary.

I met Castro. Ten minutes after he agreed to an interview, a cablegram arrived from Eisenhower breaking off diplomatic relations. Goddammit, Ike, it was *your* fault I never got that interview.

At the Havana Riviera, Cubans were busy mounting anti-aircraft guns atop the cabañas lining the swimming pool. News reports from the U.S. labeled it all a "comic opera." That was before the Bay of Pigs.

On television an old movie is playing, and Desi Arnaz sings, once again, *I'm Spic and Spanish.* You think I'm kidding? I'm not kidding.

* * *

Hippies, black people, Viet Cong—they're all expendable. It's not far-fetched to draw a link between sentencing a young person to prison for smoking flowers and dropping napalm on a suspected guerrilla stronghold. What these acts have in common is the exercise of power without compassion.

The way to accomplish that is, you have to transform human beings into abstractions. One day you manufacture Accent to dull their taste buds; the next day you hire an ad agency to present it as a public service.

So, on one side of the coin, *Newsday* quotes an ammunition-loader on the USS *Morton* off Vietnam: "I'm against the war historically, politically, legally and morally. The only way I can do this job is by telling myself that these are not shells that are going to fall and kill people. I keep telling myself that all I'm doing is moving objects, just objects, from one spot to another. I couldn't do the job otherwise."

And, on the other side of that coin, in an interview in a Havana paper, Cuba's Ambassador to North Vietnam says of the NLF: "Even the bomb craters are used as fish-ponds. Moreover, sections of planes shot down are being used to make plows and agricultural equipment."

"I never said God is on our side," Dean Rusk confessed to the Foreign Policy Association.

Maybe nobody ever *asked*.

"Mr. Rusk, sir, *is* God on our side?"

"Yup—went to the highest bidder."

I don't want to see a single American killed in Vietnam, but in a battle between right and wrong, one must take sides. How many years can you go on listening to General Westmoreland say that we have to continue the bombing as long as they keep using those anti-aircraft guns?

Obviously, though, rightness and wrongness are subjective qualities. Don't take my word for it. Ask any Nazi.

At the AFL-CIO convention in Miami Beach, following a forty-minute debate on organized labor's Vietnam policy, only about half a dozen out of 1,200 delegates dissented from a resolution supporting "that lonely man in the White House." The quote belongs to George Meany, who said he'd read in the Communist *Worker* that same opposition policy. The Commies, incidentally, have come out unanimously against air pollution.

At the annual meeting of the American Anthropological Association, Professor Andrew Vayda of Columbia University cited studies indicating that war may help to satisfy certain social needs: the redistribution of people to relieve problems of local population pressures; the creation of deterrents to discourage one group from attacking or trespassing against its neighbors; and as a safety-valve "to keep such variables as anxiety, tension, and hostility from exceeding certain limits."

Between the emotion of labor and the rationale of anthropology, an imaginary leader named General Consensus is telling a convention of Gold Star mothers in limbo that the International Communist Conspiracy is more threatening than ever. They desperately need this reassurance that their sons have not died in vain insanity.

Ironically, returning *killers* could bring about the legalization of marijuana: 75% of 'em smoke there. Bust a Vietnam *veteran* for pot? The American Legion will, of course, lead his defense.

Meanwhile, Lynda Bird is on her honeymoon, but she's still a virgin. At least, according to Leonard Lyons in the *New York Post*, "She doesn't drink lest it set an example, particularly while a war is being waged in Asia."

* * *

It was the Diggers—the activist end of the hippie spectrum—who brought food, toys and joints over to Newark during the insurrection. And it was a hippie bail fund—the now-broke Jade Companions of the Flower Dance, Inc.—which put up $200 of Rap Brown's $15,000 bail.

This was originally intended as a drug bust trust, but the board of directors decided that getting arrested for transporting a rifle over the Louisiana state line was certainly psychedelic—especially since one board member, cherubic Jim Fouratt, had been bailed out when he got arrested in Newark for refusing to say whether he was a boy or girl, an increasing perception problem for police. Naked, he tucked his genitals out of sight between his legs, and the cops suddenly felt sorry for the ordeal they'd put her through.

In Haight-Ashbury, a mimeographed Communications Company sheet consists of one word: "Diggersareniggers"; and in Harlem, as if to say *Amen*, a young black man stops a hippie on the street and says, "Hey, you guys are the new niggers." For a long while, there has been a certain resentment by blacks and Hispanics—who never had a *choice*—toward hippies who had *decided* to forego middle-class society. But now they're increasingly learning how much they have in common, including the enemy: coercive authority.

Their spiritual coalescence was inadvertently summed up by Nancy Reagan. "Today's runaway," she said, "will be tomorrow's PTA secretary."

Item: Philadelphia hippies have filed suit requesting a temporary injunction to halt the police and park guards from "chasing and threatening" them.

Item: Chicago and New York landlords have attempted to drive out retail stores which cater to the freaky tastes of hippies; a Miami head shop is suing the city.

Item: The media have been busy massing misinformation on what they call "The Death of Hippies," a milestone marked by the extremely exploitable murder of Groovy and Linda.

Every week the *National Enquirer* headlines a story about a mother who chopped her child into little pieces which she proceeded to fry, put between slices of whole wheat bread and distribute as sandwiches to her neighbors, but we have yet to see a resultant article anywhere on "The Death of the Straight World."

All of the reports stated that Linda Fitzpatrick was raped four times. I wondered how they could tell. I was so curious, in fact, that I decided to check into it. This is the statement of Dr. Elliot Gross, Medical Examiner, who performed the autopsy on Linda: "I don't know where they got that information from. We haven't released *any* of the findings of the autopsy other than the cause of death. Maybe the police department gave it out as something one of the suspects said." That's unlikely, however, inasmuch as the suspects are pleading innocent.

No, hippies aren't dead, they're just evolving into guerrilla warriors.

What blacks and hippies and Vietnamese share is a goal: *to have power over their own lives.* The notion is crystallized by an SDS button on draft resistance: "Not with *my* life you don't." It doesn't matter whether or not you take LSD, have an abortion, vote, drop out; the only thing that matters is your right to do with your body and soul what *you* will.

The tragedy of our time is that Our National Purpose has become the imposition of our will upon others. American arrogance was personified in one sentence of a news story about the drowning of Australian Prime Minister Harold Holt: "President Johnson led world leaders in mourning Holt's loss."

"These are unhappy times for New York's hippies," said a telegram from *Time*, which led U.S. magazines in mourning Groovy and Linda's loss. "As a result, we feel we must cancel our press party, which was scheduled in connection with the publication of *The Hippies*. The book itself, of course, is proceeding on schedule..."

Things are getting more and more surrealistic. The Hare Krishna people advertised in the *East Village* for a "Professional Typist needed to type for publication a 400-page manuscript for the *Bhagavad-Gita*. We cannot pay much, but we assure liberation...."

* * *

You don't really think that LBJ didn't know in advance—*and* approve of—what Lynda Bird was writing for *McCall's*, do you? There had been the foolish gossip all along, but there would be no doubt when word got out that the First Couple sleep in separate bedrooms, so that intimations of impotence at the White House had become rampant. But now here was a way, through his daughter, to let the truth reach the public.

The scene is inspiring.

Lyndon pulls Lady Bird into bed by the ears—an act which never fails to arouse him. "Look, honey, I'm escalatin'." Later, Lynda Bird peers through the keyhole and hears her Daddy verbalizing his pre-orgasmic tension: "Oh, Lady Bird!... *Oh, Lady Bird!... OH, LADY BIRD!...* With a heavy heart, your President is coming...."

And so is the Second American Revolution.

Street events will be attended by theater critics. Draft resistance will become a fraternity initiation rite. Guerrilla warfare will be preceded by press conferences. Teenyboppers will burn their birth certificates in front of radio stations. Tax refusers will be framed as dope pushers. Black militants will be pacified with saltpeter in concentration camps. White liberals will take full-page "We Protest!" ads in the *New York Times*. Armed violence will be interrupted by TV commercials. The mood of neo-Christianity will be: "Fuck them, oh, Lord, they know *exactly* what they do."

Coincidental with the Democrats' convention there's going to be a Youth International Party—YIP—and Chicago will be invaded by a mass of *Yippies!* You've just witnessed the birth of a word.

No more marches. No more rallies. No more speeches. The dialogue is over, baby. Tolerance of rational dissent has become an insidious form of repression. The goal now is to disrupt an insane society.

We've already applied for the permit.

Revolution for the Hell of It

Abbie Hoffman

February 16, 1968

Stokely:

It's been a year since I last saw you in Washington and a lot has happened. I have left Liberty House to others. It is going well, but PPC has just been able to hold its own in Mississippi. Living on the Lower East Side I was naturally aware of this whole hippie business and started to organize around here: bail funds, Free Stores, smoke-ins, be-ins. We threw out money at the stock exchange in a wild event I'm sure you heard about. We threw soot on Con Ed executives and dumped smoke bombs in their lobby. Exorcising the Pentagon of its evil spirits, back to New York and a blood bath for Dean Rusk in which we threw seventeen gallons of blood at cops, Rusk, limousines. Lots of other things. I'm enclosing an article for you to read and maybe comment on.

We are working on a huge Youth Festival in Chicago at the time of the Democratic Convention. I hope I get to participate. I'm currently on trial for supposedly hitting a cop with a bottle in a demonstration. I can't imagine what they are talking about, me being a flower child and all that. I am also working on getting a group of longhairs along with a rock band to visit Cuba. I hear Castro is interested. I have been reading a good deal about Cuba and having talks with its UN Embassy. I would

Excerpts from Abbie Hoffman, *Revolution for the Hell of It*, New York: The Dial Press, 1968, pp. 53–64. Reprinted with permission of the author.

very much like to go. Julius Lester and I talked the other night about it. I see Mendy Sampstein every once in awhile but he has a job as a cab driver and isn't involved in the Movement any more. I saw you in a movie by Peter Brook last night. It was a rotten movie—very boring. Nothing like *Planet of the Apes*, which is a trip and half. I was in Washington last week, we busted up McCarthy's talk with some guerrilla theater. I tried to call you but you are hard to find. I thought your book was blah compared to some exciting TV shots of your talk in France with a huge photo of Ché behind you. I see Timothy Leary a lot. He has just done a whole turnabout. He's supporting Gregory for President and joining us in bringing people to Chicago. His little drop-out shelter in Millbrook gets busted about once a week by the cops and it's had an effect in getting him involved. I would like very much to talk to you if you come to New York. Maybe a get-together down here. I got some fantastic stuff that a friend brought back from Vietnam and it ain't napalm. It'll make your ears fall off.

In freedom,

* * *

TALKING IN MY SLEEP—AN EXERCISE IN SELF-CRITICISM

A mythical interview of questions that are asked and answers that are given. Interviews are always going on. Here's one with myself.

* * *

You're planning to drop out?
Well, dropping out is a continual process. I don't see anything really definite in the future. I just don't want to get boxed-in to playing a predetermined role. Let's say, so much of what we do is theater—in life I just don't want to get caught in a Broadway show that lasts five years, even if it is a success. The celebrity bag is another form of careerism. But you see, celebrity status is very helpful in working with media. It's my problem and I'll deal with it just like any other problem. I'll do the best I can.

Is that why the Yippies were created? To manipulate the media?
Exactly. You see, we are faced with this task of getting huge numbers of people to come to Chicago along with hundreds of performers, artists, theater groups, engineers. Essentially, people involved in trying to work out a new society. How do you do this starting from scratch, with no organization, no money, nothing? Well, the answer is that you create a myth. Something that people can play a role in, can relate to. This is especially true of media people. I'll give you an example. A reporter was interviewing us once and he liked what we were doing. He said "I'm going to tell what good ideas you guys really have. I'm going to tell the truth about the Yippies." We said, "That won't help a bit. Lie about us." It doesn't matter as long as he gets Yippie! and Chicago linked together in a magical way. The myth is about LIFE vs. DEATH. That's why we are headed for a powerful clash.

You don't want the truth told?
Well, I don't want to get philosophical but there is really no such animal. Especially when one talks of creating a myth. How can you have a true myth? When newspapers distort a story they become participants in the creation of the myth. We love distortions. Those papers that claim to be accurate, i.e., the New York *Times, Village Voice, Ramparts, The Nation, Commentary,* that whole academic word scene is a total bore. In the end they probably distort things more than the *Daily News.* The New York *Times* is the American Establishment, not the *Daily News.* The *Daily News* creates a living style. You know: "Pot-smoking, dirty, beatnik, pinko, sex-crazy, Vietnik, so-called Yippies." Compare that to the New York *Times:* "Members of the newly formed Youth International Party (YIP)." The New York *Times* is death. The *Daily News* is the closest thing to TV. Look at its front page, always a big picture. It looks like a TV set. I could go on and on about this. It's a very important point. Distortion is essential to myth-making.

* * *

That's some fantasy.
Of course. It'll come true, though. Fantasy is the only truth. Once we had a demonstration at the *Daily News* Building. About three hundred people smoked pot, danced, sprayed the reporters with body deodorant, burned money, handed out leaflets to all the employees that began:

"Dear fellow member of the Communist conspiracy..." We called it an "Alternative Fantasy." It worked great.

What do you mean, it worked great?
Nobody understood it. That is, nobody could explain what it all meant yet everyone was fascinated. It was pure information, pure imagery, which in the end is truth. You see, the New York *Times* can get into very theoretical discussions on the critical level of what we are doing. The *Daily News* responds on a gut level. That's it. The New York *Times* has no guts.

Then being understood is not your goal?
Of course not. The only way you can understand is to join, to become involved. Our goal is to remain a mystery. Pure theater. Free, with no boundaries except your own. Throwing money onto the floor of the Stock Exchange is pure information. It needs no explanation. It says more than thousands of anticapitalist tracts and essays. It's so obvious that I hesitate to discuss it, since everyone reading this already has an image of what happened there. I respect their images. Anything I said would come on like expertise. "Now, this is what *really* happened." In point of fact nothing happened. Neither we nor the Stock Exchange exist. We are both rumors. That's it. That's what happened that day. Two different rumors collided.

Can you think of any people in the theater that influence you?
W.C. Fields, Ernie Kovacs, Ché Guevara, Antonin Artaud, Alfred Hitchcock, Lenny Bruce, the Marx Brothers—probably the Beatles have the most influence. I think they have the perfect model for the new family. They have unlimited creativity. They are a continual process, always changing, always burying the old Beatles, always dropping out.

Can you pursue that a little?
Well, the Beatles are a new family group. They are organized around the way they create. They are communal art. They are brothers and, along with their wives and girlfriends, form a family unit that is horizontal rather than vertical, in that it extends across a peer group rather than descending vertically like grandparents-parents-children. More than horizontal, it's circular with the four Beatles the inner circle, then their wives and kids and friends. The Beatles are a small circle of friends, a tribe. They are far more than simply a musical band. Let's say, if you

want to begin to understand our culture, you can start by comparing Frank Sinatra and the Beatles. It wouldn't be perfect but it would be a good beginning. Music is always a good place to start.

Why is that?
Well, a revolution always has rhythm. Whether it's songs of the Lincoln Brigade, black soul music, Cuban love songs by José Martí, or white psychedelic rock. I once heard songs of the Algerian rebels that consisted mostly of people beating guns on wooden cases. It was fantastic. What is the music of the system? Kate Smith singing the National Anthem. Maybe that's Camp, but it's not Soul.

* * *

THE YIPPIES ARE GOING TO CHICAGO

Last December a group of us in New York conceived the Yippie! idea. We had four main objectives:

1. The blending of pot and politics into a potlitical grass leaves movement—a cross-fertilization of the hippie and New Left philosophies.
2. A connecting link that would tie together as much of the underground as was willing into some gigantic national get-together.
3. The development of a model for an alternative society.
4. The need to make some statement, especially in revolutionary action-theater terms, about LBJ, the Democratic Party, electoral politics, and the state of the nation.

To accomplish these tasks required the construction of a vast myth, for through the notion of myth large numbers of people could get turned on and, in that process of getting turned on, begin to participate in Yippie! and start to focus on Chicago. *Precision was sacrificed for a greater degree of suggestion.* People took off in all directions in the most sensational manner possible:

"We will burn Chicago to the ground!"
"We will fuck on the beaches!"

"We demand the Politics of Ecstasy!"
"Acid for all!"
"Abandon the Creeping Meatball!"
And, all the time: "Yippie! Chicago—August 25-30."

Reporters would play their preconceived roles: "What is the difference between a hippie and a Yippie?" A hundred different answers would fly out, forcing the reporter to make up his own answers; to distort. And distortion became the life-blood of the Yippies.

Yippie! was in the eye of the beholder.

Perhaps Marshall McLuhan can help.

This is taken from an interview in the current Columbia University yearbook:

MCLUHAN: Myth is the mode of simultaneous awareness of a complex group of causes and effects... We hear sounds from everywhere, without ever having to focus... Where a visual space is an organized continuum of a uniform connected kind, the ear world is a world of simultaneous relationships. Electric circuitry confers a mythic dimension on our ordinary individual and group actions. Our technology forces us to live mythically, but we continue to think fragmentarily, and on single, separate planes.

INTERVIEWER: What do you mean by myth?

MCLUHAN: Myth means putting on the audience, putting on one's environment. The Beatles do this. They are a group of people who suddenly were able to put on their audience and the English language with musical effects—putting on a whole vesture, a whole time, a Zeit.

INTERVIEWER: So it doesn't matter that the Pentagon didn't actually levitate?"

MCLUHAN: Young people are looking for a formula for putting on the universe—participation mystique. They do not look for detached patterns—for ways of relating themselves to the world, a la nineteenth century.

So there you have it, or rather have it suggested, because myth can never have the precision of a well-oiled machine, which would allow it to be trapped and molded. It must have the action of participation and the magic of mystique. It must have a high element of risk, drama, excitement and bullshit.

Let's return to history. Remember a guy named Lyndon Johnson? He was so predictable when Yippie! began. And then *pow!* He really fucked us. He did the one thing no one had counted on. He dropped out. "My God," we exclaimed. "Lyndon is out-flanking us on our hippie side."

Then Go-Clean-for-Gene and Hollywood-Bobby. Well, Gene wasn't much. One could secretly cheer for him the way you cheer for the Mets. It's easy, knowing he can never win. But Bobby, there was the real threat. A direct challenge to our theater-in-the-streets, a challenge to the charisma of Yippie!

Remember Bobby's Christmas card: psychedelic blank space with a big question mark—"Santa in '68?" Remember Bobby on television stuttering at certain questions, leaving room for the audience to jump in and help him agonize, to battle the cold interviewer who knew all the questions and never made a mistake.

Come on, Bobby said, *join the mystery battle against the television machine.* Participation mystique. Theater-in-the-streets. He played it to the hilt. And what was worse, Bobby had the money and power to build the stage. We had to steal ours. It was no contest.

Yippie stock went down quicker than the money we had dumped on the Stock Exchange floor. Every night we would turn on the TV set and there was the young knight with long hair, holding out his hand (a gesture he learned from the Pope): "Give me your hand—it is a long road ahead."

When young longhairs told you how they'd heard that Bobby turned on, you knew Yippie! was *really* in trouble.

We took to drinking and praying for LBJ to strike back, but he kept melting. Then Hubert came along exclaiming the "Politics of Joy" and Yippie! passed into a state of catatonia which resulted in near permanent brain damage.

Yippie! grew irrelevant.

National action seemed meaningless.

Everybody began the tough task of developing new battlegrounds. Columbia, the Lower East Side, Free City in San Francisco. Local action became the focus and by the end of May we had decided to disband Yippie! and cancel the Chicago festival.

It took two full weeks of debate to arrive at a method of dropping-out which would not further demoralize the troops. The statement was all ready when up stepped Sirhan Sirhan, and in ten seconds he made it a whole new ball game.

We postponed calling off Chicago and tried to make some sense out of what the hell had just happened. It was not easy to think clearly. Yippie!, still in a state of critical shock because of LBJ's pullout, hovered close to death somewhere between the 50/50 state of Andy Warhol and the 0/0 state of Bobby Kennedy.

The United States political system was proving more insane than Yippie!.

Reality and unreality had in six months switched sides.

It was *America* that was on a trip; we were just standing still.

How could we pull our pants down? America was already naked.

What could we disrupt? America was falling apart at the seams.

Yet Chicago seemed more relevant than ever. Hubert had a lock on the convention: it was more closed than ever. Even the squares who vote in primaries had expressed a mandate for change. Hubert canned the "Politics of Joy" and instituted the "Politics of Hope"—some switch—but none of the slogans mattered. We were back to power politics, the politics of big-city machines and back-room deals.

The Democrats had finally got their thing together by hook or crook and there it was for all to see—fat, ugly, and full of shit. The calls began pouring into our office. They wanted to know only one thing: "When do we leave for Chicago?"

What we need now, however, is the direct opposite approach from the one we began with. We must sacrifice suggestion for a greater degree of precision. We need a reality in the face of the American political myth. We have to kill Yippie! and still bring huge numbers to Chicago.

If you have any Yippie! buttons, posters, stickers or sweatshirts, bring them to Chicago. We will end Yippie! in a huge orgasm of destruction atop a giant media altar. We will in Chicago begin the task of building Free America on the ashes of the old and from the inside out.

A Constitutional Convention is being planned. A convention of visionary mind-benders who will for five long days and nights address themselves to the task of formulating the goals and means of the New Society.

It will be a blend of technologists and poets, of artists and community organizers, of anyone who has a vision. We will try to develop a Community of Consciousness.

There will be a huge rock-folk festival for free. Contrary to rumor, no groups originally committed to Chicago have dropped out. In fact, additional ones have agreed to participate. In all about thirty groups and performers will be there.

Theater groups from all over the country are pledged to come.

They are an integral part of the activities, and a large amount of funds raised from here on in will go for the transportation of street theater groups.

Workshops in a variety of subjects such as draft resistance, drugs, commune development, guerrilla theater and underground media will be set up. The workshops will be oriented around problem-solving while the Constitutional Convention works to developing the overall philosophical framework.

There will probably be a huge march across town to haunt the Democrats.

People coming to Chicago should begin preparations for five days of energy-exchange. Do not come prepared to sit and watch and be fed a cared for. It just won't happen that way. It is time to become a life-actor. The days of the audience died with the old America. If you don't have a thing to do, stay home, you'll only get in the way.

All of these plans are contingent on our getting a permit, and it is toward that goal that we have been working. A permit is a definite contradiction in philosophy since we do not recognize the authority of the old order, but tactically it is a necessity.

We are negotiating, with the Chicago city government, a six-day treaty. All of the Chicago newspapers as well as various pressure groups have urged the city of Chicago to grant the permit. They recognize full well the huge social problem they face if we are forced to use the streets of Chicago for our action.

They have tentatively offered us use of Soldiers' Field Stadium or Navy Pier (we would have to re-name either, of course) for our convention. We have had several meetings, principally with David Stahl, Deputy Mayor of Chicago, and there remains but to iron out the terms of the treaty—suspension of curfew laws, regulations pertaining to sleeping on the beach, etc.—for us to have a bona fide permit in our hands.

The possibility of violence will be greatly reduced. There is no guarantee that it will be entirely eliminated.

This is the United States, 1968, remember. If you are afraid of violence you shouldn't have crossed the border.

This matter of a permit is a cat-and-mouse game. The Chicago authorities do not wish to grant it too early, knowing this would increase the number of people that descend on the city. They can ill afford to wait too late, for that will inhibit planning on our part and create more chaos.

It is not our wish to take on superior armed troops who outnumber us on unfamiliar enemy territory. It is not their wish to have a Democrat nominated amidst a major bloodbath. The treaty will work for both sides.

There is a further complicating factor: the possibility of the Convention being moved out of Chicago. Presently there are two major strikes taking place by bus drivers and telephone and electrical repairmen in addition to a taxi strike scheduled to begin on the eve of the Convention.

If the Convention is moved out of Chicago we will have to adjust our plans. The best we can say is, keep your powder dry and start preparing. A good idea is to begin raising money to outfit a used bus that you can buy for about $300, and use locally before and after Chicago.

Prepare a street theater skit or bring something to distribute, such as food, poems or music. Get sleeping bags and other camping equipment. We will sleep on the beaches. If you have any free money we can cannel this into energy groups already committed. We are fantastically broke and in need of funds.

In Chicago contact *The Seed*, 837 N. LaSalle St.; in New York, the Youth International Party, 32 Union Sq. East. Chicago has rooming facilities for 25 organizers. Write us of your plans and watch the underground papers for the latest developments.

The point is, you can use Chicago as a means of pulling your local community together. It can serve to open up a dialogue between political radicals and those who might be considered hippies. The radical will say to the hippie: "Get together and fight, you are getting the shit kicked out of you." The hippie will say to the radical: "Your protest is so narrow, your rhetoric is so boring, your ideological power plays so old-fashioned."

Each can help the other, and Chicago—like the Pentagon demonstration before it—might well offer the medium to put forth the message.

POSTSCRIPT

The preceding article, borrowed from *The Realist*, July 7, 1968, is the only article I wrote about Chicago prior to the Convention. It was quoted by Jack Mabley of the Chicago *American* as "proof" of my serious revolutionary goals. It was also quoted in a subsequent article in the Chicago *Sun-Times*, entitled "Cops Watch Top Yippies," an article which showed only that they watched what we wrote in the underground press. Both news articles quote the opening section of my piece, the part with the numbers (both, incidentally, changed the word "potlitical" back to "political"). STRUCTURE IS MORE IMPORTANT THAN CONTENT IN THE TRANSMISSION OF INFORMATION. It is the same as saying "the medium is the message." The fact that they quoted the section with the numbers reminds me of how I used to bull my way through college exams. If I didn't know the answer to a question such as "Why did the Tasmanian Empire collapse?" I made a point of structuring the answer in the following manner:

> Economically, the Tasmanian Empire suffered from bureaucratic excesses and internal corruption. It became...
> Culturally, a decline could be noted in the quality and character of artistic output. In previous times...
> Politically, the Tasmanians, although they had developed one of the most advanced forms of government, found themselves with a system which steadily grew more unworkable. It was necessary...

The teacher always considered this "structure" worthy of serious consideration. I never studied in college, I just practiced outlines, played games, and got laid.

Festival of Life

Ed Sanders

PREDICTIONS FOR YIPPIE ACTIVITIES

1. Poetry readings, mass meditation, flycasting exhibitions, demagogic yippie political arousal speeches, rock music, and song concerts will be held on a precise timetable throughout the week August 25–30.

2. A dawn ass-washing ceremony with 10's of 1000's participating will occur each morning at 5:00 AM as yippie revellers and protesters prepare for the 7:00 AM volleyball tournaments.

3. Several hundred Yippie friends with press passes will gorge themselves on 800 pounds of cocktail onions and puke in unison at the nomination of Hubert H. Pastry.

4. Psychedelic long haired mutant-jissomed peace leftists will consort with known dope fiends, spilling out onto the sidewalks in porn-ape disarray each afternoon.

5. The Chicago offices of the National Biscuit Company will be hijacked on principle to provide bread & cookies for 50,000 as a gesture of goodwill to the youth of America.

6. Universal Syrup Day will be held on Wednesday when a movie will be shown at Soldiers Field in which Hubert Humphrey confesses to Allen Ginsberg of his secret approval of anal intercourse.

7. Filth will be worshipped.

Ed Sanders, "Predictions for Yippie Activities," *The Berkeley Barb*, August 2–8, 1968, p. 13.

8. The Yippie Ecological Conference will spew out an angry report denouncing scheiss-poison in the lakes and streams industrial honky-fumes from white killer industrialists, and exhaust murder from a sick hamburger society of automobile freaks; with precise total assault solutions to these problems.

9. There will be public fornication whenever and wherever there is an aroused appendage and willing aperture.

10. Poets will re-write the bill of rights in precise language, detailing ten thousand areas of freedom in OUR OWN LANGUAGE, to replace the confusing and vague rhetoric of 200 years ago.

11. Reporters and media representatives will be provided free use of dope and consciousness altering thrill-chemicals for their education and re-freshment.

12. Pissed off hordes of surly draft eligible poets will somehow confront conventioneers with 16 tons of donated fish eyes.

* * *

PRECAUTIONS AND SUGGESTIONS

a. Don't accept shit as a form of communication from any public official, pig, service employee or anybody. Demand respect from the stodgy porcupines that control the Blob Culture.

b. Share your food, your money, your bodies, your energy, your ideas, your blood, your defenses. Attempt peace.

c. Plan ahead of time how you will probably respond to various degrees of provocation, hate & creep-vectors from the opposition. Know carefully your responses.

d. Learn the Internationale.

e. Bring sleeping bags, extra food, blankets, bottles of fireflies, cold cream, lots of handkerchiefs and canteens to deal with pig-spray, love beads, electric toothbrushes, see-thru blouses, manifestoes, magazines, tenacity.

Remember, we are the
life forms evolving in
our own brain.

Buddhism and the Coming Revolution

Gary Snyder

Buddhism holds that the universe and all creatures in it are intrinsically in a state of complete wisdom, love and compassion; acting in natural response and mutual interdependence. The personal realization of this from-the-beginning state cannot be had for and by one—"self"—because it is not fully realized unless one has given the self up, and away.

In the Buddhist view, what obstructs the effortless manifestation of this state is ignorance, which projects into fear and needless craving. Historically, Buddhist philosophers have failed to analyze out the degree to which ignorance and suffering are caused by social factors, considering fear-and-desire to be given facts of the human condition. Consequently the major concern of Buddhist philosophy is epistemology and "psychology" with no attention paid to historical or sociological problems. Although Mahayana Buddhism has a grand vision of universal salvation, the ACTUAL achievement of Buddhism has been the development of practical systems of meditation toward the end of liberating a few dedicated invididuals from psychological hangups and cultural conditionings. Institutional Buddhism has been conspicuously ready to accept or ignore the inequalities and tyrannies of whatever political system it found itself under. This can be death to Buddhism, because it is death to any meaningful function of compassion. Wisdom without compassion feels no pain.

Gary Snyder, "Buddhism and the Coming Revolution," *The Berkeley Barb*, November 15–21, 1968, p. 90.

No one today can afford to be innocent, or indulge himself in ignorance of the nature of contemporary governments, politics, and social orders. The national politics of the modern world maintain their existence by deliberately fostered craving and fear: monstrous protection rackets. The free world has become economically dependant on a fantastic system of stimulation of greed which canot be fulfilled, sexual desires which cannot be satiated, and hatred which has no outlet except against oneself, the persons one is supposed to love, or the revolutionary aspirations of pitiful poverty-striken marginal societies like Cuba or Vietnam. The conditions of the cold war have turned all modern societies—Communist included—into vicious distorters of man's true potential. They create populations of "preta"—hungry ghosts with giant appetites and throats no bigger than needles. The soil, the forests, and all animals life are being consumed by these cancerous collectivities; the air and water of the planet is being fouled by them.

There is nothing in human nature or the requirements of human social organization which intrinsically requires that a culture be contradictory, repressive, and productive of violent and frustrated personalities. Recent findings in anthropology and psychology make this more and more evident. One can prove it for himself by taking a good look at his own nature through meditation. Once a person has this much faith and insight, he must be led to a deep concern with the need for radical social change through a variety of hopefully non-violent means.

The joyous and voluntary poverty of Buddhism becomes a positive force. The traditional harmlessness and refusal to take life in any form has nation-shaking implications. The practice of meditation, for which one needs "only the ground beneath one's feet" wipes out mountains of junk being pumped into the mind by the mass media and universities. The belief in a serene and generous fulfillment of natural loving desires destroys ideologies which blind, maim, and repress and points the way to a kind of community which would amaze "moralists" and eliminate armies of men who are fighters because they cannot be lovers.

Avatamsaka (Kegon) Buddhist philosophy sees the world as a vast inter-related network in which all objects and creatures are necessary and illuminated. From one standpoint, governments, wars, or all that we consider evil are uncompromisingly contained in this totalistic realm. The hawk, the swoop, and the hare are one. From the "human" standpoint we cannot live in those terms unless all beings see with the same enlightened eye. The Bodhisattva lives by the sufferer's standard, and he must be effective in aiding those who suffer.

The mercy of the West has been social revolution; the mercy of the East has been individual insight into the basic self/void. We need both. They are both contained in the traditional three aspects of the Dharma; wisdom (prajna), meditation (dhyana), and morality (sila). Wisdom is intuitive knowledge of the mind of love and charity that lies beneath one's ego-driven anxieties and aggressions. Meditation is going into the mind to see this for yourself—over and over again, until it becomes the mind you live in. Morality is bringing it back out in the way you live, through personal example and responsible action, ultimately toward the true community (sangha) of "all beings." This last aspect means, for me, supporting any cultural and economic revolution that moves clearly toward a free, international, classless world. It means using such means as civil disobedience, outspoken criticism, protest, pacifism, voluntary poverty, and even gentle violence if it comes to a matter of restraining some impetuous redneck. It means affirming the widest possible spectrum of non-harmful individual behavior—defending the right of individuals to smoke hemp, eat peyote, be polygunous, polyandrous, or homosexual. Worlds of behavior and custom long banned by the Judaeo-Capitalist-Christian, Marxist West. It means respecting intelligence and learning, but not as greed or means to personal power. Working on one's own responsiblity, but willing to work with a group. "Forming the new society within the shell of the old"—the IWW slogan of fifty years ago.

The traditional cultures are in any case, doomed and rather than cling to their good aspects hopelessly it should be remembered that whatever is or was in any other culture can be reconstructured from the unconscious, through meditation. In fact, it is my own view that the coming revolution will close the circle and link us in many ways with the most creative aspects of our archaic past. If we are lucky we may eventually arrive at a totally integrated world culture with matrilineal descent, free-form marriage, natural-credit communist economy, less industry, far less population and lots more national parks.

People's Park: Free for All

Stew Albert

We began building a Park last Sunday. There were no speeches or long debates. Several hundred Berkeley Freemen showed up for work on the mud swamp between Dwight and Haste in back of Telegraph, and if you stopped working for five seconds somebody grabbed your shovel and said "it's my turn."

The land belonged to the University, it bought it up and tore down some of the most beautiful housing in Berkeley. A cement parking lot and then dormitories were supposed to be built but Ronald Reagan cut off the bread and the land just stayed there and turned into a swamp with automobiles on it.

Some green seeking people got the idea for a People's Park and then went ahead and built it.

There wasn't much advance notice, a proclamation in the *Barb* by Robin Hoods Park Commissioner and a leaflet given out on the Avenue.

For a week the Avenue merchants were panhandled. They were told of our plans and responded as modestly as a midwestern virgin on her first time around. Some anonymous types kicked in about seven hundred dollars and we were ready to go.

All sorts of straight and freaky people showed up at the Park. First the land was bulldozed and then we shovelled the rocks and assorted shit into barrels. A morning chill gave way to sweat and more creators kept pouring into what was becoming a Park.

A truck arrived with rolled up grass—that is, sod. We picked the

Stew Albert, "People's Park: Free for All," *The Berkeley Barb*, April 25–May 1, 1969, p. 5.

rolls off the truck and carried them over to a cluster of old and soon to be exciting trees. This would be the first green and after the land was watered the sod was put down. It seemed eternally natural like it was always there.

When we were through several hundred square yards were put down and some people began to say that they had never noticed those trees until grass was rolled out under them.

Flower and vegetable gardens were planted around the trees and it was like a small universe of beauty being created at the roots of a giant one.

Nursery swings and a sliding board appeared and so did children to play on them. Old benches and some newly-made ones were fine for sitting down and being amazed at what was happening.

At some point in the early afternoon a pig appeared and wasn't sure if our Park was disturbing the peace. It looked like those guys liked what was going on but a lifetime of conditioning made it impossible for them to act it out.

A couple of baby trees were set down on the optimistic intuition that we and our children would take shade from them grown to their fullest height and embrace.

The Black Panthers showed up and loved it. Bobby Seale kept laughing in total and happy amazement.

"Are you going to call it PEOPLES Park, listen we got to have some Panthers down here working, this is really socialistic."

As the afternoon turned late, the chill returned but with it rock music and a warming fire, people danced and celebrated, the weed was passed and an appropriate height of accomplishment was part of what we vibrated to.

The night came and people began splitting. The water vulture fire department showed up and put out our source of heat and warm food. A weird thing happened; some fuzz present tried to talk the fire fighters out of their little murder and praised our work. The waters came, people were pissed and the Park's first day was over. People were really happy. The sense of victory of having eliminated something ugly, of just doing something that was uncompromising and truthful was a very powerful trip. A few madmen hallucinated a Park and by the darkness it really was there even for the most pessimistic eye.

In the last couple of days the Park has continued to happen. Two cats showed up and planted a Corn patch, a few new trees sprung up and we sat on new benches and it was still beyond our belief.

Free food was served without announcement or boast and orange-robed Hare Krishna singers sat and chanted as people wrote poetry and some guy tried to play folk guitar.

Several hundred dollars were raised in the Park and on the Avenue and we will be able to put down lots of new grass and shrubbery next Sunday. Anytime you want to work is the time to come to the Park but Sunday will be our next big Commune Day.

Anyone is welcome, but if you want to be a gawking tourist why not check out the Police Station?

For the first time in my life I enjoyed working. I think lots of people had that experience. Ever since I was eighteen I hated every job and either quit or was fired. But this was something different, with aching back and sweat on my brow, there was no boss. What we were creating was our own desires, so we worked like madmen and loved it.

Who Owns the Park?: A Leaflet

F.J. Bardacke

Someday a petty official will appear with a piece of paper, called a land title, which states that the University of California owns the land of the People's Park. Where did that piece of paper come from? What is it worth?

A long time ago the Costanoan Indians lived in the area now called Berkeley. They had no concept of land ownership. They believed that the land was under the care and guardianship of the people who used it and lived on it.

Catholic missionaries took the land away from the Indians. No agreements were made. No papers were signed. They ripped it off in the name of God.

The Mexican Government took the land away from the Church. The Mexican Government had guns and an army. God's word was not as strong.

The Mexican Government wanted to pretend that it was not the army that guaranteed them the land. They drew up some papers which said they legally owned it. No Indians signed those papers.

The Americans were not fooled by the papers. They had a stronger army than the Mexicans. They beat them in a war and took the land. Then they wrote some papers of their own and forced the Mexicans to sign them.

The American Government sold the land to some white settlers. The Government gave the settlers a piece of paper called a land title in exchange for some money. All this time there were still some Indians around who claimed the land. The American army killed most of them.

The piece of paper saying who owned the land was passed around

among rich white men. Sometimes the white men were interested in taking care of the land. Usually they were just interested in making money. Finally some very rich men, who run the University of California, bought the land.

Immediately these men destroyed the houses that had been built on the land. The land went the way of so much other land in America—it became a parking lot.

We are building a park on the land. We will take care of it and guard it, in the spirit of the Costanoan Indians. When the University comes with its land title we will tell them: "Your land title is covered with blood. We won't touch it. Your people ripped off the land from the Indians a long time ago. If you want it back now, you will have to fight for it again."

Do It!

Jerry Rubin

ELVIS PRESLEY KILLED IKE EISENHOWER

The New Left sprang, a predestined pissed-off child, from Elvis' gyrating pelvis.

> tell ya somethin' brother
> found a new place to dwell
> down on the end of Lonely Street
> it's Heartbreak Hotel.

On the surface the world of the 1950's was all Eisenhower calm. A cover story of "I Like Ike" father-figure contentment.

Under the surface, silent people railed at the chains upon their souls. A latent drama of repression and discontent.

Amerika was trapped by her contradictions.

Dad looked at his house and car and manicured lawn, and he was proud. All of his material possessions justified his life.

He tried to teach his kids: he told us not to do anything that would lead us from the path of Success.

> **work** don't play
> **study** don't loaf

Jerry Rubin, *Do It!*, New York: Simon and Schuster, 1970, pp. 17–20; 106–108; 132–133; 209–215. Copyright © 1970 by the Social Education Foundation. Reprinted by permission of SIMON & SCHUSTER, a Division of Gulf & Western Corporation.

obey don't ask questions
fit in don't stand out
be sober don't take drugs
make money don't make waves

We were conditioned in self-denial:
We were taught that fucking was bad because it was immoral. Also in those pre-pill days a knocked-up chick stood in the way of Respectability and Success.
We were warned that masturbation caused insanity and pimples.
And we were confused. We didn't dig why we needed to work toward owning bigger houses? bigger cars? bigger manicured lawns?
We went crazy. We couldn't hold it back any more.

Elvis Presley ripped off Ike Eisenhower by turning our uptight young awakening bodies around. Hard animal rock energy beat/surged hot through us, the driving rhythm arousing repressed passions.
Music to free the spirit.
Music to bring us **together.**
Buddy Holly, the Coasters, Bo Diddley, Chuck Berry, the Everly Brothers, Jerry Lee Lewis, Fats Domino, Little Richard, Ray Charles, Bill Haley and the Comets, Fabian, Bobby Darin, Frankie Avalon: they all gave us the life/beat and set us free.
Elvis told us to *let go!*
let go!
let go!
let go!
let go!
let go!
let go!
let go!
let go!
let go!
let go!
let go!
let go!

Affluent culture, by producing a car and car radio for every middle-class home, gave Elvis a base for recruiting.

While a car radio in the front seat rocked with "Turn Me Loose," young kids in the back seat were breaking loose. Many a night was spent on dark and lonely roads, balling to hard rock beat.

The back seat produced the sexual revolution, and the car radio was the medium for subversion.

Desperate parents used permission to drive the car as a power play in the home: "If you don't obey, you can't have the car Saturday night."

It was a cruel weapon, attacking our gonads and our means of getting together.

The back seat became the first battleground in the war between the generations.

Rock 'n' roll marked the beginning of the revolution.

THE MIDDLE OF THE BEAST

Che stood before us in the Ministry of Labor auditorium. He was shorter than we expected, about 5 feet 10 inches tall. He wore an olive-green military uniform with a revolver at his hip. He embraced us with his intensity and joy.

We were 84 Amerikan students visiting Cuba illegally in 1964. We had to travel 14,000 miles, via Czechoslovakia, to reach Cuba, 90 miles off the Florida coast.

As Che rapped on for four hours, we fantasized taking up rifles. Growing beards. Going into the hills as guerrillas. Joining Che to create revolutions throughout Latin America. None of us looked forward to returning home to the political bullshit in the United States.

Then Che jolted us out of our dream of the Sierra Madre. He said to us:

You North Amerikans are very lucky. You live in the middle of the beast.
You are fighting the most important fight of all, in the center of the battle.
If I had my wish, I would go back with you to North Amerika to fight there.

I envy you.

* * *

EVERY REVOLUTIONARY NEEDS A COLOR TV

Walter Cronkite is SDS's best organizer. Uncle Walter brings out the map of the U.S. with circles around the campuses that blew up today. The battle reports.

Every kid out there is thinking, "Wow! I wanna see *my* campus on that map!"

Television proves the domino theory: one campus falls and they all fall.

The first "student demonstration" flashed across the TV tubes of the nation as a myth in 1964. That year the first generation being raised from birth on TV was 9, 10 and 11 years old. "First chance I get," they thought, "I wanna do that too."

The first chance they got was when they got to junior high and high school five years later—1969! And that was the year America's junior high and high schools exploded! A government survey shows that three out of every five high schools in the country had "some form of active protest" in 1969.

TV is raising generations of kids who want to grow up and become demonstrators.

Have you ever seen a boring demonstration on TV? Just being on TV makes it exciting. Even picket lines look breathtaking. Television creates myths bigger than reality.

Demonstrations last hours, and most of that time nothing happens. After the demonstration we rush home for the six o'clock news. The drama review. TV packs all the action into two minutes—a commercial for the revolution.

The mere idea of a "story" is revolutionary because a "story" implies disruption of normal life. Every reporter is a dramatist, creating a theater out of life.

Crime in the streets is news; law and order is not. A revolution is news; the status quo ain't.

The media does not *report* "news," it creates it. An event *happens* when it goes on TV and becomes myth.

The media is not "neutral." The presence of a camera transforms a demonstration, turning us into heroes. We take more chances when the press is there because we know whatever happens will be known to the entire world within hours.

Television keeps us escalating our tactics; a tactic becomes ineffective when it stops generating gossip or interest—"news."

Politicians get air time just by issuing statements. Rockefeller doesn't have to carry a picket sign to make a point. But ordinary people must take to the streets to get on television. One person, doing the right thing at the right time, can create a myth. The disruption of Nixon's speech reduces Nixon to background.

TV time goes to those with the most guts and imagination.

I never understand the radical who comes on TV in a suit and tie. Turn off the sound and he could be the mayor!

The *words* may be radical, but television is a non-verbal instrument! The way to understand TV is to shut off the sound. No one remembers any words they hear; the mind is a technicolor movie of images, not words.

I've never seen "bad" coverage of a demonstration. It makes no difference what they *say* about us. The pictures are the story.

Our power lies in our ability to strike fear in the enemy's heart: so the more the media exaggerate, the better. When the media start saying nice things about us, we should get worried.

If the yippies controlled national TV, we could make the Viet Kong and the Black Panthers the heroes of swooning Amerikan middle-aged housewives everywhere within a week.

The movement is too puritanical about the use of the media. After all, Karl Marx never watched television!

You can't be a revolutionary today without a television set—it's as important as a gun!

Every guerrilla must know how to use the terrain of the culture that he is trying to destroy!

* * *

REVOLUTION IS THEATER-IN-THE-STREETS

You are the stage.
You are the actor.
Everything is for real.
There is no audience.

The goal is to turn on everybody who can be turned on and turn off everybody else.

Theater has no rules, forms, structure, standards, traditions—it is pure, natural energy, impulse, anarchy.

The job of the revolution is to smash stage sets, start fires in movie theaters and then scream, "Fire!"

The theatrical geniuses of today are creating the drama of Vietnam in occupied school administration buildings across Amerika.

The Living Theater, a far-out guerrilla theater group, came to Berkeley while people were fighting the National Guard in the streets. As pacifists they opposed the street action.

Living Theater eliminated the stage and joined the audience. Revolutionary theater.

"I am not allowed to smoke marijuana," one Living Theater member sobbed. He was offered five joints.

Another cried, "I can't take off my clothes!" Around him people stripped naked.

At the end of the performance, everyone left to take the revolution to the streets. The cast stopped at the front door.

Revolution-in-the-auditorium is a contradiction. We get pissed when our revolutionary energy is wasted with a play that is defined by walls and exit doors, by starting and ending times, by ticket prices.

The only role of theater is to take people out of the auditorium and into the streets. The role of the revolutionary theater group is to make the revolution.

* * *

BURN DOWN THE SCHOOLS

A sunny day on the Berkeley campus. Students are carrying ten pounds of books from one class to the next.

We nonstudent fuck-ups say, "Excuse me, student. Did you know the sun is shining?"

They look at us like we're crazy.

We invade libraries yelling, "The sun is shining! The sun is shining!"

We go into a psychology class on "Thinking," a huge lecture hall with 300 students. The professor is up front, diagraming behavior on the blackboard. Everybody writes down in their notebook every word he spews.

His first words are, "Good morning, class."

The guy next to me copies down, "Good morning, class."

Somebody raises his hand and asks: "Do we have to know that for the exam?"

The classroom is an authoritarian environment. Teacher up front and rows of students one after another. Do not lose your temper, fuck, kiss, hug, get emotional or take off your clothes.

The class struggle begins in class.

We roll a few joints and start smoking in the middle of the classroom. The smell is overpowering, but no one seems to notice it.

The Viet Kong could attack with mortar shells, and everybody would still be taking notes.

It's an assembly line.

The professor talks; students copy.

Everyone is 99 percent asleep.

Marvin Garson takes off his shirt and begins tongue-kissing with his chick Charlie. I rip off my shirt and start soul-kissing with Nancy.

There we are in the middle of the class, shirts off, kissing, feeling each other up and smoking pot.

Everyone gets itchy and nervous because of us. No one can take notes anymore. The professor stutters. Pens stop. People squirm. Everyone's looking at us—no one at the professor. But the students are too repressed and shy to say anything.

Finally a girl in the middle of the room can't stand it any more. "Could these people please stop making a disturbance?" she pants.

Nancy leaps to her feet: "This is a class on thinking! We're thinking! You can't separate thinking from kissing, feeling, touching.

"We're the laboratory part of the class. Anybody who wants to come, join us. Anybody who wants to listen to the lecture part of the class move to the other part of the room."

The professor then reveals his soul. "In *my* class," he says with authority, "*I* do the teaching."

Scratch a professor and find a pig.

(His assistant goes to get the uniformed pig, so we split.)

TWO HUNDRED PSYCHOLOGICAL TERRORISTS COULD DESTROY ANY MAJOR UNIVERSITY—WITHOUT FIRING A SHOT.

Schools—high schools and colleges—are the biggest obstacle to education in Amerika today.

Schools are a continuation of toilet training.

Taking an exam is like taking a shit. You hold it in for weeks, memorizing, just waiting for the right time. Then the time comes, and you sit on the toilet.

Ah!

Um!

It feels so good.

You shit it right back on schedule—for the grade. When exams are over, you got a load off your mind. You got rid of all of the shit you clogged your poor brain with. You can finally relax.

The paper you write your exam on is toilet paper.

Babies are zen masters, curious about everything.

Adults are serious and bored.

What happened?

Brain surgery by the schools.

I lost my interest in books in literature class. I lost my interest in foreign languages in language class. I lost my interest in biology in biology class.

Dig the environment of a university! The buildings look like factories, airports, army barracks, IBM cards in the air, hospitals, jails. They are designed to wipe out all individuality, dull one's senses, make you feel small.

Everyone should bring dayglow paint to campus and psychedelicize the buildings as the first act of liberation.

"Critical" or "abstract thinking" is a trap in school.

Criticize, criticize, criticize.

Look at both sides of the argument, take no action, take no stands, commit yourself to nothing, because you're always looking for more arguments, more information, always examining, criticizing.

Abstract thinking turns the mind into a prison. Abstract thinking is the way professors avoid facing their own social impotence.

Our generation is in rebellion against abstract intellectualism and critical thinking.

We admire the Viet Kong guerrilla, the Black Panther, the stoned hippie, not the abstract intellectual vegetable.

Professors are put-ons, writing and talking in fancy, scientific, big motherfucking words, so the people on the street won't dig that they're not saying shit.

They're so thankful for their "intellectual freedom in Amerika" that they're not going to waste it fighting on issues like poverty, war, drugs, and revolution. They insist upon the freedom to be irrelevant.

We judge our teachers as men first and teachers second. How can you teach us about World War I if you weren't in the streets of Czechago?

The goal of the revolution is to eliminate all intellectuals, create a society in which there is no distinction between intellectual and physical work: a society without intellectuals. Our task is to destroy the university and make the entire nation a school with on-the-job living.

School addicts people to the heroin of middle-class life: busy work for grades (money) stored in your records (banks) for the future (death). We become replaceable parts for corporate Amerika!

School offers us cheap victories—grades, degrees—in exchange for our souls: We're actually supposed to be happy when we get a better grade than somebody else! We're taught to compete and to get our happiness from the *un*happiness of others.

For us education is the creation of a free society. Anyone who wants to teach should be allowed to "teach." Anybody who wants to learn should be allowed to "learn." There is no difference between teachers and students, because we teach and learn from each other.

The professors and the students are the dropouts—people who have dropped out of Life. The dropouts from school are people who have dropped into Living. Our generation is making history in the streets, so why waste our lives in plastic classrooms?

High school students are the largest oppressed minority in Amerika. We know what *freedom is* when we hear the bell dismissing school. *"School's out, I'm free at last!"*

Teachers know that unless they control our toilet training, we'd never stay in class. You gotta raise your hand to get permission to go take a shit. The bathrooms are the only liberated areas in school.

DROP OUT!

Why stay in school? To get a degree? *Print your own!* Can you smoke a diploma?

We are going to invade the schools and free our brothers who are prisoners. We will burn the buildings and the books. We will throw pies in the faces of our professors.

We will give brooms and pails to the administrators so they can be useful and sweep the place up. Fuck bureaucrats, especially the "nice" Deans of Men who put one hand around our shoulders while the other hand gropes for our pants. We'll take all the records, grades, administrative shit and flush it down the toilet.

The same people who control the universities own the major capitalist corporations, carry out the wars, fuck over black people, run the police forces and eat money and flesh for breakfast. They are absentee dictators who make rules but don't live under them.

Universities are feudal autocracies.

Professors are house niggers and students are field niggers.

Demonstrations on campuses aren't "demonstrations"—they're jail breaks. Slave revolts.

The war on the campuses is similar to the war in Vietnam: a guerrilla people's war.

By closing down 100 universities in one day, we, the peasants, can level the most powerful blow possible against the pigs who run Amerikan society.

We'll force the President of the United States to come on his hands and knees to the conference table.

We're using the campus as a launching pad to foment revolution everywhere.

Ronnie Reagan, baby, you're right!

449

Been Down So Long
It Looks Like Up to Me

Konstantin Berlandt

I stood on the street corner tired from the long drive to El Paso. A man backed his white car up to me.

"I'm too tired to trick tonight," I said through the open window on my side of his car, "but could you tell me where the gay bars are?"

I'm in El Paso to run some gay liberation workshops and a homosexual happening at the National Students Association convention.

The gay bars were four blocks from the convention hotels. Dancing is allowed. I dance with my brothers.

I'm at a radical party. I ask no one to dance. Everyone is playing straight. In mixed company straights have always been in command.

The drama of the happening's first act was to get you over your fear of dancing with another boy or another girl someone else of your sex, even in mixed company.

The tape of rock 'n' roll continued into a second act of dancing and making it: "You Turn Me On," "Light My Fire," "Your Love Takes Me Higher and Higher," a Mitch Ryder/James Brown spliced together orgasm ("Sock It to Me" entry; "Wow, I Feel Good, I Got You" delivery and waking up in the morning to recall that "Double Shot of My Baby's Love."

And Act III began with the refrain "Everybody Loves a Lover" bopping along with the Shirelles, and then the ensuing guilt and hiding

Konstantin Berlandt. "Been Down So Long It Looks Like Up to Me, *The Berkeley Tribe*, September 12–18, 1969, p. 5.

attached to an oppressed homosexual identity. "Meeting in Smoky Places, hiding in shadowy corners, dancing where no one knows our faces, sharing love stolen in the night in Smoky Places."

Now seeing the lies that put you there:

The Purpose of a Man is to love a woman
The purpose of a woman is to love a man
... Come on Baby let's play the game of love.

Now realizing that you have always listened to the radio from a narrow heterosexual perspective, now recognizing the parallels between your struggle and other freedom struggles, now moving with the same self-love:

We're a winner
And never let anybody say,
"Ah, you can't make it, cause the people's
    minds are in your way."
No more tears do we cry, and we have finally
    dried our eyes,
And we're moving on up.

That's the message that came across in posters that advertised the happening and homosexual freedom workshops and were torn off the walls. "Gay is good," "Homosexuality is Healthy," "Conquer your fear, get on that motorcycle."

That's the message that came across in the private conversations I had with homosexual delegates at the convention.

That's the message that came across from the free people who came to the workshops.

That's the message that came across from the 50 homosexuals from the community and the convention who came to the happening.

"I saw one man with his arm around another's leg and I freaked," said a woman delegate, pretty radical in other areas.

It came across in the homosexual freedom resolution.

The Resolution:

The United States National Student Association, opposing racism in any form and supporting the struggles of oppressed people against that racism, affirms its support of the Homosexual Liberation Movement. NSA will not discriminate on the basis of sexual orientation in their hiring practices, programs, social activities or public statements, and will urge student governments and other organizations to adopt this same policy.

We recognize this policy is only the beginning of seeing the widespread discrimination against homosexuals on the campuses and in the country. This discrimination goes deep into the minds of homosexuals themselves, moving in fear, suppressing any displays of their sexuality and affection in public or even with their family, closest friends and potential lovers.

But self-hate is only half the problem. We recognize too the dangerous anti-social manifestations of anti-homosexuality (and lack of self-acceptance) in various forms of projected hate—in the violent policeman swinging his club, in the racist and male chauvinist, in pigs of all kinds.

Freedom for Homosexuals and Homosexual Freedom for Everyone.

But the oppression came across in the general public silence of gay convention delegates.

No one signed. People weren't interested, people were more concerned about other things, people were afraid to put their names down on a blank sheet of paper supporting homosexuals.

NSA wouldn't pay my expenses for coming down to El Paso, staying and going back. They were very low on money and didn't think homosexual liberation was important enough.

"I feel like a black man asking a white board to say I'm important."

But one officer, in pity, gave me his own meal tickets (he didn't like the food) and said, "I'll get you a bed to sleep in. I don't want you to have to sleep on the floor." The bed turns out to be his own bed. "I'm gay too," he tells me in his room.

He makes me, and I feel exploited. I deserve my own bed, my own room, my own meal tickets, my plane fare and expenses. If gay liberation were strong as black liberation they would find the money. He tells me it may cast aspersions on him if anyone finds out I'm in his room, so please don't tell anyone.

"You're the first homosexual I've ever met," says a dark-haired girl, delegate from El Paso.

"I'm the first person you ever met who told you he was a homosexual," I say.

"I want to kiss you," I tell an attractive friend in the Plaza Hotel lobby.

His answer, "I'm concerned that some of the things you are doing are for political rather than personal reasons. And I'm concerned about my own effectiveness here. And there's a time and a place for everything."

We went up to his room. He turned out the lights and we went to bed together.

I put my hand on his back. It became very heavy there, like a big weight, getting heavier and heavier, going to push right through him, feeling very uncomfortable and uptight. I was the pervert trying to make a straight, normal man. Can I do it delicately without freaking him, without turning him off?

What the fuck are you in bed together for? What do you think he is afraid of? What do you think you're going to do?

What do you want to do?

Rubbing your shoulders, rubbing your neck, sliding my hand down your arm, tracing your ear and jaw, moving through your hair, sweeping my hand down your back—like rolling down a hill, a smooth and natural pace down your smooth back. What I am doing is a loving thing, is loving, is love. There is no pervert in bed with us. He is out there trying to tell us we are.

We had breakfast in the delegate cafeteria, I sat at his table and we talked for the people around us as if we'd never touched.

Another conversation in the cafeteria alone with a delegate from the East. He hadn't come to the workshops, or happening.

"I'm content with the arrangement I've worked out, being gay and not telling any of my friends." He tells me about a job interview to be an investigator for the government. "What if you had to reveal someone was homosexual?" they asked him. "And all the time I was answering I was wondering what would happen if they found out I was a homosexual."

I talk about the now automatic suppression he probably practiced on himself, so automatic that he may be almost ignoring his oppression. "In conversation you'll automatically switch the gender of your boyfriend, you'll suppress any gay thoughts and just bullshit along with what other people want to talk about." And as we talked, a friend of his came up, set down her purse and went to get some tea.

"This is where the conversation ends," he says. "That's the rules of the game."

"That's our oppression," I say.

I talked to a politico from the East who keeps his homosexuality secret because he wants to teach children. I talked to a boy from the West who rubbed up against me when no one was looking, but he wouldn't come to the sessions and joined in choked laughter with his friends when I said I was doing gay liberation work.

I talked with a boy from a commune who thinks his friends probably know he is bisexual but would feel uptight being homosexual around them.

I have always been uptight about being homosexual around anyone who might be straight, but now I do it, often with angry determination. And I always feel strong afterwards.

Conclusion, Closet homosexuals are keeping themselves in chains. They can't get on their own picket line, sign their own resolution, attend their own freedom workshops. They laugh defensively when their rights are brought up.

Straight people don't care about you. They don't feel your oppression. They can give you only pity and wish you could be cured as they hear you cry from your anonymous knees.

"Too bad these faggots are the way they are."

And you can only say, "Yes, it is too bad." (So bad I can't tell you, can't whisper this darkest truth about myself; I like you. I want to kiss you. I want to have sex with you, make love to you.)

But watch,

"No, it's not too bad. I like being gay."

Watch the liberal's quick slide over rejection, "Yes, but you're not a swishy fag."

"But you're not a motorcycle cop. All heterosexuals except the ones I know are motorcycle cops, and even some of the straights I know have tendencies in that direction. Occasionally I notice their strong wrists ready to wield a club, the way their words are sometimes gruff and insensitive, the way they let their paunches stick out and still think they're irresistible, the way they brag about the chicks they made like the heads they beat in. They think they are some sort of master race. I go into the Tenderloin in San Francisco and see drunken heterosexuals falling all over each other, shouting at passing cars, being really flagrant.

"Queens are an exciting aspect of the homosexual scene, and they have been the strongest people in it, the only faggots strong enough to say, 'Fuck you; I don't care what you think,' to the straight and disapproving world."

"And there is swishy fag—camp and fuck—in all of us. The club-swinging motorcycle cop is hating that part of himself, trying to maintain it doesn't exist. WHAP! WHAP! WHAP! Faggot!"

Sock it to me with your cock. We'll both feel better.

And to hell with liberal positions like Jayne Graves', radical in educational reform, who ran totalitarian classroom exercises at the convention, who said she didn't mind bisexuality but didn't like homosexuals because they cut themselves off.

You can't very well sleep with another guy without being homosexual at the time. But you tell me you'll tolerate that as long as I hurry up and sleep with a girl soon. You're still telling me, "You've got to sleep with women." I'll do what I want to do. Nothing I have to do is enjoyable till I make it what I want to do.

Ten minutes of trying to hitch back to California from an El Paso freeway on ramp when a Texas State trooper pulled up and asked me to get out of the sun into his car.

He asked me questions: where was I going? where was I coming from? what had I been doing in El Paso? "Running homosexual liberation workshops at NSA." He wrote down "SDS" not "NSA."

I was cooperative because I thought hitching might be illegal in Texas.

Then, conversationally, I asked, "What are you writing this up for?" "It's for the central crime investigation computer," he said.

Now whenever they ask for a report on me they'll read I ran homosexual liberation workshops at NSA in August 1969. My computer identity is punched homosexual.

But I'm not worried any more about their finding out. And I won't be worried much more about your finding out. I'm movin' on up.

And everybody knows it too
We just keep on pushin'
We're a winner.

Radical Psychiatry and Community Organizing

Joy Marcus

For some time now, radicals in the mental health field have been using their skills to provide "movement people" with direct services. Also, at least in Berkeley, we've been teaching others—mostly non-professionals—how to provide psychiatric help to each other and our allies. These services are increasingly being provided through "counter institutions"—rap centers, psychiatric emergency centers, free clinics, and so forth.

However, while our counter-institutions are important and must be nurtured, I do not see that they alone will insure the kind of thoroughgoing change needed for the health of this country. Nor is it economically possible or even necessarily attractive for most people to "drop out." In order to build the massive base which will be the ultimate guarantee of radical change in our society many people will have to create countermovements within establishment institutions and agencies to gain control over them, thus taking power over the working conditions of their chosen occupation, which is one of the most basic needs of human life. The transcript of our discussion at the Free University shows how we tackled some of the many problems of self-determination and community control posed by establishment institutions—in this case, Contra Costa County Hospital in Martinez, California.

Joy Marcus, "Radical Psychiatry and Community Organizing," in Claude Steiner et al., *Readings in Radical Psychiatry*, New York: Grove Press, 1975, pp. 123–25, 141. Reprinted with permission of the author.

For example: a therapist whom everyone in the day-care program valued greatly had been told he would be fired because he hadn't met a certain civil service requirement. The requirement had to do with a technicality about credentials. Some of the patients brought up the subject in a community meeting; the possibility of losing one of the most effective and loved workers in the program made many people feel unhappy and helpless. Then one of us said, "Wait a sec. Maybe we don't have to take this flat on our backs." This bit of dynamite produced an avalanche of talk and determination in the patients to "take care of business." More community meetings were held, during which the politics of the situation, as well as people's experiences in it, were discussed.

These meetings encouraged a group of five or six patients plus a few staff people to make an intense argument at the civil service commission hearing. Most of the commission members were astonished to hear the community assert its right to keep the therapist on the staff. But they listened and we won.

If it's possible to separate the two notions, we won in political terms and also in therapeutic terms. Politically, what we won—and "we" means the patient-staff coalition—was not controlling power over the institution but a certain amount of influence, a veto power that would make it possible for us to determine the people we would work with. The therapeutic results were that the patients gained a heightened awareness of some of the forces that oppress them and valuable experience in working cooperatively to change an oppressive condition. Not only were they learning about external oppressive conditions, such as the ancient and totally useless civil service system, but in order to be effective at the civil service hearing these patients—who up until then had had precious little sense of their own potency—also had to fight against their internalized oppression (their images of themselves as crazy, impotent, invisible, unworthy). If acquiring the skills and strength to control the internal oppressor isn't a measure of growth or psychiatric success, I don't know what is.

It was an opening. We don't yet have a particularly clear image of what "the complete take-over" of a hospital will look like. I only know that if one must work in an establishment institution, doing it with allies—with people who share the same visions—to gain power and control over our own lives is a more satisfying, more integrative experience than the one we've been taught to expect and accept.

* * *

SUMMARY

- Radial psychiatry and community organizing are interchangeable in their practice.

- The basic theories and techniques of radical psychiatry can be transferred to broader political arenas than therapy groups.

- Just as in effective psychiatry, effective political action requires that people feel permission to: (1) define problems—see, think, feel; (2) be angry; (3) fight back; (4) have vision, use imagination, have fun; (5) work cooperatively; (6) organize; and (7) follow-through.

- Being engaged in a community organizing process is therapeutic for people; in order to take political power we need to rid ourselves of internalized oppression; while being engaged in the process of taking power, we feel more alive and are able to experience ourselves as intelligent and powerful, thus ridding ourselves of old "tapes" about being "crazy," "stupid," "worthless," "weak," "incompetent."

- Effective political action is a good indicator of psychiatric success.

- The most pleasurable kind of organizing occurs when people act in behalf of their own liberation, rather than entering a situation from a markedly one-up (and guilty) position to "Rescue" an oppressed class.

6   THE WOMEN'S REBELLION

Valerie Solanis became a cause célèbre in June of 1968 after she shot and wounded her employer, artist and film director Andy Warhol. This well-publicized "media event" was a dramatic introduction for many to the issue of women's liberation. S.C.U.M. stands for "The Society for Cutting Up Men." Solanis's current whereabouts are unknown.

Anne Koedt's first persentation of "The Myth of the Vaginal Orgasm" appeared in the original issue of Notes from the First Year, published in June 1968 by New York Radical Women. The "first year" refers to the opening phase of the women's liberation movement. This highly influential article prompted many new left women to reconsider the physiological basis of their sexual pleasure and the worth of their heterosexual relationships.

Kate Millett's "Sexual Politics: A Manifesto for Revolution" was written at Barnard/Columbia University in the rebellious atmosphere that was created by the 1968 student strike. Her piece was authored in conjunction with the founding of the university's first women's liberation group. The phrase "sexual politics," used in the document reprinted here, would become the title of Millett'e best-selling book and be commonly used by feminists of the 1970s to analyze women's cultural oppression.

Birth Control Pills and Black Children: The Sisters Reply was one of the few collectively authored feminist documents written in the late 1960s by Third World women. It was a protest against a point of view prevalent in the black nationalist movement that, due to the threat of genocide against black people, women's primary role in the revolution was to bear children.

Former New York National Organization for Women Chapter President Ti-Grace Atkinson's "Declaration of War" was authored in April 1969. The piece was written in a then-popular militaristic tone and laid down the gauntlet of feminist anger. It is fully representative of the sharp division between the sexes that was emerging in some quarters of the radical movement.

Shulamith Firestone's Dialectic of Sex was one of the most influential radical feminist writings of 1970. A former new left activist, Firestone appropriated the dialectical method to portray all women as an oppressed "sex-class." Frances Beale's article "Double Jeopardy: To Be Black and Female" was a formative study of black women's social status. The phrase "double jeopardy" would become, in the 1970s, the term most frequently used to describe the condition of Third World women.

Robin Morgan's "Goodbye to All That," published in January 1970, reflects a growing rebellion against the new left's misogyny. A timely and provocative piece, it appeared at a time when the majority of heterosexual Movement relationships were ending in bitterness. "To a White Male Radical" by "a Berkeley Sister" was published in The Berkeley Barb in May 1970.

The article is typical of radical women's disillusionment with Movement men. Many countercultural women, however, rejected the drastic conclusions drawn by those feminists who had participated in new left political organizations. Genie Plamondon, a leader of the countercultural White Panther Party in Ann Arbor. Michigan, wrote "Hello to All That" in response to Morgan's declaration.

Karen Durkin's "Alphabet Soup," which described the various women's liberation activities that blossomed in 1970, was published in WIN, a revolutionary pacifist magazine. Like the new left from which it emerged, the early women's liberation movement was extremely pluralistic.

The S.C.U.M. Manifesto

Valerie Solanis

...[T]he male is...obsessed with screwing; he'll swim a river of snot, wade nostril-deep through a mile of vomit, if he thinks there'll be a friendly pussy awaiting him. He'll screw a woman he despises, any snaggle-toothed hag, and, further, pay for the opportunity. Why? Relieving physical tension isn't the answer, as masturbation suffices for that. It's not ego satisfaction; that doesn't explain screwing corpses and babies.... He hates his passivity, so he projects it onto women, defines the male as active, then sets out to prove that he is ("prove he's a Man"). His main means of attempting to prove it is screwing (Big Man with a Big Dick tearing off a Big Piece). Since he's attempting to prove an error, he must "prove" it again and again.... The male claims that females find fulfillment through motherhood and sexuality reflects what males think THEY'D find fulfilling if they were female. Women, in other words, don't have penis envy; men have pussy envy. When the male accepts his passivity, defines himself as a woman...and becomes a transvestite he loses his desire to screw (or to do anything else, for that matter; he fulfills himself as a dragqueen) and gets his cock chopped off. Screwing is, for a man, a defense against his desire to be female.... The male, because of his obsession to compensate for not being female combined with his inability to relate and feel compassion, has made of the world a shitpile...many females would, even assuming complete economic equality between the sexes, prefer residing with males or peddling their asses on the street, thereby having most of their time for themselves, to

Excerpts from Valerie Solanis, "S.C.U.M. Manifesto," *The Berkeley Barb*, June 7–13, 1968, p. 4.

spending many hours of their days doing boring, stultifying, non-creative work for somebody else, functioning...as machines, or at best—if able to get a "good" job—co-managing the shitpile. What will liberate women, therefore, from male control is the total elimination of the money-work system, not the attainment of economic equality with men within it.... The effect of fatherhood on males, specifically, is to make them "Men," that is, highly defensive of all impulses to passivity, faggotry and of desire to be female. Every boy wants to imitate his mother, be her, fuse with her, but Daddy forbids this; HE is the mother; HE gets to fuse with her. So he tells the boy, sometimes directly, sometimes indirectly, to not be a sissy, to act like a "Man." The boy, scared shitless of and "respecting" his father, complies and becomes just like Daddy, that model of "Man"-hood, the all-American ideal—the well-behaved heterosexual dullard.... Wanting to become a woman, he strives to be constantly around females, the closest he can get to becoming one, so he created a "society" based on the family—a male-female couple and their kids (the excuse for the family's existence).... A true community consists of individuals...not couples—respecting each other's individuality and privacy while at the same time interacting with each other mentally and emotionally—free spirits in free relation to each other—and cooperating with each other to achieve a common end, because each man's end is all the pussy for himself.... The male can't progress socially, but merely swings back and forth from isolation to gangbanging.... Wanting the female (Mama) to guide him, but unable to accept this fact (He is, after all, a MAN), wanting to play Woman, to usurp her function as Guider and Protector, he sees to it that all authorities are male.... There's no reason why a society...should have a government, laws or leaders.... The male's inability to relate to anybody or anything makes his life pointless and meaningless (The ultimate male insight is that life is absurd), so he invented philosophy and religion. Being empty, he looks outward, not only for guidance and control, but for salvation and for the meaning of life. Happiness impossible on this earth, he invented Heaven.... A woman not only takes her identity and individuality for granted, but knows instinctively that the only wrong is to hurt others and the meaning of life is love.... No genuine social revolution can be accomplished by the male, as the male on top wants the status quo, and all the male on the bottom wants is to be the male on top.... The male changes only when forced to do so by technology, when he has no choice, when "society" reaches the stage when he must change or die. We're at that stage now; if women don't fast get their asses in gear, we may very well all die.... The male, being completely self-centered and unable to relate to anything outside himself, his "conversation" is a strained, compulsive attempt to impress the female...only completely self-confident, arrogant, outgoing, proud, tough-minded females are capable of intense, bitchy, witty conversation.... Having stripped the world of conversation, friendship and love, the male offers us as paltry substitutes—"Great Art" and "Culture"... The true artist is every self-confident, healthy female, and in a female society the only Art, the only Culture, will be conceited, kookie, funkie females grooving on each other and on everything else in the universe.... Sex is the refuge of the mindless. And the more mindless the woman, the more deeply embedded in the male "culture," in short, the nicer she is, the more sexual she is. The nicest women in our "society" are raving sex maniacs. But, being just awfully, awfully nice, they don't, of course, descend to fucking—that's uncouth but rather they make love, commune by means of their bodies and establish sensual rapport; the literary ones are attuned to the throb of Eros and attain a clutch of the Universe; the religious have spiritual communion with the Divine Sensualism; the mystics merge with the Erotic Principle and blend with the cosmos and the acid heads contact their erotic cells. On the other hand, those females least embedded in the male "culture," in short, the least nice, those crass and simple souls who reduce fucking to fucking, who are too childish for the grown-up world of suburbs, mortgages, mops and baby shit, too selfish to raise kids and husbands, too uncivilized to give one shit for anyone's opinion of them other than their own, too arrogant to respect Daddy, the "Greats" or the deep wisdom of the Ancients, who trust only their own animal, gutter instincts, who equate Culture with chicks, whose sole diversion is prowling for emotional thrills and excitement, who are given to disgusting, nasty, upsetting "scenes," hateful, violent bitches given to slamming those who unduly irritate them in the teeth, who'd sink a shiv into a man's chest or ram an icepick up his asshole as soon as look at him, if they knew they could get away with it, in short, those who, by the standards of our "culture," are SCUM...these females are cool and...skirting asexuality. Unhampered by propriety, niceness, discretion, public opinion, "morals," the "respect" of assholes, always funky, dirty, low-down, SCUM gets around...and around and around...they've seen the whole show—every bit of it—the fucking scene, the sucking scene, the dick scene, the dyke scene—they've covered the whole waterfront, been under every dock and pier—the peter pier, the pussy pier.... You've got to go through a lot of sex to get to anti-sex, and SCUM's been through it all, and now they're ready for a new show; they want to crawl out from under the dock, move, take off, sink out. But SCUM doesn't yet prevail; SCUM's still in the gutter of our "society," which if it's not deflected from its present course and if the Bomb doesn't drop on it, will hump itself to death.... The male's chief delight—in so far as the tense, grim male can ever be said to delight in anything—is exposing others. It doesn't matter much what they're exposed as, as long as they're exposed; it distracts attention from himself. Exposing others as enemy agents (Communists and Socialists) is one of his favorite exposés, as it removes the source of the threat to him, not only from himself, but from the country and even further yet, from the Western world. The bugs up his ass aren't in him; they're in Russia....

The Myth of the Vaginal Orgasm

Anne Koedt

Whenever female orgasm and frigidity is discussed, a false distinction is made between the vaginal and clitoral orgasm. Frigidity has generally been defined by men as the failure of women to have vaginal orgasms. Actually the vagina is not a highly sensitive area and is not constructed to achieve orgasm. It is the clitoris which is the center of sexual sensitivity and which is the female equivalent of the penis.

I think this explains a great many things: First of all, the fact that the so-called frigidity rate among women is phenomenally high. Rather than tracing female frigidity to the false assumptions about female anatomy, our "experts" have declared frigidity a psychological problem of women. Those women who complained about it were recommended psychiatrists, so that they might discover their "problem"—diagnosed generally as a failure to adjust to their role as women.

The facts of female anatomy and sexual response tell a different story. There is only one area for sexual climax, although there are many areas for sexual arousal; that area is the clitoris. All orgasms are extensions of sensation from this area. Since the clitoris is not necessarily stimulated sufficiently in the conventional sexual positions, we are left "frigid."

Aside from physical stimulation, which is the common cause of orgasm for most people, there is also stimulation through primarily mental processes. Some women, for example, may achieve orgasm through sexual fantasies, or through fetishes. However, while the stimulation may be psychological, the orgasm manifests itself physically. Thus, while the cause is psychological, the *effect* is still physical, and the orgasm necessarily takes place in the sexual organ equipped for sexual climax—the clitoris. The orgasm experience may also differ in degree of intensity—some more localized, and some more diffuse and sensitive. But they are all clitoral orgasms.

All this leads to some interesting questions about conventional sex and our role in it. Men achieve orgasms essentially by friction with the vagina, not the clitoral area, which is external and not able to cause friction the way penetration does. Women have thus been defined sexually in terms of what pleases men; our own biology has not been properly analyzed. Instead, we are fed the myth of the liberated woman and her vaginal orgasm—an orgasm which in fact does not exist.

What we must do is redefine our sexuality. We must discard the "normal" concepts of sex and create new guidelines which take into account mutual sexual enjoyment. While the idea of mutual enjoyment is liberally applauded in marriage manuals, it is not followed to its logical conclusion. We must begin to demand that if certain sexual positions now defined as "standard" are not mutually conducive to orgasm, they no longer be defined as standard. New techniques must be used or devised which transform this particular aspect of our current sexual exploitation.

FREUD—A FATHER OF THE VAGINAL ORGASM

Freud contended that the clitoral orgasm was adolescent, and that upon puberty, when women began having intercourse with men, women should transfer the center of orgasm to the vagina. The vagina, it was assumed, was able to produce a parallel, but more mature, orgasm than the clitoris. Much work was done to elaborate on this theory, but little was done to challenge the basic assumptions.

To fully appreciate this incredible invention, perhaps Freud's general attitude about women should first be recalled. Mary Ellman, in *Thinking About Women*, summed it up this way:

Everything in Freud's patronizing and fearful attitude toward women follows from their lack of a penis, but it is only in his essay *The Psychology of Women* that Freud makes explicit...the deprecations of women which are implicit in his work. He then prescribes for them the abandonment of the life of the mind, which will interfere with their sexual function. When the psychoanalyzed patient is male, the analyst sets himself the task of developing the man's capacities; but with women patients, the job is to resign them to the limits of their sexuality. As Mr. Rieff puts it: For Freud, "Analysis cannot encourage in women new energies for success and achievement, but only teach them the lesson of rational resignation."

It was Freud's feelings about women's secondary and inferior relationship to men that formed the basis for his theories on female sexuality.

Once having laid down the law about the nature of our sexuality, Freud not so strangely discovered a tremendous problem of frigidity in women. His recommended cure for a woman who was frigid was psychiatric care. She was suffering from failure to mentally adjust to her "natural" role as a woman. Frank S. Caprio, a contemporary follower of these ideas, states:

> ...whenever a woman is incapable of achieving an orgasm via coitus, provided her husband is an adequate partner, and prefers clitoral stimulation to any other form of sexual activity, she can be regarded as suffering from frigidity and requires psychiatric assistance. (*The Sexually Adequate Female*, p. 64.)

The explanation given was that women were envious of men— "renunciation of womanhood." Thus it was diagnosed as an anti-male phenomenon.

It is important to emphasize that Freud did not base his theory upon a study of woman's anatomy, but rather upon his assumptions of woman as an inferior appendage to man, and her consequent social and psychological role. In their attempts to deal with the ensuing problem of mass frigidity, Freudians created elaborate mental gymnastics. Marie Bonaparte, in *Female Sexuality*, goes so far as to suggest surgery to help women back on their rightful path. Having discovered a strange connection between the non-frigid woman and the location of the clitoris near the vagina,

> it then occurred to me that where, in certain women, this gap was excessive, and clitoridal fixation obdurate, a clitoridal-vaginal

reconciliation might be effected by surgical means, which would then benefit the normal erotic function. Professor Halban, of Vienna, as much a biologist as surgeon, became interested in the problem and worked out a simple operative technique. In this, the suspensory ligament of the clitoris was severed and the clitoris secured to the underlying structures, thus fixing it in a lower position, with eventual reduction of the labia minora. (p. 148.)

But the severest damage was not in the area of surgery, where Freudians ran around absurdly trying to change female anatomy to fit their basic assumptions. The worst damage was done to the mental health of women, who either suffered silently with self-blame, or flocked to the psychiatrists looking desperately for the hidden and terrible repression that kept from them their vaginal destiny.

LACK OF EVIDENCE?

One may perhaps at first claim that these are unknown and unexplored areas, but upon closer examination this is certainly not true today, not was it true even in the past. For example, men have known that women suffered from frigidity often during intercourse. So the problem was there. Also, there is much specific evidence. Men knew that the clitoris was and is the essential organ for masturbation, whether in children or adult women. So obviously women made it clear where *they* thought their sexuality was located. Men also seem suspiciously aware of the clitoral powers during "foreplay," when they want to arouse women and produce the necessary lubrication for penetration. Foreplay is a concept created for male purposes, but it works to the disadvantage of many women, since as soon as the woman is aroused the man changes to vaginal stimulation, leaving her both aroused and unsatisfied.

It has also been known that women need no anesthesia inside the vagina during surgery, thus pointing to the fact that the vagina is in fact not a highly sensitive area.

Today, with extensive knowledge of anatomy, with Kinsey, and Masters and Johnson, to mention just a few sources, there is no ignorance on the subject. There are, however, social reasons why this knowledge has not been popularized. We are living in a male society which has not sought change in women's role.

ANATOMICAL EVIDENCE

Rather than starting with what women *ought* to feel, it would seem logical to start out with the anatomical facts regarding the clitoris and vagina.

The Clitoris is a small equivalent of the penis, except for the fact that the urethra does not go through it as in the man's penis. Its erection is similar to the male erection, and the head of the clitoris has the same type of structure and function as the head of the penis. G. Lombard Kelly, in *Sexual Feeling in Married Men and Women*, says:

> The head of the clitoris is also composed of erectile tissue, and it possesses a very sensitive epithelium or surface covering, supplied with special nerve endings called genital corpuscles, which are peculiarly adapted for sensory stimulation that under proper mental conditions terminates in the sexual orgasm. No other part of the female generative tract has such corpuscles. (Pocketbooks; p. 35.)

The clitoris has no other function than that of sexual pleasure.

The Vagina—Its functions are related to the reproductive function. Principally, (1) menstruation, (2) receive penis, (3) hold semen, and (4) birth passage. The interior of the vagina, which according to the defenders of the vaginally caused orgasm is the center and producer of the orgasm, is:

> like nearly all other internal body structures, poorly supplied with end organs of touch. The internal entodermal origin of the lining of the vagina makes it similar in this respect to the rectum and other parts of the digestive tract. (Kinsey, *Sexual Behavior in the Human Female*, p. 580.)

The degree of insensitivity inside the vagina is so high that "Among the women who were tested in our gynecologic sample, less than 14% were at all conscious that they had been touched." (Kinsey, p. 580.)

Even the importance of the vagina as an *erotic* center (as opposed to an orgasmic center) has been found to be minor.

Other Areas—Labia minora and the vestibule of the vagina. These two sensitive areas may trigger off a clitoral orgasm. Because they can be effectively stimulated during "normal" coitus, though infrequent, this kind of stimulation is incorrectly thought to be vaginal orgasm. However, it is important to distinguish between areas which can stimulate the clitoris, incapable of producing the orgasm themselves, and the clitoris:

> Regardless of what means of excitation is used to bring the individual to the state of sexual climax, the sensation is perceived by the genital corpuscles and is localized where they are stimulated: in the head of the clitoris or penis. (Kelly, p. 49.)

Psychologically Stimulated Orgasm—Aside from the above mentioned direct and indirect stimulations of the clitoris, there is a third way an orgasm may be triggered. This is through mental (cortical) stimulation, where the imagination stimulates the brain, which in turn stimulates the genital corpuscles of the glans to set off an orgasm.

WOMEN WHO SAY THEY HAVE VAGINAL ORGASMS

Confusion—Because of the lack of knowledge of their own anatomy, some women accept the idea that an orgasm felt during "normal" intercourse was vaginally caused. This confusion is caused by a combination of two factors. One, failing to locate the center of the orgasm, and two, by a desire to fit her experience to the male-defined idea of sexual normalcy. Considering that women know little about their anatomy, it is easy to be confused.

Deception—The vast majority of women who pretend vaginal orgasm to their men are faking it to, as Ti-Grace Atkinson says, "get the job." In a new best-selling Danish book, *I Accuse* (my own translation), Mette Ejlersen specifically deals with this common problem, which she calls the "sex comedy." This comedy has many causes. First of all, the man brings a great deal of pressure to bear on the woman, because he considers his ability as a lover at stake. So as not to offend his ego, the woman will comply with the prescribed role and go through simulated ecstasy. In some of the other Danish women mentioned, women who were left frigid were turned off to sex, and pretended vaginal orgasm to hurry up the sex act. Others admitted that they had faked vaginal orgasm to catch a man. In one case, the woman pretended vaginal orgasm to get him to leave his first wife, who admitted being vaginally frigid. Later she was forced to continue the deception, since obviously she couldn't tell him to stimulate her clitorally.

Many more women were simply afraid to establish their right to equal enjoyment, seeing the sexual act as being primarily for the man's benefit, and any pleasure that the woman got as an added extra.

Other women, with just enough ego to reject the man's idea that they needed psychiatric care, refused to admit their frigidity. They wouldn't accept self-blame, but they didn't know how to solve the problem, not knowing the physiological facts about themselves. So they were left in a peculiar limbo.

Again, perhaps one of the most infuriating and damaging results of this whole charade has been that women who were perfectly healthy sexually were taught that they were not. So in addition to being sexually deprived, these women were told to blame themselves when they deserved no blame. Looking for a cure to a problem that has none can lead a woman on an endless path of self-hatred and insecurity. For she is told by her analyst that not even in her one role allowed in a male society—the role of a woman—is she successful. She is put on the defensive, with phony data as evidence that she better try to be even more feminine, think more feminine, and reject her envy of men. That is, shuffle even harder, baby.

WHY MEN MAINTAIN THE MYTH

1. *Sexual Penetration is Preferred*—The best stimulant for the penis is the woman's vagina. It supplies the necessary friction and lubrication. From a strictly technical point of view this position offers the best physical conditions, even though the man may try other positions for variation..

2. *The Invisible Woman*—One of the elements of male chauvinism is the refusal or inability to see women as total, separate human beings. Rather, men have chosen to define women only in terms of how they benefited men's lives. Sexually, a woman was not seen as an individual wanting to share equally in the sexual act, any more than she was seen as a person with independent desires when she did anything else in society. Thus, it was easy to make up what was convenient about women; for on top of that, society has been a function of male interests, and women were not organized to form even a vocal opposition to the male experts.

3. *The Penis as Epitome of Masculinity*—Men define their lives greatly in terms of masculinity. It is a *universal*, as opposed to racial, ego boosting, which is localized by the geography of racial mixtures.

The essence of male chauvinism is not the practical, economic services women supply. It is the psychological superiority. This kind of negative definition of self, rather than positive definition based upon one's own achievements and development, has of course chained the victim and the oppressor both. But by far the most brutalized of the two is the victim.

An analogy is racism, where the white racist compensates his feelings of unworthiness by creating an image of the black man (it is primarily a male struggle) as biologically inferior to him. Because of his power in a white male power structure, the white man can socially enforce this mythical division.

To the extent that men try to rationalize and justify male superiority through physical differentiation, masculinity may be symbolized by being the *most* muscular, the most hairy, the deepest voice, and the biggest penis. Women, on the other hand, are approved of (i.e., called feminine) if they are weak, petite, shave their legs, have high soft voices, and no penis.

Since the clitoris is almost identical to the penis, one finds a great deal of evidence of men in various societies trying to either ignore the clitoris and emphasize the vagina (as did Freud), or, as in some places in the Mideast, actually performing clitoridectomy. Freud saw this ancient and still practiced custom as a way of further "feminizing" the female by removing this cardinal vestige of her masculinity. It should be noted also that a big clitoris is considered ugly and masculine. Some cultures engage in the practice of pouring a chemical on the clitoris to make it shrivel up into proper size.

It seems clear to me that men in fact fear the clitoris as a threat to their masculinity.

4. *Sexually Expendable Male*—Men fear that they will become sexually expendable if the clitoris is substituted for the vagina as the center of pleasure for women. Actually this has a great deal of validity if one considers *only* the anatomy. The position of the penis inside the vagina, while perfect for reproduction, does not necessarily stimulate an orgasm in women because the clitoris is located externally and higher up. Women must rely upon indirect stimulation in the "normal" position.

Lesbian sexuality could make an excellent case, based upon anatomical data, for the extinction of the male organ. Albert Ellis says something to the effect that a man without a penis can make a woman an excellent lover.

Considering that the vagina is very desirable from a man's point of view, purely on physical grounds, one begins to see the dilemma for men. And it forces us as well to discard any "physical" arguments explaining why women go to bed with men. What is left, it seems to me, are primarily psychological reasons why women select men at the exclusion of women as sexual partners.

5. *Control of Women*—One reason given to explain the Mideastern practice of clitoridectomy is that it will keep the women from straying. By removing the sexual organ capable of orgasm, it must be assumed that her sexual drive will diminish. Considering how men look upon their women as property, particularly in very backward nations, we should begin to consider a great deal more why it is not in the men's interest to have women totally free sexually. The double standard, as practiced for example in Latin America, is set up to keep the woman as total property of the husband, while he is free to have affairs as he wishes.

6. *Lesbianism and Bisexuality*—Aside from the strictly anatomical reasons why women might equally seek other women as lovers, there is a fear on men's part that women will seek the company of other women on a full, human basis. The establishment of clitoral orgasm as fact would threaten the heterosexual *institution*. For it would indicate that sexual pleasure was obtainable from either men *or* women, thus making heterosexuality not an absolute, but an option. It would thus open up the whole question of *human* sexual relationships beyond the confines of the present male-female role system.

BOOKS MENTIONED IN THIS ESSAY

Sexual Behavior in the Human Female, Alfred C. Kinsey, Pocketbooks
Female Sexuality, Marie Bonaparte, Grove Press
Sex Without Guilt, Albert Ellis, Grove Press
Sexual Feelings in Married Men and Women, G. Lombard Kelly, Pocketbooks
I Accuse (Jeg Anklager), Mette Ejlersen, Chr. Erichsens Forlag (Danish)
The Sexually Adequate Female, Frank S. Caprio, Fawcett Gold Medal Books
Thinking About Women, Mary Ellman; Harcourt, Brace & World
Human Sexual Response, Masters and Johnson; Little, Brown

Also see:
The ABZ of Love, Inge and Sten Hegeler, Alexicon Corp.

Sexual Politics:
A Manifesto for Revolution

Kate Millett

When one group rules another, the relationship between the two is political. When such an arrangement is carried out over a long period of time it develops an ideology (feudalism, racism, etc.). All historical civilizations are patriarchies: their ideology is male supremacy.

Oppressed groups are denied education, economic independence, the power of office, representation, an image of dignity and self-respect, equality of status, and recognition as human beings. Throughout history women have been consistently denied all of these, and their denial today, while attenuated and partial, is nevertheless consistent. The education allowed them is deliberately designed to be inferior, and they are systematically programmed out of and excluded from the knowledge where power lies today—e.g., in science and technology. They are confined to conditions of economic dependence based on the sale of their sexuality in marriage, or a variety of prostitutions. Work on a basis of economic independence allows them only a subsistence level of life—often not even that. They do not hold office, are represented in no positions of power, and authority is forbidden them. The image of women fostered by cultural media, high and low, then and now, is a marginal and demeaning existence, and one outside the human condition—which is defined as the prerogative of man, the male.

Kate Millett, "Sexual Politics: A Manifesto for Revolution," *Notes from the Second Year*, New York: Radical Feminism, 1970, pp. 111–112. Reprinted with permission of the author.

Government is upheld by power, which is supported through consent (social opinion), or imposed by violence. Conditioning to an ideology amounts to the former. But there may be a resort to the latter at any moment when consent is withdrawn—rape, attack, sequestration, beatings, murder. Sexual politics obtains consent through the "socialization" of both sexes to patriarchal policies. They consist of the following:

1) the formation of human personality along stereotyped lines of sexual category, based on the needs and values of the master class and dictated by what he would cherish in himself and find convenient in an underclass: aggression, intellectuality, force and efficiency for the male; passivity, ignorance, docility, "virtue," and ineffectuality for the female.

2) the concept of sex role, which assigns domestic service and attendance upon infants to all females and the rest of human interest, achievement and ambition to the male; the charge of leader at all times and places to the male, and the duty of follower, with equal uniformity, to the female.

3) the imposition of male rule through institutions: patriarchal religion, the proprietary family, marriage, "The Home," masculine oriented culture, and a pervasive doctrine of male superiority.

A Sexual Revolution would bring about the following conditions, desirable upon rational, moral and humanistic grounds:

1) the end of sexual repression—freedom of expression and of sexual mores (sexual freedom has been partially attained, but it is now being subverted beyond freedom into exploitative license for patriarchal and reactionary ends).

2) Unisex, or the end of separatist character-structure, temperament and behavior, so that each individual may develop an entire—rather than a partial, limited, and conformist—personality.

3) re-examination of traits categorized into "masculine" and "feminine," with a total reassessment as to their human usefulness and advisability in both sexes. Thus if "masculine" violence is undesirable, it is so for both sexes; "feminine" dumb-cow passivity likewise. If "masculine" intelligence or efficiency is valuable, it is so for both sexes equally, and the same must be true for "feminine" tenderness or consideration.

4) the end of sex role and sex status, the patriarchy and the male supremacist ethic, attitude and ideology—in all areas of endeavor, experience, and behavior.

5) the end of the ancient oppression of the young under the patriarchal proprietary family, their chattel status, the attainment of the human rights presently denied them, the professionalization and therefore improvement of their care, and the guarantee that when they enter the world, they are desired, planned for, and provided with equal opportunities.

6) Bisex, or the end of enforced perverse heterosexuality, so that the sex act ceases to be arbitrarily polarized into male and female, to the exclusion of sexual expression between members of the same sex.

7) the end of sexuality in the forms in which it has existed historically—brutality, violence, capitalism, exploitation, and warfare—that it may cease to be hatred and become love.

8) the attainment of the female sex to freedom and full human status after millennia of deprivation and oppression, and of both sexes to a viable humanity.

Birth Control Pills and Black Children: The Sisters Reply

The Brothers are calling on the Sisters to not take the pill. It is this system's method of exterminating Black people here and abroad. To take the pill means that we are contributing to our own GENOCIDE.

However, in not taking the pill, we must have a new sense of value. When we produce children, we are aiding the REVOLUTION in the form of NATION building. Our children must have pride in their history, in their heritage, in their beauty. Our children must not be brainwashed as we were.

PROCREATION is beautiful, especially if we are devoted to the Revolution which means that our value system be altered to include the Revolution as the responsibility. A good deal of the Supremacist (White) efforts to sterilize the world's (Non-whites) out of existence is turning toward the black people of America. New trends in Race Control have led the architects of GENOCIDE to believe that Sterilization projects aimed at the black man in the United States can cure American internal troubles.

Under the cover of an alleged campaign to "alleviate poverty,' white supremacist Americans and their dupes are pushing an all-out drive to put rigid birth control measures into every black home. No such drive exists within the White American world. In some cities, Peekskill, Harlem, Mississippi and Alabama, welfare boards are doing their best to force black women receiving aid to submit to Sterilization. This disguised attack on black future generations is rapidly picking up popularity among determined genocidal engineers. This country is prepared to exterminate people by the pill or by the bomb; therefore, we must draw strength from ourselves.

Reprinted with permission of Patricia Robinson.

You see why there is a Family Planning Office in the Black Community of Peekskill.

THE SISTERS REPLY

September 11, 1968

Dear Brothers:

Poor black sisters decide for themselves whether to have a baby or not to have a baby. If we take the pills or practise birth control in other ways, it's because of poor black men.

Now here's how it is. Poor black men won't support their families, won't stick by their women—all they think about is the street, dope and liquor, women, a piece of ass, and their cars. That's all that counts. Poor black women would be fools to sit up in the house with a whole lot of children and eventually go crazy, sick, heartbroken, no place to go, no sign of affection—nothing. Middle class white men have always done this to their women—only more sophisticated like.

So when whitey put out the pill and poor black sisters spread the word, we saw how simple it was not to be a fool for men any more (politically we would say men could no longer exploit us sexually or for money and leave the babies with us to bring up). That was the first step in our waking up!

Black women have always been told by black men that we were black, ugly, evil, bitches and whores—in other words, we were the real niggers in this society—oppressed by whites, male and female, and the black man, too.

Now a lot of the black brothers are into a new bag. Black women are being asked by militant black brothers not to practice birth control because it is a form of whitey committing genocide on black people. Well, true enough, it takes two to practise genocide and black women are able to decide for themselves, just like poor people all over the world, whether they will submit to genocide. For us, birth control is freedom to fight genocide of black women and children.

Like the Vietnamese have decided to fight genocide, the South American poor are beginning to fight back, and the African poor will fight back, too. Poor black women in the U.S. have to fight back out of our own experience of oppression. Having too many babies stops us from supporting our children, teaching them the truth or stopping the brainwashing as you say, and fighting black men who still want to use and exploit us.

But we don't think you are going to understand us because you are a bunch of little middle class people and we are poor black women. The middle class never understands the poor because they always need to use them as you want to use poor black women's children to gain power for yourself. You'll run the black community with your kind of black power—you on top!

Mt. Vernon, N.Y.

Patricia Haden—welfare recipient
Sue Rudolph—housewife
Joyce Hoyt—domestic
Rita Van Lew—welfare recipient
Catherine Hoyt—grandmother
Patricia Robinson—housewife and psychotherapist

Poor Black Women

Patricia Robinson

It is time to speak to the whole question of the position of poor black women in this society and this historical period of revolution and counterrevolution. We have the foregoing analysis of their own perspective and it offers all of us some very concrete points.

First, that the class hierarchy as seen from the poor black woman's position is one of white male in power, followed by the white female, then the black male and lastly the black female.

Historically, the myth in the black world is that there are only two free people in the United States, the white man and the black woman. The myth was established by the black man in the long period of his frustration when he longed to be free to have the material and social advantages of his oppressor, the white man. On examination of the myth, this so-called freedom was based on the sexual prerogatives taken by the white man on the black female. It was fantasized by the black man that she enjoyed it.

The black woman was needed and valued by the white female as a domestic. The black female diluted much of the actual oppression of the white female by the white male. With the help of the black woman, the white woman had free time from mother and housewife responsibilities and could escape her domestic prison overseered by the white male.

The poor black woman still occupies the position of a domestic in

Patricia Robinson, *Poor Black Women*, Boston: New England Free Press, 1968, pp. 3–4. Reprinted with permission of the author.

481

this society, rising no higher than public welfare, when the frustrated male deserts her and the children. (Public welfare was instituted primarily for poor whites during the depression of the thirties to stave off their rising revolutionary violence. It was considered as a temporary stop-gap only.)

The poor black male deserted the poor black female and fled to the cities where he made his living by his wits—hustling. The black male did not question the kind of society he lived in other than on the basis of racism: "The white man won't let me be up 'cause I'm black!" Other rationalizations included blaming the black woman, which has been a much described phenomenon. The black man wanted to take the master's place and all that went with it.

Simultaneously, the poor black woman did not question the social and economic system. She saw her main problem as...social, economic and psychological oppression by the black man. But awareness in this case has moved to a second phase and exposes an important fact in the whole process of oppression. It takes two to oppress, a proper dialectical perspective to examine at this point in our movement.

An examination of the process of oppression in any or all of its forms shows simply that at least two parties are involved. The need for the white man, particularly, to oppress others reveals his own anxiety and inadequacy about his own maleness and humanity. Many black male writers have eloquently analyzed this social and psychological fact. Generally a feeling of inadequacy can be traced to all those who desperately need power and authority over others throughout history.

In other words, one's concept of oneself becomes based on one's class or power position in a hierarchy. Any endangering of this power position brings on a state of madness and irrationality within the individual which exposes the basic fear and insecurity beneath— politically speaking, the imperialists are paper tigers.

But the oppressor must have the cooperation of the oppressed, of those he must feel better than. The oppressed and the damned are placed in an inferior position by force of arms, physical strength, and later, by threats of such force. But the long-time maintenance of power over others is secured by psychological manipulation and seduction. The oppressed must begin to believe in the divine right and position of kings, the inherent right of an elite to rule, the supremacy of a class or an ethnic group, the power of such condensed wealth as money and private property to give to its owners high social status. So a gigantic and complex myth has been woven by those who have power in this society of the inevitability of classes and the superiority and inferiority of certain groups. The oppressed begin to believe in their own inferiority and are left in their lifetime with two general choices: to identify with the oppressor (imitate him) or to rebel against him. Rebellion does not take place as long as the oppressed are certain of their inferiority and the innate superiority of the powerful, in essence a neurotic illusion. The oppressed appear to be in love with their chains.

In a capitalist society, all power to rule is imagined in male symbols and, in fact, all power in a capitalist society *is* in male hands. Capitalism is a male supremacist society. Western religious gods are all male. The city, basis of "civilization," is male as opposed to the country which is female. The city is a revolt against earlier female principles of nature and man's dependence on them. All domestic and international political and economic decisions are made by men and enforced by males and their symbolic extension—guns. Women have become the largest oppressed group in a dominant, male, aggressive, capitalistic culture. The next largest oppressed group is the product of their wombs, the children, who are ever pressed into service and labor for the maintenance of a male-dominated class society.

If it is granted that it takes two to oppress, those who neurotically need to oppress and those who neurotically need to be oppressed, then what happens when the female in a capitalist society awakens to the reality? She can either identify with the male and opportunistically imitate him, appearing to share his power and giving him the surplus product of her body, the child, to use and exploit. Or she can rebel and remove the children from exploitative and oppressive male authority.

Rebellion by poor black women, the bottom of a class hierarchy heretofore not discussed, places the question of what kind of society will the poor black woman demand and struggle for. Already she demands the right to have birth control, like middle class black and white women. She is aware that it takes two to oppress and that she and other poor people no longer are submitting to oppression, in this case genocide. She allies herself with the have-nots in the wider world and their revolutionary struggles. She has been forced by historical conditions to withdraw the children from male dominance and to educate and support them herself. In this very process, male authority and exploitation are seriously weakened. Further, she realizes that the children will be used as all poor children have been used through history—as poorly paid mercenaries fighting to keep or put an elite group in power. Through these steps...she has begun to question aggressive male domination and the class society which enforces it, capitalism. This question, in time, will be posed to the entire black movement in this country.

Declaration of War[1]

Ti-Grace Atkinson

Almanina Barbour, a black militant woman in Philadelphia, once pointed out to me: "The Women's Movement is the first in history with a war on and no enemy." I winced. It was an obvious criticism. I fumbled about in my mind for an answer. Surely the enemy must have been defined at some time. Otherwise, what had we been shooting at for the last couple of years? into the air?

Only two responses came to me, although in looking for those two I realized that it was a question carefully avoided. The first and by far the most frequent answer was "society." The second, infrequently and always furtively, was "men."

If "society" is the enemy, what could that mean? If women are being oppressed, there's only one group left over to be doing the oppressing: men. Then why call them "society"? Could "society" mean the "institutions" that oppress women? But institutions must be maintained, and the same question arises: by whom? The answer to "who is the enemy?" is so obvious that the interesting issue quickly becomes "why has it been avoided?"

The master might tolerate many reforms in slavery but none that would threaten his essential role as master. Women have known this, and since "men" and "society" are in effect synonymous, they have feared confronting him. Without this confrontation and a detailed understanding of what *his* battle strategy[2] has been that has kept us so

---

Excerpts from Ti-Grace Atkinson, "Declaration of War," *Amazon Odyssey*, New York: Links Books, 1974, pp. 47–55. Reprinted with permission.

successfully pinned down, the "Women's Movement" is worse than useless. It invites backlash from men, and no progress for women.

There has never been a feminist analysis. While discontent among women and the attempt to resolve this discontent have often implied that women form a class, no political or *causal* class analysis has followed. To rephrase my last point, the persecution of women has never been taken as the starting point for a political analysis of society.

Considering that the last massing of discontent among women continued some 70 years (1850–1920) and spread the world and that the recent accumulation of grievances began some three years ago here in America, the lack of a structural understanding of the problem is at first sight incomprehensible. It is the understanding of the *reasons* for this devastating omission and of the *implications* of the problem that forces one to "radical feminism."

Women who have tried to solve their problems as a class have proposed not solutions but dilemmas. The traditional feminists want equal rights for women with men. But on what grounds? If women serve a different *function* from men in society, wouldn't this necessarily affect women's "rights"? For example, do *all* women have the "right" not to bear children? Traditional feminism is caught in the dilemma of demanding equal treatment for unequal functions, because it is unwilling to challenge political (functional) classification by sex.

Radical women, on the other hand, grasp that women as a group somehow fit into a political analysis of society, but err in refusing to explore the significance of the fact that women form a class, the uniqueness of this class, and the implications of this description to the system of political classes. Both traditional feminists and radical women have evaded questioning any part of their *raison d'être:* women are a class, and the terms that make up this initial assumption must be examined.

The feminist dilemma is that it is as women—or "females"—that women are persecuted, just as it was as slaves—or "blacks"—that slaves were persecuted in America. In order to improve their condition, those individuals who are today defined as women must eradicate their own definition. Women must, in a sense, commit suicide, and the journey from womanhood to a society of individuals is hazardous. The feminist dilemma is that we have the most to do, and the least to do it with. We must create, as no other group in history has been forced to do, from the very beginning.

The "battle of the sexes" is a commonplace, both over time and distance. But it is an inaccurate description of what has been happening. A "battle" implies some balance of powers, whereas when one side suffers all the losses, such as in some kinds of raids (often referred to as the "rape" of an area), that is called a *massacre*. Women have been massacred as human beings over history, and this destiny is entailed by their definition. As women begin massing together, they take the first step from *being* massacred to *engaging in* battle (resistance). Hopefully, this will eventually lead to negotiations—in the *very* far future—and peace.

When any person or group of persons is being mistreated or, to continue our metaphor, is being attacked, there is a succession of responses or investigations

(1) depending on the severity of the attack (short of an attack on life), the victim determines how much damage was done and what it was done with

(2) where is the attack coming from?—from whom?—located where?

(3) how can you win the immediate battle?—defensive measures?—holding actions?

(4) why did he attack you?

(5) how can you win (end) the war?—offensive measures. —moving within his boundaries.

These first five questions are necessary but should be considered diplomatic maneuvers. They have never been answered by the so-called "Women's Movement," and for this reason I think one cannot properly call that Movement "political." It could not have had any direction relevant to women as a class.

If diplomacy fails, that is, if your enemy refuses to stop attacking you, you must force him to stop. This requires a strategy, and this strategy requires a map of the relevant landscape, including such basic information as

(1) who is the enemy?

(2) where is he located?

(3) is he getting outside support? —material? —manpower? —from whom?

(4) where are his forces massed?

(5) what's the best ammunition to knock them out?

(6) what weapons is he using?

(7) how can you counteract them?

(8) what is your plan of attack on him to force diplomatic negotiations? —program of action (including priorities). —techniques.

I am using some military terminology, and this may seem incongruous. But why should it? We accept the phrase "battle of the sexes." It is the proposal that *women* fight *back* that seems incongruous. It has been necessary to program women's psychic structure to nonresistance on their own behalf—for obvious reasons—they make up over half the population of the world.

* * *

With this introduction to the significance of a feminist analysis, I will outline what we have so far.

As I mentioned before, the *raison d'être* of all groups formed around the problem of women is that women are a class. What is meant by that? What is meant by "women" and what is meant by "class"?

Does "women" include all women? Some groups have been driven back from the position of *all* women to some proposed "special" class such as "poor" women and eventually concentrated more on economic class than sexual class.[3] But if we're interested in women and how women *qua* women are oppressed, this class must include *all* women.

What separates out a particular individual from other individuals as a "woman"? We recognize it's a sexual separation and that this separation has two aspects, "sociological" and "biological." The term for the sociological function is "woman" (wifman); the term for the biological function is "female" (to suckle). Both terms are descriptive of functions in the interests of someone other than the possessor.

And what is meant by "class"? We've already briefly covered the meaning as the characteristic by which certain individuals are grouped together. In the "Women's Movement" or "feminism," individuals group together to *act* on behalf of women as a class in opposition to the *class* enemies of women. It is the interaction between classes that defines political action. For this reason I call the feminist analysis a *causal class analysis*.

* * *

If women were the first political class, and political classes must be defined by individuals outside that class, who defined them, and why, and how? It is reasonable to assume that at some period in history the population was politically undifferentiated; let's call that mass "Mankind" (generic).

The first dichotomous division of this mass is said to have been on the grounds of sex: male and female. But the genitals *per se* would be no more grounds for the human race to be divided in two than skin color or height or hair color. The genitals, in connection with a particular activity, have the *capacity* for the initiation of the reproductive process. But, I submit, it was because one half the human race bears the *burden* of the reproductive *process* and because man, the "rational" animal, had the wit to take advantage of that that the childbearers, or the "beasts of burden," were corralled into a political class. The biologically contingent burden of childbearing was equivocated into a political (or necessary) penalty, thereby modifying those individuals' definition thereby defined from the human to the functional—or animal.

There is no justification for using any individual as a function of others. Didn't *all* members of society have the right to decide if they even *wanted* to reproduce? Because one half of humanity was and still is forced to bear the burden of reproduction at the will of the other half, the first political class is defined not by its sex—sexuality was only relevant originally as a means to reproduction—but by the function of being the *container* of the reproductive process.

Because women have been taught to believe that men have protective feelings toward women (men have protective feelings toward their functions [property], *not* other human beings!), we women are shocked by these discoveries and ask ourselves *why* men took and continue to take advantage of us.

Some people say that men are naturally, or biologically, aggressive. But this leaves us at an impasse. If the values of society are power-oriented, there is no chance that men would agree to be medicated into an humane state.

The other alternative that has been suggested is to eliminate men as biologically incapable of humane relationships and therefore a menace to society. I can sympathize with the frustration and rage that leads to this suggestion.

But the proposal to eliminate men, as I understand it, assumes that men constitute a kind of social disease, and that by "men" is meant those individuals with certain typical genital characteristics. These genital characteristics are held to determine the organism in every biochemical respect thus determining the psychic structure as well. It may be that as in other mental derangements, and I do believe that men behave in a mentally deranged manner toward women, there is a biochemical correspondence, but this would be ultimately behaviorally determined, not genetically.

I believe that the sex roles—both male and female—must be destroyed, not the individuals who happen to possess either a penis or a vagina, or both, or neither. But many men I have spoken with see little to choose from between the two positions and feel that without the role they'd just as soon die.

Certainly it is the master who resists the abolition of slavery, especially when he is offered no recompense in power. I think that the *need* men have for the role of Oppressor is the source and foundation of all human oppression. Men suffer from a disease peculiar to mankind which I call "metaphysical cannibalism." Men must, at the very least, cooperate in curing themselves.

NOTES

1.   April, 1969; written at the request of *Maclean's* magazine (Canada's version of *Life*); rejected as too esoteric; published in *Notes from the Second Year*, Shulamith Firestone and Anne Koedt, eds. (New York: 1970), pp. 32–37.

2.   See *Strategy and Tactics: A Presentation of Political Lesbianism*, pp. 135–189, for a fuller development of the concept of "strategy."

3.   See footnote 4 in *Radical Feminism and Love*, p. 42.

The Dialectic of Sex

Shulamith Firestone

Sex class is so deep as to be invisible. Or it may appear as a superficial inequality, one that can be solved by merely a few reforms, or perhaps by the full integration of women into the labor force. But the reaction of the common man, woman, and child—"*That?* Why you can't change *that!* You must be out of your mind!"—is the closest to the truth. We are talking about something every bit as deep as that. This gut reaction—the assumption that, even when they don't know it, feminists are talking about changing a fundamental biological condition—is an honest one. That so profound a change cannot be easily fit into traditional categories of thought, e.g., "political," is not because these categories do not apply but because they are not big enough: radical feminism bursts through them. If there were another word more all-embracing than *revolution* we would use it.

Until a certain level of evolution had been reached and technology had achieved its present sophistication, to question fundamental biological conditions was insanity. Why should a woman give up her precious seat in the cattle car for a bloody struggle she could not hope to win? But, for the first time in some countries, the preconditions for feminist revolution exist—indeed, the situation is beginning to *demand* such a revolution.

The first women are fleeing the massacre, and, shaking and tottering,

From pp. 1–12 "Sex class is so deep...eradicate all class systems," in *The Dialectic of Sex* by Shulamith Firestone. Copyright © 1970 by Shulamith Firestone. By permission of William Morrow & Company.

are beginning to find each other. Their first move is a careful joint observation, to resensitize a fractured consciousness. This is painful: No matter how many levels of consciousness one reaches, the problem always goes deeper. It is everywhere. The division yin and yang pervades all culture, history, economics, nature itself; modern Western versions of sex discrimination are only the most recent layer. To so heighten one's sensitivity to sexism presents problems far worse than the black militant's new awareness of racism: Feminists have to question, not just all of Western culture, but the organization of culture itself, and further, even the very organization of nature. Many women give up in despair: if *that's* how deep it goes they don't want to know. Others continue strengthening and enlarging the movement, their painful sensitivity to female oppression existing for a purpose: eventually to eliminate it.

Before we can act to change a situation, however, we must know how it has arisen and evolved, and through what institutions it now operates. Engels' "[We must] examine the historic succession of events from which the antagonism has sprung in order to discover in the conditions thus created the means of ending the conflict." For feminist revolution we shall need an analysis of the dynamics of sex war as comprehensive as the Marx-Engels analysis of class antagonism was for the economic revolution. More comprehensive. For we are dealing with a larger problem, with an oppression that goes back beyond recorded history to the animal kingdom itself.

In creating such an analysis we can learn a lot from Marx and Engels: Not their literal opinions about women—about the condition of women as an oppressed class they know next to nothing, recognizing it only where it overlaps with economics—but rather their *analytic method.*

Marx and Engels outdid their socialist forerunners in that they developed a method of analysis which was both *dialectical* and *materialist.* The first in centuries to view history dialectically, they saw the world as process, a natural flux of action and reaction, of opposites yet inseparable and interpenetrating. Because they were able to perceive history as movie rather than as snapshot, they attempted to avoid falling into the stagnant "metaphysical" view that had trapped so many other great minds. (This sort of analysis itself may be a product of the sex division....) They combined this view of the dynamic interplay of historical forces with a materialist one, that is, they attempted for the first time to put historical and cultural change on a real basis, to trace the development of economic classes to organic causes. By understanding thoroughly the mechanics of history, they hoped to show men how to master it.

Socialist thinkers prior to Marx and Engels, such as Fourier, Owen, and Bebel, had been able to do no more than moralize about existing social inequalities, positing an ideal world where class privilege and exploitation should not exist—in the same way that early feminist thinkers posited a world where male privilege and exploitation ought not exist—by mere virtue of good will. In both cases, because the early thinkers did not really understand how the social injustice had evolved, maintained itself, or could be eliminated, their ideas existed in a cultural vacuum, utopian. Marx and Engels, on the other hand, attempted a scientific approach to history. They traced the class conflict to its real economic origins, projecting an economic solution based on objective economic preconditions already present: the seizure by the proletariat of the means of production would lead to a communism in which government had withered away, no longer needed to repress the lower class for the sake of the higher. In the classless society the interests of every individual would be synonymous with those of the larger society.

But the doctrine of historical materialism, much as it was a brilliant advance over previous historical analysis, was not the complete answer, as later events bore out. For though Marx and Engels grounded their theory in reality, it was only a *partial* reality. Here is Engels' strictly economic definition of historical materialism from *Socialism: Utopian or Scientific*:

> Historical materialism is that view of the course of history which seeks the *ultimate* cause and the great moving power of all historical events in the economic development of society, in the changes of the modes of production and exchange, in the consequent division of society into distinct classes, and in the struggles of these classes against one another. (Italics mine)

Further, he claims:

> ...that all past history with the exception of the primitive stages was the history of class struggles; that these warring classes of society are always the products of the modes of production and exchange—in a word, of the economic conditions of their time; that the *economic* structure of society always furnishes the real basis, starting from

which we can alone work out the *ultimate* explanation of the whole superstructure of juridical and political institutions as well as of the religious, philosophical, and other ideas of a given historical period. (Italics mine)

It would be a mistake to attempt to explain the oppression of women according to this strictly economic interpretation. The class analysis is a beautiful piece of work, but limited: although correct in a linear sense, it does not go deep enough. There is a whole sexual substratum of the historical dialectic that Engels at times dimly perceives, but because he can see sexuality only through an economic filter, reducing everything to that, he is unable to evaluate in its own right.

Engels did observe that the original division of labor was between man and woman for the purposes of child-breeding; that within the family the husband was the owner, the wife the means of production, the children the labor; and that reproduction of the human species was an important economic system distinct from the means of production.*

But Engels has been given too much credit for these scattered recognitions of the oppression of women as a class. In fact he acknowledged the sexual class system only where it overlapped and illuminated his economic construct. Engels didn't do so well even in this respect. But Marx was worse: There is a growing recognition of Marx's bias against women (a cultural bias shared by Freud as well as all men of culture), dangerous if one attempts to squeeze feminism into an orthodox Marxist framework—freezing what were only incidental insights of Marx and Engels about sex class into dogma. Instead, we must enlarge historical materialism to *include* the strictly Marxian, in the same way that the physics of relativity did not invalidate Newtonian physics so much as it drew a circle around it, limiting its application—but only through comparison—to a smaller sphere. For an economic diagnosis traced to ownership of the means of production, even of the means of reproduction, does not explain everything. There is a level of reality that does not stem directly from economics.

The assumption that, beneath economics, reality is psychosexual is often rejected as ahistorical by those who accept a dialectical materialist view of history because it seems to land us back where Marx began:

---

* His correlation of the interdevelopment of these two systems in *Origin of the Family, Private Property and the State* on a time scale might read as in Figure 1.

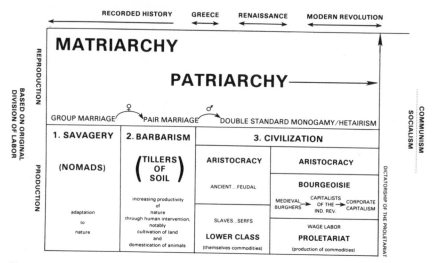

Figure 1.

groping through a fog of utopian hypotheses, philosophical systems that might be right, that might be wrong (there is no way to tell), systems that explain concrete historical developments by *a priori* categories of thought; historical materialism, however, attempted to explain "knowing" by "being" and not vice versa.

But there is still an untried third alternative: We can attempt to develop a materialist view of history based on sex itself.

The early feminist theorists were to a materialist view of sex what Fourier, Bebel, and Owen were to a materialist view of class. By and large, feminist theory has been as inadequate as were the early feminist attempts to correct sexism. This was to be expected. The problem is so immense that, at first try, only the surface could be skimmed, the most blatant inequalities described. Simone de Beauvoir was the only one who came close to—who perhaps has done—the definitive analysis. Her profound work *The Second Sex*—which appeared as recently as the early fifties to a world convinced that feminism was dead—for the first time attempted to ground feminism in its historical base. Of all feminist theorists De Beauvoir is the most comprehensive and far-reaching, relating feminism to the best ideas in our culture.

It may be this virtue is also her one failing: she is almost too sophisticated, too knowledgeable. Where this becomes a weakness—and this is still certainly debatable—is in her rigidly existentialist interpretation of feminism (one wonders how much Sartre had to do with this).

This in view of the fact that all cultural systems, including existentialism, are themselves determined by the sex dualism. She says:

> Man never thinks of himself without thinking of the Other; he views the world under the sign of duality *which is not in the first place sexual in character*. But being different from man, who sets himself up as the Same, it is naturally to the category of the Other that woman is consigned; the Other includes woman. (Italics mine)

Perhaps she has overshot her mark: Why postulate a fundamental Hegelian concept of Otherness as the final explanation—and then carefully document the biological and historical circumstances that have pushed the class "women" into such a category—when one has never seriously considered the much simpler and more likely possibility that this fundamental dualism sprang from the sexual division itself? To posit *a priori* categories of thought and existence—"Otherness," "Transcendence," "Immanence"—into which history then falls may not be necessary. Marx and Engels had discovered that these philosophical categories themselves grew out of history.

Before assuming such categories, let us first try to develop an analysis in which biology itself—procreation—is at the origin of the dualism. The immediate assumption of the layman that the unequal division of the sexes is "natural" may be well-founded. We need not immediately look beyond this. Unlike economic class, sex class sprang directly from a biological reality: men and women were created different, and not equally privileged. Although, as De Beauvoir points out, this difference of itself did not necessitate the development of a class system—the domination of one group by another—the reproductive *functions* of these differences did. The biological family is an inherently unequal power distribution. The need for power leading to the development of classes arises from the psychosexual formation of each individual according to this basic imbalance, rather than, as Freud, Norman O. Brown, and others have, once again overshooting their mark, postulated, some irreducible conflict of Life against Death, Eros vs. Thanatos.

The *biological family*—the basic reproductive unit of male/female/infant, in whatever form of social organization—is characterized by these fundamental—if not immutable—facts:

1) That women throughout history before the advent of birth control were at the continual mercy of their biology—menstruation,

menopause, and "female ills," constant painful childbirth, wet-nursing and care of infants, all of which made them dependent on males (whether brother, father, husband, lover, or clan, government, community-at-large) for physical survival.

2) That human infants take an even longer time to grow up than animals, and thus are helpless and, for some short period at least, dependent on adults for physical survival.

3) That a basic mother/child interdependency has existed in some form in every society, past or present, and thus has shaped the psychology of every mature female and every infant.

4) That the natural reproductive difference between the sexes led directly to the first division of labor at the origins of class, as well as furnishing the paradigm of caste (discrimination based on biological characteristics).

These biological contingencies of the human family cannot be covered over with anthropological sophistries. Anyone observing animals mating, reproducing, and caring for their young will have a hard time accepting the "cultural relativity" line. For no matter how many tribes in Oceania you can find where the connection of the father to fertility is not known, no matter how many matrilineages, no matter how many cases of sex-role reversal, male housewifery, or even empathic labor pains, these facts prove only one thing: the amazing *flexibility* of human nature. But human nature is adaptable *to* something, it is, yes, determined by its environmental conditions. And the biological family that we have described has existed everywhere throughout time. Even in matriarchies where woman's fertility is worshipped, and the father's role is unknown or unimportant, if perhaps not on the genetic father, there is still some dependence of the female and the infant on the male. And though it is true that the nuclear family is only a recent development, one which, as I shall attempt to show, only intensifies the psychological penalties of the biological family, though it is true that throughout history there have been many variations on this biological family, the contingencies I have described existed in all of them, causing specific psychosexual distortions in the human personality.

But to grant that the sexual imbalance of power is biologically based is not to lose our case. We are no longer just animals. And the Kingdom of Nature does not reign absolute. As Simone de Beauvoir herself admits:

The theory of historical materialism has brought to light some important truths. Humanity is not an animal species, it is a historical reality. Human society is an antiphysis—in a sense it is against nature; it does not passively submit to the presence of nature but rather takes over the control of nature on its own behalf. This arrogation is not an inward, subjective operation; it is accomplished objectively in practical action.

Thus, the "natural" is not necessarily a "human" value. Humanity has begun to outgrow nature: we can no longer justify the maintenance of a discriminatory sex class system on grounds of its origins in Nature. Indeed, for pragmatic reasons alone it is beginning to look as if we *must* get rid of it....

The problem becomes political, demanding more than a comprehensive historical analysis, when one realizes that, though man is increasingly capable of freeing himself from the biological conditions that created his tyranny over women and children, he has little reason to want to give this tyranny up. As Engels said, in the context of economic revolution:

It is the law of division of labor that lies at the basis of the division into classes [Note that this division itself grew out of a fundamental biological division]. But this does not prevent the ruling class, once having the upper hand, from consolidating its power at the expense of the working class, from turning its social leadership into an intensified exploitation of the masses.

Though the sex class system may have originated in fundamental biological conditions, this does not guarantee once the biological basis of their oppression has been swept away that women and children will be freed. On the contrary, the new technology, especially fertility control, may be used against them to reinforce the entrenched system of exploitation.

So that just as to assure elimination of economic classes requires the revolt of the underclass (the proletariat) and, in a temporary dictatorship, their seizure of the means of *production*, so to assure the elimination of sexual classes requires the revolt of the underclass (women) and the seizure of control of *reproduction*: not only the full restoration to women of ownership of their own bodies, but also their (temporary) seizure of control of human fertility—the new population biology as well as all the social institutions of childbearing and childrearing. And just as the end goal of socialist revolution was not only the elimination of the economic class *privilege* but of the economic class *distinction* itself, so the end goal of feminist revolution must be, unlike that of the first feminist movement, not just the elimination of male *privilege* but of the sex *distinction* itself: genital differences between human beings would no longer matter culturally. (A reversion to an unobstructed *pansexuality*—Freud's "polymorphous perversity"—would probably supersede hetero/homo/bi-sexuality.) The reproduction of the species by one sex for the benefit of both would be replaced by (at least the option of) artificial reproduction: children would be born to both sexes equally, or independently of either, however one chooses to look at it; the dependence of the child on the mother (and vice versa) would give way to a greatly shortened dependence on a small group of others in general, and any remaining inferiority to adults in physical strength would be compensated for culturally. The division of labor would be ended by the elimination of labor altogether (cybernation). The tyranny of the biological family would be broken.

And with it the psychology of power. As Engels claimed for strictly socialist revolution:

> The existence of not simply this or that ruling class but of any ruling class at all [will have] become an obsolete anachronism.

That socialism has never come near achieving this predicted goal is not only the result of unfulfilled or misfired economic preconditions, but also because the Marxian analysis itself was insufficient: it did not dig deep enough to the psychosexual roots of class. Marx was onto something more profound than he knew when he observed that the family contained within itself in embryo all the antagonisms that later develop on a wide scale within the society and the state. For unless revolution uproots the basic social organization, the biological family—the vinculum through which the psychology of power can always be smuggled—the tapeworm of exploitation will never be annihilated. We shall need a sexual revolution much larger than—inclusive of—a socialist one to truly eradicate all class systems.

Double Jeopardy:
To Be Black and Female

Frances Beale

In attempting to analyze the situation of the Black woman in America, one crashes abruptly into a solid wall of grave misconceptions, outright distortions of fact, and defensive attitudes on the part of many. The system of capitalism (and its afterbirth—racism) under which we all live has attempted by many devious ways and means to destroy the humanity of all people, and particularly the humanity of Black people. This has meant an outrageous assault on every Black man, woman, and child who reside in the United States.

In keeping with its goal of destroying the Black race's will to resist its subjugation, capitalism found it necessary to create a situation where the Black man found it impossible to find meaningful or productive employment. More often than not, he couldn't find work of any kind. And the Black woman likewise was manipulated by the system, economically exploited and physically assaulted. She could often find work in the white man's kitchen, however, and sometimes became the sole breadwinner of the family. This predicament has led to many psychological problems on the part of both man and woman and has contributed to the turmoil that we find in the Black family structure.

Unfortunately, neither the Black man nor the Black woman understood the true nature of the forces working upon them. Many Black

---

Excerpts from Frances Beale, "Double Jeopardy: To Be Black and Female," in Toni Cade, ed., *The Black Woman*, New York: New American Library, 1970. Reprinted with permission of the author.

women tended to accept the capitalist evaluation of manhood and womanhood and believed, in fact, that Black men were shiftless and lazy, otherwise they would get a job and support their families as they ought to. Personal relationships between Black men and women were thus torn asunder and one result has been the separation of man from wife, mother from child, etc.

America has defined the roles to which each individual should subscribe. It has defined "manhood" in terms of its own interests and "femininity" likewise. Therefore, an individual who has a good job, makes a lot of money, and drives a Cadillac is a real "man," and conversely, an individual who is lacking in these "qualities" is less of a man. The advertising media in this country continuously informs the American male of his need for indispensable signs of his virility—the brand of cigarettes that cowboys prefer, the whiskey that has a masculine tang, or the label of the jock strap that athletes wear.

The ideal model that is projected for a woman is to be surrounded by hypocritical homage and estranged from all real work, spending idle hours primping and preening, obsessed with conspicuous consumption, and limiting life's functions to simply a sex role. We unqualitatively reject these respective models. A woman who stays at home caring for children and the house often leads an extremely sterile existence. She must lead her entire life as a satellite to her mate. He goes out into society and brings back a little piece of the world for her. His interests and his understanding of the world become her own and she cannot develop herself as an individual having been reduced to only a biological function. This kind of woman leads a parasitic existence that can aptly be described as legalized prostitution.

Furthermore it is idle dreaming to think of Black women simply caring for their homes and children like the middle-class white model. Most Black women have to work to help house, feed, and clothe their families. Black women make up a substantial percentage of the Black working force, and this is true for the poorest Black family as well as the so-called "middle-class" family.

Black women were never afforded any such phony luxuries. Though we have been browbeaten with this white image, the reality of the degrading and dehumanizing jobs that were relegated to us quickly dissipated this mirage of womanhood. The following excerpts from a speech that Sojourner Truth made at a Women's Rights Convention in the nineteenth century show us how misleading and incomplete a life this model represents for us:

... Well, chilern, whar dar is so much racket dar must be something out o' kilter. I tink dat 'twixt de niggers of de Souf and de women at de Norf all a talkin' 'bout rights, de white man will be in a fix pretty soon. But what's all dis here talkin' 'bout? Dat man ober dar say dat women needs to be helped into carriages, and lifted ober ditches, and to have de best place every whar. Nobody ever help me into carriages, or ober mud puddles, or gives me any best places... and ar'nt I a woman? Look at me! Look at my arm! ... I have plowed, and planted, and gathered into barns, and no man could head me—and ar'nt I a woman? I could work as much as a man (when I could get it), and bear de lash as well—and ar'nt I a woman? I have borne five chilern and I seen 'em mos' all sold off into slavery, and when I cried out with a mother's grief, none but Jesus heard—and ar'nt I a woman?

Unfortunately, there seems to be some confusion in the Movement today as to who has been oppressing whom. Since the advent of Black power, the Black male has exerted a more prominent leadership role in our struggle for justice in this country. He sees the system for what it really is for the most part, but where he rejects its values and mores on many issues, when it comes to women, he seems to take his guidelines from the pages of the *Ladies' Home Journal*. Certain Black men are maintaining that they have been castrated by society but that Black women somehow escaped this persecution and even contributed to this emasculation.

Let me state here and now that the Black woman in America can justly be described as a "slave of a slave." By reducing the Black man in American to such abject oppression, the Black woman had no protector and was used, and is still being used in some cases, as the scapegoat for the evils that this horrendous system has perpetrated on Black men. Her physical image has been maliciously maligned; she has been sexually molested and abused by the white colonizer; having been forced to serve as the white woman's maid and wet nurse for white offspring while her own children were more often than not starving and neglected. It is the depth of degradation to be socially manipulated, physically raped, used to undermine your own household, and to be powerless to reverse this syndrome.

It is true that our husbands, fathers, brothers, and sons have been emasculated, lynched, and brutalized. They have suffered from the cruelest assault on mankind that the world has ever known. However, it is a gross distortion of fact to state that Black women have oppressed Black men. The capitalist system found it expedient to enslave and oppress them and proceeded to do so without consultation or the signing of any agreements with Black women.

It must also be pointed out at this time that Black women are not resentful of the rise to power of Black men. We welcome it. We see in it the eventual liberation of all black people from this corrupt system of capitalism. Nevertheless, this does not mean that you have to negate one for the other. This kind of thinking is a product of miseducation; that it's either X or it's Y. It is fallacious reasoning that it order for the Black man to be strong, the Black woman has to be weak.

Those who are exerting their "manhood" by telling Black women to step back into a domestic, submissive role are assuming a counter-revolutionary position. Black women likewise have been abused by the system and we must begin talking about the elimination of all kinds of oppression. If we are talking about building a strong nation, capable of throwing off the yoke of capitalist oppression, then we are talking about the total involvement of every man, woman, and child, each with a highly developed political consciousness. We need our whole army out there dealing with the enemy and not half an army.

There are also some Black women who feel that there is no more productive role in life than having and raising children. This attitude often reflects the conditioning of the society in which we live and is adopted from a bourgeois white model. Some young sisters who have never had to maintain a household and accept the confining role which this entails tend to romanticize (along with the help of a few brothers) this role of housewife and mother. Black women who have had to endure this kind of function are less apt to have these utopian visions.

Those who project in an intellectual manner how great and rewarding this role will be and who feel that the most important thing that they can contribute to the Black nation is children are doing themselves a great injustice. This line of reasoning completely negates the contributions that Black women have historically made to our struggle for liberation. These Black women include Sojourner Truth, Harriet Tubman, Mary McLeod Bethune, and Fannie Lou Hamer, to name but a few.

We live in a highly industrialized society and every member of the Black nation must be as academically and technologically developed as possible. To wage a revolution, we need competent teachers, doctors, nurses, electronics experts, chemists, biologists, physicists, political scientists, and so on and so forth. Black women sitting at home reading bedtime stories to their children are just not going to make it.

ECONOMIC EXPLOITATION OF BLACK WOMEN

The economic system of capitalism finds it expedient to reduce women to a state of enslavement. They oftentimes serve as a scapegoat for the evils of this system. Much in the same way that the poor white cracker of the South, who is equally victimized, looks down upon Blacks and contributes to the oppression of Blacks, so, by giving to men a false feeling of superiority (at least in their own home or in their relationships with women), the oppression of women acts as an escape valve for capitalism. Men may be cruelly exploited and subjected to all sorts of dehumanizing tactics on the part of the ruling class, but they have someone who is below them—at least they're not women.

Women also represent a surplus labor supply, the control of which is absolutely necessary to the profitable functioning of capitalism. Women are systematically exploited by the system. They are paid less for the same work that men do, and jobs that are specifically relegated to women are low-paying and without the possibility of advancement. Statistics from the Women's Bureau of the U.S. Department of Labor show that in 1967 the wage scale for white women was even below that of Black men; and the wage scale for non-white women was the lowest of all:

White Males	$6704
Non-White Males	$4277
White Females	$3991
Non-White Females	$2861

Those industries which employ mainly Black women are the most exploitive in the country. Domestic and hospital workers are good examples of this oppression; the garment workers in New York City provide us with another view of this economic slavery. The International Ladies Garment Workers Union (ILGWU), whose overwhelming membership consists of Black and Puerto Rican women, has a leadership that is nearly all lily-white and male. This leadership has been working in collusion with the ruling class and has completely sold its soul to the corporate structure.

To add insult to injury, the ILGWU has invested heavily in business enterprises in racist, apartheid South Africa—with union funds. Not only does this bought-off leadership contribute to our continued exploitation in this country by not truly representing the best interests of its membership, but it audaciously uses funds that Black and Puerto Rican women have provided to support the economy of a vicious government that is engaged in the economic rape and murder of our Black brothers and sister in our Motherland, Africa.

The entire labor movement in the United States has suffered as a result of the super-exploitation of Black workers and women. The unions have historically been racist and chauvinistic. They have upheld racism in this country and have failed to fight the white skin privileges of white workers. They have failed to fight or even make an issue against the inequities in the hiring and pay of women workers. There has been virtually no struggle against either the racism of the white worker or the economic exploitation of the working woman, two factors which have consistently impeded the advancement of the real struggle against the ruling class.

This racist, chauvinistic, and manipulative use of Black workers and women, especially Black women, has been a severe cancer on the American labor scene. It therefore becomes essential for those who understand the workings of capitalism and imperialism to realize that the exploitation of Black people and women works to everyone's disadvantage and that the liberation of these two groups is a steppingstone to the liberation of all oppressed people in this country and around the world.

BEDROOM POLITICS

I have briefly discussed the economic and psychological manipulation of Black women, but perhaps the most outlandish act of oppression in modern times is the current campaign to promote sterilization of non-white women in an attempt to maintain the population and power imbalance between the white haves and the non-white have-nots.

These tactics are but another example of the many devious schemes that the ruling-class elite attempt to perpetrate on the Black population in order to keep itself in control. It has recently come to our attention that a massive campaign for so-called "birth control" is presently being promoted not only in the underdeveloped non-white areas of the world, but also in Black communities here in the United States. However, what the authorities in charge of these programs refer to as "birth control" is in fact nothing but a method of outright surgical genocide.

The United States has been sponsoring sterilization clinics in non-white countries, especially in India, where already some three million young men and boys in and around New Delhi have been sterilized in makeshift operating rooms set up by the American Peace Corps workers. Under these circumstances, it is understandable why certain countries view the Peace Corps not as a benevolent project, not as evidence of America's concern for underdeveloped areas, but rather as a threat to their very existence. This program could more aptly be named the Death Corps.

Vasectomy, which is performed on males and takes only six or seven minutes, is a relatively simple operation. The sterilization of a woman, on the other hand, is admittedly major surgery. This operation (salpingectomy)* must be performed in a hospital under general anesthesia. This method of "birth control" is a common procedure in Puerto Rico. Puerto Rico has long been used by the colonialist exploiter, the United States, as a huge experimental laboratory for medical research before allowing certain practices to be imported and used here. When the birth-control pill was first being perfected, it was tried out on Puerto Rican women and selected Black women (poor), using them as human guinea pigs, to evaluate its effect and its efficiency.

Salpingectomy has now become the commonest operation in Puerto Rico, commoner than an appendectomy or a tonsillectomy. It is so widespread that it is referred to simply as la operación. On the island, 10 percent of the women between the ages of 15 and 45 have already been sterilized.

And now, as previously occurred with the pill, this method has been imported into the United States. These sterilization clinics are cropping up around the country in the Black and Puerto Rican communities. These so-called "maternity clinics" specifically outfitted to

---

*Salpingectomy: Through an abdominal incision, the surgeon cuts both fallopian tubes and ties off the separated ends, after which act there is no way for the egg to pass from the ovary to the womb.

purge Black women or men of their reproductive possibilities are appearing more and more in hospitals and clinics across the country.

A number of organizations have been formed to popularize the idea of sterilization, such as the Association for Voluntary Sterilization and the Human Betterment (!!!?) Association for Voluntary Sterilization, Inc., which has its headquarters in New York City.

Threatened with the cut-off of relief funds, some Black welfare women have been forced to accept this sterilization procedure in exchange for a continuation of welfare benefits. Black women are often afraid to permit any kind of necessary surgery because they know from bitter experience that they are more likely than not to come out of the hospital without their insides. (Both salpingectomies and hysterectomies are performed.)

We condemn this use of the Black woman as a medical testing ground for the white middle class. Reports of the ill effects, including deaths, from the use of the birth control pill only started to come to light when the white privileged class began to be affected. These outrageous Nazi-like procedures on the part of medical researchers are but another manifestation of the totally amoral and dehumanizing brutality that the capitalist system perpetrates on Black women. The sterilization experiements carried on in concentration camps some twenty-five years ago have been denounced the world over, but no one seems to get upset by the repetition of these same racist tactics today in the United States of America—land of the free and home of the brave. This campaign is as nefarious a program as Germany's gas chambers, and in a long-term sense, as effective and with the same objective.

The rigid laws concerning abortions in this country are another vicious means of subjugation and, indirectly, of outright murder. Rich white women somehow manage to obtain these operations with little or no difficulty. It is the poor Black and Puerto Rican woman who is at the mercy of the local butcher. Statistics show us that the non-white death rate at the hands of the unqualified abortionist is substantially higher than for white women. Nearly half of the childbearing deaths in New York City are attributed to abortion alone and out of these, 79 percent are among non-whites and Puerto Rican women.

We are not saying that Black women should not practice birth control. *Black women have the right and the responsibility to determine when it is in the interest of the struggle to have children or not to have them, and this right must not be relinquished to anyone.* It is also her right and responsibility to determine when it is in her own best interests to have children, how many she will have, and how far apart. The lack of the availability of safe birth-control methods, the forced sterilization practices, and the inability to obtain legal abortions are all symptoms of a decadent society that jeopardizes the health of Black women (and thereby the entire Black race) in its attempts to control the very life processes of human beings. This is a symptom of a society that believes it has the right to bring political factors into the privacy of the bedchamber. The elimination of these horrendous conditions will free Black women for full participation in the revolution, and thereafter, in the building of the new society.

Goodbye to All That

Robin Morgan

So. *Rat* has been liberated, for this week, at least. Next week? If the men return to reinstate the porny photos, the sexist comic strips, the "nude-chickie" covers (along with their patronizing rhetoric about being in favor of Women's Liberation)—if this happens, our alternatives are clear. *Rat* must be taken over permanently by women—or *Rat* must be destroyed.

Why *Rat?* Why not EVO or even the obvious new pornzines (Mafia-distributed alongside the human pornography of prostitution)? First, they'll get theirs—but it won't be a takeover, which is reserved for something at least *worth* taking over. Nor should they be censored. They should just be helped not to exist—by any means necessary. But *Rat*, which has always tried to be a really radical *cum* life-style paper—that's another matter. It's the liberal co-optative masks on the face of sexist hate and fear, worn by real nice guys we all know and like, right? We have met the enemy and he's our friend. And dangerous. "What the hell, let the chicks do an issue; maybe it'll satisfy 'em for a while, it's a good controversy, and it'll maybe sell papers"—runs an unheard conversation that I'm sure took place at some point last week.

And that's what I wanted to write about—the friends, brothers, lovers in the counterfeit male-dominated Left. The good guys who think they know what "Women's Lib," as they so chummily call it, is all about—and who then proceed to degrade and destroy women by almost everything they say and do: The cover on the last issue of *Rat*

Robin Morgan, "Goodbye to All That," *The Rat*, February, 9–23, 1970, pp. 6–7.

(front *and* back). The token "pussy power" or "clit militancy" articles. The snide descriptions of women staffers on the masthead. The little jokes, the personal ads, the smile, the snarl. No more, brothers. No more well-meaning ignorance, no more co-optation, no more assuming that this thing we're all fighting for is the same: one revolution under *man*, with liberty and justice for all. No more.

Let's run it on down. White males are most responsible for the destruction of human life and environment on the planet today. Yet who is controlling the supposed revolution to change all that? White males (yes, yes, even with their pasty fingers back in black and brown pies again). It just could make one a bit uneasy. It seems obvious that a legitimate revolution must be led by, *made* by those who have been most oppressed: black, brown, and white *women*—with men relating to that the best they can. A genuine Left doesn't consider anyone's suffering irrelevant or titillating; nor does it function as a microcosm of capitalist economy, with men competing for power and status at the top, and women doing all the work at the bottom (and functioning as objectified prizes or "coin" as well). Goodbye to all that.

Run it all the way down.

Goodbye to the male-dominated peace movement, where sweet old Uncle Dave can say with impunity to a woman on the staff of *Liberation*, "The trouble with you is you're an aggressive woman."

Goodbye to the "straight" male-dominated Left: to PL who will allow that some workers are women, but won't see all women (say, housewives) as workers (just like the System itself); to all the old Leftover parties who offer their "Women's Liberation caucuses" to us as if that were not a contradiction in terms; to the individual anti-leadership leaders who hand-pick certain women to be leaders and then relate only to them, either in the male Left or in Women's Liberation—bringing their hang-ups about power-dominance and manipulation to everything they touch.

Goodbye to the WeatherVain, with the Stanley Kowalski image and theory of free sexuality but practice of sex on demand for males. "Left Out!"—not Right On—to the Weather Sisters, who, and they know better—they know, reject their own radical feminism for that last desperate grab at male approval that we all know so well, for claiming that the *machismo* style and the gratuitous violence is their own style by "free choice" and for believing that this is the way for a woman to make her revolution...all the while, oh my sister, not meeting my eyes because WeatherMen chose Manson as their—and your—Hero. (Honest, at least...since Manson is only the logical extreme of the normal American male's fantasy [whether he is Dick Nixon or Mark Rudd]: master of a harem, women to do all the shitwork, from raising babies and cooking and hustling to killing people on order.) Goodbye to all that shit that sets women apart from women; shit that covers the face of any Weatherwoman which is the face of any Manson Slave which is the face of Sharon Tate which is the face of Mary Jo Kopechne which is the face of Beulah Saunders which is the face of me which is the face of Pat Nixon which is the face of Pat Swinton. *In the dark, we are all the same*—and you better believe it: we're in the dark, baby. (Remember the old joke: Know what they call a black man with a Ph.D.? A nigger. Variation: Know what they call a Weatherwoman? A heavy cunt. Know what they call a Hip Revolutionary Woman? A groovy cunt. Know what they call a radical militant feminist? A crazy cunt. Amerika is a land of free choice—take your pick of titles.) Left Out, my Sister—don't you see? Goodbye to the illusion of strength when you run hand in hand with your oppressors; goodbye to the dream that being in the leadership collective will get you anything but gonorrhea.

Goodbye to RYM II, as well, and all the other RYMs—not that the Sisters there didn't pull a cool number by seizing control, but because they let the men back in after only *a day or so* of self-criticism on male chauvinism. (And goodbye to the inaccurate blanket use of that phrase, for that matter: male chauvinism is an *attitude*—male supremacy is the *objective reality, the fact*.) Goodbye to the Conspiracy who, when lunching with fellow sexist bastards Norman Mailer and Terry Southern in a bunny-type club in Chicago, found Judge Hoffman at the neighboring table—no surprise: *in the light they are all the same.*

Goodbye to Hip Culture and the so-called Sexual Revolution, which has functioned toward women's freedom as did the Reconstruction toward former slaves—reinstituted oppression by another name. Goodbye to the assumption that Hugh Romney is safe in his "cultural revolution," safe enough to refer to "our women, who make all our clothes" without somebody not forgiving that. Goodbye to the arrogance of power indeed that lets Czar Stan Freeman of the Electric Circus sleep without fear at night, or permits Tomi Ungerer to walk unafraid in the street after executing the drawings for the Circus advertising campaign against women. Goodbye to the idea that Hugh Hefner is groovy 'cause he lets Conspirators come to parties at the Mansion—goodbye to Hefner's dream of a ripe old age. Goodbye to Tuli and the Fugs and all the boys in the front room—who always knew they hated the women they loved. Goodbye to the notion that good ol' Abbie is any different from any other up and coming movie star (like, say Cliff Robertson) who ditches the first wife and kids, good enough for the old days but awkward once you're Making It. Goodbye to his hypocritical double standard that reeks through all the tattered charm. Goodbye to lovely pro-Women's-Liberation Paul Krassner, with all his astonished anger that women have lost their sense of humor "on this issue" and don't laugh anymore at little funnies that degrade and hurt them; farewell to the memory of his "Instant Pussy" aerosol-can poster, to his column for *Cavalier*, to his dream of a Rape-In against legislators' wives, to his Scapegoats and Realist Nuns and cute anecdotes about the little daughter he sees as often as any proper divorced Scarsdale middle-aged (38) father; goodbye forever to the notion that he is my brother who, like Paul, buys a prostitute for the night as a birthday gift for a male friend, or who, like Paul, reels off the names in alphabetical order of people in the Women's Movement he has fucked, reels off names in the best lockerroom tradition—as proof that *he's* no sexist oppressor.

Let it all hang out. Let it seem bitchy, catty, dykey, frustrated, crazy, Solanisesque, nutty, frigid, ridiculous, bitter, embarrassing, man-hating, libelous, pure, unfair, envious, intuitive, low-down, stupid, petty, liberating. We are the women that men have warned us about.

And let's put one lie to rest for all time: the lie that men are oppressed, too, by sexism—the lie that there can be such a thing as "men's liberation groups." Oppression is something that one group of people commits against another group specifically because of a "threatening" characteristic shared by the latter group—skin color or sex or age, etc. The oppressors are indeed *fucked up* by being masters (racism hurts whites, sexual stereotypes are harmful to men) but those masters are not *oppressed.* Any master has the alternative of divesting himself of sexism or racism—the oppressed have no alternative—for they have no power—but to fight. In the long run, Women's Liberation will of course free men—but in the short run it's going to *cost* men a lot of privilege, which no one gives up willingly or easily. Sexism is *not* the fault of women—kill your fathers, not your mothers.

Run it on down. Goodbye to a beautiful new ecology movement that could fight to save us all if it would stop tripping off women as earth-mother types or frontier chicks, if it would *right now* cede leadership to those who have *not* polluted the planet because that action implies power and women haven't had any power in about 5,000 years, cede leadership to those whose brains are as tough and clear as any man's but whose bodies are also unavoidably aware of the locked-in relationship between humans and their biosphere—the earth, the tides, the atmosphere, the moon. Ecology is no big *shtick* if you're a woman—it's always been there.

Goodbye to the complicity inherent in the Berkeley Tribesmen being part publishers of Trashman Comics; goodbye, for that matter, to the reasoning that finds whoremaster Trashman a fitting model, however comic-strip far out, for a revolutionary man—somehow related to the same Supermale reasoning that permits the first statement on Women's Liberation and male chauvinism that came out of the Black Panther Party to be made *by a man*, talkin' a whole lot 'bout how the Sisters should speak up for themselves. Such ignorance and arrogance ill befits a revolutionary.

We know how racism is worked deep into the unconscious by our System—the same way sexism is, as it appears in the very name of The Young Lords. What are you if you're a "macho woman"—a female Lord? Or, god forbid, a Young Lady? Change it, change it to The Young Gentry if you must, or never assume that the name itself is innocent of pain, of oppression.

Theory and practice—and the light-years between them. "Do it!" says Jerry Rubin in *Rat's* last issue—but he doesn't, or every *Rat* reader would have known the pictured face next to his article as well as they know his own much-photographed face: it was Nancy Kurshan, the power behind the clown.

Goodbye to the New Nation and Earth People's Park, for that matter, conceived by man, announced by men, led by men—doomed before its birth by the rotting seeds of male supremacy which are to be transplanted in fresh soil. Was it my brother who listed human beings among the *objects* which would be easily available after the Revolution: "Free grass, free food, free women, free acid, free clothes, etc."? Was it my brother who wrote "Fuck your women till they can't stand up" and said that groupies were liberated chicks 'cause they dug a tit-shake instead of a handshake? The epitome of female exclusionism—"men will make the Revolution—and their chicks." Not my brother, no. Not my revolution. Not one breath of my support for the new counterleft Christ—John Sinclair. Just one less to worry about for ten years. I do not choose my enemy for my brother.

Goodbye, goodbye. The hell with the simplistic notion that automatic freedom for women—or non-white peoples—will come about ZAP! with the advent of a socialist revolution. Bullshit. Two evils pre-date capitalism and have been clearly able to survive and post-date socialism: sexism and racism. Women were the first property when the Primary Contradiction occurred: when one half of the human species decided to subjugate the other half, because it was "different," alien, the Other. From there it was an easy enough step to extend the Other to someone of different skin shade, different height or weight or language—or strength to resist. Goodbye to those simple-minded optimistic dreams of socialist equality all our good socialist brothers want us to believe. How liberal a politics that is! How much further we will have to go to create those profound changes that would give birth to a genderless society. *Profound*, Sister. Beyond what is male or female. Beyond standards we all adhere to now without daring to examine them as male-created, male-dominated, male-fucked-up, and in male self-interest. *Beyond all known standards*, especially those easily articulated revolutionary ones we all rhetorically invoke. Beyond, to a species with a new name, that would not dare define itself as Man.

I once said, "I'm a revolutionary, not just a woman," and knew my own lie even as I said the words. The pity of that statement's eagerness to be acceptable to those whose revolutionary zeal no one would question, i.e., any male supremacist in the counterleft. But to become a true revolutionary one must first become one of the oppressed (not organize or educate or manipulate them, but become one of them)—or realize that you *are* one of them already. No woman wants that. Because that realization is humiliating, it hurts. It hurts to understand that at Woodstock or Altamont a woman could be declared uptight or a poor sport if she didn't want to be raped. It hurts to learn that the Sisters still in male-Left captivity are putting down the crazy feminists to make themselves look okay and unthreatening to our mutual oppressors. It hurts to be pawns in those games. It hurts to try and change *each day of your life right now*—not in talk, not "in your head," and not only conveniently "out there" in the Third World (half of which is women) or the black and brown communities (half of which are women) but in your own home, kitchen, bed. No getting away, no matter how else you are oppressed, from the primary oppression of being female in a patriarchal world. It hurts to hear that the Sisters in the Gay Liberation Front, too, have to struggle continually against the male chauvinism of their gay brothers. It hurts that Jane Alpert was cheered when rapping about imperialism, racism, the Third World, and All Those Safe Topics but hissed and booed by a Movement crowd of men who wanted none of it when she began to talk about Women's Liberation. The backlash is upon us.

They tell us the alternative is to hang in there and "struggle," to confront male domination in the counterleft, to fight beside or behind or beneath our brothers—to show 'em we're just as tough, just as revolushunerry, just as whatever-image-they-now-want-of-us-as-once-they-wanted-us-to-be-feminine-and-keep-the-home-fire-burning. They will bestow titular leadership on our grateful shoulders, whether it's being a token woman on the Movement Speakers Bureau Advisory board, or being a Conspiracy groupie or one of the "respectable" chain-swinging Motor City Nine. Sisters all, with only one real alternative: to seize our own power into our own hands, all women, separate and together, and make the Revolution the way it must be made—no priorities this time, no suffering group told to wait until after.

It is the job of revolutionary feminists to build an ever stronger independent Women's Liberation Movement, so that sisters in counter-left captivity will have somewhere to turn, to use their power and rage and beauty and coolness in their own behalf for once, on their own terms, on their own issues, in their own style—whatever that may be. Not for us in Women's Liberation to hassle them and confront them the way their men do, nor to blame them—or ourselves—for what any of us are: an oppressed people, but a people raising our consciousness toward something that is the other side of anger, something bright and smooth and cool, like action unlike anything yet contemplated or carried out. It is for us to survive (something the white male radical has the luxury of never really worrying about, what with all his options), to talk, to plan, to be patient, to welcome new fugitives from the counterfeit Left with no arrogance but only humility and delight, to plan, to push—to strike.

There is something every woman wears around her neck on a thin chain of fear—an amulet of madness. For each of us, there exists somewhere a moment of insult so intense that she will reach up and rip the amulet off, even if the chain tears at the flesh of her neck. And the last protection from seeing the truth will be gone. Do you think, tugging furtively every day at the chain and going nicely insane as I am, that I can be concerned with the puerile squabbles of a counterfeit Left that laughs at my pain? Do you think such a concern is noticeable when set alongside the suffering of more than half the human species for the past 5,000 years—due to a whim of the other half? No, no, no, goodbye to all that.

Women are Something Else. This time, we're going to kick out all the jams, and the boys will just have to hustle to keep up, or else drop out and openly join the power structure of which they are already the illegitimate sons. Any man who claims he is serious about wanting to divest himself of cock privilege should trip on this: all male leadership out of the Left is the only way; and it's going to happen, whether through men stepping down or through women seizing the helm. It's up to the "brothers"—after all, sexism is their concern, not ours; we're too busy getting ourselves together to have to deal with their bigotry. So they'll have to make up their own minds as to whether they will be divested of just cock privilege or—what the hell, why not say it, *say it?*—divested of cocks. How deep the fear of that loss must be, that it can be suppressed only by the building of empires and the waging of genocidal wars!

Goodbye, goodbye forever, counterfeit Left, counterleft, male-dominated cracked-glass-mirror reflection of the Amerikan Nightmare. Women are the real Left. We are rising, powerful in our unclean bodies; bright glowing mad in our inferior brains; wild hair flying, wild eyes staring, wild voices keening; undaunted by blood we who hemorrhage every twenty-eight days; laughing at our own beauty we who have lost our sense of humor; mourning for all each precious one of us might have been in this one living time-place had she not been born a woman; stuffing fingers into our mouths to stop the screams of fear and hate and pity for men we have loved and love still; tears in our eyes and bitterness in our mouths for children we couldn't *not* have, or didn't want, or didn't want *yet*, or wanted and had in this place and this time of horror. We are rising with a fury older and potentially greater than any force in history, and this time we will be free or no one will survive. Power to all the people or to none. All the way down, this time.

Free Kathleen Cleaver!   Free Kim Agnew!
Free Anita Hoffman!   Free Holly Krassner!
Free Bernadine Dohrn!   Free Lois Hart!
Free Donna Malone!   Free Alice Embree!
Free Ruth Ann Miller!   Free Nancy Kurshan!
Free Leni Sinclair!   Free Lynn Phillips!
Free Jane Alpert!   Free Dinky Forman!
Free Gumbo!   Free Sharon Krebs!
Free Bonnie Cohen!   Free Iris Luciano!
Free Judy Lampe!   Free Robin Morgan!

Free Valerie Solanis!

FREE OUR SISTERS!   **FREE OURSELVES!**

To a White Male Radical

A Berkeley Sister

It is the hardness of your face when I am with you that prevents me from telling you what hurts so much. Every time we part I feel a sense of overwhelming relief; coupled by a sense of personal disintegration. I feel almost sick with hunger for what you refuse to give, while my dislike of you grows.

You probably do not even know how you oppress me, or other women. But you do. Each time we meet you spell out the business of your schedule while I am supposed to marvel at this important male world to which you belong? I sometimes see very little difference between a conventional bourgeois chauvinist who thinks that his work is his whole life and a radical activist who also escapes the risk of being known by another through his intensive avoidance of free time.

Closeness. Something I have never felt with you after the first time you held me. You even dictate when I may be affectionate, for upon your body there is a sign that says "don't touch, unless I make it clear that I want it." Affection seems only proper with you when you are the initiator. Holding, touching, cuddling, these seem alien to you. Your body only expresses warmth in lovemaking. The rest of the time you are "self reliant," the word you repeat over and over again in hopes that someday you will no longer need anyone at all?

The tenderness and warmth that you suppress are as much your loss as mine. And you really seem tough and for this I dislike you; you are truly the John Wayne of the radical set.

A Berkely Sister, "To a White Male Radical," *The Berkeley Tribe*, May 15–22, 1970, p. 8.

Everyone has "work" and obligations. The only difference is that most people forget about the side of life that is equally important, that of deep and profound giving and taking with others. These are usually the people that will someday be offed. What shall we do with you on that day? Will anyone really distinguish you from a thousand other men who live for their work and cannot balance people and goals. Because of the things you choose to do you have successfully picked the most socially acceptable way in our radical world of avoiding the risk that follows when you give a little of yourself to another person. If you did it for fame and money in the straight world we would see you as another of the mad, neurotic, sublimated males with which this nation is overpopulated. Ah, but because you are contemplating the next activity and meeting. On to the busy world in which one struggles through competition, fights, struggles for the highest glories... the image itself resembles closely the Madison Ave. executive. No you don't sell out politically tho many think you do... no, you sell out your life.

Why am I writing this? Because you don't understand yet what it means not to oppress a woman. In everything we have done together I feel that I have been unable to tell you what a chauvinist you are. From the tough John Wayne facade to the empty and closed hours I have spent with you it really hurts to be a woman near you. So I will stay far away. You never allow me the privilege of asking you to spend time with me; no rather you always inform me of the time you can spend with me. I could love you someday if I stayed near you long enough. But then I would hate you as much. I would rather stay away and let others take your shit. You represent to me on a personal level what women in Women's Liberation have been discussing so long. You are the embodiment of male chauvinism and what is so sick about it is that you self-importantly deny it. Like all the white male liberals who abound over this shitty earth you are forever denying your elitism and prejudice while you oppress others. And when I bring up the problem you feel threatened. Well good! FEEL threatened because someday women will see through your facade and you will become the visible enemy. Yes you feel threatened because I a woman will no longer be treated as an object but demand my existence as a person. Because I a woman am demanding that you treat me as an equal and not as part of your agenda. Because I am a woman bringing the revolution home. Because I a woman have seen through your compulsive need for ego gratification and see the suppression and sickness of your goals.

I suppose it is far easier to oust me into a nagging woman role than deal with the fundamental issue at hand. To be self reliant after all means to need no one. To need no one means to possess a superior power by which you can fulfill all your own needs. Others become inessential, thus they are inferior to you. Self reliance is a luxury of the unoppressed. Though you may continue to feel haunted by the John Wayne mystique and continue to feel the need to conform to that miserable role, I hope you realize how counterrevolutionary and how reactionary it is in fact to seek self reliance.

Thoreau after all did not cause a revolution. His acts were as American as yours; firmly planted within the traditional American role of the male; a sick role. Perhaps you have never understood what real equality between the sexes means to us. It does not mean that women take on the supremely sick and neurotic role of men in this society. It means that both sexes give up the passive feminine–aggressive masculine limited roles they play in favor of becoming totally androgynous personalities. Women no longer fear their powers and act on them; men become softer, gentler, more in need of the warmth and understanding they have never attributed to themselves. I therefore will not accept your ridiculous role of self reliance; it is inhuman, counterrevolutionary and opposed to the goals of Women's Liberation.

Your reluctance to be close and open when all is said and done indicates that you make a rather limited socialist after all. Refusing vulnerability you are refusing friendship. Refusing acts of sharing you seem so sadly alone. Long ago, earlier feminists wanted to be tough like you. Only fifty years later did they realize how they had assumed the role of the oppressor. Like many Blacks they had silently slipped into the oppressor's habits and therefore truly failed. That is why you are an enemy.

Hello to All That

Genie Plamondon

So many deeds cry out to be done,
And always urgently;
The world rolls on,
Time presses.
Ten thousand years are too long,
Seize the day, seize the hour!

—*Chairman Mao*

I really feel like I've got to answer Robin Morgan's article in the first issue of the Women's Rat—wow—you see, I'm one of the founders of the White Panther Party—not many people know that, and before now I never really cared who knew it—I can say without feeling badly about it at all that the White Panther Party has been male chauvinist in the past, I was the only woman on the Central Committee and my first title was Corresponding Secretary, which, I found out later, really pissed a lot of people off—they figured we were male chauvinist, and I guess they were right, even though me and Leni *were* actually the only chicks playing an active role in the Party at the time of its birth in November '68...and Leni just didn't care to be listed on the Central Committee. We never related to women's liberation until revolutionary women made it a definite issue that we couldn't overlook. As the

Genie Plamondon, "Hello to All That," *The Berkeley Tribe*, March 6–13, 1970, p. 13.

concept of male chauvinism began to sink in I was forced at the same time to become more and more revolutionary, to accept more responsibility, forced to realize that I can't be free until everyone is free, until the whole planet has been liberated...I can't give anyone priorities when it comes to freedom, we *all* need it *now*, and there will be vanguards in women's liberation, and there will be vanguards in the liberation of the black colony and in the liberation of the youth colony, in the liberation of *all* colonialized oppressed peoples—but we all have the same oppressor, the same enemy—and we're all fighting side by side despite our differences—everyone should be working their hardest to make it continue that way and become even *more* of a united front.

Now I'm Minister of Communication—and I have been educated to the need for emphasizing women's liberation within the struggle to liberate all the people on the planet—but I have to say right here right now that I'm into women's liberation to educate women to become *revolutionaries*—Revolution means Change—I cannot accept a woman as a revolutionary woman who says of John Sinclair "Just one less to worry about for ten years. I do not choose my enemy for my brother."

She leaves no room for change, for revolution—she assumes that since John Sinclair was male chauvinist a year and a half ago he must be male chauvinist now and for the rest of his life—and she assumes that throughout her article.

I'm not into that at all—I'm into intensifying the struggle on all levels, dealing with concrete problems in a revolutionary fashion that will make us *come together*. I cannot accept her as a revolutionary when she says "Goodbye" to so many of the people and movements that have brought us to the point in history we have reached now—I say *hello* to all the things and people she spoke of—*hello from a new revolutionary woman who is now ready to deal with you as a revolutionary*, and we'll go on from here—we'll go on to revolutionize the whole planet and *everyone* on it—including John Sinclair, who, along with brother Pun Plamondon and sister Leni Sinclair, was most instrumental in revolutionizing myself, forcing me to realize my own potential, demanding that I study, demanding that I dedicate my life to the revolution and to serving the people...demanding it by their own daily lives so intertwined with mine—I almost have to hang my head in sorrow when I realize all the frustration pent up in all of us—I keep seeing pure examples of what Fritz Fanon was talking about in *Wretched of the Earth* when he said that brothers and sisters who can't reach the real oppressor start striking out at each other—but I'm not going to hang my head in sorrow any more (except in private, at night, when I go to bed without Pun, knowing he is out there somewhere in the belly the beast, an outlaw, forced underground with a phoney conspiracy and bombing charge, I really miss him)—there's no time for that—there's too much to say hello to, too much revolutionizing to do—too many things to change, too many "simple-minded optimistic dreams" that are going to take a lot of hard work to make realities—no, I'm gonna raise my head and my *fist* in anger and love, and join my brothers and sisters in demanding and working and fighting for *Freedom now—by any means necessary*—I'm not going to join any women who want a "genderless society"—they can have their own genderless tribe, I'm not down on that—I love to fuck, I love being a woman, I love women, and I love *men*—oh yes I do—Nor am I going to join any woman, any body, who wants to "take over the movement"—bullshit—I align myself with all revolutionary people who are dedicated to serving the people and liberating the planet from *all* oppressive forces—the White Panther Party is dedicated, Rising Up Angry is dedicated, the Young Patriots and Young Lords are dedicated, the Weathermen are dedicated, the Vietnamese are dedicated, the Koreans the Cubans and Chinese and Africans are dedicated—and we are all *revolutionaries*, we are all for *change*—on the planet and within ourselves, anyone not prepared to change will *die*, and I won't waste my time saying goodbye....

    Seize the time outlaws!!!!!!

Alphabet Soup

Karen Durbin

In attempting to put together an alphabet soup of the women's liberation movement, I began to feel that I was assembling some sort of descriptive telephone book for a small city. With each new discovered and defined group came inklings of a dozen others just beyond, until it became apparent that whatever else the movement is, its numbers are legion and no comprehensive list could be got ready by deadline time.

In a recent article (November 21) on "the new feminism," *Time* magazine reported that there are "at least 50 groups in New York...35 in the San Francisco Bay Area...30 in Chicago, 25 in Boston and a scattering of others in cities ranging from Gainesville, Fla. to Toronto." I can add to that list an indeterminate number of British groups and a large movement in Berlin (where radical feminists have organized into communes, opened childcare and information centers and operate a mobile health care service). Fifty in New York? At least. Furthermore, the groups vary greatly in type. Some are small, informal consciousness-raising groups. Others are organized around a single issue central to the movement such as abortion or free child-care, some along extra-feminist lines (for example, professional groups such as Media Women or the numerous high school, college and graduate school groups). Still others are feminist caucuses within organizations that are, to put it mildly in some cases, not primarily feminist (e.g. YSA Women, the Women's Rights Caucus of the New Democratic Coalition, SDS Women). Finally, there are the groups whose organization and politics are primarily

---

Karen Durbin, "Alphabet Soup," *Win* magazine, January 1970.

feminist, independent and non-feminist professional and political affiliations, and who operate in a wider sphere than the informal consciousness-raising groups. I don't have a complete list of these groups—as far as I know, no one does, since it is a characteristic peculiar to the women's liberation movement that it cuts across all social divisions of class and race and that it is as politically complex and fluid as a movement can be. New groups are constantly forming, old ones divide and multiply into new or undergo radical transformations as women strive for a new and truer definition not only of themselves but of politics as well, I began this project with the idea of producing a neat diagram of the movement, a tidy, conscientious parsing of its elements. That idea had been abandoned; how does one diagram upheaval? Instead, what follows is an attempt to describe briefly six groups whose differences of style and concentration will yield a rough measure of the movement as a whole.

"Citywide" women's liberation coalition. This group properly has no name and doesn't particularly want one, but is generally referred to as "Citywide." It began in the spring of 1969 as a coalition of revolutionary women, some from other feminist groups, many from non-feminist radical organizations (e.g. SDS, Newsreel, *Leviathan* and later, RYM II), who met every other Thursday evening to concentrate on women's liberation issues. It has a fluctuating attendance membership of 50–70 women, who tend to believe that while capitalism/imperialism and male chauvinism maintain each other, the greater power and therefore the focus of attack resides in the system rather than in male chauvinism. They are distinct from much of the rest of the women's liberation movement by the fact that they acknowledge the possibility of strategic alliances with male-dominated radical groups. They see women's liberation as essential to any real revolution, but do not always place primary emphasis on it. Suggesting that "freedom is the recognition of necessity" one woman active in the coalition gave as an example the need for black and brown women to multiply in order to combat "American genocidal policies" as more important than the demand for control over their bodies, i.e. free abortion and birth control. The same woman pointed out, however, that there was a growing trend in the coalition toward a more strictly feminist approach. According to another member, the coalition has organized separate day-care, abortion and health collectives and is in the process of developing others. A propaganda collective is planned, as well as others to work with high school and college students, and people are moving to Brooklyn and Queens to organize there. The

coalition is also willing to assist any women in starting their own consciousness-raising groups....

The Feminists. Self-described as "a political organization to annihilate sex roles" The Feminists began on October 17, 1968 as a breakaway group from N.O.W. which they considered too hierarchical and superficial in its approach to women's liberation. An intense and highly disciplined group, they meet twice a week and conduct frequent workshops and special meetings as well. Penalties for irregular attendance are temporary loss of voting privileges and, if necessary, expulsion from the group. They require further that not more than one third of their membership be either married or living with a man, on the basis that such arrangements are inherently inequitable. They are also insistently democratic: the chair and secretary of each meeting are chosen by lot, and all work, whether menial or demanding of special skills, is assigned by lot with provision against the same sort of task—writing a position paper, for example—falling to one member twice before it has made the round of the group.

The Feminists' rules reflect their political theory which states, in part, that "all political classes grew out of the male-female role system.... The pathology of oppression can only be fully comprehended in its primary development, the male-female division. Because the male-female system is primary, the freedom of every oppressed individual depends upon the freeing of every individual from every aspect of the male-female system." They demand that marriage and the family be eliminated, that children be cared for by the society as a whole and not "belong" to anyone and that extra-uterine means of reproduction be developed as "a humane goal." They also oppose sexual intercourse ("at present its psychology is dominance-passivity") and suggest the exploration of other means of sexual gratification as a way toward "physical relations...(that) would be an extension of communication between individuals." In a demonstration at the Marriage License Bureau and City Hall the Feminists made additional demands for economic and educational reparations for women and repeal of all state laws pertaining to marriage, divorce and annulment....

National Organization for Women. NOW was founded in 1966 by Betty Friedan, author of *The Feminine Mystique.* It has more than 5000 members, including some 100 men, with chapters in all the major cities of the U.S. It is the most politically moderate of the feminist organizations and concentrates on working within the system with a program of legislative demands for full equality for women. Those demands include passage of an Equal Rights Amendment to the Constitution which reads, "Equality of Rights under the Law shall not be denied or abridged by the United States or by any State on account of sex." NOW also demands the repeal of all abortion laws, the establishment of free, state-supported child-care centers and the revision of the tax laws to permit full deduction of all housekeeping and child-care expenses for working parents. The organization functions as an effective legislative pressure group and is considered to be largely responsible for the barring of sexual categorization in Want Ads and was instrumental in winning the fight by airline stewardesses to marry and stay on the job after age 32. NOW is the only currently active feminist organization that did not develop out of New Left-oriented radical politics, a fact that is reflected, perhaps, not only in its tendency to focus somewhat exclusively on specific legislative inequities without going on to scrutinize the social and political system in which these inequities flourish but also in the structure of the organization itself. Not only is NOW hierarchical—there is a board of directors, as well as national and local officers, all elected for fixed terms—but among its male members there is even a chapter president, a phenomenon that one might safely guess has not been duplicated elsewhere in women's liberation. There is evidence, however, that a radical trend is developing in NOW which should be interesting to watch....

Redstockings. Formed in January 1968, Redstockings insist on the need for a completely new political analysis based on their personal experience as women. Much of their energy has been devoted to personal consciousness-raising, not as "therapy...but as the only method by which we can ensure that our program for liberation is based on the concrete realities of our lives." They have participated regularly in women's liberation demonstrations since the start of the movement; however, they recently disrupted and took over an abortion hearing in New York at which women were denied places on the panel. Their persistence in sticking to their slogan, "We will not ask what is 'revolutionary' or 'reformist' only what is good for women," has, on occasion, put them very much at odds with the Citywide faction of the movement. (It's impossible, for example, to imagine Redstockings accepting the Citywide interpretation of the priorities of black and brown women in regard to abortion and birth control.)

Redstockings flatly blames men for women's oppression, stating in their manifesto that "all other forms of exploitation and oppression (racism, capitalism, imperialism, etc.) are extensions of male supremacy: men dominate women, a few men dominate the rest." The group is opposed to marriage and the nuclear family but does not attempt to legislate the sexual lives of its members. They further "call on all men to give up their male privileges and support women's liberation," a demand that reflects their own personal pledge to "repudiate all economic, racial, educational or status privileges that divide us from other women." They hold an orientation meeting for new women on the first Sunday of every month and they also have a selection of interesting literature for sale....

   The Stanton-Anthony Brigade of the Radical Feminists. Just begun in November by a group of women already active in women's liberation who felt the need for a group that would concentrate specifically on creating a mass movement. The Brigade, by virtue of the political history of its members, is radical-leftist but emphasizes feminism as the core of its politics. Their program is one of "consciousness-raising actions," demonstrations designed to focus national attention on radical feminism and to draw as many women as possible into the movement. They feel that too many women's liberation actions in the past have been politically self-indulgent (for example, wearing arm bands mourning the death of Ho Chi Minh at the Miss America demonstration) and have as a result turned women away from a movement that should properly be inviting them in. They also welcome publicity (many groups don't at this point, largely out of fear and distrust) and when planning demonstrations will take into account ways to circumvent distortion and misunderstanding of their actions. They have begun with a core group of around 20 women and welcome new members. As their membership grows it is to be divided into separate "brigades" of fifteen women each. So far they have met once a week, usually on Monday nights, and a meeting for new people is planned for the near future....

   Women's International Terrorist Conspiracy from Hell (WITCH). WITCH surfaced on Halloween Day, 1968, with an "Up against the Wall Street" action involving day-long street theatre in the financial district and talk sessions with the women who work there. It is a flamboyant action-oriented organization with more than thirty autonomous covens around the country. Like most of women's liberation it has no official leaders and functions by consensus. WITCH is opposed to marriage and the nuclear family but its distinctiveness lies less in its ideology than in its style, which is by turns exuberant, rude, funny and extravagant. On the bus ride to Atlantic City for last summer's Miss America demonstration, a coven sitting in the back produced several fine, rowdy songs and chants for the demonstration when the bus was barely out of New York. WITCH, more than any other group, suggests

in its tone that women's liberation can be fun. A few excerpts from their manifesto:

> WITCH is an all-woman Everything. It's theater, revolution, magic, terror, joy, garlic flowers, spells. It's an awareness that witches and gypsies were the original guerrillas and resistance fighters against oppression... Witches were the first Friendly Heads and Dealers, the first birth-control practitioners and abortionists, the first alchemists... WITCH lives and laughs in every woman. She is the free part of each of us, beneath the shy smiles, the acquiescence to absurd male domination... if you are a woman and dare to look within yourself, you are a witch...you are free and beautiful... Whatever is repressive, solely male-oriented, greedy, puritanical, authoritarian—those are your targets....you are pledged to free our brothers from oppression and stereotyped sexual roles as well as ourselves. You are a witch by saying aloud, "I am a Witch," three times, and thinking about that. You are a witch by being female, untamed, angry, joyous, and immortal.

WITCH also quotes the Bible (Judges): "for rebellion is as the sin of witchcraft...."

Index

Central Committee (Soviet), 89
Central Intelligence Agency, (see
 CIA)
Chaney, James, 9
Charles, Ray, 440
Cherne, Leo, 281–282
Chicago, 31–35
Chicago American, 426
Chicago Conspiracy Trial, (see Chi-
 cago 8/7)
Chicago 8/7, 42–46, 47, 53,
 62n.90, 174, 252, 256, 272,
 273, 361–392
Chicago National Action, 247,
 254–263, (see also Days of
 Rage)
Chicago Sun-Times, 426
China, 222, 223, 263, 267, 276,
 303, 311
Church, Senator Frank, 62n., 308
CIA (Central Intelligence Agency),
 28, 58n.23, 89, 282, 284, 287
"Citywide," 525–526
Civic Action teams, 284
Civil Rights Act (1964), 9, 118
Civil rights movement, 6–9, 12–13,
 22–23, 56, 105–171, 193,
 198, 265–266, 267, (see also
 Sit-ins, Montgomery Bus Boy-
 cott)
Clark, Mark, 27, 54, 62n.90
Clark, Ramsey, 45
Class:
 and sex, 483, 485, 488–489, 491,
  496
 struggle, 493, 498–499
 upper, 177
 working, 88, 409
Clay, Cassius, (see Ali, Muhammad)
Cleaver, Eldridge, 24, 59n.48
Cleaver, Kathleen, 26, 516
Coasters, The, 440

Coffin, William S., 61n.81
Cohen, Bonnie, 516
COINTELPRO, 26–27, 60n.55
Cold war, 2, 14, 73–85, 176, 177,
 190, 218, 276, 400
Coleman, Henry, 238
Collectives, revolutionary, 255, 258
Collins, Judy, 44
Collins, General Lawton, 280, 282
Columbia University, 30–31, 174,
 233–246, 267, 413, 422, 423,
 460
Commentary, 419
Common Market, 207
Communes, 30, 39, 52, 240, 424,
 524
Communism:
 and suppression in U.S., 2,
  56n.1, 305
 Vietnamese, 14, 15, 219, 221,
  222, 226, 276, 277, 280,
  281, 286, 287, 298, 300,
  309, 319, 338, 343
Communist Party, 2, 5, 10, 26, 102,
 310, 311, 335, 413, 432
Communists, 15, 36, 55, 255, 256,
 263, 333, 420, 465
Community organizing, 244,
 257–258
Computers, 11, 197, 391, (see also
 Cybernation)
Concentration camps, 94, 157, 179,
 209, 219, 335, 337, 339, 416
Congress of Racial Equality, (see
 CORE)
Consciousness raising, 48, 515,
 524–525, 527, 528
CORE (Congress of Racial Equali-
 ty), 8, 106, 129, 234
Cornell University, 38
Counterculture, 15, 19–22, 28, 40,
 41, 44, 52, 107, 402–458

The turbulent decade of the 1960s has been analyzed and interpreted by numerous journalists and scholars. In *The Sixties Papers*, former movement leaders Judith Clavir Albert and Stewart Edward Albert "tell it like it was," presenting material generated by the social protest movements. Challenging the prevailing view that the decade failed to produce influential enduring ideas, the authors demonstrate that the new left and counterculture produced a coherent body of critical thought about the nature of American society.

"I don't know how we did so long without such a book. Not only does it restore a vital part of American radical history to us, but it is especially pertinent to the struggles and challenges we face in the 1980s."
Barbara Ehrenreich, author *Hearts of Men: American Dreams and the Flight from Commitment*

"At last, a panorama of the '60s, possibly one of the most memorable decades in American history, prepared by two who lived a great deal of it. *The Sixties Papers* was well worth the long wait."
William M. Kunstler, civil rights attorney; president, Center for Constitutional Rights

"This book is essential reading for anyone who wants to know where America is coming from."
Robert Allen, author *Black Awakening in Capitalist America*

"*The Sixties Papers* is a profoundly enlightening, necessary documentation of recent American history. It is like a lamp by which the middle aged, who were confused, and the youth of America can guide their feet through the next few decades. To read *The Sixties Papers* is to realize the history of our rebellion: a gallant quest for first class humanism."
Bobby Seale

"A political nostalgia tour that brings back the smell of tear-gas, the sounds of protest, and the excitement of a decade well worth remembering."
Robert Friedman, editor *Columbia Daily Spectator*, 1968–69

ISBN 0-03-063617-5

Buddhism and the Coming Revolution

Gary Snyder

Buddhism holds that the universe and all creatures in it are intrinsically in a state of complete wisdom, love and compassion; acting in natural response and mutual interdependence. The personal realization of this from-the-beginning state cannot be had for and by one— "self"—because it is not fully realized unless one has given the self up, and away.

In the Buddhist view, what obstructs the effortless manifestation of this state is ignorance, which projects into fear and needless craving. Historically, Buddhist philosophers have failed to analyze out the degree to which ignorance and suffering are caused by social factors, considering fear-and-desire to be given facts of the human condition. Consequently the major concern of Buddhist philosophy is epistemology and "psychology" with no attention paid to historical or sociological problems. Although Mahayana Buddhism has a grand vision of universal salvation, the ACTUAL achievement of Buddhism has been the development of practical systems of meditation toward the end of liberating a few dedicated invididuals from psychological hangups and cultural conditionings. Institutional Buddhism has been conspicuously ready to accept or ignore the inequalities and tyrannies of whatever political system it found itself under. This can be death to Buddhism, because it is death to any meaningful function of compassion. Wisdom without compassion feels no pain.

Gary Snyder, "Buddhism and the Coming Revolution," *The Berkeley Barb*, November 15–21, 1968, p. 90.

No one today can afford to be innocent, or indulge himself in ignorance of the nature of contemporary governments, politics, and social orders. The national politics of the modern world maintain their existence by deliberately fostered craving and fear: monstrous protection rackets. The free world has become economically dependant on a fantastic system of stimulation of greed which canot be fulfilled, sexual desires which cannot be satiated, and hatred which has no outlet except against oneself, the persons one is supposed to love, or the revolutionary aspirations of pitiful poverty-striken marginal societies like Cuba or Vietnam. The conditions of the cold war have turned all modern societies—Communist included—into vicious distorters of man's true potential. They create populations of "preta"—hungry ghosts with giant appetites and throats no bigger than needles. The soil, the forests, and all animals life are being consumed by these cancerous collectivities; the air and water of the planet is being fouled by them.

There is nothing in human nature or the requirements of human social organization which intrinsically requires that a culture be contradictory, repressive, and productive of violent and frustrated personalities. Recent findings in anthropology and psychology make this more and more evident. One can prove it for himself by taking a good look at his own nature through meditation. Once a person has this much faith and insight, he must be led to a deep concern with the need for radical social change through a variety of hopefully non-violent means.

The joyous and voluntary poverty of Buddhism becomes a positive force. The traditional harmlessness and refusal to take life in any form has nation-shaking implications. The practice of meditation, for which one needs "only the ground beneath one's feet" wipes out mountains of junk being pumped into the mind by the mass media and universities. The belief in a serene and generous fulfillment of natural loving desires destroys ideologies which blind, maim, and repress and points the way to a kind of community which would amaze "moralists" and eliminate armies of men who are fighters because they cannot be lovers.

Avatamsaka (Kegon) Buddhist philosophy sees the world as a vast inter-related network in which all objects and creatures are necessary and illuminated. From one standpoint, governments, wars, or all that we consider evil are uncompromisingly contained in this totalistic realm. The hawk, the swoop, and the hare are one. From the "human" standpoint we cannot live in those terms unless all beings see with the same enlightened eye. The Bodhisattva lives by the sufferer's standard, and he must be effective in aiding those who suffer.

Been Down So Long
It Looks Like Up to Me

Konstantin Berlandt

I stood on the street corner tired from the long drive to El Paso. A man backed his white car up to me.

"I'm too tired to trick tonight," I said through the open window on my side of his car, "but could you tell me where the gay bars are?"

I'm in El Paso to run some gay liberation workshops and a homosexual happening at the National Students Association convention.

The gay bars were four blocks from the convention hotels. Dancing is allowed. I dance with my brothers.

I'm at a radical party. I ask no one to dance. Everyone is playing straight. In mixed company straights have always been in command.

The drama of the happening's first act was to get you over your fear of dancing with another boy or another girl someone else of your sex, even in mixed company.

The tape of rock 'n' roll continued into a second act of dancing and making it: "You Turn Me On," "Light My Fire," "Your Love Takes Me Higher and Higher," a Mitch Ryder/James Brown spliced together orgasm ("Sock It to Me" entry; "Wow, I Feel Good, I Got You" delivery and waking up in the morning to recall that "Double Shot of My Baby's Love."

And Act III began with the refrain "Everybody Loves a Lover" bopping along with the Shirelles, and then the ensuing guilt and hiding

Konstantin Berlandt. "Been Down So Long It Looks Like Up to Me, *The Berkeley Tribe*, September 12–18, 1969, p. 5.

TWO HUNDRED PSYCHOLOGICAL TERRORISTS COULD DESTROY ANY MAJOR UNIVERSITY—WITHOUT FIRING A SHOT.

Schools—high schools and colleges—are the biggest obstacle to education in Amerika today.

Schools are a continuation of toilet training.

Taking an exam is like taking a shit. You hold it in for weeks, memorizing, just waiting for the right time. Then the time comes, and you sit on the toilet.

Ah!

Um!

It feels so good.

You shit it right back on schedule—for the grade. When exams are over, you got a load off your mind. You got rid of all of the shit you clogged your poor brain with. You can finally relax.

The paper you write your exam on is toilet paper.

Babies are zen masters, curious about everything.
Adults are serious and bored.
What happened?
Brain surgery by the schools.

I lost my interest in books in literature class. I lost my interest in foreign languages in language class. I lost my interest in biology in biology class.

Dig the environment of a university! The buildings look like factories, airports, army barracks, IBM cards in the air, hospitals, jails. They are designed to wipe out all individuality, dull one's senses, make you feel small.

Everyone should bring dayglow paint to campus and psychedelicize the buildings as the first act of liberation.

"Critical" or "abstract thinking" is a trap in school.

Criticize, criticize, criticize.

Look at both sides of the argument, take no action, take no stands, commit yourself to nothing, because you're always looking for more arguments, more information, always examining, criticizing.

Abstract thinking turns the mind into a prison. Abstract thinking is the way professors avoid facing their own social impotence.

the blackboard. Everybody writes down in their notebook every word he spews.

His first words are, "Good morning, class."

The guy next to me copies down, "Good morning, class."

Somebody raises his hand and asks: "Do we have to know that for the exam?"

The classroom is an authoritarian environment. Teacher up front and rows of students one after another. Do not lose your temper, fuck, kiss, hug, get emotional or take off your clothes.

The class struggle begins in class.

We roll a few joints and start smoking in the middle of the classroom. The smell is overpowering, but no one seems to notice it.

The Viet Kong could attack with mortar shells, and everybody would still be taking notes.

It's an assembly line.

The professor talks; students copy.

Everyone is 99 percent asleep.

Marvin Garson takes off his shirt and begins tongue-kissing with his chick Charlie. I rip off my shirt and start soul-kissing with Nancy.

There we are in the middle of the class, shirts off, kissing, feeling each other up and smoking pot.

Everyone gets itchy and nervous because of us. No one can take notes anymore. The professor stutters. Pens stop. People squirm. Everyone's looking at us—no one at the professor. But the students are too repressed and shy to say anything.

Finally a girl in the middle of the room can't stand it any more. "Could these people please stop making a disturbance?" she pants.

Nancy leaps to her feet: "This is a class on thinking! We're thinking! You can't separate thinking from kissing, feeling, touching.

"We're the laboratory part of the class. Anybody who wants to come, join us. Anybody who wants to listen to the lecture part of the class move to the other part of the room."

The professor then reveals his soul. "In *my* class," he says with authority, "*I* do the teaching."

Scratch a professor and find a pig.

(His assistant goes to get the uniformed pig, so we split.)

The goal is to turn on everybody who can be turned on and turn off everybody else.

Theater has no rules, forms, structure, standards, traditions—it is pure, natural energy, impulse, anarchy.

The job of the revolution is to smash stage sets, start fires in movie theaters and then scream, "Fire!"

The theatrical geniuses of today are creating the drama of Vietnam in occupied school administration buildings across Amerika.

The Living Theater, a far-out guerrilla theater group, came to Berkeley while people were fighting the National Guard in the streets. As pacifists they opposed the street action.

Living Theater eliminated the stage and joined the audience. Revolutionary theater.

"I am not allowed to smoke marijuana," one Living Theater member sobbed. He was offered five joints.

Another cried, "I can't take off my clothes!" Around him people stripped naked.

At the end of the performance, everyone left to take the revolution to the streets. The cast stopped at the front door.

Revolution-in-the-auditorium is a contradiction. We get pissed when our revolutionary energy is wasted with a play that is defined by walls and exit doors, by starting and ending times, by ticket prices.

The only role of theater is to take people out of the auditorium and into the streets. The role of the revolutionary theater group is to make the revolution.

* * *

BURN DOWN THE SCHOOLS

A sunny day on the Berkeley campus. Students are carrying ten pounds of books from one class to the next.

We nonstudent fuck-ups say, "Excuse me, student. Did you know the sun is shining?"

They look at us like we're crazy.

We invade libraries yelling, "The sun is shining! The sun is shining!"

We go into a psychology class on "Thinking," a huge lecture hall with 300 students. The professor is up front, diagraming behavior on

Television keeps us escalating our tactics; a tactic becomes ineffective when it stops generating gossip or interest—"news."

Politicians get air time just by issuing statements. Rockefeller doesn't have to carry a picket sign to make a point. But ordinary people must take to the streets to get on television. One person, doing the right thing at the right time, can create a myth. The disruption of Nixon's speech reduces Nixon to background.

TV time goes to those with the most guts and imagination.

I never understand the radical who comes on TV in a suit and tie. Turn off the sound and he could be the mayor!

The *words* may be radical, but television is a non-verbal instrument! The way to understand TV is to shut off the sound. No one remembers any words they hear; the mind is a technicolor movie of images, not words.

I've never seen "bad" coverage of a demonstration. It makes no difference what they *say* about us. The pictures are the story.

Our power lies in our ability to strike fear in the enemy's heart: so the more the media exaggerate, the better. When the media start saying nice things about us, we should get worried.

If the yippies controlled national TV, we could make the Viet Kong and the Black Panthers the heroes of swooning Amerikan middle-aged housewives everywhere within a week.

The movement is too puritanical about the use of the media. After all, Karl Marx never watched television!

You can't be a revolutionary today without a television set—it's as important as a gun!

Every guerrilla must know how to use the terrain of the culture that he is trying to destroy!

* * *

REVOLUTION IS THEATER-IN-THE-STREETS

You are the stage.
You are the actor.
Everything is for real.
There is no audience.

Who Owns the Park?: A Leaflet

F.J. Bardacke

Someday a petty official will appear with a piece of paper, called a land title, which states that the University of California owns the land of the People's Park. Where did that piece of paper come from? What is it worth?

A long time ago the Costanoan Indians lived in the area now called Berkeley. They had no concept of land ownership. They believed that the land was under the care and guardianship of the people who used it and lived on it.

Catholic missionaries took the land away from the Indians. No agreements were made. No papers were signed. They ripped it off in the name of God.

The Mexican Government took the land away from the Church. The Mexican Government had guns and an army. God's word was not as strong.

The Mexican Government wanted to pretend that it was not the army that guaranteed them the land. They drew up some papers which said they legally owned it. No Indians signed those papers.

The Americans were not fooled by the papers. They had a stronger army than the Mexicans. They beat them in a war and took the land. Then they wrote some papers of their own and forced the Mexicans to sign them.

The American Government sold the land to some white settlers. The Government gave the settlers a piece of paper called a land title in exchange for some money. All this time there were still some Indians around who claimed the land. The American army killed most of them. The piece of paper saying who owned the land was passed around among rich white men. Sometimes the white men were interested in taking care of the land. Usually they were just interested in making money. Finally some very rich men, who run the University of California, bought the land.

Immediately these men destroyed the houses that had been built on the land. The land went the way of so much other land in America—it became a parking lot.

We are building a park on the land. We will take care of it and guard it, in the spirit of the Costanoan Indians. When the University comes with its land title we will tell them: "Your land title is covered with blood. We won't touch it. Your people ripped off the land from the Indians a long time ago. If you want it back now, you will have to fight for it again."

Our generation is in rebellion against abstract intellectualism and critical thinking.

We admire the Viet Kong guerrilla, the Black Panther, the stoned hippie, not the abstract intellectual vegetable.

Professors are put-ons, writing and talking in fancy, scientific, big motherfucking words, so the people on the street won't dig that they're not saying shit.

They're so thankful for their "intellectual freedom in Amerika" that they're not going to waste it fighting on issues like poverty, war, drugs, and revolution. They insist upon the freedom to be irrelevant. We judge our teachers as men first and teachers second. How can you teach us about World War I if you weren't in the streets of Czechago?

The goal of the revolution is to eliminate all intellectuals, create a society in which there is no distinction between intellectual and physical work: a society without intellectuals. Our task is to destroy the university and make the entire nation a school with on-the-job living.

School addicts people to the heroin of middle-class life: busy work for grades (money) stored in your records (banks) for the future (death). We become replaceable parts for corporate Amerika!

School offers us cheap victories—grades, degrees—in exchange for our souls: We're actually supposed to be happy when we get a better grade than somebody else! We're taught to compete and to get our happiness from the unhappiness of others.

For us education is the creation of a free society. Anyone who wants to teach should be allowed to "teach." Anybody who wants to learn should be allowed to "learn." There is no difference between teachers and students, because we teach and learn from each other. The professors and the students are the dropouts—people who have dropped out of Life. The dropouts from school are people who have dropped into Living. Our generation is making history in the streets, so why waste our lives in plastic classrooms?

High school students are the largest oppressed minority in Amerika. We know what *freedom is* when we hear the bell dismissing school. *"School's out, I'm free at last!"*

Teachers know that unless they control our toilet training, we'd never stay in class. You gotta raise your hand to get permission to go take a shit. The bathrooms are the only liberated areas in school.

DROP OUT!

Why stay in school? To get a degree? *Print your own!* Can you smoke a diploma!

We are going to invade the schools and free our brothers who are prisoners. We will burn the buildings and the books. We will throw pies in the faces of our professors.

We will give brooms and pails to the administrators so they can be useful and sweep the place up. Fuck bureaucrats, especially the "nice" Deans of Men who put one hand around our shoulders while the other hand gropes for our pants. We'll take all the records, grades, administrative shit and flush it down the toilet.

The same people who control the universities own the major capitalist corporations, carry out the wars, fuck over black people, run the police forces and eat money and flesh for breakfast. They are absentee dictators who make rules but don't live under them. Universities are feudal autocracies.

Professors are house niggers and students are field niggers. Demonstrations on campuses aren't "demonstrations"—they're jail breaks. Slave revolts.

The war on the campuses is similar to the war in Vietnam: a guerrilla people's war.

By closing down 100 universities in one day, we, the peasants, can level the most powerful blow possible against the pigs who run Amerikan society.

We'll force the President of the United States to come on his hands and knees to the conference table.

We're using the campus as a launching pad to foment revolution everywhere.

Ronnie Reagan, baby, you're right!

People's Park: Free for All

Stew Albert

We began building a Park last Sunday. There were no speeches or long debates. Several hundred Berkeley Freemen showed up for work on the mud swamp between Dwight and Haste in back of Telegraph, and if you stopped working for five seconds somebody grabbed your shovel and said "it's my turn."

The land belonged to the University, it bought it up and tore down some of the most beautiful housing in Berkeley. A cement parking lot and then dormitories were supposed to be built but Ronald Reagan cut off the bread and the land just stayed there and turned into a swamp with automobiles on it.

Some green seeking people got the idea for a People's Park and then went ahead and built it.

There wasn't much advance notice, a proclamation in the *Barb* by Robin Hoods Park Commissioner and a leaflet given out on the Avenue.

For a week the Avenue merchants were panhandled. They were told of our plans and responded as modestly as a midwestern virgin on her first time around. Some anonymous types kicked in about seven hundred dollars and we were ready to go.

All sorts of straight and freaky people showed up at the Park. First the land was bulldozed and then we shovelled the rocks and assorted shit into barrels. A morning chill gave way to sweat and more creators kept pouring into what was becoming a Park.

A truck arrived with rolled up grass—that is, sod. We picked the

Stew Albert, "People's Park: Free for All," *The Berkeley Barb*, April 25–May 1, 1969, p. 5.

The mercy of the West has been social revolution; the mercy of the East has been individual insight into the basic self/void. We need both. They are both contained in the traditional three aspects of the Dharma; wisdom (prajna), meditation (dhyana), and morality (sila). Wisdom is intuitive knowledge of the mind of love and charity that lies beneath one's ego-driven anxieties and aggressions. Meditation is going into the mind to see this for yourself—over and over again, until it becomes the mind you live in. Morality is bringing it back out in the way you live, through personal example and responsible action, ultimately toward the true community (sangha) of "all beings." This last aspect means, for me, supporting any cultural and economic revolution that moves clearly toward a free, international, classless world. It means using such means as civil disobedience, outspoken criticism, protest, pacifism, voluntary poverty, and even gentle violence if it comes to a matter of restraining some impetuous redneck. It means affirming the widest possible spectrum of non-harmful individual behavior—defending the right of individuals to smoke hemp, eat peyote, be polygunous, polyandrous, or homosexual. Worlds of behavior and custom long banned by the Judaeo-Capitalist-Christian, Marxist West. It means respecting intelligence and learning, but not as greed or means to personal power. Working on one's own responsiblity, but willing to work with a group. "Forming the new society within the shell of the old"—the IWW slogan of fifty years ago.

The traditional cultures are in any case, doomed and rather than cling to their good aspects hopelessly it should be remembered that whatever is or was in any other culture can be reconstructured from the unconscious, through meditation. In fact, it is my own view that the coming revolution will close the circle and link us in many ways with the most creative aspects of our archaic past. If we are lucky we may eventually arrive at a totally integrated world culture with matrilineal descent, free-form marriage, natural-credit communist economy, less industry, far less population and lots more national parks.